Students and Politics in Developing Nations

Students and Politics
in
Developing Nations

Edited by
DONALD K. EMMERSON

FREDERICK A. PRAEGER, *Publishers*
New York • Washington • London

FREDERICK A. PRAEGER, PUBLISHERS
111 Fourth Avenue, New York, N.Y. 10003, U.S.A.
5, Cromwell Place, London S.W. 7, England

Published in the United States of America in 1968
by Frederick A. Praeger, Inc., Publishers

Library of Congress Catalog Card Number: 68–19507

Printed in the United States of America

FOREWORD

The purpose of this book is to explore the political attitudes and behavior of university students in Africa, Asia, and Latin America. The task requires analysis of student bodies and student organizations, of university structures and university climates, and of the sometimes shattering reciprocal impacts of campus and national politics. Eleven chapters explore these contexts in as many national settings. The concluding chapter is comparative.

The phrase "developing nations" contains more hope than fact, and its use here is a matter more of convention than of preference. In particular, the term is not meant to suggest the existence of some preordained social trajectory toward prosperity and enlightenment, let alone toward what the West understands as democracy. Nor is the book's coverage meant to be rigidly comprehensive; a larger compilation might have included chapters on the nations of South Asia, the Middle East, East Africa, or Central America, while perhaps exluding South Africa as an anomaly. The criteria used in commissioning chapters were simply three: the interest of the national case, its location in Africa, Asia, or Latin America, and the availabilty of a qualified author to handle it.

I am grateful to Professor Joseph LaPalombara of Yale University for an encouraging comment on a graduate seminar paper that first started me thinking in the broader terms of this book; to Professor Philip Altbach of the University of Wisconsin, formerly with the Comparative National Development Project at Harvard University, for suggesting many of the contributors; to the Social Science Research Council and the American Council of Learned Societies for supporting me financially as a Foreign Area Fellow in New Haven and Djakarta during the preparation of the manuscript; to my wife, Carolyn, for helping put together the index; and, most important of all, to the authors themselves, who weathered my editorial pedantry with the patience of Job.

DONALD K. EMMERSON

Djakarta, Indonesia
June 1968

v

Contents

Students and Politics in Developing Nations

1. ALGERIA

DAVID B. OTTAWAY

UGEMA: The Years of Glory

The General Union of Muslim Algerian Students (*Union Générale des Etudiants Musulmans Algériens,* or UGEMA) was founded in Paris in July 1955, nine months after the outbreak of the Algerian revolution.

Algerian students had contributed little to the liberation struggle before the creation of UGEMA, being for the most part sons of a landed aristocracy and urban bourgeoisie that had long accepted coexistence with the French settlers (*colons*) and advocated Algeria's assimilation into France. Although some students had joined nationalist organizations, few if any belonged to the small dissident group that broke away from the sterile politicking of the old parties to launch the revolution on November 1, 1954.[1] But once the war for independence was under way, Algerian students en masse joined the National Liberation Front (FLN), convinced of the futility of continuing to agitate for parliamentary reforms, as their fathers had done, and of the necessity for direct action.

For a Muslim student, it had never been easy to act. In the first place, there were few Muslims at the University of Algiers or, for that matter, in any French schools. Prior to World War II only a tiny number of carefully selected Muslim students had been allowed to enter the hallowed halls of the University.[2] A change in French

The research for this chapter was carried out in Algiers in the fall of 1966, while the author was working as a correspondent for *The New York Times*. I wish to express my thanks to student leaders and to officials of the Ministry of Information, who gave their time in interviews and discussions that greatly helped to clarify the complex and turbulent history of the Algerian student union.

3

educational policies after the war considerably increased the number of Algerians in French schools, but by 1954 there were still only 6,260 Muslims (or one out of every 125 of high school age) in French *lycées* in Algeria and only 589 attending the University of Algiers (about one-tenth of the student body) .[3] Perhaps another 300 Algerians were studying in universities in France.

The sons of French *colons* dominated the *Association Générale des Etudiants* (AGE) at the University of Algiers,[4] while Muslim students were strictly forbidden to form their own union. Algerians and their fellow students from Morocco and Tunisia managed to evade this prohibition by setting up "cultural associations" in Algiers and Paris. The first such organization, called an *amicale* ("friendly society") , was formed in Algiers in 1920.[5] Six years later, under the leadership of Ferhat Abbas, a young pharmacy student at the University of Algiers, the *amicale* became the *Association des Etudiants Musulmans d'Afrique du Nord*. In 1927, a similar *Association des Etudiants Musulmans Nord-Africains* (AEMNA) was organized in Paris.

While the Tunisian and Moroccan students in AEMNA were in this period in the vanguard of the nationalist movements in their countries, the Algerians remained almost until World War II under the moderating influence of Ferhat Abbas. As late as 1936, Abbas still contended that Algeria was not, and had never been, a nation; he believed that the destiny of his people was inextricably bound to that of France. He advocated complete equality of rights between Algerian Muslims and Frenchmen, but also fought for the preservation of Algeria's Arab-Islamic culture.

Shortly before World War II, many Algerian university students began to switch their allegiance from Abbas' party, the Democratic Union of the Algerian Manifesto (UDMA), to the more revolutionary and dynamic Party of the Algerian People (PPA) of Messali Hadj, the man who first called for Algeria's independence in 1924. High school students in the French *lycées* and Muslim *medersas* were becoming active in nationalist politics. Future leaders like Benyoucef Ben Khedda, M'hammed Yazid, and Saad Dahlab began their political careers in this period as high school students in Blida, where they were secretly active in the youth branch of Messali Hadj's party.

In the immediate postwar period, North African students in Paris became increasingly active, and AEMNA sought to bring together the many North African student organizations that had sprung up at universities throughout France. Finally, meeting in Tunis in 1950, the AEMNA Congress named a permanent secretariat to draw up plans for a unified Maghreb student union.[6] But these plans were never carried out. The nationalist movements in the three countries took quite different courses in the early 1950's, because France showed a willingness to carry out political reforms in Tunisia and Morocco, but not in Algeria. In that country, the French grip had tightened and repression of nationalist activities grew steadily worse. Messali Hadj's party, then called the Movement for the Triumph of Democratic Liberties (MTLD), was forced underground and its terrorist wing, the Special Organization (OS), uprooted.[7]

In July 1953, Tunisian students jumped the gun on their North African colleagues and created in Paris a separate *Union Générale des Etudiants de Tunisie* (UGET). Plans for a united movement of all Maghreb students were shunted aside, and Algerian students turned their attention to the formation of their own national union. But they were still just talking when the revolution broke out on November 1, 1954. It took another nine months to get the project off the ground. In February 1955, the Algiers section of AEMNA unanimously adopted a motion calling for the creation of a national union. Two months later, a preparatory meeting was held in Paris to plan a constituent First Congress for July.

Before the Congress opened on July 8 at the Palais de la Mutualité in Paris, a fierce battle over the orientation and membership of the proposed union took place, primarily between nationalist and Communist students. The new *Union Générale des Etudiants Musulmans Algériens* (UGEMA) was finally defined as a movement dedicated to "the restoration and spread of the national culture,"[8] i.e., Islam and the Arabic language. This gave the Union a cultural façade that enabled it to exist under French laws. The adjective "Muslim" in its name also served to keep out French Algerians, particularly members of the Communist *Union des Etudiants Algériens* (UEA), who were trying to take over the new student movement and who still questioned the justice of the nationalist cause. The creation of UGEMA marked the demise of the short-lived UEA.

The true political character of UGEMA—its alignment with the National Liberation Front—was no secret. UGEMA considered itself essentially a "unit of combat" in the struggle for independence; the real condition for membership in the Union was support for the revolution. UGEMA was not just an appendage of the FLN, however. The Union kept its autonomy almost until the end of the war.

UGEMA had sections in some twenty-five countries where Algerians were studying, but its leaders could maintain only irregular contact with students beyond the Mediterranean area. The Union's headquarters were located first in Paris, then in Lausanne, and finally in Tunis, but never in Algeria. UGEMA was supposed to hold annual congresses to renew its leadership, but only four were held in the seven years before independence because of the cost and difficulties involved in bringing together delegates from so many countries. There was nevertheless a rapid turnover in leadership during the early years because of numerous arrests. Then, in December 1957, Messaoud Ait Chaalal became President and held the reins of power undisputedly for the next four years.

The founders and first leaders of UGEMA were students who had been active for many years in the youth branches of the MTLD and the UDMA. Such was UGEMA's first President, Ahmed Taleb, a medical student and son of Cheikh Bachir el-Ibrahimi, one of the leaders of the reformist Islamic movement. As a student at the University of Algiers, Taleb had founded a French-language newspaper, the *Jeune Musulman* (*Young Muslim*), in which he urged young French-educated Algerians not to forget their Islamic cultural heritage.[9] Another key figure was Belaid Abdesselam. His involvement in the nationalist movement dated back to May 8, 1945 (V-E Day), when as a sixteen-year old *lycée* student he was arrested for participating in anticolonial demonstrations that were brutally repressed by the French police at the cost of several thousand Algerian lives. In 1953, he became President of the AEMNA branch at the University of Algiers. Along with two other student activists, Lamine Khene and Mohamed Ben Yahia, he organized the Algiers Section of UGEMA.

Ait Chaalal, the son of a wealthy landowner from the region of Constantine, was an exception among UGEMA leaders in that he had not belonged to any of the nationalist parties before becoming active in UGEMA. This may explain his relatively late rise to the Union's top ranks. But he quickly gained the respect of his peers at international conferences, where he was regarded as one of the shrewdest negotiators and most capable student leaders around.

The creation of UGEMA immediately brought relations between the Algerian and French student communities to the breaking point. When the Union conducted the first of its many campaigns for solidarity with imprisoned FLN members in January 1956, provocations and discrimination against Algerian students in France intensified sharply. At the University of Algiers, right-wing French students formed a *Comité d'Action Universitaire* and proposed the creation of a special student corps to help wipe out the "rebellion."

At its Second Congress, held in Paris at the end of March 1956, UGEMA passed a resolution calling for Algerian independence. The declaration sparked off a wave of arrests of Muslim students in France and Algeria. At the University of Algiers, in particular, conditions for Muslim students became unbearable. The torture and killing of a young high school student at the Lycée Ben Aknoun, the latest in a growing list of hideous crimes committed by the French army and police, provoked UGEMA's Algiers Section into action. On May 16, 1956, Section leaders Ben Yahia and Alloum Ben Baatouche called a general, unlimited boycott of classes:

> We will not make better corpses with one more diploma. And what good are these diplomas [the French] continue to offer us while our people are heroically struggling, our mothers, wives and sisters are being raped, and our children and grandparents are falling under the fire of guns, bombs and napalm? . . . Our passivity before the war being waged in front of our eyes makes us accomplices [of those who level] ignoble accusations against our courageous national army. The false tranquillity in which we now live can no longer satisfy our consciences.[10]

The declaration ended with an appeal to all Muslim students to join the Army of National Liberation (ALN) and fight in the *maquis* (underground) for Algeria's independence.

The Algiers Section had acted on its own initiative, but UGEMA's Directing Committee in Paris quickly endorsed the strike and urged Algerian students in France, Morocco, and Tunisia to boycott their classes in solidarity with their brothers inside Algeria. The boycott was a spectacular success, particularly at the University of Algiers, where nearly all of the 520 Algerian students went on strike. Between 5,000 and 6,000 high school students throughout Algeria also went on strike.[11] Led by Lamine Khene and Ben Baatouche, hundreds of university students joined the ALN. Some became medics, messengers, radio operators, or regular soldiers; others helped run makeshift army hospitals and schools.[12]

The contribution of the students to the armed struggle under way inside Algeria should not be overrated. As some ALN officers later remarked bitterly, many students preferred the safety and glamour of international diplomacy to the rigors and dangers of actual combat. In the *maquis*, intense jealousies between students and uneducated peasant guerrillas sometimes led to violence. Many guerrilla leaders, like Colonel Amirouche, considered students physically and psychologically unable to withstand the hard life of the resistance fighter and ordered them to leave for Tunisia and Morocco. The guerrillas mistrusted the "intellectuals" and often suspected them of being French agents or potential rivals for power. Few students rose to prominent positions in the ALN. Among the exceptions was Youcef Khatib, a medical student who, as Colonel Si Hassan, became commander of one of the ALN's six *wilayas* (military zones). Ben Baatouche became a major and an assistant *wilaya* chief before dying on the battlefield.

The students, distrusted in the *maquis*, got a better reception from the Provisional Government of the Algerian Republic (GPRA) and the ALN General Staff, both located in Tunisia. As the center of political gravity slowly moved from the field of battle to the conference table, student leaders like Khene, Redha Malek, and Ben Yahia left UGEMA and turned their talents to diplomacy. Others, like Cherif Belkacem and Abdelaziz Bouteflika, became first subordinates of Army General Staff Chief Colonel Houari Boumedienne and later his political allies.[13]

UGEMA's most important contribution to the nationalist cause was undoubtedly its propaganda campaign in the international student world. In President Ait Chaalal's words:

> Our goal was clear: to inform and explain the tragic reality of Algeria, to demystify the student world that fails to distinguish cultural France from colonial France, to win sympathy for our just cause, [and] to obtain the concrete commitment of the international student community to the struggle in which we are engaged. To do this, we had to follow a policy of active presence—and such [indeed] was our policy.[14]

UGEMA's leaders set about these tasks with the skill of expert players in a game of chess, and such indeed was the nature of international student politics in a world divided into two antagonistic blocs. UGEMA exploited Cold War rivalries and tensions to obtain moral and material aid from both the Western International Student Conference (ISC) and the Communist International Union of Students (IUS).

Examples of French repression were used very effectively by UGEMA to arouse student opinion against the French government and win support for the Union's cause. UGEMA could cite innumerable cases of illegal arrests, shoddy trials, torture, and assassination. UGEMA President Ahmed Taleb was arrested in February 1957 and detained almost four years without a proper trial. In November of the same year, UGEMA Secretary General Mohamed Khemisti was arrested in Montpellier, France, without being charged with any offense, and whisked away to Barberousse Prison in Algiers, where he was kept incommunicado for several months and then summarily tried and sentenced by a military tribunal.[15] One of the most famous cases of torture was that of Djamila Bouhired. Arrested by French paratroopers on charges of terrorist activity in April 1957, Miss Bouhired underwent eight days of torture before she was condemned to death by a military court.

The attempted suppression of UGEMA by French authorities was also adroitly exploited by the Union's leaders to benefit their cause. On January 22, 1958, the French government declared UGEMA dissolved because of "anti-national activities" and "collusion with the FLN."[16] The Union's Executive Committee members were arrested a few days later along with fifty other student leaders throughout France. After their release, the Union leaders fled France for good and re-established UGEMA's headquarters in Switzerland.

The measures taken by the French government cut off UGEMA leaders from Algerian students in France and badly shook the Union's structure. The Third Congress could not be held until August 1960, more than four years after the Second. But clandestine activity continued in France despite the mounting risks. In December 1958, the French police arrested thirty more student leaders, who were found guilty of "reconstituting a dissolved league [UGEMA]."[17] Three months later, a right-wing French terrorist group known as the Red Hand proved that Algerian students were not even safe in neutral countries like Belgium. On March 9, 1959, a young medical student in Brussels, Akli Aissiou, walked out of his apartment into a fatal hail of bullets.

UGEMA's first international objective was to gain recognition from the powerful *Union Nationale des Etudiants de France* (UNEF) and thereby turn French student opinion against the war. But UNEF was four years in making its peace with the "upstart" Algerian union. The French student community was deeply divided over the issue, with the right wing opposed to any kind of *entente* with UGEMA and the left too weak to impose its will. After a brief flirtation, the two unions broke off all contact in

December 1956. It was not until June 1960, after UNEF had come out clearly in favor of Algerian independence, that the two organizations were finally able to issue a joint appeal, calling upon the French government to negotiate directly with the FLN to end the war.

Seeking to circumvent the hostility of UNEF, Algerian student leaders took their case to the Sixth International Student Conference, held in Ceylon in September 1956. There the UNEF delegation played every card it had against UGEMA. The Algerian union, they correctly argued, represented only a minority of the students at the University of Algiers, since it excluded the French Algerians studying there. For this reason, continued the French delegates, UGEMA could not be considered a representative national organization.

This time the "Muslim" in UGEMA's name was a handicap for the Algerian student leaders, who had to convince prospective supporters that the word was there only to appease the French authorities and did not mean the union was either racist or religious in character. As for the argument that French students in Algeria were excluded from its ranks, UGEMA countered by noting that these French students were already represented in UNEF through the Algiers AGE, while Muslim Algerians had never had an organization to defend their own interests.

After a hot debate, under the threat of a walkout by UNEF and its supporters, the Conference plenary voted 36 to 5, with 7 abstentions, to seat UGEMA and grant it the right to vote as a national union of students. Legalities had been cast aside, the nationalist cause implicitly endorsed, and UNEF isolated within the ISC.

But UGEMA's tough-minded leaders did not stop there. They proceeded to demand a resolution condemning outright the French repression of Algerian students and calling for Algeria's independence. Many delegates invoked Conference legalities to stall off a vote, but UGEMA pressed the issue. The ISC was faced with a potential schism that could only benefit its Communist-sponsored rival, the IUS. If the Conference had turned its back on this burning colonial issue, a growing number of national student unions from Africa and Asia would have gravitated toward the IUS.

The American delegates of the United States National Student Association (USNSA), understanding what was at stake, negotiated a toned-down motion with UGEMA and then introduced it. The resolution went through on a 28-18 vote with only two European nations, Italy and Yugoslavia, lining up with USNSA and the delegates from developing countries. UNEF and its Western European allies did not walk out—they had no place to go; they sought to force through a substitute motion, which was narrowly defeated.[18]

The Ceylon Conference was a turning point not only for UGEMA, but for the ISC as well. UGEMA had won the battle for recognition and made Algerian independence the cause of dozens of student unions. At the same time, the ISC had been diverted from its primary concern with the Cold War and related issues, which had provided the basic rationale for the Conference. The ISC in ensuing years opened its agenda to the anticolonial students of the "Third World," and UGEMA turned out to have been the thin edge of an intensely political wedge that eventually split the Conference apart.

A few months after the Ceylon Conference, UGEMA became an associate member of the IUS, turning down full membership in order not to compromise its relations with the ISC. The battle to win, Algerian student leaders realized, was the one inside the Western-influenced Conference, where UNEF and its allies were active. UGEMA's leaders were not interested in embracing the political orientation of either international organization, but wanted instead to use both bodies for their own purposes and on their own terms. The Union's associate membership in the IUS became an effective political lever in its dealings with the ISC and the latter's Coordinating Secretariat of National Unions of Students (COSEC).

The shrewd international tactics of Algeria's student leaders were clearly illustrated after the French government dissolved UGEMA in France in January 1958. The Union turned down an IUS offer to organize a massive joint solidarity meeting, preferring to make first use of COSEC to counter the French action. In April, COSEC and the British national student union convened an emergency conference in London; twenty-two national unions attended in an impressive show of solidarity. The conference condemned the French government for its treatment of Algerian students, called for Algerian independence, and launched a vast campaign to raise scholarship funds for the approximately 500 Algerian students who had fled from France to neighboring European countries.

No sooner did the London conference end than UGEMA leaders went on a highly profitable IUS-sponsored fund-raising and

propaganda tour of Eastern Europe. With the dissolution of
UGEMA in France, the importance of the IUS for the baseless
union became much greater. The number of Algerians studying
in the East on scholarships provided by the IUS grew steadily,
while the Western affiliates of the ISC were less successful in meeting UGEMA's demands. The Union's French-educated leaders
undoubtedly would have preferred to send their members to universities in Western Europe, but of an estimated 350 students who
in 1960 held scholarships obtained by UGEMA, approximately 200
were in Communist countries, a meager 21 in the United States,
and the rest scattered over Western Europe.[19]

Aside from participating actively in the ISC and the IUS,
UGEMA attended every major international youth or student
meeting held during this period. In addition, delegations went
on propaganda tours to Communist China (1957, 1960), Scandi-
navia (1958), Eastern Europe (1958–59), South America (1959),
and North America (1959–60).[20] This was UGEMA's policy of "active presence," and it proved highly successful. In many countries
where the Provisional Government (GPRA) had no official recognition, the Union's emissaries were received with open arms by top
government officials, and the Algerian cause was warmly embraced
by the national student union. While Washington cold-shouldered
the Provisional Government, UGEMA found USNSA one of its
best allies; while Moscow held off official recognition of the GPRA
until the last days of French Algeria, Soviet student leaders did
their best to bring UGEMA into the councils of the IUS.

Throughout their diplomatic campaign, Algerian student leaders strenuously avoided taking sides in the Cold War. "We have
refused to become involved in the polemics and partisan struggles
that are tearing apart the student world," said Ait Chaalal, "because we know these conflicts . . . were not made to serve our cause."
But neutrality did not mean abstention. In 1959, the *Confédéra-
tion Nord-Africaine des Etudiants* (CNAE), led by UGEMA,
joined Polish and Italian student leaders in promoting a "round
table" meeting of national student unions from East and West.
"We used the full weight of our influence," Ait Chaalal said later,
"in a manner we believed conducive to cooperation and unity in
the [international] student movement, to the maintenance of peace
in the world, and to the coming of a new era of liberty and progress
in a climate of respect and friendship among all peoples."[21]

But the new era never came. In the ISC, UGEMA found itself
in a mixed minority of radical Latin American leftists and European

seekers of *détente*. At the Ninth ISC in Switzerland in 1960, after losing a close vote on the proposed round table meeting, the UGEMA delegates walked out, but were persuaded to return. Two years later, at the Tenth ISC in Quebec in June-July 1962, the Algerians withdrew again, in a group led by Latin American radicals angered by the Conference's refusal to recognize a student group favoring Puerto Rican independence—the *Federación Universitaria Pro-Independencia*—as the national union of students of Puerto Rico. UGEMA's decision was largely emotional. First, the issue evoked the Algerian union's own past history and battle for recognition. Second, the leftists—with IUS members and sympathizers in their ranks—were virtually the only supporters within the Conference of UGEMA's drive for "world student unity."[22]

This time the Algerian delegation did not return. On the sixth day of the Conference—July 1, 1962—the Algerian people voted for their country's independence. A few days later the "Algerian problem" came to an end, and with it UGEMA's years of glory.

Independence: The Morning After

Independence immediately plunged Algeria into a civil war that shattered into a thousand pieces the nationalist dream that liberation would usher in a golden age. The hidden quarrels and rivalries among leaders, which had plagued the National Liberation Front throughout the war, burst into the open for the first time. The commanders of the guerrilla forces inside Algeria turned against the General Staff of the ALN and the troops it commanded, who had sat out the last four years of the independence struggle on Tunisian and Moroccan soil. The GPRA tried to depose the three top officers of the General Staff, whom it suspected of wanting to seize power. Other leaders of the nationalist movement, among them Ahmed Ben Bella, were released from French prisons shortly before independence, and sought to make a comeback onto the political scene.

The contending nationalist leaders divided into two uneasy coalitions. On one side stood Ben Bella, the General Staff, and the troops under Colonel Boumedienne, and a few guerrilla leaders and their forces. On the other side stood the GPRA under President Benyoucef Ben Khedda and the bulk of the guerrilla units. The struggle for power degenerated into civil war in late August. The faction led by Ben Bella finally triumphed, thanks to the support of Colonel Boumedienne's well-disciplined army, which slowly crushed the divided guerrilla forces. By mid-September the

GPRA had lost the battle. Elections for a constituent National Assembly took place on September 20, and eight days later Ben Bella was elected the first Prime Minister of independent Algeria.

The brief but bloody civil war dealt a psychological blow to most educated Algerians, who were appalled and ashamed at the behavior of their leaders. In the midst of this crisis, the students turned to face their own problems. The standard-bearers of an impossible dream—world-wide student unit—returned home to discover the cruel reality that there were no grounds for unity even within their own ranks.

The civil war certainly contributed to the splintering of UGEMA, but the Union's weaknesses dated back to earlier days. UGEMA had hardly begun to organize itself when repression of the strike of 1956 put an end to its activities inside Algeria. Then came the banning by French authorities in 1958, which ended the Union's overt existence in France and drove its leaders first to Lausanne and then to Tunis. UGEMA's leadership had been cut off from its base and that base in turn cut up and scattered abroad. The Union was bound to find itself in trouble after independence when Algerian students, educated under divergent Communist, Western, and Islamic influences, came home to face one another and discover their differences.

UGEMA's problems were further complicated by the interference of the Provisional Government, which in December 1961 dissolved the Union's Executive Committee and replaced it with a nine-man University Section of the FLN. For the GPRA, this was part of an effort to bring all the national organizations, which had led an independent existence within the loosely knit Front during the war, more directly under its control. For UGEMA, it was the *coup de grâce*.

There is some evidence that the Provisional Government's action reflected concern over UGEMA's rapprochement with the IUS and apprehension over the future role of students educated in Communist countries. The dissolution was kept secret because the GPRA feared a public scandal and UGEMA a loss of face internationally. Meanwhile, the University Section, supposedly the future nucleus of a new Algerian student union, went about its task of preparing the first UGEMA Congress in independent Algeria.[23]

The civil war in the summer of 1962, which split the students into factions allied to the opposing leaders, made it very difficult for the FLN University Section to organize the Congress. Nonetheless, UGEMA's homecoming Fifth Congress, after several post-ponements, finally opened in Algiers on September 5. The civil war was still raging just south of the city, and the country still lacked any real government.[24]

One student leader described the Congress as "a miniature United Nations of students from over twenty countries with different backgrounds, educations, and ideologies."[25] It should have been a constituent assembly to launch a new national union and decide the orientation of independent Algeria's student community. But these issues were hardly touched. The spirit of civil war prevailed instead.

Two thousand students were reportedly present for the opening ceremonies at the University of Algiers campus in Ben Aknoun, but it was virtually impossible to distinguish delegates from observers.[26] Many delegates' mandates were challenged, and the Credentials Committee immediately bogged down in hot debate. The University Section came under heavy attack for numerous "irregularities" in its preparation of the Congress—notably the disproportionate representation given to the delegations from France and Algiers—but refused to render any account of its activities.[27]

Various delegations had apparently been stacked with students, loyal to one FLN leader or another, who were interested primarily in taking over UGEMA's leadership. The delegation from Algiers was tagged "pro–Ben Bella," and that from the University Section, "pro–Ben Khedda." The delegates from France supported Mohamed Boudiaf, an FLN leader who opposed both Ben Bella and the GPRA, and the representatives of students from the ALN were close to Abdelhafid Boussouf, the GPRA's Minister of Intelligence and Communications. Communist students, many of whom had studied in East European countries, formed another faction.

Before the Congress really got under way, thirteen delegations stormed out of the hall over the question of representation.[28] The smaller sections, from the Middle East, the Communist countries, and the United States, were determined to avoid a takeover by the University Section or by the large delegations from France and Algiers. At the initiative of the delegates from the ALN and the Middle Eastern countries, the Congress was finally converted into a "national conference" whose only task was to elect a preparatory committee for a new Fifth Congress in 1963. But even this proved impossible.

Many delegates felt that before the election of any committee, the question of defining UGEMA's orientation and policies until the 1963 Congress, as well as the Union's future relations with the FLN, should be discussed and settled. The University Section members and the delegations from France and Algiers, all for different reasons, were against the principle of UGEMA's independence from party or government control. The other delegations, although sharply divided over the issue of "Arabization"[29] raised by the students returning from Middle Eastern countries, could at least agree that UGEMA should maintain its proud tradition of autonomy.

The delegates finally voted a motion to uphold the principle of autonomy and prohibit the future preparatory committee from deciding any question of Union orientation or policy until the Fifth Congress could be held.[30] However, even after arguing into the early hours of the morning, they were unable to elect a preparatory committee for the Congress, and the conference broke up in total confusion. The Union's collapse was complete. Observers from East and West alike were appalled at the state of UGEMA. Few had guessed the disarray and discord latent within the Union that had for so long held the spotlight in their councils.

The breakdown of UGEMA marked the beginning of the psychological demobilization of the Algerian student community. The students' wartime *esprit de corps* disappeared overnight. Like all Algerians, they were exhausted after nearly eight years of guerrilla warfare, clandestine living, police repression, and OAS terrorism. Many wanted above all to "live a little," and many preferred to do it abroad. The government had to launch a full-scale campaign to bring the students back.[31]

Life in Algiers was hardly equal to that on the Left Bank. Still, the students now had their own café, the *Cercle Taleb,* on Algiers' most fashionable boulevard, a five-story student center, the palm-shaded campus at Ben Aknoun, and, above all, the University itself, once the third-largest in France and still a leading institution in Africa.[32]

French terrorists had blown up the University library in June 1962, destroying most of its 500,000 volumes. Roughly 6,000 French students had left the country, as had many French professors. Nevertheless, after an intensive recruiting campaign for both students and professors, the University finally opened in mid-December; the President and almost all of the 230 professors were French. An Algerian was named President the following year, but as late as 1965 Algerians held only one-fourth of the teaching positions at the University.[33]

The University is still oriented toward France. Attempts toward "Arabization" have not gone much beyond the creation of a department of Arabic language and literature, the establishment of a school to train Arabic-speaking instructors, and the teaching of some history and geography courses in Arabic.[34] Most Algerian students still show a marked preference for French diplomas and little interest in Arab-Islamic culture.

The government took two major steps toward reforming higher education, one to "democratize" it, the other to divert university students from law and literature to science and medicine. Democratization entailed granting every student a scholarship equivalent to $60 a month. This payment—called a *présalaire* by leftist French student leaders, who viewed the university student as an "intellectual worker" entitled to receive a "pre-salary" for his academic "labor"—was aimed at enabling the sons of peasants and workers to attend the University. But it will be at least a few more years before any significant change takes place in the composition of the student body, which is today overwhelmingly of bourgeois origin.

The University also sought to accommodate those whose studies had been interrupted by the war. Special entrance exams brought about 2,000 students without the normal French *baccalauréat* into the University, while some 3,000 others were offered accelerated courses to prepare for the *baccalauréat*. This "social promotion" measure proved quite controversial. Many students and professors feared the University would become a second-rate institution, a "servant of the state," or a breeding ground for half-educated "revolutionaries." Significantly, the government dropped its talk of a "People's University" after 1964.[35]

The problem of attracting more students to the sciences was largely solved within two years by simply cutting off all scholarships to study law or literature abroad and giving higher "pre-salaries" to science and medical students.[36]

Those to whom the government offered so many advantages were expected in return to abandon their "ivory towers." In December 1962, President Ben Bella told the students what he wanted:

> Our young intellectuals responded to our call in a revolutionary fashion during the 1956 strike. A heavy responsibility lies on their shoulders. The Tripoli Program [the first ideological charter of the FLN, approved at a meeting in Tripoli in May 1962] calls for the union of the peasants and the intellectuals. I am convinced it is the university that will give

us the avant-garde. The students have to understand that they must lead the peasants. They must go into the interior and participate in the reconstruction campaign, just as the students in Cuba go help cut sugar cane.[37]

The students proved considerably less enthusiastic than Ben Bella about this "revolutionary" role; only a small group of leftists answered his call. At the end of 1962, Ben Bella was still considerably to the left of the leaderless Union.

Even before Ben Bella's election at the end of September 1962, the FLN Political Bureau under his control contacted student leaders to fill the vacuum left by the collapse of the UGEMA conference earlier that month. Talks with Djamal Khiari, who had led the Belgrade delegation; Laadi Flici, head of the powerful Algiers Section; and Rabah Belaid, Cairo delegation leader, led to the formation on September 19 of a seven-man provisional executive committee, with Flici acting as President.[38] This group held elections for the leadership of the Algiers and Constantine Sections of UGEMA,[39] put out the first issues of a Union magazine, *Révolution à l'Université*, organized an impromptu demonstration before the United States Information Center in early October during the Cuban missile crisis, and helped set up an Algerian-Cuban Solidarity Committee. But it was unable to do much more.

The provisional Executive was on shaky grounds from the start; pro-Communist students contested its representativeness and defections began to occur. In late November, Flici withdrew on the pretext of ill health. Khiari took over, but soon found himself at odds with Belaid; the latter profited from Khiari's absence in January 1963 to make a controversial speech in which he accused the pro-Communist students of seeking to undermine the executive committee's position.

When Khiari returned in early February, an emergency assembly was called. Members from the powerful Algiers Section attended, along with delegates from Oran and Constantine. The meeting was more a "public trial" than anything else. The students' charges against the executive ranged from embezzling Union funds to traveling abroad too much. Belaid, who had in fact spent much time abroad, did not dare show up for the confrontation. After a protracted and bitter debate, when few students were left in the hall, an ex-ALN officer, Mokhtar Mokhtefi, succeeded in getting himself elected President of a new executive committee. He didn't last long, either. In early April, the FLN convoked a national student conference that swept the house clean and elected a third executive committee led by Moustafa Mekideche.[40]

More important for the future of UGEMA was the creation, at the same time, of a twelve-man "control commission" charged with preparing the Fifth Congress. Among the commission's members was Houari Mouffok, a twenty-six-year old alumnus of East German universities. Mouffok was the prototype of the "new militant" then emerging in UGEMA. He had no war record, having kept to his studies (economics and planning) in Leipzig and East Berlin until late 1962. At one point, he had led the UGEMA section in East Germany. Whether he attended the abortive 1962 Algiers conference or not is unclear; if he did, he made no impression and played no role. In short, Mouffok was a newcomer with few credentials. He found the door wide open and walked in.[41]

The rise of Mouffok and his allies began with the takeover of the Algiers Section, which was the real center of power in UGEMA. Among the members of this Section was a group of extremely militant students, many of them beneficiaries of the "social promotion." Nourredine Zenine, Mouffok's right-hand man, became head of the Algiers Section in early 1963. Under his leadership, the militant students took initiatives such as the formation of a *Comité d'Action Révolutionnaire des Etudiants à la Campagne* to help the peasants run the huge nationalized French farms.[42] The initiative was largely a failure, since the students could do little to help the peasants, but it showed that the Algiers Section had taken Ben Bella's speech seriously. Later during the summer, these same students embarked upon a number of government-sponsored volunteer projects that also achieved modest results. Only about 350 of the 3,000 students at the University signed up for the Cuban-style national literacy campaign, for service in hospitals, or for work in village reconstruction or reforestation projects.[43] The bulk of the "volunteers" for the latter campaign had to be rounded up by the party youth organization (JFLN) from among the unemployed, semiliterate teenagers with time on their hands.

On June 9, a general assembly of the Algiers Section elected Zenine to head its delegation to the Fifth Congress. The assembly also passed a motion calling for UGEMA to become a full member of the Communist-sponsored IUS, an issue that was to be debated at the Congress. Later, however, 254 students protested Zenine's election, signing a petition in which they pointed out that the assembly had been scheduled early on a Sunday morning just before exams and that only 98 of the 900 members of the Section had been present.[44]

Meanwhile, UGEMA's provisional leadership, which had no legal right to take decisions affecting the Union's orientation, played host in mid-May 1963 to a well publicized meeting of the IUS Executive Committee. Naceur Saada, an ally of Mouffok in charge of foreign relations, signed a joint declaration with the Cuban national union of students, which included an offer of twenty scholarships to attend Cuban universities. Shortly thereafter, Saada flew back to Sofia, where he was studying, and signed a similar joint declaration with the Bulgarian student union.[45] If he was overstepping his mandate, his actions were not out of step with Ben Bella's foreign policy. The JFLN had already organized a five-day "Youth Day Against Colonialism" with the Communist-sponsored World Federation of Democratic Youth (WFDY) in Algiers.

UGEMA's Fifth Congress finally got under way on August 10, 1963. The preparatory committee and the key Algiers Section were in the hands of Mouffok and his allies, now the undisputed leaders of the militantly radical wing. The FLN, and Ben Bella himself, watched UGEMA with growing concern. If the Union's new leaders were "going to the people" as Ben Bella had asked them to do in his December speech, they were also showing a potentially troublesome spirit of independence.

In his speech to the Fifth UGEMA Congress, Ben Bella tried to appease both the Marxist left, by showing he was as socialist as they were, and the more conservative upholders of Islam in Algeria, by showing he was not an atheist:

> We are for scientific socialism. We only ask one thing: that you leave us our God, Allah. Aside from this, we are ready to go further than any other scientific socialism. . . .
>
> I respect those who are not believers and I believe they can be good militants. But they had better not try to make us adopt their atheism. I would say they are in the majority in this hall. I ask in all friendliness that all brothers watch out for a dangerous evil: partisanship. Our brothers in Cuba suffer from this.[46]

UNEA: The Politics of Partisanship

"The students have to understand," Ben Bella had said in December, "that they must lead the peasants." Mouffok and his militants understood well enough. In the words of the charter of the new *Union Nationale des Etudiants Algériens* (UNEA), as the Congress renamed UGEMA:[47]

> The classical conception of the student, which represents him as a privileged and bourgeois character, must be banned. Indeed, the student must consider himself a useful and productive worker taking his place in the ranks of the working masses.
>
> It is the contact with the hard realities of constructive work amidst the peasant and worker brothers that will form the revolutionary conscience of the students, and that will give our country a revolutionary intellectual elite.[48]

The new charter defended the Union's autonomy more emphatically than ever. The only concession to the party, then striving to unite all youth groups under its wing, was a proposal for a committee to "coordinate" the various national organizations. But at least an open break between party and students had been avoided. Like the Algerian Communist Party at the time, the new Union was willing to give conditional support to the regime and to back all government actions it judged "revolutionary."

The Union's demands—student "self-management" of the University campus and certain student restaurants and cafés, a student majority on the government's national Scholarship Committee, and something more than "symbolic representation" in the University's ruling Higher Council and University Services—exceeded what the government was willing to give.[49] On a number of other issues, however, UNEA and the Ben Bella regime spoke the same language. At the top of the list of UNEA's "national objectives" were "the struggle against colonialism, neocolonialism, and imperialism" and the building of an "authentic socialist economy."

In keeping with this new, more radical orientation, the Congress decided to exchange delegate for mere observer status in the ISC, while retaining associate membership in the Communist IUS. The decision was justified on the grounds that in its "anti-imperialist struggle," UNEA stood closer to the IUS than to the Western ISC. Only the protests of delegations from the Middle East and the United States kept UNEA from voting to become a full member of the IUS. The delegates defeated a motion for friendly relations with the USNSA, once a stanch ally, ending all but the most formal contacts between the two.

The Congress had hotly debated the Union's new policies, but the real battle came over the election of a twenty-seven-man Directing Committee to implement them. A skirmish over the credentials of two Moscow delegations, one of them Communist and the other sponsored by the Algerian government, provoked the walkout of seven delegations from Arab countries (Syria, Iraq, Kuwait, Egypt, Libya, Tunisia, and Morocco [Fez]). Only 132 of the original 180 delegates were left in the hall. Only 101 finally took part in the election, 50 of them Algiers Section delegates under Mouffok's control. The Directing Committee, which proceeded to name Mouffok President and Zenine Vice-President of UNEA, had been elected by a thin majority of all the delegates, whose discipline and organization had prevailed over the protests of a large but easily fragmented minority.[50]

The election of Mouffok and his supporters did little to change the basic apathy and conservatism of the vast majority of students in Algeria; if anything, it hardened these attitudes. The number of hard-core militants who regularly turned out to join FLN-led demonstrations against the "counterrevolution" or to vote resolutions and shout slogans condemning "imperialism" in Cuba, the Congo, and Viet-Nam, never numbered much more than 300.[51] Only the brief clash with Morocco over a disputed frontier in October 1963 again roused the nationalist fervor of the students: around 600 answered Ben Bella's call for volunteers. Earlier that year, student opposition to plans for a compulsory summer program of civic service had been so strong that Ben Bella had withdrawn the project.

The antisocialist sentiments of the student community in Algeria were clearly shown in a 1965 government survey. Three-fourths of the students sampled chose a freely competitive over a planned economy as the model developing countries should follow.[52]

If UNEA's militant leaders failed to arouse the students, they did succeed in using the Union as a steppingstone in their own political careers. Mouffok, Zenine, and UNEA Secretary-General Nourredine Hassani were particularly active in national politics. They helped prepare the FLN Congress, held in April 1964, Hassani even sitting on the committee that drew up the Charter of Algiers, the country's new ideological platform. Later, Zenine traveled throughout the country, lecturing on the Charter as though he were an official party spokesman.

Ben Bella, however, like the GPRA in 1961, had always intended to organize an FLN student wing to take over UNEA in a "democratic" fashion from the inside. This had been impossible in 1962, when there were only seven students in Algiers who were members of the party. But in 1963 they numbered 150, and by December they had begun infiltrating the Algiers Section, just as Mouffok had done before them.[53] Mouffok and Zenine decided to avoid an open conflict by playing along with the party in public while working in private to retain control. In the spring of 1964, the party students—led by Mohamed Berdi, Abdelaziz Bouchaib, and Abdel Sadok—formed a committee within the ranks of UNEA and tried to promote the party's position and win support away from Mouffok's group.

Ben Bella told one Western ambassador he was determined to bring Mouffok and his followers to heel before the Sixth Congress, and some observers expected him to intervene in May 1964 in the elections of the Algiers Section leaders. He did neither. He may have misjudged the strength of the party students, thinking they could oust Mouffok at the Congress without his help. He was also preoccupied at the time with the rebellion of one of his military commanders, Colonel Chaabani, and had little time to deal with the students.[54] In any case, the Sixth Congress opened on August 3, 1964, and Mouffok was re-elected President, thanks once again to the disarray in the ranks of his opponents.

At the 1964 Congress there were three different centers of opposition to Mouffok's group. The most important was the pro-FLN faction, which opposed the incumbent leadership on the question of UGEMA's autonomy. A second center consisted of the delegations from the Arab countries and the United States. These students objected to the Marxist orientation of UNEA and to Mouffok's plan to make allegiance to the Charter of Algiers a prerequisite for Union membership. A third source of opposition was the nine-man Paris delegation, which supported the Front of Socialist Forces, a dissident group then engaged in armed insurrection against the Ben Bella regime in the Kabylia region. After prolonged debate, this third group was condemned for its "counter-revolutionary" stand and excluded from the Congress. After its exclusion, while the Congress was meeting, the Paris delegation founded a short-lived *Union Générale des Etudiants Démocratiques Algériens.*[55]

In a long report to the Congress, Mouffok stressed the Union's political activities—demonstrations, declarations, and voluntary service schemes—in "defense of the socialist revolution." He prided himself on having maintained UNEA's autonomy while still cooperating with the Party. But he admitted that UNEA's house was still in disorder. Contacts with the Union's thirty-four sections were "irregular," and only about 2,500 out of 6,000 students in Algeria carried UNEA cards, most of these only to benefit from discount prices at theaters, movie houses, restaurants, and shops.

The Education Ministry's survey later found that 80 per cent of the students interviewed were "members" of the UNEA, but nearly half of these said they were not active members. The survey also showed that the majority of students sampled (60 per cent) thought UNEA's primary role was to look after "material conditions," while only 17 per cent regarded "political education" as its chief task. But UNEA, as Mouffok admitted to the Congress, had done little to improve the students' welfare and still barely had a voice in "on-campus" issues, i.e., in the University Services or on the Scholarship Committee.[56]

At the Sixth Congress, UNEA's foreign policy took a decisive turn toward the IUS camp; the pro-Communist students pushed through a vote that the Union opt for full membership in the Moscow-sponsored international organization. The Union thus abandoned its long-standing tradition of neutrality in international student politics. Mouffok himself had no use for the Western ISC; he was more interested in developing ties with the "revolutionary" student unions of Asia and Latin America (notably Cuba). He also sought for UNEA a leading pan-African role. This latter ambition was fulfilled during the Sixth Congress, which coincided with the Third Pan-African Student Conference in Nairobi. Out of the meeting of twenty-eight delegations in Kenya emerged, at least on paper, a Pan-African Student Movement, with UNEA elected to the top post of Secretary General and Algiers selected as the movement's headquarters. It was the crowning glory of UNEA, and Mouffok, abroad.

Ironically, elections for UNEA's leadership under way at home showed that Mouffok's popularity, or control, was definitely on the wane. With the Algiers Section (47 out of 148 Congress delegates) now divided between pro-FLN and pro-Communist factions, Mouffok was elected to the enlarged thirty-one-man Directing Committee only on the second ballot.[57] Still, a slim 17–14 majority on the Committee in favor of Mouffok's faction assured him control of the executive and his reelection as President.

Mouffok had congratulated himself at the Congress on the "climate of confidence" that existed between the party and UNEA. Ben Bella's absence from the meeting belied this claim. Indeed, after the narrow failure of the party students, Ben Bella decided to take a direct hand in UNEA's affairs. He made his move against the pro-Communist student leadership in November 1964.

Algiers had just been chosen the site of the IUS- and WFDY-backed Ninth World Youth Festival, the first to be held outside Europe, and Ben Bella wanted to control UNEA before it took place. He was also anxious to make the change before the Eighth IUS Congress, scheduled to meet in Sofia in December. As a first step, the FLN students were reorganized. A meeting held November 8 in Ben Bella's presence named Berdi coordinator and Bouchaib head of a "vigilance committee." Then a meeting between FLN and UNEA leaders took place November 16–17. The result was a compromise: Mouffok stayed, but Berdi became Vice-President for Foreign Relations and Bouchaib, Secretary General. Two other party students took over North African affairs and relations with sections in the Arab world. The party now at least had control over UNEA's foreign policy and a voice in its internal affairs. Mouffok later told a press conference that the shuffle was UNEA's "contribution" to the unification of Algeria's youth movements. In fact, the FLN had simply taken over.[58]

The tide had now turned. Berdi organized FLN student committees inside the University to infiltrate UNEA and squeeze out Mouffok's appointees. When elections for the Algiers Section leaders came up in mid-January 1965, the FLN candidates elected their candidates with little trouble.[59] Mouffok had finally lost his major base of power. The coup d'état of June 19, 1965, that toppled Ben Bella only speeded the end of Mouffok's stormy two-year rule over UNEA.

After Ben Bella: The Politics of Impotence

The fall of Ben Bella set the Union back three years, to the crisis situation of September 1962. Once again, Algerian students split into pro– and anti–Ben Bella factions. The pro–Ben Bella students this time took to the streets to denounce the man who had ousted their leader: Colonel Houari Boumedienne. The turnout was not spectacular, never much more than a thousand at best, but still well above those Algiers had seen for Cuba, Viet-Nam, or Angola.[60] It was enough to scare Boumedienne, who sent out army troops and police reinforcements to disperse the students with water trucks and tear gas. The demonstrations were quickly over, but they contributed to the tense atmosphere in Algiers, and thus indirectly to the postponement of the Afro-Asian Summit Conference, scheduled to take place there in June.

The pro–Ben Bella students were undoubtedly pleased by the loss of face Boumedienne suffered when the Afro-Asian meeting was finally canceled, but they found themselves the next victims of the sharp drop in Algeria's international prestige set in motion by the coup. On June 24, the International Preparatory Committee for the World Youth Festival met in Algiers, without inviting any Algerian youth officials to attend, and canceled the event. The cancellation particularly humiliated the JFLN, which had been at work on the preparations for months.

In the wake of the coup d'état, UNEA disintegrated. Mouffok joined the Communist-backed clandestine opposition and was finally arrested in Algiers on October 7. Zenine and others went into hiding. Some of them later moved to Paris to set up, with the support of the IUS and the French Communists, an External Delegation to challenge the new UNEA leadership.[61] The FLN students, however, agreed to cooperate with the new regime, and in late September 1965 took over UNEA; Berdi became President of still another provisional executive. But for the party it was an empty victory. With the left-wing militants who had animated UNEA for two years gone, the party-appointed leaders found themselves in control of a lifeless organization virtually without followers.

Only in the Algiers Section was there still a spark of life, which flared up briefly against the regime on January 29, 1966, when around 1,500 students demonstrated in downtown Algiers. It is hard to say who was more surprised, the government or UNEA. The demonstration began as a protest against the Moroccan government over the kidnaping in Paris of a Moroccan leftist leader, Mehdi Ben Barka, but before long some of the marchers were shouting "Free Mouffok!" and "Boumedienne, assassin!" The police immediately broke up the protest and arrested some twenty students, but the regime's embarrassment remained.

That same night, police raided the University campus, searched the rooms, and arrested thirteen Moroccan and Algerian students. This intrusion irritated even the students who were indifferent to or favored the Boumedienne regime. UNEA leaders were totally discredited in student eyes by their silence during these events, a silence not even broken when the party dissolved the Algiers Section and ten students were dismissed from the University.

But the Algiers Section, spurred clandestinely by its old leaders, did react: a three-day boycott of classes began January 31. Nearly all the University's 8,000 students joined the strike. The party-controlled press ran pages of messages from FLN sections condemning the strike, but this only served to inflate its importance.[62] Despite the strike's success, the government did not release the imprisoned students or reinstate the leaders of the Algiers Section. A second strike, unlimited this time, was called for February 23. The FLN had learned its lesson, and completely ignored the boycott, which limped on for five days, then collapsed. The University had warned that four absences from class would prevent a student from taking exams. To most students, the cause was not worth the risk.

After the demonstration and the first strike, Berdi and his fellow appointees were swept out of office and the party installed a new group led by Laadi Flici, who had headed UGEMA's first provisional executive in September 1962. Flici's appointment provoked one last outburst from the old militant leftist students still in Algeria. At the May Day parade organized by the General Union of Algerian Workers (UGTA), which was sympathetic to their cause, a group of perhaps forty students stopped directly in front of the reviewing stand where Boumedienne was sitting and shouted, *"Pas de parachutage!,"* i.e., "Stop imposing [parachuting] UNEA leaders!"

But Flici kept his position. Under his leadership, UNEA became a faithful reflection of the regime's ideals and phobias. He stressed the need to put UNEA's affairs in order and attend to bread-and-butter issues of student welfare. The Union's once shabby and ill-kept headquarters on Boulevard Amirouche were cleaned up, socialist slogans and banners taken down from the walls, and bookshelves of Marxist literature thrown out. Rooms formerly in disuse were turned into badly needed study halls, a mimeographing service was established to provide copies of university lectures, and a student art gallery set up. Voluntary community work projects were dropped as "impractical," and there were to be no more demonstrations for distant causes.

Flici was one of the few student leaders who remained in Algeria throughout the war. His appointment as President of UNEA was in step with Boumedienne's policy of promoting former guerrilla leaders to top posts in the regime. Like the country's new leaders, Flici reacted strongly to foreign, particularly Communist, pressure. He felt especially bitter toward those students who had left the battlefield to continue their studies abroad during the war and had returned after independence to give lessons on "revolutionary democracy." In this sense, he was the perfect antithesis of Mouffok, just as Boumedienne was of Ben Bella. UNEA's principal role, Flici believed, should be to help the government and University produce "technicians," not a "revolutionary avant-garde."[63]

Here again, Flici was following the lead of Boumedienne, who by late 1966 had brought into his government a number of "technicians," among them some of the original founders of UGEMA. They were Ahmed Taleb (Minister of Education), Belaid Abdesselam (Ministry of Industry and Energy), Lamine Khene (Minister of Public Works), and Mohamed Ben Yahia (Minister of Information). Ait Chaalal, who like Taleb had openly opposed the Ben Bella regime, became Ambassador to Rome. All these men were highly politicized, but hardly "revolutionaries" as Mouffok understood the term.

Whether UNEA in its present state will produce men of this caliber is doubtful. Its leaders since independence have yet to measure up to those who launched and led UGEMA during the war. UNEA has failed to attract the best minds and most serious students; on the contrary, they have been repelled by the petty politicking and partisanship that have characterized the Union since 1962. Monthly meetings called by the Union have not attracted more than 100–150 students at best.

In late 1966, there was little cause for optimism. At a conference of 180 "militant party students" in late October, the party ousted Flici and his group, the third executive committee to be dismissed in less than eighteen months. Ironically, Flici had spent too much time on practical matters and not enough at FLN headquarters, where another group of faithfuls had reorganized the party students.

The party students fared no better than Flici had; they too were isolated from the main student body and at odds with the few truly "militant" members of the Union, those who followed the former leaders of the Algiers Section. The latter finally made a comeback in early 1967. During a tumultuous general assembly on April 15, some of the leftists succeeded in being re-elected to the executive of the Algiers Section, after an all-night struggle with the party students. The FLN only grudgingly accepted this election, and several members of the new executive were arrested on April 29. Two days later, the leftist students from the Algiers Section were prevented from marching in the May Day parade, the party apparently fearing they would shout antigovernment slogans as they had done the previous year.

In mid-1967, the outcome of the struggle between the party students and the leftists remained uncertain. The leftists had proven that they had more support in the student body than the discredited "parachuted" leaders. However, the latter had the support of the party, which undoubtedly would intervene again should the party students be in danger of losing control over UNEA.

Summary and Conclusion

UGEMA's "crisis of reconversion" was an ordeal all Algerian national organizations faced when independence came. The FLN, the UGTA, the women's union (UFA), and UGEMA had all been created by and for the revolution. Existing outside the country and largely independent from one another and from the GPRA in Tunis, none of them had any real roots in the country. When independence finally arrived, they all moved into Algeria to organize their members for the first time on national soil and to define their peacetime roles.

Each organization was a front of factions fighting for leadership and for a chance to impose their own conception of the role the organization should play in socialist Algeria. The internal problems were compounded by the FLN's efforts to impose its control over all the national organizations. Although most leaders of the national organizations agreed that the FLN should be the nation's sole party, few of them accepted the corollary that they should give up their autonomy to it. The fact that the FLN was weak and poorly organized made it possible for them to engage in a tug of war with party leaders.

The crisis of reconversion was especially painful for UGEMA. Structurally and ideologically, the Union was a front, comprising independent sections in more than twenty countries where Algerian students had absorbed differing ideological orientations. These differences came to the surface in the debate within UGEMA just after independence. But the language of their conflict could not hide its essence: a struggle for power. Algerian politics, at both the national and student levels, has always been a highly personal affair of contending groups and clans in which ideology plays only a secondary role.

For almost a year no faction within UGEMA was strong enough to prevail, and the party was too weak to step in and settle the question. But after their rivals walked out of the 1963 Congress, the leftist students took over and imposed their "revolutionary" line. Most of Mouffok's supporters were students admitted into the University without French *baccalauréats* thanks to the "social promotion"—those who had benefited most from Algeria's chosen socialist path. These students, together with the distinctly nonintellectual youths of the FLN, were the only "revolutionary" upholders of socialism the regime could call upon. The students of the social promotion were looked down upon by their colleagues with regular pre-university degrees. In the latter group, the majority were antisocialist, as the Education Ministry's survey makes clear, but they tended to be apathetic or dared not speak out. Had they opposed him, Ben Bella would certainly have acted against them much faster than he did against Mouffok.

The takeover of the Union by Mouffok's faction was not promoted by Ben Bella—on the contrary, we have noted his concern over UNEA's self-proclaimed autonomy—but it was definitely favored by the political climate Ben Bella helped to create. Ben Bella had allowed members of the Algerian Communist Party (PCA) into the top ranks of the FLN. The Communist newspaper *Alger République* sang his praise and backed his policies. Mouffok, whether or not he was actually a member of the Communist Party, had extremely close ties with PCA Secretary General Bachir Hadj Ali and with the editors of *Alger République* (notably with its chief editor, the French Communist Henri Alleg). He also had direct access to Ben Bella's office and home.

Moreover, Mouffok's ideas echoed the doctrine Ben Bella expounded. The students' demand for management of their own academic and social affairs was in line with the spirit of the "self-management" decrees of March 1963, intended to give peasants and workers direct control over the running of abandoned or nationalized French farms and factories. UNEA's foreign policy paralleled that of Ben Bella, who was forging ties with the Soviet Union and other Communist countries. The Union's relations with the FLN were marred primarily by the issue of autonomy, a question ultimately solved in the party's favor by the 1965 coup d'état.

The history of UNEA illustrates two different types of party-student relationship in a single-party system where the party, not as tightly organized as in Communist countries, is not always able to control the activities of national organizations. Under Mouffok, the Union was more the FLN's ally than its subordinate, an ally that wanted to establish the terms of the alliance. After the coup, UNEA became wholly dependent on the party.

There was a third position the students might have assumed toward the party, that of outright opposition, but they never took such a stand. This can be explained on two grounds. First, neither regime really oppressed the students as a group. Ben Bella even backed down on the matter of compulsory summer civic service, as he did when a proposal to suppress the scholarships of students deemed insufficiently "militant" met with equally strong student criticism. Moreover, Algerian students were being taught by French professors in a French-style university where academic freedom was still largely a reality. Second, the majority of Algerian students were apathetic, or considered the risks of open opposition—including imprisonment and possible injury—as too high a potential price to pay. The militant students were simply too few to make an impact on the government through opposition activity.

Mouffok's conception of the party-student relationship was undoubtedly the most difficult to apply. It required considerable diplomatic skill to make just enough concessions to the regime to keep it from interfering, but not enough to give it control. This was the formula that would have permitted the students to have some influence on government policy.

An autonomous or semi-autonomous UNEA, by stimulating and sustaining political discussion among the students, might have helped achieve the stated goal of both regimes: democracy within a single-party system. In reality, UNEA under Mouffok's leadership never became a center of political debate where students could come to exchange ideas without fear of being branded "counter-revolutionaries." A few attempts were made, some seminars organized, but the difficult game of autonomy played with Ben Bella absorbed nearly all the talents and energies of the militant student leaders. Maintaining the Union's autonomy became, of necessity, an end in itself and not the means to other ends. As for UNEA's role "on campus," Mouffok admitted to the Sixth Congress that the Union had done little in this domain, despite his ambitious program for establishing a system of student management in the University.

The Union's post-coup subordination to the party should make it in theory a recruiting and training ground for future party cadres, as UGET has been in neighboring Tunisia. In practice, UNEA's leadership since June 1965 has been too isolated from the student community to permit the Union to play this role. On campus, UNEA has become primarily an extension of the University administration. It has provided some useful services, but has not gained the students a voice in any basic decisions affecting their lives or studies. Nor has it become any more of a center for debate than under Mouffok, for the leadership has remained as inflexible and exclusive as before.

One is obliged to conclude that UNEA largely failed in all the roles it tried to play in independent Algeria. The Union has become isolated and partisan because of the apathy of the student community, while that apathy has in turn increased because of the partisanship of Union leaders. The students are unlikely to break out of this vicious circle on their own initiative. Any leadership dynamic enough to spark enthusiasm, and possibly opposition, among the students—in short, to mobilize them again—will immediately be shoved aside by the Boumedienne regime. Any party-controlled leadership—unable and afraid to make choices or stir controversy—will meet only indifference in the student body. It will take a total regeneration of the political life of the country to awaken the students from their present apathy, which is a reflection of the fatigue and disillusionment that grip the entire nation after the first five years of independence.

NOTES

1. Only one of the nine founders of the National Liberation Front, the so-called historic leaders, had set foot inside a French university. He was Hocine Ait Ahmed, a Kabyle, who completed at least the first part of his French *baccalauréat* degree and is said to have attended the Sorbonne as a law student. The other eight founders were Ahmed Ben Bella, Mohamed Khider, Mohamed Boudiaf, Rabah Bitat, Belkacem Krim, Mohamed Larbi Ben M'Hidi, Moustafa Ben Boulaid, and Mourad Didouche. The last three died during the independence war. Of the surviving six, only one is in power today: Rabah Bitat, Minister of State. Ben Bella, who was Algeria's first President, was deposed in a military coup d'état on June 19, 1965, and is now in prison in Algeria. Khider was assassinated in Madrid in January 1967. Boudiaf lives in exile in Paris, while Krim has retired from politics and is living in Algiers.

2. The University of Algiers was established in 1879. According to Ferhat Abbas, in his book *Le jeune algérien* (Paris: Editions de la Jeune Parque, 1931), there were only fifty Algerian students at the University in 1930. Jacques Berque, in his book, *Le Maghreb entre deux guerres* (Paris: Editions du Seuil, 1962), p. 284, cites French government statistics showing that there were only 142 students from Algeria, Morocco, and Tunisia enrolled in the University of Paris in 1935.

3. Secretariat Social d'Alger, *L'Algérie et sa jeunesse* (Algiers, 1957), pp. 60–64, citing French government statistics.

4. The AGE was controlled by right-wing extremists during the Algerian war. Its President in 1957 was Pierre Lagaillarde, who led the assault upon government buildings in Algiers in the attempted army coup of May 1958 that brought General de Gaulle to power in France. Another AGE President was Jean-Jacques Susini, the "ideologist" of the French terrorist Secret Army Organization (OAS).

5. UGEMA, *IVe Congrès National de l'UGEMA* (Leiden: Coordinating Secretariat of National Unions of Students, 1960), p. 11.

6. See UGEMA, *UGEMA, les étudiants algériens en lutte* (Prague: International Union of Students, 1960).

7. See Roger Le Tourneau, *Evolution politique de l'Afrique du nord musulmane, 1920–1961* (Paris: Librairie Armand Colin, 1962).

8. *UGEMA, les étudiants algériens en lutte*, p. 13.

9. Ahmed Taleb, *Lettres de prison, 1957–61* (Algiers: Editions Nationales Algériennes, 1966), p. 21.

10. *UGEMA, les étudiants algériens en lutte*, p. 45.

11. The estimates are those of B. Hammiche, Assistant Director of Orientation and Planning in the Ministry of Education, interviewed by the author in Algiers in October 1966.

12. It is extremely difficult to determine even the approximate number of students who actually joined the ALN. Most student leaders interviewed agreed that "hundreds" passed through the ALN; apparently many did not stay for long. Of the 520 students at the University in 1956, only 250 returned after the strike ended in 1957 (Hammiche interview), but many of the remainder may have left the country to study abroad.

13. Belaid Abdesselam became Secretary General of the GPRA under President Benyoucef Ben Khedda. Having held the same post under Ferhat Abbas, Mohamed Ben Yahia later became a top GPRA negotiator at the French-Algerian talks in Evian, which ended in the peace agreement of March 1962. After independence, Ben Yahia served the Ben Bella government as Ambassador to Moscow. Redha Malek was named editor in chief of the principal FLN journal, *El Moudjahid*. He later became Ambassador to Belgrade under Ben Bella and to Paris under Boumedienne. Cherif Belkacem (alias Major Si Djamal) became a member of the western wing of the ALN General Staff based in Oujda, Morocco. He later served as Minister of Education and Orientation in Ben Bella's government and was given the key position of Coordinator of the FLN's Executive Secretariat after the June 1965 coup d'état. Abdelaziz Bouteflika has been Algeria's Foreign Minister since 1963.

14. Messaoud Ait Chaalal, speaking to UGEMA's Fourth Congress in Tunis in 1960, in *IVe Congrès National de l'UGEMA*, p. 34.

15. After independence, Khemisti served as Foreign Minister in Ben Bella's first government. He was assassinated in April 1963 in Algiers. The convicted killer, declared insane, committed suicide.

16. Research and Information Commission (RIC), *Report on Higher Education and Culture in Algeria* (Leiden: Coordinating Secretariat of National Unions of Students, 1959), p. 18.

17. *Ibid.*, p. 13.

18. See the "Minutes of the 6th International Student Conference" (mimeo.; Coordinating Secretariat of National Unions of Students, Leiden, 1956).

19. Figures compiled for a 1960 RIC report on Algeria showed the following distribution of students: France (500), Egypt (150), East Germany (106), Iraq (100), Syria (100), Switzerland (91), Kuwait (50), Morocco (50), Tunisia (26, plus 750 in traditional Islamic studies), Czechoslovakia (24), West Germany (24), Yugoslavia (23), United States (21), Bulgaria (20), Belgium (13), Soviet Union (8), Hungary (6), Rumania (6), Albania (5), Poland (5), Spain (2), and Sweden (1). Many of the Algerians studying in North Africa and the Middle East were given scholarships directly by their host governments.

20. *UGEMA, les étudiants algériens en lutte*, pp. 36–37.

21. *IVe Congrès National de l'UGEMA*, pp. 32–33. The CNAE had been created in January 1958 in Tunis at a meeting of the three Maghreb student unions: UGEMA, UGET, and the *Union Nationale des Etudiants du Maroc* (UNEM), formed in 1956. The CNAE and its 1960 successor, the *Con-*

fédération des Etudiants du Maghreb (CEM), were authorized to speak at international conferences in the name of all three organizations. A widening breach between UGET and the other two unions left the CEM in limbo after 1964.

22. See the "Summary of the Minutes of the 10th International Student Conference" (mimeo.; Coordinating Secretariat of National Unions of Students, Leiden, 1962).

23. Several student leaders interviewed considered growing Communist influence one of the key motives behind the GPRA's decision to set up the University Section. Mohamed Mokrane headed the Section. For information on its activities, see its *Bulletin Spécial* (Algiers), April 16–20, 1962.

24. A mixed French-Algerian caretaker government at Rocher Noir thirty miles outside Algiers was theoretically in charge of running the country until elections could be held. In fact, it ran very little.

25. Laadi Flici, interviewed by the author in Algiers, October 1966.

26. The figure 2,000 is from *Le Monde*, September 12, 1962. The number of delegates was never made clear, but must have been around 200.

27. *Alger Républicain* (Algiers) and *Le Peuple* (Algiers), September 5–15, 1962.

28. They were from the Soviet Union, the United States, West Germany, Egypt, Kuwait, Iraq, Syria, Jordan, Libya, Yugoslavia, Morocco, Tunisia, and the ALN.

29. The term "Arabization" generally refers to the teaching of courses in Arabic rather than French. In colonial Algeria, Arabic was treated as a "foreign" language and its use discouraged at all levels of education. As late as 1966–67, there was still such a shortage of Arabic-speaking educators in the country that, despite the help of roughly 2,000 teachers from the Middle East, instruction could be carried out wholly in Arabic in the first grade only. The term also refers to demands for greater emphasis in education on the history and culture of Islam and the Arab world.

30. *Alger Républicain*, September 15, 1962.

31. From October to December 1962, the Ministry of Education published a series of communiqués appealing to students abroad to return home.

32. By 1966–67, the University of Algiers had fourteen faculties and *Grandes Ecoles*, seven institutes, and its own French-staffed nuclear center, and had acquired over $2-million worth of electronic equipment. Approximately 20 per cent of the students were foreigners: Africans, Arabs, and French.

The student-run café had been named after a UGEMA martyr, Abderrahmane Taleb, an Algiers University chemistry student condemned to death for manufacturing FLN explosives and guillotined in Algiers in April 1958. The upper floors of the student center on Boulevard Amirouche had been blown up by French terrorists and were largely unusable for three years after independence.

33. Abdelaziz Ouabdesalam took over as President of the University in 1963, replacing the French historian Henri Gautier. Malek Bennabi, a nationalist and writer, replaced another French historian (André Mandouze) as Director of Higher Education. France, implementing its cooperation agreement with Algeria, furnished eighty-two full professors in 1965. The Soviet Union provided eight professors, while the Arab countries, notably Tunisia and the U.A.R., also sent personnel. Figures from *Maghreb*, No. 12 (November-December 1965), p. 20.

34. There were only 115 students enrolled in Arabic studies at the University in 1963. (Ministry of Education, *Informations Statistiques*, July 1964.) In 1964, the teacher training school had only eight students. (Dr. Malek Bennabi, interviewed in Algiers, November 1964.)

35. Other reforms, equally controversial, have been carried out to make the University an institution of the state. The El-Harrach School of Agriculture was placed directly under the supervision of the Agrarian Reform Ministry, while the medical school was detached from the University and put directly under the purview of the Ministry of Social Affairs. The length of studies in medicine was cut by one year, but the academic year for medical students was extended to eleven months. After finishing their studies, medical students must serve two years in the interior with the state medical corps.

36. The monthly scholarship for medical and science students is $80 and for those attending the Polytechnical School of El-Harrach, $90. The "pre-salary" is given out even during the summer vacation. In the 1964–65 school year, there were 1,822 students in sciences and 1,555 in letters. (Figures from Ministry of Education officials interviewed in Algiers, October 1966.) Most of the approximately 1,600 Algerians on scholarships abroad are studying sciences.

37. *Al Chaab* (Algiers), December 18, 1962, reporting Ben Bella's speech at the University's opening day ceremony.

38. Information on the formation of the provisional executive was given by Djamal Khiari, interviewed in Algiers, September 1966.

39. There were faculties of law and medicine in Oran and also in Constantine. The government, pursuing a policy of decentralization to relieve the pressure for admission to the University of Algiers, hoped to open a university in Oran and another in Constantine. The University of Oran was finally inaugurated in December 1966.

40. *Al Chaab*, April 11, 1964.

41. See *The New York Times*, August 25, 1964.

42. See *Al Chaab*, February 7 and 13, 1963.

43. Estimate based on figures given by Zenine at a press conference in Algiers, July 17, 1963. According to Zenine, the Algiers Section had signed up 258 students for the summer literacy campaign, and 50 medical students had volunteered to work in hospitals. See also *Al Chaab*, July 18, 1963.

44. See *Alger Républicain* and *Al Chaab*, April 10, 1963, and "Algeria, the Revolution, Ben Bella and Youth," *Youth and Freedom* (New York), VII, No. 2 (1965), 5.

45. See *Alger Républicain*, May 31 and June 12, 1963.

46. *Al Chaab*, August 14, 1963.

47. This was not merely a matter of words. The "M" in UGEMA had served to keep French and Algerian Communists out of the organization and had symbolized the assertion of Algeria's indigenous personality and Arab-Islamic heritage in the face of secular French culture. The Marxists who obtained its deletion at the Congress thereby pointed the Union in a wholly different direction.

48. *Ve Congrès de l'UGEMA et le programme de l'UNEA* (Algiers: Imprimerie le Peuple, 1965).

49. See Mouffok's speech to the Fifth Congress, in *ibid.*

50. "Algeria, the Revolution, Ben Bella and Youth," p. 5.

51. This estimate is based on Mouffok's speech to the Sixth Congress of

UNEA, in *VIe Congrès National* (Algiers: Imprimerie le Peuple, 1965), and the author's conversations with students in Algiers at the time.

52. Ministry of Education, *Bulletin Intérieur*, No. 13–14 (April 4, 1966). The survey was administered in February-March 1965 to a sample of 400 students chosen at random from all the faculties of the University of Algiers. The students were asked (among other questions) whether there was greater advantage to a developing country in using planning and control techniques or in allowing free competition in the following fields: exploitation of natural resources, use of manpower, training of cadres, and allocation of trained personnel. In each field, between 74 and 77 per cent of the students favored allowing free competition. On a question asking for preferred place of study, over half the respondents said they would rather study abroad (notably in France), but of these only 4 per cent specified a Communist country.

53. See the interview with Mohamed Berdi, a party student, in the JFLN weekly, *Jeunesse*, November 13, 1964.

54. Colonel Mohamed Chaabani, a member of the FLN Political Bureau, headed the 4th Military Region. He refused a promotion to the Army General Staff and instead took to the hills with 1,500 soldiers at the end of June 1964. He was captured on July 8 by Colonel Boumedienne's troops and, after a military trial, executed in early September.

55. See *Alger Républicain*, August 8–9, 1964. The Front of Socialist Forces, led by Hocine Ait Ahmed, was launched in September 1963 and became a hit-and-run terrorist organization of small guerrilla bands operating in the Kabylia mountains sixty miles east of Algiers. Two-thirds of Colonel Boumedienne's 50,000-man army was tied up in the mountains fighting against these bands. Ait Ahmed's capture in October 1964 ended the Front's activities.

56. See Mouffok's speech to the Sixth Congress, in *VIe Congrès National*. Of the 80 per cent in the Ministry's survey who said they belonged to UNEA, 46 per cent described themselves as "mere adherents" and only 22 per cent as "active members." Twenty-seven per cent of the entire sample said they joined the Union because they considered themselves "union militants," 23 per cent out of "conformity or duty," 16 per cent for "material advantages," and 5 per cent as "political militants." (Ministry of Education, *Bulletin Intérieur*, No. 13–14 [April 4, 1966].)

57. Mouffok was elected with 63 votes. Zenine was elected on the first ballot with 68 votes, while both Berdi and Bouchaib, the party students, got 65 and 63 votes respectively on the first ballot. *Le Peuple*, August 15, 1964.

58. See *ibid.*, November 9 and 18, 1964.

59. *Jeunesse*, No. 31 (January 22, 1965).

60. Author's estimate, based on personal observation.

61. The External Delegation, based in Paris, undoubtedly enjoyed the support of the majority of Algerian students in France. One UNEA official told the author its own Paris section had no more than seventy-five followers. The Delegation was far more active, putting out its own *Révolution Université*. AEMNA in Paris, the IUS in Prague, student unions in Communist countries, and several African student organizations supported the Delegation internationally.

62. See, for example, *El Moudjahid* (Algiers), February 1–4, 1966.

63. Flici interview, October 1966.

2. THE CONGO

JEAN-CLAUDE WILLAME

In comparison with their counterparts in Asia and Latin America, African student political movements are notable for both their scarcity and their weakness. The university is still something of a newcomer in black Africa,[1] and nationalist traditions are comparatively short. This is particularly true of the Republic of the Congo.

This chapter seeks to explore and explain the striking contrast in the Congo between the intellectual's respected status in society and his negligible impact on politics. After briefly reviewing colonial education, we shall examine the various political roles played by students and student organizations since 1960, the year of Congolese independence. We shall then focus on the social condition and political behavior of students at the nation's major university. A brief conclusion will summarize our findings.

Colonial Education

As it began to develop after 1892, when the first school was opened, education in the Belgian Congo reflected the general principles of Belgian colonialism. The colonizer's stated objective was "to lift the Congolese masses to a fuller economic and social life, and thus give the population as a whole a personal stake in a productive and prosperous nation."[2] The Congolese child was to be prepared for his role as a producer of primary goods and, by the inculcation

The research on which this chapter is based was conducted at Lovanium University in 1966. Special thanks are owed to Professor Benoit Verhaegen, Director of the University's Center of Political Studies, for his inspiration and guidance. Yvon Bongoy, André Ilunga-Kabongo, and Laurent Monnier, research assistants at Lovanium, also contributed valuable advice and information. The chapter has been translated from the French by Donald Emmerson.

in him of a deep religious faith, immunized against the temptations of politics.[3]

Until 1948, post-primary education in the Congo centered on teacher training schools, where pupils were taught "the love of work, the habit of sustained effort . . . and respect for authority"; commercial schools where clerks, accountants, and typists were trained; and professional schools producing technically qualified personnel for business and the civil service.[4] The Catholic missions enjoyed a near total monopoly over this system. Any young Congolese who wanted to complete his intellectual education was obliged to go through one of the many seminars established to develop a native African clergy.

The quantitative growth of mass education was remarkable. In 1908, when the Congo Free State became a Belgian colony, school enrollment stood below 100,000. Fifty years later, the figure had risen fifteen-fold to nearly 1.5 million, encompassing well over half the total school-age population.[5] Literacy, estimated at 50 per cent at the time of Congolese independence, was among the highest in Africa.

But however broad its base, the colonial educational pyramid had no top. Academic secondary education was not made available until 1948. Not until 1954 did opportunities for university education in the Congo exist; in that year, near Léopoldville, Lovanium University first opened its doors.[6] In 1955, a Belgian Congo–Ruanda Urundi State University was established in Elisabethville (now Lubumbashi).[7] In contrast to the latter institution, from the start a majority of the students at Lovanium were African,[8] giving rise to the myth of Lovanium as "the African university."

In 1959, over 400 Africans were enrolled in these two institutions.[9] Nevertheless, when independence came the following year, there were only about thirty Congolese with university degrees (awarded for the most part in the social sciences, business administration, and education) .

Students and Political Power

Three periods can be distinguished in the history of relations between students and political authority in the Congo. The first extended from the "Economic Round Table" conference of April-June 1960 to the dissolution of the *Collège des Commissaires* the following February. This phase ended with the passing of the "intellectual as technician" from the Congolese political scene. In the second period, a Congolese student movement emerged and tried to organize itself. Its leaders began to turn toward radical options, the year 1963 marking the height of student political opposition. The third period, dating from July 1964, when Moise Tshombe, as Prime Minister, began his second political career, was a time of crisis for the student movement. During this phase, the students failed to play more than a peripheral political role.

The Economic Round Table conference, convened in Belgium on April 26, 1960, marked the political debut of the university-trained Congolese intellectual. The conference, called together through the efforts of Minister of Congo Economic Affairs Raymond Scheyven, was an extension of the political "Round Table" of January-February 1960, which had scheduled Congolese independence for June 30 of that year. Belgium was particularly concerned over the future of her investments in the Congo and hoped the second meeting would yield reassurances regarding the financial policies of the state to be. The categories of representation at the political Round Table were again present at the economic conference: Belgian government and parliamentary delegates on the one hand, Congolese political party spokesmen on the other. But unlike its predecessor, the Economic Round Table allocated seats to a number of Congolese university students and recent graduates. These "technical experts" attended as representatives of the *Collège Exécutif Général*,[10] which had been established as the transitional administrative authority in Léopoldville.

The *Collège Exécutif* had already been discredited for its inefficiency and lack of cohesion. Its delegates at the conference fared no better. The Congolese politicians wanted from the Economic Round Table an inventory of the national assets of their future state, and the Belgian government hoped the meeting would lead to an agreement on post-independence economic and financial cooperation.[11] The Congolese "experts" found themselves caught between conflicting alternative roles. On the one side, they were expected to advance the interests of the Congo in technical fields where the politicians were on unsure ground. On the other, they were expected to be sufficiently impartial and understanding to attenuate the politicians' more radical demands.

In the course of the discussions, the delegates of the *Collège Exécutif* tended to favor the Belgians' procedural points and, to a degree, their substantive arguments as well. The students' sojourn in Belgium had made them, or so it seemed, less able to share the suspicions or endorse the demands of their politician colleagues. The students and ex-students did on occasion take positions opposed to those of the Belgium delegates, but "expert-vs.-politician" tensions among the Congolese persisted.

The politicians, more sensitive to the electoral implications of the talks, tended to view the experts as overly Belgian-influenced. A leader of the African Solidarity Party (PSA), Gabriel Yumbu, even accused the students of being outright "neocolonialists." Mario Cardoso, then a research assistant at Lovanium, tried to coordinate the Congolese representation, but failed. Several groups boycotted the Conference; Patrice Lumumba and Joseph Kasavubu were among those absent from the closing session.[12]

The months May through September 1960 were critical ones. The legislative elections, the mutiny of the *Force Publique,* and the conflict between President Kasavubu and his Prime Minister, Lumumba, marked a period of brutal intertribal, interfactional violence. The politicians reigned supreme, albeit in chaos. While recognizing the need to grant responsibility to the technically skilled, the new state's leaders saw in the students in Europe a potential threat to their own recently gained monopolies of power.

In September, Colonel Mobutu decided to "neutralize" the Lumumba-Kasavubu strife. As a journalist and friend of Lumumba, Joseph Mobutu had maintained a strong interest in politics, but he had also retained a taste for professionalism and discipline acquired during seven years of service in the *Force Publique.* On September 14, he announced he would

> launch a solemn appeal to all our students, to all our African technicians in Europe and elsewhere. They must return as quickly as possible to assume the administration of the country. . . . After this short revolutionary period, we will, with the agreement of our young students, return power to the politicians.[13]

In what must be one of the few occasions in human history when the reins of state have been formally handed over to a nation's university-educated youth, Mobutu formed a *Collège des Commissaires* (College of Commissioners), staffed it with the students and recent graduates who responded to his appeal, and gave them the awesome task of governing the Congo.

Each General Commissioner, assisted by one or more Commissioners received a portfolio related, if possible, to his academic major. The General Commissioners for Justice and Public Health, for example, were law and medical students respectfully. On September 19, the new student government declared:

> To the call of the nation, the technicians have answered, "Present."

All the education we have received, all our capabilities, we place at the disposal of the country. This is how the elite of the country comes to the aid of the elected. However, this elite has neither the intention nor the right to replace the elected. That is why the technicians who have been called upon refuse to become ministers, refuse to seize power from the elected. . . .

In the distribution of posts, ability will be applied as the sole criterion, without any tribal discrimination whatsoever. Our task is above all to run the administration. The administrative machinery must operate to give the politicians time and the material possibilities to reach agreement.[14]

Promise is one thing, performance another. The size of the *Collège*, initially set at twenty-four members, increased rapidly to thirty-nine under pressure from the students themselves, particularly those who had dropped their studies to come home, and because of the need to balance regions and tribes. The institution became unwieldy, its deliberations often paralyzed by younger members fresh from the university and without political or administrative experience of any kind.

Furthermore, from the outset, the Commissioners' functions were ill defined. Despite the students' public renunciation of any desire for political power and their self-portrayal as interim technicians fending off anarchy,[15] many members of the *Collège* sought to play political-ministerial roles. Such activity did not even violate the limits of their authority, which had been specifically decreed to encompass both the legislative and executive realms.[16]

Three different tendencies quickly developed within the *Collège*.[17] The *technicians,* who had interrupted their studies or left their jobs to answer Colonel Mobutu's appeal, were the most numerous and, politically, the least effective. The *defenders of Mobutu* and his coup d'état, while opposing the politicians, maneuvered for political power (under first Mobutu's, later Kasavubu's, protection). In this category were students and ex-students who had already clashed with the politicians at the Economic Round Table earlier the same year. Among them, Mbeka, Ndele, and the ex-student leader Lihau (see Note 10, above) were the driving force of the *Collège*.

The *political Commissioners* filled a third category. Overtly active in politics, either as individuals or in line with some partisan group, they included the President of the *Collège,* Justin Bomboko, and General Commissioners Albert Bolela and Ferdinand Kazadi.

Aside from Bomboko,[18] the Commissioners had no base of mass support. In the still hyperpolitical atmosphere of the Congo, the *Collège* was neither an effective power, an efficient authority, nor an electoral force of any weight.

The students' and the politicians' skills differed greatly. The students' advantage lay in the scientific knowledge they had acquired in the classroom. But the politicians excelled in the art of political communication; their visionary language, as Jacques Berque has remarked in another context, could "touch the heart of a changing society more profoundly than any other instrument." As a wielder of effective, day-to-day power, wrote Berque, the politician "is nothing. As a representative of the people, he is little. But as a symbol, he is everything. . . ."[19]

The Commissioners were overtaken by events they could not control. As the weeks went by, political power slipped like sand through their fingers and was quickly gathered up by various factions: President Kasavubu's clique, certain members of the Ileo cabinet,[20] the security police (*Sûreté*), the Congolese National Army (ANC), and other elements. Internationally, the Commissioners antagonized certain radical African states (notably Ghana, Guinea, and the UAR) and, in Léopoldville, conducted a violent press campaign against them. Domestically, the *Collège* was shaken by a succession of political and military setbacks: the ANC's failure in battle against the dissident regime of Anicet Kashamura in Bukavu, the mutiny at Camp Hardy in Thysville, and the assassination of Patrice Lumumba in Katanga in January 1961, the last an event in which certain members of the *Collège* were indirectly implicated.

The myth of the "student-technician" collapsed. While their predecessors fell back before the advancing politicians, a new generation of students began organizing in the universities to defend and reorient the crumbling Congolese polity.

Students in Opposition

The late arrival of universities in the Congo, as we have noted, delayed the birth of a student movement. Tensions between the predominantly European student body at the State University in Elisabethville and the African student majority at Lovanium further impeded the development of a national organization.

Two Congolese students[21] from Lovanium attended the Seventh International Student Conference in Ibadan, Nigeria, in September 1957. They did not represent the students at the newly established State University in Elisabethville and were therefore not granted the right to vote for the Congo. The Conference instead called for the establishment of a national union of Congolese students.

Plans for the new union foundered on the insistence by the European majority in Elisabethville that the proposed organization affiliate with the Federation of Belgian Students in the metropole. A protocol between the students at Lovanium and Elisabethville was finally signed, but arguments soon broke out again. Not until March 1960, less than four months before the Congo became independent, was the National Union of Students of the Congo and Ruanda-Urundi (*Union Nationale des Etudiants du Congo et du Ruanda-Urundi,* or UNECRU) finally inaugurated.[22] Created (as its name indicates) in the colonial framework, UNECRU played no role in events leading to independence.

The failure of their elders in the *Collège des Commissaires* and an awareness of their growing numbers led the students to confront their responsibilities in the new, rapidly (but only partially) decolonized Congo. Meeting at Lovanium May 4–7, 1961, they formed the General Union of Congolese Students (*Union Générale des Etudiants Congolais,* or UGEC). Most of the delegates to this constituent First Congress were Lovanium students, but representatives from Belgium, France, and the United States also took part. The secessionist government of Katanga lent a note of urgency to the students' hopes for national unity and reconciliation by preventing the attendance of a delegation from Elisabethville.[23]

Two ex-students, Henri Takizala and Nestor Watum, were elected UGEC President and Secretary for National Affairs, respectively.[24] The new Union's constitution, in fact, specified that the President should be a recent university graduate and empowered him to draw a salary from the organization. Takizala, a former Commissioner and a key UNECRU leader, remained an important figure in Congolese student politics for some time to come.

The political positions taken by the Congress were anguished in tone, but relatively moderate in substance. In their resolution on the political situation in the Congo, the delegates denounced "the politicians in power" for having compromised with foreign powers, for having rejected good advice,[25] for refusing to agree among themselves, for seeking only money and power, and "because they bathe in blood and violence." The resolution condemned "all political executions without trial," but did not mention the killing of Lumumba only four months before. The Congress went on to recommend that a "Government of Public Safety" be allowed to rule for two years, Parliament relegated to a consultative role, and a strong central government organized atop a federal state structure.[26] In their vague delimitation of the proposed government's purview, the delegates showed a poor grasp of constitutional law.

It was on the subject of education—where the students had direct experience—that the resolutions were most thoroughly developed. The delegates demanded that education be adapted to African conditions, urged university students to study in the Congo if at all possible, recommended the expansion of adult education, and expressed the hope that students and professors together might govern the Congo's universities and defend their autonomy against regionalist or ideological pressure.

These resolutions went almost completely unnoticed outside the congress hall. With the opening of Parliament in July 1961, the politics of legislative maneuver began again. The government of Cyrille Adoula, with U.N. aid and substantial foreign support, gained in power and stability as it sought to quell the dissident regimes in Stanleyville and Elisabethville. UGEC stayed fairly quiet through these events and into 1962, speaking out only toward the climax of the struggle against Moise Tshombe's secession in Katanga and during a bitter conflict between the central government and the trade unions.

The students' lethargy lasted until the beginning of 1963. In that year, tribal and regional discontent, the systematic removal of radical nationalist leaders, and the increasing weight of a political elite swollen by the multiplication and subdivision of territorial units, all worked to intensify opposition to the Adoula government. In February, the Union of Congolese Workers (UTC) struck the Office of Congolese Transport (OTRACO); many arrests were made. In May and again in August, certain leaders of the General Federation of Congolese Workers (FGTK) were arrested for anti-government activity. In August, Pierre Mulele organized an armed revolt in Kwilu province. In September, the Lumumbist Congolese National Movement (MNC–L) and the African Solidarity Party (PSA) took to the streets of Léopoldville to protest the detention of Antoine Gizenga, President of the PSA and formerly Vice Premier in Lumumba's government. In October, several opposition groups formed the National Committee of Liberation (CNL) in Brazzaville, 25,000 school teachers were reported on strike, military police rule was clamped down on the city of Léopoldville to suppress "subversion," and the founding member-parties of the CNL (among them the MNC–L and the Gizengist PSA) were outlawed.[27]

As the repression mounted, UGEC threw off its torpor. The frequency, unanimity, and coherence of its positions and the importance they were given by the political public testified to the fact that for the first time since its birth, UGEC had become a real political force.

UGEC's Second Congress, held in Léopoldville August 4–11, 1963, showed the new strength of radical sentiment in Congolese student politics. The importance of the meeting was underscored by the presence, among others, of opposition leaders Christophe Gbenye and Egide Bocheley-Davidson (who later inspired the rebellions of 1964–65). UTC President André Bo-Boliko, and several East European diplomats.

The Congress debated more than thirty different topics and passed fifty mimeographed pages of resolutions. The delegates' options, for the most part, paralleled those of the opposition parties and trade unions, especially the MNC–L and the PSA. Correcting the omission of the First Congress in 1961, the meeting proclaimed Patrice Lumumba a national martyr-hero. The students demanded that Gizenga be immediately released, the condition of the Congolese worker improved, and "imperialist" intervention via the American Embassy in Léopoldville brought to an end.[28]

Under UGEC's new slogan, "All for the People and their Revolution!," the delegates orated in the language of radical African nationalism: the nationalization of private enterprise; the defeat of colonialism, neocolonialism, and imperialism; a diplomatically neutral, domestically socialist ideological option; the installation of a strong presidential regime as in Ghana and Guinea; an end to nuclear tests above African soil; and the erection of a monument to the memory of Patrice Lumumba.

At the Congress, the notion of the student as intellectual technician ceded to an image of the student as political activist. One resolution pledged "unshakable solidarity" with the "working masses" in their struggle against the government. In another, the delegates judged the actions of the "old" student generation of the *Collège des Commissaires:*

> Whereas the General Commissioners aggravated the Congolese crisis by adopting partisan political positions;
>
> Whereas the General Commissioners were remote-controlled by foreign powers with an interest in the Katangese secession and opposed to the territorial integrity of the Congo;
>
> Whereas these General Commissioners are in part responsible for the assassination of the Congolese leader, the NATIONAL HERO Patrice LUMUMBA. . . .
>
> Whereas the behavior of the General Commissioners has discredited the entire Congolese intellectual class. . . .
>
> UGEC denounces, before national and international opinion, the sinister conduct of the General Commissioners. . . .[29]

With these words, the students broke with their past. The Congress decided that henceforth all members of the National Executive Committee would have to be students. The mandate of Henri Takizala, who had become Vice Rector of the State University in Elisabethville, was not renewed; Ferdinand Kayukwa-Kimoto, formerly head of the Union's section in Belgium, was elected to replace him as President of UGEC.

The attempt to penetrate the society of which the students wanted so much to be a part—an attempt at all costs *to be heard* by that society—characterized UGEC during this period. The radical utopianism and verbal extravagance of their views reflected the students' search for a place in the nation and a role in her salvation.

After the Congress, UGEC's new President demanded the dissolution of Parliament and the election of a national constituent assembly to prepare a new constitution for popular approval.[30] When later invited to send delegates to an appointed Constitutional Commission, scheduled to meet in Luluabourg to draw up a national constitution, UGEC flatly refused.[31]

The increasingly intransigent stands taken by UGEC leaders in the latter half of 1963 provoked some criticism among their fellow students. Condemning UGEC's refusal to help draw up the new constitution, the Association of Bakongo Students denounced the UGEC leaders for their "dictatorial partisan policy," their "ambitions for power," and their infatuation with radical slogans.[32] UGEC claimed this opposition had been stimulated by the Adoula government in an attempt to divide the students. Otherwise of little consequence, the criticism did underscore the fragility of UGEC, whose leaders, authoritarian in style but lacking effective means of coercion, had little control over their fellow students. This fragility and lack of control could be seen most clearly in the severe internal crisis UGEC underwent as a result of Moise Tshombe's unexpected re-entrance to stage center in the Congolese political drama.

The Students Divided

In the Congo, the birth, growth, and death of political groups is largely a function of shifting interpersonal relationships. Political ideologies, in any formal sense, are little more than superstructures of convenient myth. The Congolese polity must be viewed in this light, as a collection of simultaneously linked and conflictive interfactional networks of support and hostility whose configurations may break or merge in easy violation of ideological boundaries. Only when we realize that the Congolese political spectrum is calibrated not so much from left to right as in degrees of personal influence can we understand what at first glance appears inexplicable: the installation of a Tshombe government in Léopoldville only eighteen months after the end of the Katangese secession.

Tshombe's sudden comeback proved disastrous for a student movement still searching for its own identity and unity. Tshombe seemed the very negation of the radical values of UGEC and of everything symbolized by his antagonist in life and death, Patrice Lumumba, whose martyrdom had not yet faded from the memories of African intellectuals. When the possibility of Tshombe's return to power from his self-imposed exile in Spain became known, the Union split wide open.

Endless arguments broke out between student opponents of the former Katangese secessionist and students upholding "national reconciliation." At the top, the leaders of UGEC were also divided. On the initiative of UGEC President Kayukwa-Kimoto, the National Executive Committee issued a statement on June 1, 1964, demanding the installation of an eight-man "Government of Public Safety" and the return to Léopoldville of certain "Congolese personalities being kept outside the country."[33] This stand triggered a coup d'état within the executive. Kayukwa-Kimoto was removed from office and National Affairs Secretary André Nkanza-Dolumingu was appointed interim President of UGEC.

At a press conference held not long after the installation of the Tshombe government, on July 10, 1964, Nkanza-Dolumingu and his fellow student leaders denounced the new regime in virulent terms. Their indictment resulted in the arrest of Hubert Makanda (President of AGEL, the student association at Lovanium University), Gerard Kamanda (Vice President of AGEL), and Nkanza-Dolumingu himself.

Tshombe's return split UGEC's Belgian section as well. For the "reformist" wing, led by the students at Liège, UGEC was supposed "first of all to help the students toward academic success, the primary objective justifying their presence abroad." The students of Liège held that a reform of the organization was absolutely essential "because the simple fact of being known as a member of UGEC, merely [being seen under] the UGEC banner [or behind] the UGEC label, brings public censure down on the students when they return to their country."[34]

The radical wing of the Congolese student community in Belgium continued to reject any possibility of dialogue with the new regime. In one press release, they condemned the Tshombe government and supported the CNL; in another, they denounced the U.S.-supported Belgian parachute drop on Stanleyville of November 1964.[35] Centered in Brussels, they gathered around Jules Chome, a Belgian lawyer and editorial writer for *Remarques Congolaises et Africaines,* in which their declarations frequently appeared.

To dampen the students' resistance at home, the new regime gave them, and particularly those from Kasai and Katanga, easy access to the administration. To cut down student opposition abroad, Tshombe requested that the Belgian government cancel the scholarships of the leaders of UGEC-Belgium and expel them from the country.[36]

Ideologically torn, its leaders under surveillance in the Congo and abroad, the student movement rapidly declined as a political force. The Third Congress of UGEC, scheduled for 1965, was postponed *sine die,* although in November 1965 UGEC President Nkanza-Dolumingu announced that the meeting would be held at the beginning of 1966.[37]

The Congress was finally held October 8–16, 1966, in Kinshasha (Léopoldville). Joseph Mobutu, President of the Republic since his successful military coup in November 1965, sent a message of greetings to the meeting and his government helped defray its costs.

Going into the Congress, the Union's prospects must have seemed bleak. Only two Executive Committee members were still in office: Nkanza Dolumingu, "interim" President for more than two years, and Anatole Malu, Secretary for Information. Most of the others had left the Union to accept positions in the government. Both Nkanza-Dolumingu and Malu were reelected, as President and National Affairs Secretary, respectively.[38]

The resolutions of the Third Congress were even more radical in tone than those of the Second. The delegates called for a socialist single-party state in the Congo, equipped with a "people's army" to "track down all the reactionary, opportunist elements whose action might endanger the interests of the people and the security of the State"; urged the dissolution of OCAM (the regional interstate *Organisation Commune Africaine et Malgache*), calling it "a tool in the hands of the imperialists to undermine the embryo of African unity"; and, in a series of resolutions, condemned the United States for "imperialist" intervention in Cambodia, Colombia, Cuba, the Dominican Republic, Israel, Japan, Laos, Malaysia, the Philippines, Puerto Rico, South Korea, South Viet-Nam, Taiwan, Thailand, and Venezuela.[39]

In an introduction to these resolutions, the National Executive

Committee of UGEC traced the rise and decline of a succession of types of social organization: "the primitive community, the slave-based society, the feudal society, the capitalist society, and finally the socialist society whose growth and [self-]affirmation herald the reign of Communism."[40] In this historically inevitable process

the "movements of national liberation" are a sociopolitical phenomenon of fundamental import in our time, because they not only carry on their flanks the germs of the final triumph of (scientific) socialism over capitalism, but also because they confirm from day to day the scientific precision and rigor of historical materialism as conceived and elaborated by Marx and Engels, [and as] verified and enriched by Lenin, Stalin and Mao Tse-tung in the light of revolutionary practice.[41]

The Congress also marked a general rapprochement between UGEC and the Mobutu government. With the latter moving to cut down Belgian influence in the Congolese economy, seeking to bring Moise Tshombe home to be executed on charges of treason, and working to improve its relations with radical African states, UGEC was willing for the first time to cooperate with public authority in the Congo.

In return, the Mobutu regime seemed willing, at least in the educational sphere, to cooperate with UGEC. In January 1967, under the pressure of student demands for the decolonization of higher technical education, the government replaced the Belgian director of the National Institute of Buildings and Public Works (INBTP) in Kinshasha with a Congolese, and named UGEC Vice President Malu to the INBTP Administrative Council. As he had in 1960, Mobutu sought to reintegrate the university-educated elite into the national administration. Ex-students and former student leaders from the 1961–65 period soon figured prominently among his closest advisers: among them, Gerard Kamanda (formerly President of AGEL), Jacques Bongoma, and Umba di Lutete. Five of his ministers were university graduates: Justin Bomboko, Paul Mushiete, Joseph Nsinga, Sophie Kanza-Lihau, and Athanase Ndjadi. Bomboko had been President and Mushiete a Commissioner in the *Collège des Commissaires* in 1960; Nsinga had been elected to the leadership of UGEC in 1961.

Yet there were important differences between Mobutu's styles of leadership in 1960 and in 1967. The "student government" of 1960 was strictly provisional and, in theory if not in fact, apolitical; its successor in 1967 was permanent and, in its appropriation of radical nationalist symbols, eminently political. The Mobutu government of 1967, building its legitimacy expressively through the potent symbology of Lumumbism and instrumentally through concrete measures of reform, could perhaps accomplish what none of its predecessors had been able to: gain, retain, and harness the loyalties of the Congolese student. But it was still too early to tell.

Lovanium University: A Case Study

In 1923, the Catholic University of Louvain in Belgium (from which Lovanium takes its name) founded a medical training center in the Congo.[42] But not until 1954 was Lovanium University opened, at Kimuenza near Léopoldville, to crown the work of the Catholic missions in the Congo.

Lovanium's student body, including Congolese, foreign Africans, and Europeans, expanded rapidly from 33 in 1954–55 to 485 in 1959–60.[43] In the troubled 1960–61 period, many foreign students left the University, but the following year a new wave came to the Congo to enroll.

A look at the distribution of students by faculty refutes the notion that university students in the Congo are overwhelmingly concentrated in the social sciences and humanities. In 1964–65, there were 226 Congolese students in the faculty of medicine, a figure not too far below the 341 in political, social, and economic science. Enrollment that same year in the technical and natural science faculties (130) was almost as high as the number in law, philology, and letters (146).[44] The humanistic disciplines, however, contributed a disproportionate share of the politically active students and graduates.[45]

The rapid development of Lovanium took place on two levels: physical facilities and public image. Under the impetus of its Rector, Monseigneur Luc Gillon, the University put up new academic and dormitory buildings, improved the roads, and built professors' homes, to the point where the campus at times resembled a huge construction site. The University also has scientific equipment, including a nuclear reactor and a computer, that makes it among the most modern in Africa. All these projects derive from one of the University's basic decisions: "to construct to exist and last" in a society fallen prey to so many imbalances, uncertainties, and contradictions.

Lovanium has also attended to its public image. In the words of one of the founders of Lovanium, Professor Guy Malengreau, the University must consider problems as the Africans consider them, understand them as they understand them, and travel the roads of research following their guides. . . . The University will remain alien to the African community if she fails to become an integral part of it, embodying its very personality, [and] if she fails to encompass and unify that [process of] profound acculturation, to foster [that] synthesis, from which the new Africa will grow.[46]

This language invariably recurs in the speeches and declarations of the academic authorities, who stress the necessity for Lovanium to "take part in the construction of Africa" and to "promote African cultural values and the African personality," and who boast of the University's accomplishments in this regard.[47]

The University's advancing material prosperity and the self-congratulatory conviction with which its "African" mission is advertised hide a far different reality: the chasms that separate the University from Congolese society in general and Congolese students in particular. Lovanium is, in effect, an organism whose essential structure remained sheltered from the critical phase of decolonization and whose development was thereby retarded in comparison with the pace of change in society at large.

In every sense, Lovanium is still a fundamentally alien institution. Located at a distance of more than fifteen miles from the capital, the campus has been furnished with a complete set of amenities—primary schools, a police force, a clinic, food stores, automobile transport, garages, and so on—which make it a self-servicing unit. This self-enclosed ecology strongly reinforces the University's isolation from Congolese society.

Like most of the business enterprises in the Congo, the University is largely dependent on institutions outside the country: governments, commercial firms, insurance companies, and others. Academically, Lovanium is still guided by Belgian institutions and standards. Before independence, the executive organ of the University was located in Louvain; the Rector held power only as delegated by an administrative council sitting in Belgium. Since 1960, the center of decision-making has shifted from Louvain to Lovanium, where the Rector has gradually gathered discretionary power in his own hands. But signs of continuing ties with the "mother university" still remain: among them, the existence of a Higher Academic Council and a Lovanium University Foundation headquartered in Louvain, and the high proportion of Belgian professors from Louvain now teaching at Lovanium.

Last and most important of all, the teaching, research, and administrative staff of the University in 1966 was still 80 per cent non-African (largely Belgian).[48] As Benoit Verhaegen has suggested, Africa for these foreigners is a place for interim training and experience before they resume their careers in Europe.[49] For a number of them, the "interim" dates back to the founding of the University.

In recent years, a limited number of Congolese have risen to posts of responsibility in instruction, research, and adminstration. A minority group, they tend to model their attitudes after those of the European professors and administrators, in whose images they find their own self-definition.

This situation has had a profound effect on the system of academic values at Lovanium, which are derived from the aristocratic-paternalist conception of an "Alma Mater" prevalent in the West: student subordination to professorial authority, the exclusion of the student from academic policy formation, and so on. The student is an object of, not a participant in, the educational process. The supposed beneficiary of the University, he feels a stranger there. But he is neither sufficiently organized nor ideologically armed to shake up the status quo.

Over the years, however, the increasing scope of the University, its ever expanding student body, the formation of a conscientious elite among those who entered Lovanium in 1960 and 1961, and the radicalization of student political activity have begun to erode the splendid isolation of the "inspired hill" at Kimuenza. One event—the celebration in February 1964 of the University's tenth anniversary—simultaneously crowned and closed Lovanium's era of false euphoria as a self-proclaimed "African" university.

The Student Strike of 1964

On March 8, 1964, a month after the anniversary celebration, the General Association of Students of Lovanium (*Association Générale des Etudiants de Lovanium,* or AGEL) unleashed a bitter strike, lasting a full week and observed by the entire student body. The students barricaded the campus; no one could enter or leave without their permission. To those authorities accustomed to the smooth functioning of the academic machine, the strike must have recalled the equally unexpected events of January 1959, when sudden rioting in Léopoldville led within one week to an explicit Belgian promise of Congolese independence.

This protest, the first occasion on which the students expressed their discontent en masse, is worth examining for the light it sheds on their behavior under pressure. The students demanded three things: the joint administration of the University by students and staff, the improvement of education through the hiring of full-time, internationally respected professors, and the bettering of their own material conditions.

The strike failed. Verhaegen cited three reasons: tactical errors, a lack of strategy, and the limitations on the students' action imposed by their nonrevolutionary position in society.[50]

Tactical errors occurred because the leaders of the strike did not appreciate the true distribution of power in the University. The strike, its effectiveness, and the shock it caused had unquestionably placed the students in a position of strength. But this advantage vanished when the students' representatives called off the strike in return for an agreement to create a tripartite (student-teacher-administrator) committee of purely advisory powers to study their demands. The leaders of AGEL erred further in linking their demands to those of the predominantly non-Congolese teaching staff. The goals of the two groups were fundamentally different. While the students were groping for a complete redefinition of the University, the professors merely wanted improvements in classroom and laboratory conditions.

The lack of strategy became evident during the negotiations that followed the strike. The discussions of the tripartite committee bogged down in a morass of procedural detail and personal complaint. The students, Verhaegen noted, had no over-all strategy because they had no clear long-range goal, i.e., they had not defined the new kind of University they wished to create.

Finally, the students' narrow vision of the protest led them to turn it into an ostentatious display. If for the authorities the strike was a threat to the established order, for the students it was their own celebration, their own tenth anniversary. For the first time and for eight full days, they stood alone before the footlights while their elders—academics and administrators—whispered in the corridors off-stage.

But, in Verhaegen's words,

when the parades were over, [the students'] enthusiasm crumbled. Confronting their own success, having stripped the power structure [of its pretensions], some of them began to wonder what step to take from this newly gained position of strength. . . . [Later,] after the talks had failed, renewal of the strike was unthinkable.

It is at this moment that one sees clearly the superficial and *petit bourgeois* character of the students' movement and their failure to fundamentally rethink their role in an African university. They lacked a truly revolutionary outlook and were lulled by their self-complacent pride into believing that their honor could be vindicated with material benefits instead of structural reform. All in all, the great student strike was the ceremonial equivalent, not the antithesis, of the [University's] tenth anniversary celebration.[51]

The strike at Lovanium marked a high point in the evolution of the student movement. It also revealed the nature of the students' relations with their university environment. The relationship recalls that of the colonial situation: on the one hand, a power able to take credit for outstanding accomplishments in material infrastructure, whose pseudo-progressive ideology masks a failure to identify with the subject society; on the other, a poorly organized, heterogeneous, frustrated group, lacking internal cohesion and continuity, whose numbers have realized only imperfectly that they are the objects and not the authors of action.

Factions, Reference Groups, and Social Values: The Problem of Integration

Student politics at Lovanium have been marked by a succession of internal crises. When the University was established in 1954, a student council was created to defend the interests of the student community. Despite the small number of students enrolled in this early period, the council soon developed two factions, one representing the newly matriculated students, the other their elder colleagues. The newcomers, calling themselves the "New Guard" ("*La Relève*"), accused the "old guard" leadership of having encouraged, or at least having failed to break, the politically lethargic habits of Lovanium students. The second, older group, self-styled "The Crossroads" (*Le Carrefour*), known also as the "old wolves," denied the charge.

This tension did not subside until the formation of AGEL in 1960. But during the 1962–63 academic year, new recriminations broke out along almost identical lines. On the occasion of the "baptism of the blues," an initiation ceremony marking the new students' entrance into the University, several students accused the academic authorities of interfering in the internal affairs of AGEL; two students were promptly expelled. The students countered with an unlimited strike, but it failed. Many students held the "government" of AGEL responsible for this failure, charging it with weakness and fear of the authorities. Again, the student movement seemed to break in two, the "elders," who favored negotiations, opposing the more numerous younger group advocating "direct action."

AGEL President Kahombo Mateene was replaced in 1963 by Gerard Kamanda, who proved no more successful than his predecessor in inspiring unanimity. Accused of a "lack of initiative," he was in turn replaced by Hubert Makanda. When the student strike of March 1964 helped unify the students, the Makanda "government" benefited. Makanda's prestige was further enhanced in July 1964 when, as we have noted, he was arrested for denouncing the return of Moise Tshombe.

At the time of our interviews (May 1966), AGEL was again in crisis. Two factions were disputing the Presidency: one under outgoing President Tharcisse Mwamba, the other around former AGEL Congress Chairman Paul-Maurice Yuma. Mwamba offered us a long account of the crisis, replying point by point to the students who had prevented his return to office at the beginning of 1966. But it is difficult to draw from Mwamba's testimony a clear chronology or a rational explanation of the crisis. Mwamba jumped from one grievance to another without being able to present any unifying theme linking all the charges and countercharges.

The fragility of Congolese student politics is again underscored by the great number, extravagance, and sometimes contradictory character of these grievances: the charges against Mwamba ranged from his being too radical to being too "soft" and included allegations of "tribalism," contacts with Tshombe, and collusion with the University authorities. From the moment when the personal quarrels of the two cliques overran the framework of the executive committee, there was no longer any mechanism for control or conciliation available to dampen the dispute. The objective judgment of the uninvolved student was clouded by anonymous, invective-filled flyers, written and circulated by each leader's personal entourage. These tracts were written in the emotional shorthand so often used by politicians: "tribalism," "separatism," "neocolonialism," "corruption," and so forth. Such slogans and clichés play an important role as external stimulants in the political life of Congolese students.

With what groups does the student identify and how strongly is he attracted to collective action? The student leaders we interviewed were unanimous in stressing, sometimes bitterly, the difficulty of "moving" the mass of the students in any single direction. Aside from the annual balls and general assemblies it organized, AGEL did not mean much to the average student. Within the politically active minority, the leaders also found it difficult to reconcile the zeal of the younger students, enamored of militant phrases like "direct action," with the negativism and cynicism of their older colleagues. This "Young Turk vs. old guard" basis of group identification is apparently highly salient for Lovanium students. As we have seen, it is around this particular distinction that interstudent political crises have most frequently developed.

The student is equally if not more strongly drawn to another reference group, that based on common regional origin. Regional identification plays an important role in determining both his relations with his fellow students and his contacts outside the University. "The distance between a foreign student and a Congolese student," one of our informants remarked, "is approximately the same as that between two Congolese students, even though they come from neighboring regions."

By and large, the political purpose of regionally defined student associations is to develop the closest possible ties with particular politicians. Regionalism was particularly apparent in 1962–63, when the six original provinces of the Congo were split and redrawn to become twenty-one. Some of the regional student groups were torn between attachments to quarreling provincial leaders. The Association of Students of South Kasai (AESKA) at Lovanium, for example, split in two: the partisans of *"Mulopwe"* ("Emperor") Albert Kalonji (head of the "Autonomous State" of South Kasai in 1960–62 until his ouster by the central government) opposed the supporters of Joseph Ngalula (formerly second-in-command under Kalonji in South Kasai and installed as governor in 1962). These organizations are normally as quiescent as they are fragile, becoming active only for the annual dances or when a leading "native son" of the region visits the campus.

Our student informants cited two other types of reference group. They drew a distinction by academic major between a "bloc of the humanistic sciences" and a "bloc of the exact sciences." On an ideological plane, they distinguished between students who belonged to the Catholic group (*Pax Romana*) and those who did not. The sources of student political leadership can be traced above all to the "humanistic sciences" and the Catholics of *Pax Romana*.

The students worry a great deal about their future careers, hoping for employment from a regime with almost absolute powers whose leaders may be highly suspicious of intellectuals. For the student, it is the diploma that counts. In this context, his actual education—whether in the humanistic or exact sciences—and the grades he receives are only marginally significant; more important to him is final success, symbolized by the degree.

Our informants all regretted the stultifying impact on student life of this obsession with diploma and career, and blamed much of the weakness of the student movement on these personal preoccupations. Our informants suggested that as the students move through their university years, gaining the experience needed to lead their peers, their increasing uneasiness about the future causes them to abandon radical opinions because they know such views may be ill regarded by the adult political leaders on whom their professional hopes depend. "As long as the intellectual has not destroyed this dependence," said one student interviewed, "the student movement can never become a permanent cohesive force."

In our interviews, the students focused on their role in society. When he returns to his region to visit his family or other relatives, the student is greeted, to use one informant's term, as a "god." Although he is not yet a producing member of society, he is approached, admired, and flattered from every side. His prestigious status creates a gulf between him and the village community.

During his stay in the village, he is subject to no restraints, save perhaps an overly solicitous protection from harm. Sometimes, however, he is indirectly pressured to accept the norms and customs of the traditional milieu. It is in the matter of choosing a bride that persuasive or even coercive efforts are most intense. Even when his immediate family leaves him free to select a wife by his own criteria, other relatives or "friends of the family" may put pressure on his parents to force him to conform to custom.

When he marries a foreigner or a university classmate, his bride is often reproached by his family for her independent ways. The intellectual, emancipated wife, a relatively rare phenomenon in Africa, threatens the tranquillity of rural society. Her independent behavior is seen as an intolerable contradiction of the highly integrative function traditionally assigned to her, the perpetuation and maintenance of the family community and the socialization of children. Our informants cited several instances where a fellow male student was forced by traditionalist pressures to abandon plans to marry a coed.

The student generally finds it difficult to accept the choking welcome of his home community. He is irritated by the exaggerated deference he receives and cannot easily adapt to the meager material conditions of life in the village. He finds he cannot re-establish communication with his former school pals who stayed behind while he went off to the University. His immediate reaction is to escape the embrace of the village and return to those who share his unique condition: his fellow students back in Kimuenza.

Incapable of reintegrating himself into this parochial rural milieu, the student has sometimes also had difficulty gaining acceptance among political leaders, many of whom—perhaps remembering the *Collège des Commissaires*—have treated him with a mixture of scorn and apprehension as an "intellectual" and a potential rival for power.

Administrative integration has been far more easily accomplished. The provincial government of South Kasai, for example, has created under Auguste Mabika-Kalanda (Adoula's Minister of Foreign Affairs in 1963 and a Lovanium graduate) a bureau of planning largely staffed by former university students. The students from Kivu, according to our informants, have also gained relatively easy access to administrative positions in their provincial government. In 1966, the "father" of Congolese student politics, Henri Takizala, was elected governor of Bandundu, one of several new units created when the Mobutu government reduced the number of provinces from twenty-one to twelve. In 1967, as we have already noted, a number of university graduates held important posts in the central government in Kinshasha.

Finally, the students are cognitively isolated from political realities. Our informants were unanimous in calling attention to what they considered extreme gullibility among the students regarding public affairs. The students do indeed seem particularly sensitive to rumors and hearsay about political events, transmitted in conversation or through the press. As we have already noted, their capacity for impartial analysis is further reduced by the use of emotion-laden slogans.

Summary and Conclusions

At the outset of this essay, we posed as a paradox the contrast between the intellectual's high social status and his limited political achievement. The explanation is in part historical. Not until 1952 did a Congolese (Thomas Kanza, later to represent the Lumumba government at the U.N.) set foot in a university.[52] Yet knowledge of the colonial language and a familiarity with colonial institutions were the essential prerequisites for anyone wishing to represent African interests before the colonial authority. On the stunted horizons of the Belgian Congo, only the "clerks" could aspire to this role, deriving much of their status (in African as well as

European eyes) from their proximity to the colonial trinity: the church, the administration, and the firm.[53]

Since independence in 1960, two generations have risen to power. In the first were the founders of the major political parties, the first ideologues of nationalism. It has been said that "they considered themselves physically tied to the nation they had called into existence."[54] Some gained power, some did not. Some, like Lumumba, gained it and lost it, losing their lives as well.

After this first generation came men from the middle ranks of the military, teachers, company clerks, middle-level administrators, and occasionally priests, all professional or cultural collaborators of the colonial regime. Having helped fuel the nationalist parties with their membership, they soon took command and have yet to relinquish the reins.

This second generation-in-power forms a socially homogeneous and monopolistic stratum. They are homogeneous because, as Seurin has noted in another context,[55] political leadership is recruited from their own favored occupations—particularly administration and teaching—and monopolistic because access to political power has meant for them access to wealth as well.[56]

What of the students? Their political debut in the *Collège* had been a disappointing experience. This remarkable grant of power to a group of "super-technicians," because it ran directly against the hyperpartisan political grain of the times, prefigured the irrationality of later political change. Despite his high prestige, the intellectual did not have privileged access to the channels of production and distribution, and could therefore not offer concrete material benefits to his followers in return for their support. Yet it was precisely in these immediate terms that the mass tended to allocate its loyalties. As Weiss has written,

> African societies are not inclined to entrust political power to a group that formerly had no role or function, the group that has moved furthest away from the life and concerns of the average African. . . . It was not the most educated who enjoyed popular support, but rather the victorious champions of African demands.[57]

The students missed their rendezvous with independence. In a sense, student political history since 1960 can be summarized as an attempt to remake the appointment. Largely because of numerical weakness, disunity, and inadequate organization, they failed—aside from a brief zenith in 1963–64—to make any significant impact on the polity.

At no time did the students constitute a revolutionary force. No common tradition of political action existed to inspire and unify them. Their organizations rarely enjoyed broad student support and seldom succeeded in mobilizing even their own memberships; when this was not true—as in the AGEL-led strikes of March 1964—the student leaders failed to capitalize on initial advantages to achieve concrete gains.[58] The students' slogan-ridden ideologies could not serve as lenses for sharp political vision, let alone as guides to action.

The Congolese student finds himself cast in the prototypical role of "national man"; yet, as we have seen, the homogenizing university environment does not completely blend or obliterate regional affinities and distinctions. He can aspire to play this role not because he is in contact with all the diverse forces that make up the Congo's "national" society, but on the contrary because he is detached—the essential characteristic of his condition—from all of them and therefore compromised by none. Yet as an adult he cannot survive without commitments. The logic of compromise is inescapable. And after him, the zeal of the next student generation is also destined to cool as it, in turn, is processed and ejected into society.

NOTES

1. The only institutions of higher education in black Africa in 1945 were Fourah Bay College in Sierra Leone (est. 1827) and Gordon Memorial College in the Sudan (est. 1902).

2. Helen Kitchen (ed.), *The Educated African* (New York: Frederick A. Praeger, 1952), p. 191.

3. For a discussion of the principles underlying Belgian educational policy in the Congo, see René Lemarchand, *Political Awakening in the Congo* (Berkeley: University of California Press, 1964), pp. 134–43.

4. *Projet d'organisation de l'enseignement libre au Congo Belge avec le concours des missions nationales* (Brussels, 1924), cited by Lemarchand, *op. cit.*, p. 134.

5. Kitchen (ed.), *op. cit.*, pp. 192–93. Ninety-five per cent of these pupils were in primary schools.

6. On Lovanium University, see Benoit Verhaegen, "La situation et les perspectives de l'enseignement supérieur à Léopoldville," *Etudes Congolaises,* III, No. 6 (June-July 1962), 6–16.

7. On the State University, see Roger Lallemand and Jacques-Henri Michel, "L'Université officielle du Congo à Elisabethville," *Etudes Congolaises,* V, No. 8 (October 1963), 1–33.

Since independence, a Free University has been established in Stanleyville (now Kisangani) under Protestant auspices. Propaedeutic classes were scheduled to start in October 1963, but persistent insecurity in the area and delays in construction have severely hampered the institution's development. On the origins of the University, see "La 3e Université du Congo," *ibid.*, pp. 104–6.

8. In 1959, on the eve of Congolese independence, the student body of the State University in Elisabethville formed an exact negative of the Lovanium student population. The students at Lovanium were 72 per cent African, 28 per cent European; the identical percentages held at Elisabethville, but in reverse. (Calculated from figures in Lemarchand, *op. cit.*, p. 136.)

9. From 1952 onward, a few Africans obtained scholarships to study at Belgian universities. In 1958, Congolese students in the metropole numbered fourteen.

10. Among them, Marcel Lihau, Evariste Loliki, André Mandi, and Paul Mushiete were still students; Lihau was also President of the Congolese-Ruanda-Urundi student association in Belgium. Two other *Collège* delegates, Joseph Mbeka and Albert Ndele, were recent graduates, as were party representatives Justin Bomboko and Mario Cardoso. Of the eight, only Mbeka had studied outside Belgium (at Lovanium).

11. Centre de Recherche et d'Information Socio-Politiques (hereafter cited as CRISP), *Congo 1960* (Brussels), I, 87.

12. *Ibid.*, pp. 98–99.

13. *Ibid.*, II, 869.

14. *Ibid.*, pp. 871–72.

15. See *Congo-Presse* (Léopoldville), Document No. 495 (October 28, 1960).

16. See executive order (*décret-loi*) No. 29 of September 29, 1960, *Moniteur Congolais* (Léopoldville), No. 41 (October 10, 1960).

17. This paragraph and the next are based on the discussion in CRISP, II, 881.

18. Bomboko had been President of the Congolese and Ruanda-Urundi students' organization in Belgium. He later created his own political party and became one of the Congo's most durable political figures. Bomboko served as Minister of Foreign Affairs under Prime Ministers Patrice Lumumba and Joseph Ileo, as Minister of Justice under Prime Minister Cyrille Adoula, and again as Foreign Minister in President Mobutu's government in 1966–67.

19. Jacques Berque, "Classe et histoire contemporaine des Arabes," *Cahiers Internationaux de Sociologie*, XXXVIII (1965), 182.

20. On September 11, 1960, Senate President Joseph Ileo had been named by President Kasavubu to form a new government.

21. They were Marcel Tshibamba and Cleophas Bizala. Both later held posts in the *Collège*. Bizala went on to serve the Ileo government as Minister of National Education.

22. Union Générale des Etudiants Congolais, *The Resolutions of the First UGEC Congress* (Leiden: Coordinating Secretariat of National Unions of Students, [1961]), pp. 7–8.

23. UGEC was unable to establish a section at the State University until 1963.

24. Watum had studied political science and administration. Law students Alexis Dede and Joseph Nsinga and medical student Kizito Kalala were elected to handle cultural affairs and publicity, finance, and international affairs, respectively. (*The Resolutions of the First UGEC Congress*, pp. 5–6, 19.)

25. This may have been a reference to the failure of the Commissioners.

26. *The Resolutions of the First UGEC Congress,* pp. 21–23.

27. See the chronologies in the 1963 issues of *Etudes Congolaises.*

28. "IIe Congrès National de l'U.G.E.C.," *Etudes Congolaises,* V, No. 7 (August-September 1963), 105–11, and No. 8 (October 1963), 100–104.

29. CRISP, *Congo 1963,* p. 273. As we have noted, the General Commissioners of the *Collège* were assisted by Commissioners. Among the latter was outgoing UGEC President Henri Takizala. This may explain why the resolution applied the adjective "General" throughout.

30. *Étoile du Congo* (Léopoldville), August 29, 1963.

31. *Présence Congolaise* (Léopoldville), November 12, 1963, and *Etudes Congolaises,* VI, No. 2 (February 1964), 94–96.

32. See *Le Courrier d'Afrique* (Léopoldville), December 31, 1963, and January 14, 1964.

33. *Ibid.,* June 2, 1964. Tshombe had for some time been courting UGEC from his "exile" in Spain. The secret protocol signed by Tshombe and the Gbenye wing of the CNL in Madrid in February 1964 included a sympathetic reference to UGEC, and its language recalled that of the Second UGEC Congress: e.g., "We [Tshombe and the CNL representatives] . . . have decided to unite our efforts in a true revolution to free the Republic of the Congo from the grasp of neo-colonialism." (See CRISP, *Congo 1964,* pp. 136–37.)

34. *Le Courrier d'Afrique,* March 20, 1965.

35. *Remarques Congolaises et Africaines* (Brussels), VI (1964), 383, 533. Two leaders of the radical wing, Oswald Ndeshyo and Serge-Pontien Tshilenge (respectively President and Secretary for Information and Political Affairs of UGEC-Belgium), were expelled from Belgium for signing the second statement.

36. *Ibid.,* pp. 393–94.

37. Bulletin of the *Agence Congolaise* (Léopoldville), November 24, 1965.

38. Nkanza-Dolumingu was in his fifth year as a UGEC activist. He had completed his undergraduate work at Princeton University in 1963.

39. See "Le 3e Congrès de l'U.G.E.C.," *Etudes Congolaises,* IX, Nos. 5–6 (September-December 1966), 23–103.

40. *Ibid.,* p. 30.

41. *Ibid.,* p. 37.

42. Lemarchand, *op. cit.,* p. 135.

43. *Université Lovanium, 1954/1964* (a brochure commemorating the tenth anniversary of the University). However, the percentage of Africans in the student body *declined* in this period from over ninety to under seventy-five.

44. Lovanium University, *Statistiques de l'Université Lovanium (1964–65).*

45. Of all the academic majors that could be identified for the membership of the *Collège des Commissaires* as of October 10, 1960, twenty-six were in the humanities and social sciences and only six in the natural and applied sciences. In the former category, political science ranked first with eight, sociology second with five, and economics third with four citations; law occurred only twice. (Calculated from data in CRISP, *Congo 1960,* II, 872–73, and *ibid., Annexes et Biographies,* pp. 75–132.) For the majors of UGEC leaders in 1961–63, see n. 24 above.

46. Guy Malengreau, "Vers l'Université Africaine," *Problèmes d'Afrique Centrale,* No. 36 (1957), pp. 126–27.

47. M. Bakole, "L'Université: Signification, mesure et condition de l'Africanisation," *Présence Africaine,* LIII (First Quarter 1965), 149–61.

48. In 1961–62, the staff (full- and part-time) was 97 per cent non-Congo-

lese and 85 per cent Belgian. (Calculated from figures in Verhaegen, *op. cit.*, p. 13.)

49. Benoit Verhaegen, "L'Université et les Etudiants: Sociologie d'une grève," *Présence Africaine*, LII (Fourth Quarter 1964), 135.

50. See *ibid.*, 128–42. For further analysis and documentation, see "Textes et Documents: A.G.E.L.," *Etudes Congolaises*, VI, No. 3 (March 1964), 101–6; A. R. Ilunga Kabongo, "Crise à Lovanium," *ibid.*, VI, No. 4 (April 1964), 61–78; "Textes et Documents: Lovanium," *ibid.*, 79–98; and Jacques Ceulemans, "L'U.G.E.C. et la Révolution Congolaise," *Remarques Congolaises et Africaines*, VI, 145–46.

51. Verhaegen, "L'Université et les Etudiants," p. 138.

52. Crawford Young, *Politics in the Congo: Decolonization and Independence* (Princeton: Princeton University Press, 1965), p. 94.

53. In 1954–59, for example, Lumumba worked as a postal clerk in Stanleyville, then moved to Léopoldville where he helped run a restaurant.

54. *Les conflits de génération* ("Bibliotheque prospective") (Paris: Presses Universitaires de France, 1963), p. 47.

55. J. L. Seurin, "Elites sociales et parties politiques d'Afrique Occidentale Française," *Annales Africaines* (1958), p. 137.

56. But not necessarily access to economic power. See Georges Balandier, "Problématique des classes sociales en Afrique noire," *Cahiers Internationaux de Sociologie*, XXXVIII (1965), 131–42.

57. Herbert F. Weiss, "L'évolution des élites: Comparaison entre la situation en Afrique occidentale francophone et au Congo avant l'indépendance," *Etudes Congolaises*, VIII, No. 5 (September-October 1965), 4.

58. Events in 1967, occurring well after our research was completed, are worth noting briefly.

In February 1967, five members of the Married Students' Council at Lovanium were suspended because of a minor dispute with University health authorities. A week later, on February 20, the student body took over the campus. As in March 1964, only those with permission from AGEL could enter or leave the University. The next day classes were suspended and all 1,950 students were expelled and required to apply for readmission individually; the four leaders of AGEL, it was announced, would not be readmitted. Army troops occupied the campus and quickly dismantled the students' barricades.

President Mobutu met personally with a student delegation on February 23 and obtained AGEL's reluctant agreement to accept the collective registration of the student body and end the strike. The army withdrew and classes resumed shortly thereafter.

Although triggered by a minor incident, the students' action flowed from the same conditions that underlay the March 1964 unrest. As AGEL President Nzanda-Buana explained it, the strike was really against the "retrograde and colonialist spirit" of the University. See *Actualité Mondiale* (New York), II, No. 3 (March 10, 1967), 1–2.

Since the strike, there is some indication of potentially significant change in Congolese higher education. There is now for the first time a Congolese serving as Rector of Lovanium, and student representation in the councils of the various higher educational institutes in Kinshasha, which have been brought under the direct supervision of the Ministry of Education, is increasing. Whether or not these changes, demanded by student leaders, portend a politically more effective role for Congolese students in the future, it is still too early to say.

3. GHANA

DAVID J. FINLAY
ROBERTA E. KOPLIN
CHARLES A. BALLARD, JR.

In the predawn darkness of February 24, 1966, six hundred soldiers marched on Flagstaff House, the citadel of Kwame Nkrumah, President of Ghana. A coup d'état had begun. The "revolution" was swift and successful. Its effects continue to reverberate in Ghana and throughout Africa.

Of all the recent military takeovers in Africa, Ghana's was perhaps the most striking, for at one time this small nation of 7.5 million people epitomized the strong anticolonial surge of postwar Africa. Under Kwame Nkrumah in 1957, Ghana became the first sub-Saharan colony to gain independence. Nkrumah, a strong advocate of continental unity, hailed as the initiator of the "African personality," became a major spokesman of radical African nationalism. His removal, the banning of his Convention People's Party, and the rise of a new Ghanaian leadership mark a new, still undefined phase in Ghanaian, if not African politics.

The authors would like to express their appreciation to those who have helped to make this study possible. Finlay would like to express his gratitude to the Hoover Institution on War, Revolution and Peace, the Duke University Committee on International Studies, the Office of Scientific and Scholarly Research of the University of Oregon, and the Institute of International Studies and Overseas Administration of the University of Oregon for financial assistance during various phases of research in Ghana. Koplin would like to express her appreciation to the Institute of International Studies and Overseas Administration of the University of Oregon and to the National Science Foundation for their financial assistance. Thanks are owed to B. D. G. Folson of the University of Ghana and to Belva Finlay, C. R. Schuller, and Shirley Varmette for their cooperation and assistance.

64

In this chapter, which is based on survey data gathered in Ghana in May 1963 and June 1966,[1] we shall examine the political attitudes and expectations of students at the University of Ghana before, during, and after the coup d'état. We shall be concerned with the ways in which students in Ghana adapted or reacted over time to political stimuli in the successive contexts of a radical, single-party environment, the time of transition immediately following the coup d'état, and the post-coup period.

More specifically, the chapter focuses on student politicization and student perceptions of the legitimacy of the regime. The theoretical significance of our discussion stems from the use of three systemic variables we consider critical to an understanding of the relation of students to politics in developing countries: (1) the nature of the educational system, (2) the propensity of political authorities to impose sanctions upon student political activity—particularly activity in opposition to the regime—and the student's perception of his vulnerability to sanctions, and (3) the degree of congruence between the student population and the political elite.

We shall first examine the structure of the educational system and its effects on student politicization in Ghana. We shall then assess the impact of the last two systemic variables on student political orientations and behavior during the Nkrumah regime. After a brief discussion of the coup itself and the University's reactions to it, we shall take up the second and third variables again, in the context of post-Nkrumah Ghana. Following an analysis of student politicization and legitimacy orientations in both time periods, a concluding section will summarize our findings.

The Educational System

Whether an educational system is elitist or mass in structure affects the likelihood and expectations of mobility.[2] Prospects of recruitment into high-income, high-status roles are normally very good in elitist educational systems: so few gain access to higher education that a degree virtually guarantees appropriate occupational placement. Therefore, students in such systems may tend to identify with the existing elites, and the consequences of alienation from these elites may be severe.[3] The rewards of high-status employment heighten careerist orientations among students and remove two of the most salient grounds for making political demands: dissatisfaction with mobility opportunities, and perceptions of benefits that would result from a change in government.

Education in Ghana may be characterized as a pyramid with a

relatively broad base at the primary level but narrowing significantly at the secondary and university levels. Annually in the fifteen-year period 1950–64, middle (an intermediate level, formerly "senior primary") school students as a percentage of primary school enroll-ment averaged 25.1, while secondary school students as a percent-age of middle school students averaged 10.1, and university students as a percentage of the secondary school student population averaged only 7.6.[4] Roughly one student of every 420 who started primary school eventually reached one of Ghana's universities. The *1960*

TABLE 1

ACCESS TO EDUCATION IN SEVEN NATIONS, 1963

	Primary Enrollment as a Percentage of Total 5–14 Age Group	Academic Secondary as a Percentage of Primary Enrollment	Higher Education as a Percentage of Academic Secondary Enrollment	Enrollment in Higher Education as a Percentage of Total 20–24 Age Group
United States	76.5	42.2	14.6	40.4[a]
United Kingdom	63.5	72.1	9.9	11.2
Ghana	68.0	2.4	7.5	.35
Ivory Coast	43.4	4.7	6.3	n.a.
Senegal	28.0	10.5	13.7	1.1
Sierra Leone	26.8	10.5	4.9	.32
Indonesia	41.0	7.8	8.7	.8

SOURCES: United Nations, *Statistical Yearbook, 1965* (New York: United Nations, 1966); United Nations, *Demographic Yearbook, 1965* (New York: United Nations, 1966); S. H. Steinberg (ed.), *The Statesman's Year-Book, 1965–66* (New York: St. Martin's Press, 1966); U. S. Bureau of the Census, *Statistical Abstract of the United States, 1966* (Washington, D.C.: Government Printing Office, 1967); Republic of Ghana, *1962 Statistical Year Book* (Accra: Government Printing Department, 1964); Research and Statistics Division, Ministry of Education, "Statistics" (mimeo; Accra, n.d.); "Facts and Figures" (mimeo; University of Ghana, Legon, March 1966). Absolute age-group esti-mates used in calculating percentages were for 1963 (United States, United Kingdom, and Sierra Leone), 1961 (Ivory Coast, Indonesia, and Senegal), and 1960 (Ghana).

[a] Computed as a per cent of those within the 18–21 age range, the meaningful group for comparison.

Manpower Survey of Ghana estimated that between 1960 and 1965 the demand for personnel with university degrees would far exceed university graduates for the same period.[5] With this relation between supply and demand of graduates, a major incentive to oppose the political authorities has been absent. Some comparative perspective on this pyramidal structuring of education is provided in Table 1, which compares Ghana with the United States, the United Kingdom, and selected West African and non-African nations.

A major aim of the Nkrumah government was to develop a mass educational system and eliminate illiteracy. The remarkable success of this policy can be seen in the first column of Table 1. It is in the percentage of the 20–24 age group in institutions of higher education that the marked difference between the elitist and the mass educational systems becomes apparent.[6]

Education is highly valued throughout West Africa, but despite rapid expansion at the lower levels, higher education remains the privilege of only a few.[7] There are three universities in Ghana: the University of Ghana, located at Legon, about seven miles inland from the capital city of Accra; Kumasi University of Science and Technology, 169 miles northwest of Accra; and Cape Coast University of Science Education, approximately 92 miles west of Accra on the coast. Total enrollment at the three universities during the academic year 1965–66 was 4,286, and an additional 3,410 students were reported studying abroad, although not all the latter were in universities or colleges.

The University of Ghana outranks the other two institutions both in age and in prestige. It was founded in 1948 as the University College of the Gold Coast and conferred University of London degrees until 1961. The University has grown most rapidly since 1960: in 1961–62 the student body numbered 682; by 1965–66 it had increased to 2,001. Plans to expand higher education in Ghana further have been temporarily curtailed as a result of economic problems.

The elitist nature of higher education in Ghana is not only a function of the slope of the educational pyramid and the proportion of eligible age-group members enrolled. Equally if not more important are certain characteristics of the University itself. First, the University of Ghana has always and in various ways reflected its British heritage as a West African Oxbridge, particularly in adopting customs and practices that reinforce status differences. The hierarchical organization of the University supports status-conscious attitudes among staff and students, as do the ritualistic practices associated with "high" and "low" dining tables, the wearing of academic gowns, and the like.[8] Campus life centers on the residence halls, each with its own dining facilities, common rooms, library, chapel, and systems of internal government including a student organization.[9] This decentralization lends added significance to the few occasions when events and activities engage the entire student body.

Second, the role of the University has been conceived in universalistic rather than nationalistic terms, a tradition maintained in part by the high proportion of expatriate staff at Legon.[10] Intellectual isolation has been enhanced by the University's spatial insulation in a neatly contained campus outside Accra. Students are conscious of their distinctiveness as a group enjoying high status in the society and of the great prestige bestowed in Ghana upon the educated man. Corollary to this awareness is the students' belief in the importance of their immunity from outside control. Yet they also believe, following Ghanaian custom, that authority should be obeyed. There has never been a tradition of activism in student life at Legon. Students, like the staff, have tended to remain somewhat aloof from national politics.

The curriculum at the University of Ghana has remained very much in the Oxbridge pattern. Despite the addition of an Institute of African Studies and Schools of Agriculture, Education and Public Administration, and nondegree courses in nursing and other fields, the percentage of students majoring in the arts or social sciences has been disproportionately high.[11] In the latter fields, the use of external examiners and British-derived reading lists has meant that the students cover much the same material as their peers in the United Kingdom. Despite complaints and suggestions from both the government and visiting educational experts, increases in the "African content" of higher education have come slowly.

About 90 per cent of the students are on government scholarships (bursaries), which generally obligate the recipient to serve as a secondary school teacher or civil servant for some years after graduation.[12] Table 2 shows the substantial but declining frequency of teaching as an occupational choice among University of Ghana students; careers in education dropped to second place in popularity in 1966.[13] Among the factors involved in the decline are the likelihood of being assigned to teach in a relatively isolated rural school and the availability of more attractive jobs in other fields. Changes in the percentage of students planning government careers are quite likely related to political changes in Ghana, with the figure for 1957 perhaps reflecting a heightened identification with state and nation in the year of Ghana's independence. Since then, as the range of available occupations has broadened, the students have come increasingly to prefer alternative high-income, high-status employment in business or the professions. However, the economic retrenchment stemming from recent efforts to cope with Ghana's financial crisis may well alter this picture in the short run.

Educational structure, then, is an important factor conditioning student politicization. An elitist system, of which higher education in Ghana is an example, tends to decrease the salience of political activity for the individual student: it both assures his occupational

TABLE 2

CAREER PLANS OF UNIVERSITY OF GHANA STUDENTS, 1953–66

(In Per Cent)

Type of Employment	1953 (1)	1957 (2)	1960 (3)	1963 (4)	1966 (5)
Teaching	42.4	50.9	45.4	39.3	31.1
Government	25.1	33.6	29.6	21.4	17.3
Business	—	0.9	1.9	7.3	6.9
Professional	21.8 ⎱	14.5	23.1	⎰ 20.4	31.4
Other	7.8 ⎰			⎱ 8.2	9.3
No data and no answer[a]	2.8	excl.	excl.	3.4	4.0
	(N=243)	(N=110)	(N=108)	(N=206)	(N=376)

SOURCES: *Col. 1:* Gustav Jahoda, "The Social Background of a West African Student Population: II," *British Journal of Sociology,* VI (1955), 74; *Cols. 2 and 3:* Margaret Peil, "Ghanaian University Students: The Broadening Base," *British Journal of Sociology,* XVI (1965), 26; *Cols. 4 and 5:* David J. Finlay and Roberta E. Koplin, "Social Backgrounds of University of Ghana Students" (unpublished paper, Department of Political Science, University of Oregon, 1967), p. 10.

[a] Jahoda and Peil used the "no data" category; the 1963 and 1966 figures represent "no answer." High "no data" figures in 1957 (16 students) and 1960 (46 students) have been excluded in computing percentages for these years because of the nature of Peil's data (registrar's files) and to increase comparability. It should also be noted that Peil used only arts and science degree entrants in the 1957 and 1960 data.

aspirations and insulates him physically, if not intellectually, from national politics. The resulting predisposition to accept the political world as it is, in supportive or acquiescent legitimacy orientations, will, however, be modified by the other two variables we consider crucial in assessing Ghanaian student politicization.

The Sanction Function

This variable has two interacting components: the propensity of the political authorities to punish deviant political behavior and attitudes, and the students' perception of their own vulnerability to sanctions.[14] The first component, the propensity to impose sanctions, depends on the degree to which the polity is closed—that is, the degree to which open political competition is not allowed—and on the scope and nature of demands placed upon students to conform to standards defined by the political authorities. The propensity to sanction will be examined in terms of the political system under Nkrumah, government attitudes toward students and the university, and the nature of the relationship between university and polity. The second component, the sanctionability of the student, is a measure of the extent to which he believes that he is vulnerable to sanctions—that the threatened sanction (expulsion, blacklisting, detention, fines, and the like) would deprive him of some present or future value. His perceptions of the political authorities, of the effectiveness of past sanctions against deviant political behavior, and of his own career opportunities are all relevant to the student's estimation of his sanctionability.

When sanctions are severe or appear imminent, the salience of politics is increased and one of four types of adaptive response may result: (1) increased activism, either supportive or oppositional; (2) opportunism as a means of decreasing threats and/or increasing gains; (3) acquiescence to assure safety; or (4) a retreat from all forms of involvement.[15] The choice of a particular response will depend upon the student's perception of the costs and rewards involved.

The Ghanaian political system has changed significantly over time.[16] Nkrumah's Convention People's Party (CPP) gained its strength prior to independence as a mass movement within a competitive political system. Although the CPP was a struggle group from its inception in 1949, conflict was not overly emphasized after 1951, when Nkrumah became Leader of Government Business (and later Prime Minister), because it was necessary to cooperate with colonial administrators during the transfer of power. The independence movement itself also provided a legitimate outlet for aggressive behavior.

After independence came on March 6, 1957, the ideology of conflict assumed new dimensions as the CPP began to search for enemies, even old scores, and consolidate its position. The Preventive Detention Act of 1958 was the first significant codification of this combat ideology; the sweeping provisions of the 1960 Criminal Code further permitted the power of the state to be used against political opposition groups, in Parliament and elsewhere. The use of criminal sanctions was thus institutionalized in the political process. In 1964, the dominant position of the CPP was legalized in a constitutional amendment creating a one-party state.

Justification for the increasingly authoritarian nature of the Ghanaian state was found in "Nkrumaism," the regenerative ideology that stressed unity, socialism, the "African personality," and the existence of threatening enemies. From the first, the government sought to mobilize the society for reconstruction and development. Political independence was held to be incomplete until the former colony had freed itself of reliance on technical and financial aid that might endanger the nation by permitting foreign economic manipulation and control. To this end, society had to be united; Nkrumah felt that a developing country could not afford the "luxury of political competition" and the attendant waste of resources and deflection of energy from national goals. Thus the Nkrumah government may best be described as a modernizing autocracy: while its economic goal was modernization, politically the regime was autocratic in substance and style.

Nkrumah's attitude toward the University of Ghana reflected several considerations. In the first place, the goal of economic modernization required emphasis on applied science and agriculture in the educational system. Although curricular specialization among the universities at Legon, Kumasi, and Cape Coast had been established to this end, the continuing preference of the majority of Legon students for arts and social sciences was a source of concern to the CPP and provided grounds for an attack on the autonomy of the University that permitted it.

Second, Nkrumah knew there were students and faculty members at Legon critical of his government. His estimate of the extent and threat of opposition from the two groups was grossly exaggerated, in view of their low level of political participation. His reaction must rather be understood in terms of the total societal mobilization he envisioned. Accusations that staff and students were "anti-government, that is to say . . . anti-Convention People's Party"[17] meant in effect that "those who are not with us are against us." Even political acquiescence was not entirely satisfactory when patriotism became synonymous with active support of the Party.

Third, the political opposition, until it was finally emasculated, had been led largely by a coalition of traditional tribal leaders and the Gold Coast's older intelligentsia. One major opposition leader, Dr. K. A. Busia, had been the Head of the Sociology Department at Legon. The ideology of Nkrumaism postulated the existence of "enemies within," and it seemed reasonable to look for them where they had been found in the past, particularly since the University was one of the few semi-autonomous institutions remaining in Ghana.[18] The presence of a large number of expatriate staff further increased suspicion regarding the University, as did the determined defense of academic freedom by Vice-Chancellor Conor Cruise O'Brien.

Finally, Nkrumah's attitude toward the University of Ghana cannot be understood in isolation from the general importance he placed upon mobilizing Ghana's youth. Considerable research and consultation with experts from other nations had gone into the formulation of plans for a comprehensive youth movement. The following quotation from the party press suggests the high hopes placed on politicization of youth for system maintenance:

> In our bid to build a one Party People's Democracy, the need becomes acute for a uniform ideological orientation of the broader masses. The Ghana Young Pioneer movement . . . is aimed at making the youth more conscious of their political obligations and directs them toward the cause of the Party and the national crusade. Once the youth begins to understand their roles, our Leader can rest assured that ours shall be the victory. . . . The Movement, with this ideology [Nkrumaism], aims at building itself into a strong reservoir of Party activists which could be tapped into the mother Party on maturity to play active roles. In fact it shall serve as the preparatory grounds for full adult membership.[19]

With this background, then, what was the nature of the relations between University and polity?

Before independence there was little conflict between the CPP and the University, partly because the Legon community characteristically remained somewhat aloof from political activity, but principally because the attention of the CPP was focused elsewhere. After March 6, 1957, the Party gradually increased pressure on the universities to conform to its expectations and support its programs.

By 1959, the University of Ghana was accused of being a breeding ground for unpatriotic and subversive elements and of fostering alien traditions. Nkrumah warned that if reforms were not forthcoming, the government would impose its own.[20] Tension increased as the CPP simultaneously questioned the University's role in society and redoubled its efforts to obtain converts on the campus. The Party-controlled national press kept up a sustained and increasingly vituperous flood of criticism against Legon's "ivory-towerism." The purpose of this propaganda was to isolate the University from community support and thus to prepare the way for more concrete action to bring the University into line. Nkrumah's installation as Chancellor of the Universities in 1961 was one such step, allowing him to make appointments to Legon's University Council and increasing his opportunities to forge a "proper definition" of academic freedom.

In the meantime, the Party continued its recruiting activities through auxiliary organizations. A Ghana Youth Authority was established to coordinate youth activities and the Kwame Nkrumah Ideological Institute created to train cadres for all levels of Party organization. Student response was scarcely gratifying to the Party and fed the conviction that expatriate staff members were responsible for the indifference of the university community to the CPP. In 1961, the termination of the contracts of six staff members—five expatriates and one Ghanaian—had been accomplished without undue incident, but a similar move in 1964 resulted in a student-police clash. Because this was one of the few occurrences of student protest activity, it deserves fuller comment.

The episode was apparently the culmination of a series of events dating from December 1963, when Legon students, through the National Union of Ghana Students, sent a resolution to the government protesting the dismissal of the Chief Justice of the Supreme Court.[21] The protest drew no comment from the government, which was then engaged in a massive persuasion campaign to ensure the success of the upcoming referendum to establish a one-party state. However, shortly before the referendum the government issued deportation orders to six senior staff members, and a student rally to protest these actions was dispersed by police action. The government then closed all universities for seventeen days to allow students to return home to vote in the referendum. At Legon the recess was interpreted as an attempt to intimidate and disperse potential opposition, and again the National Union of Ghana Students protested, claiming the dismissal of classes was unnecessary and disruptive to academic life.

After the referendum the CPP quickly retaliated with a march on Legon by a large crowd to demand changes in the University. Shortly thereafter, five leaders of the National Union of Ghana Students were arrested and detained, as was one Ghanaian professor, and the University as a whole was threatened and abused. The Party later formed its own student group, the Ghana National Students' Organization.

Throughout 1964, the Party's ideological offensive continued on several fronts. Reading rooms for Party literature were established in all educational institutions, an inspection committee set about removing "anti-socialist and anti-Party" books from libraries and bookstores in Ghana, and other student organizations, including the Junior Common Room governments at Legon, were infiltrated and pressured into line. In the fall of 1964, the government required all students entering the universities to take a two-week indoctrination course at the Ideological Institute at Winneba. Twenty students had already undergone an intensive summer course at Winneba to serve as Party leaders. When Party branches were re-established at Legon in the fall, students were urged to "systematically expose" lecturers who were not in tune with the "African Revolution."[22]

Only one incident occurred at Legon to mar this smooth façade of Party domination. In early February 1965, the "doyen of Gold Coast politics," J. B. Danquah, died in detention. (Danquah had led the opposition to the colonial administration up to 1949 and subsequently to Nkrumah as well.) During dinner at Commonwealth Hall, a student called on his colleagues to stand and observe two minutes of silence in honor of Danquah. Despite protests by the CPP activists present, the students complied. Sometime that night, the CPP flag at the University was taken down, ripped up, and thrown in a fishpond. Three students, including the one who had proposed honoring Danquah, were immediately arrested.

The position of the University on the whole was defensive as it retreated in the face of Party attacks. Selective deportations and dismissals were effective weapons against the largely expatriate faculty, as was the use of preventive detention against the students and Ghanaian faculty. The lack of any further student protest indicates the effectiveness of the government's sanctions. It remains to consider the second component of the sanction function: the sanctionability of students and their adaptive response to Party pressures on the University.

Students generally defended the universalistic conception of the University and their role in it as students rather than Party activists. The friction between polity and University resulted from the students' disinclination, as one put it, "to be tied down to the apron strings of any one political party or ideology."[23] Another student expressed what seemed to be the majority attitude: "The students with all sincerity crave for a stop to this relentless Press propaganda" alleging that students lived in an ivory tower divorced from the community and the "African Revolution."[24]

Although the students were accused of being antigovernment, they did not see themselves in this way. When asked in 1963, "It has been suggested that students at the University are antigovernment. Do you think this is true?," only 24 per cent of those sampled agreed. This is not an altogether accurate self-assessment, as will be shown later. The 1963 survey revealed that students were highly critical of government behavior in certain areas such as civil liberties, while at the same time they agreed with the Party on some important nationalistic issues. Thus, on strictly political questions, the students tended to be ambivalent toward Nkrumah and the Party rather than consistently critical from a well-defined ideological position. Students who spoke out openly on political matters were rare: private views and public utterances were deftly separated, out of fear of informers and the increasing probability of sanctions. The few student organizations were neither militant nor active, nor did they serve as catalysts for the existing, but diffused, opposition.

The lack of a reformist ideology among students is also related to their overwhelming preoccupation with career goals. They realistically assessed these goals as attainable. Prerequisite, however, was a university degree. Most students saw the degree as a key to future mobility and to the type of life they desired. To attain these goals they were willing to compromise their beliefs and make some accommodation with the Party. As one interviewed student put it:

I must get my degree! My mother is an illiterate trader, you know, and she once told me, "Kofi, I'll be so happy when you get your degree, because then you can buy a car. All I'd want you to do would be to let your driver take me to the market every morning so I can sell my *kenkey* [a local foodstuff]. Then he could take you to your office. When you get your degree I'll be so proud and happy." I can't let my mother down. Why should I oppose Nkrumah and run the risk of being arrested?

The CPP, however, was not satisfied with quiet acquiescence, and it was increasingly difficult for students to avoid politics and a confrontation with an elite that held most of the keys to mobility.

Both the students and the political elite perceived each other's intentions and attitudes in negative terms that did little to facilitate communication or resolve differences. The students were not simply apolitical or "rightist." Their response to the Party's criticisms was to retreat still further from political engagements that might jeopardize their position at the University and, by extension, their career prospects. They were afraid the Preventive Detention Act would be used against them, although only a few students were ever actually detained. The intensity of the CPP attack was surely in disproportion to any threat actually posed by the University. The non-intellectual character of the CPP made it resentful of the University, as did the University's semi-autonomy from Party control and its elitist atmosphere.[25] The students contributed to this resentment by their general refusal to affiliate with the Party, their critical attitudes toward certain policies of and trends within the Party, and their appeals to the universalistic value of academic freedom when confronted with nationalistic demands for mobilization.

The use of sanctions against a group that feared them effectively prevented overt opposition, but the CPP policy was self-defeating in terms of the broader government-Party goal of gaining active support. When the salience of politics increased, most students opted either to acquiesce or to retreat from all forms of political involvement. Only a few exercised the option of opportunism by joining the CPP or one of its student auxiliaries. The nature of the political system effectively deterred any from the choice of increased oppositional activism, for the students' perceived political efficacy was radically diminished by the total sanction function.[26]

Elite Congruity

In establishing degrees of congruity or incongruity between students and political elites, we must consider at least three factors. The first concerns structural elements defining each group, such as similarity or differences in social backgrounds and recruitment. The second is the existence and extent of competition among elites. A more or less pluralistic elite structure tends to place competing demands upon students, and it offers them alternatives when congruity with political elites is low. On the other hand, if a single group holds the keys to mobility and students are not "sons of the establishment," their position is precarious. The third factor is the extent of shared (or opposed) attitudes, beliefs, and values. It is important to consider the degree to which students identify with or oppose the political elites, for attitudinal congruity can mitigate the effects of structural incongruity.

When one examines student–political elite congruity, it is necessary to keep in mind the elitist intellectual tradition in Ghana and to recall that leading opponents of the CPP, J. B. Danquah and K. A. Busia, were both products of this tradition. K. E. de Graft-Johnson, a Ghanaian sociologist, characterized the Convention People's Party, when it broke away from Danquah's predominantly intellectual United Gold Coast Convention in 1949, in these terms:

> It could be said that it represented a symbolic break with the intelligentsia as an incipient class. The new category that came into prominence and won power . . . were mostly lower-middle class—clerks, school teachers, trade unionists, farmers' representatives, storekeepers.[27]

De Graft-Johnson anticipated the continuing existence of three separate elite groups in Ghana: the traditional chiefs, the intelligentsia, and the new political elite. Each represented different cultural values and, despite some overlap, he viewed them as basically incompatible. Although Nkrumah rejected the first two elites, he tried to appeal to those groups in society that accorded political legitimacy to either the chiefs or the intelligentsia by adopting the traditional title "Osagyefo,"[28] by incorporating some elements of the traditional panoply of Akan culture into the new state ritual, by emphasizing his (honorary) academic title of Doctor, and by stressing the new, African, and socialistic intellectualism of the Party.

Party ideology was not, strictly speaking, anti-intellectual; rather it redefined intellectualism in terms of "the African Revolution versus neo-colonialism" and "Marxism versus capitalism."[29] This conflict ideology dichotomized intellectuals into those who sought a fundamental transformation of society and those who defended the status quo or advocated only minor change. Because of their predominantly European academic training and their less-than-enthusiastic embrace of Nkrumaism, Legon intellectuals were seen as "lacking the necessary sympathy with the people" and as "walking in the clouds with their feet dangling in the air."[30]

The Convention People's Party was, from the beginning, the party of the "common man." Dennis Austin described the CPP in its early stages as representing "the ordinary people—the commoners—as opposed to the chiefs and the intelligentsia,"[31] and as "a commoner's movement led by the elementary-school leavers."[32] As it gained strength, of course, it recruited from other social strata, but neither the urban professionals, the traditional ruling groups, nor the older intelligentsia felt at ease in the CPP. Recruitment into the upper ranks of the Party came to be ascriptive and, as his rule grew increasingly personalistic, to depend on the whims and fears of Nkrumah. His reluctance to share power or to designate an "heir apparent," and his growing fears for his personal safety, led to insecurity of tenure in the top ranks of the Party and government. But however great the turnover in the upper echelons of political authority, the role occupants at this level were still representative of the founders and militants of the Party.

A structural comparison of the political elite with the student population suggests that students represented a broader cross-section of the population than the political leadership.[33] While it is true that the children of the professional and business classes are overrepresented in proportion to their strength in the total Ghanaian population, those coming from families of lower economic status—the children of farmers and manual workers—have not been

TABLE 3

OCCUPATION: UNIVERSITY OF GHANA STUDENTS' FATHERS COMPARED WITH ALL GHANAIAN ADULT MALES

(In Per Cent)

Occupational Group	1950 All Adult Males (1)	1960 All Adult Males (2)	1953 Student Fathers (3)	1963 Student Fathers (4)	1966 Student Fathers (5)
Agriculture, fishing	70.0	63.1	25.8	38.7	41.8
Manual, crafts, skilled and semi-skilled	23.0	24.0	7.4	10.5	15.8
All others[a]	7.0	12.9	66.8 (N=431)	50.8 (N=181)	42.3 (N=366)

SOURCES: *Cols. 1 and 3:* Gustav Jahoda, "The Social Background of a West African Student Population: I," *British Journal of Sociology,* V (1954), 361; *Col. 2:* Computed from B. Gil, A. F. Aryee, D. K. Ghansah, *1960 Population Census of Ghana, Special Report "E": Tribes in Ghana* (Accra: Census Office, 1964), Table 20; *Col. 4:* Peil, *op. cit.,* p. 23. Sample includes all women, all science students and a 50 per cent random sample of men entering for a B.A. or B.Sc. (Econ.) degree; *Col. 5:* Finlay and Koplin, *op. cit.,* p. 5.

[a] Includes civil service, teaching, professions, and business.

excluded from the University. As Table 3 shows, students from lower-status backgrounds have steadily increased their representation at Legon.

Similar trends are evident with regard to the educational attainments of the students' parents. In a largely illiterate population, those who come from families in which there is some experience of education have a better chance of getting into the University than those who do not. Yet the percentage of students with illiterate fathers has steadily increased, as Table 4 indicates.[34]

TABLE 4

LEVEL OF EDUCATIONAL ATTAINMENT: UNIVERSITY OF GHANA
STUDENTS' PARENTS COMPARED WITH WHOLE ADULT POPULATION

(In Per Cent)

Father's Education	1953 (1)	1963 (2)	1966 (3)	1960 Census: Educational Attainment (4) All Adult Males Age 25 or Over
None	26.1	23.6	30.6	78.8
Elementary and middle school	44.1	50.5	38.1	18.4
Secondary, technical, and teacher training	27.3	21.3	22.1	2.5
University	2.5 (N=238)	4.5 (N=178)	9.3 (N=371)	0.27
Mother's Education				All Adult Females Age 25 or Over
None	65.6	59.0	51.1	94.1
Elementary and middle school	27.7	33.7	41.6	5.1
Secondary, technical, and teacher training	6.7	6.7	7.3	0.72
University	— (N=238)	0.6 (N=178)	— (N=368)	0.08

SOURCES: *Col. 1:* Gustav Jahoda, "The Social Background of a West African Student Population: II," p. 72; *Cols. 2 and 3:* Finlay and Koplin, *op. cit.*, p. 8; *Col. 4:* Computed from Gil, Aryee, Ghansah, *op. cit.*, Table 17, and B. Gil, K. T. de Graft-Johnson, A. F. Aryee, *1960 Population Census of Ghana*, Vol. III: *Demographic Characteristics* (Accra: Census Office, 1964), Table 5.

Access to the University is open to youth from all social strata. But the breadth of their social backgrounds does not necessarily mean that students identify with the "common man" or with his self-styled vanguard, the CPP. Almost all secondary schools in Ghana are boarding schools, where the student lives in isolation from his family and village for up to seven academic years. The university extends this isolation in an atmosphere marked by elitist attitudes and modern physical amenities, both of which are usually in striking contrast with the way of life at home.[35] Thus, the isolation and sense of privilege associated with education create a relatively homogeneous body of students, who take themselves as their major reference group.[36]

The second important factor affecting congruity between the political elite and the students is the existence of alternative elites with whom the latter might identify. In Nkrumah's Ghana, teaching and the civil service were occupations in which loyalty to the Party, although to the applicant's advantage, was not a prime requisite for employment.

Education had, of course, been politicized. The CPP's evangelism at Legon has already been discussed. A similar campaign mounted against secondary school headmasters eventually forced the retirement of the Ghanaian Headmaster of Achimota College, who had come to personify noncooperation in this branch of the intelligentsia. To facilitate the entrance of CPP ideology into the schools, the older headmasters were replaced whenever possible by younger, less experienced, but more tractable men.[37] Yet even these attempts did not completely destroy the operation of professional values in recruitment and advancement.

The civil service had been largely Africanized by independence, but it continued to reflect British traditions and norms and, in the opinion of some, tended to prefer British administrators to the African politicians who replaced them.[38] A general suspicion between the CPP and the civil service resulted. Nkrumah announced his intention "to tighten up the regulations and to wipe out the disloyal elements in the civil service, even if by so doing we suffer some temporary dislocation of the service . . . for disloyal civil servants are not better than saboteurs."[39] Predictably, well-qualified university graduates often found themselves passed over for better civil service positions, which appeared to be reserved for Party stalwarts, regardless of qualification.

The shift in student career choices away from government and education (Table 2) reflected the CPP's increasing use of prior support for the Party as a criterion of advancement to higher-level positions in these fields and the students' reluctance to make this accommodation. But although the civil service and the educational system were under pressure from the CPP, they nevertheless represented elite groups with whom the University graduates had more in common—in professional attitudes and academic background—than with the CPP. Neither elite had political influence comparable to that of the CPP, but each enjoyed high-income positions and considerable social prestige. To some extent, then, the existence of alternative elites and opportunities reduced the necessity for the students to come to terms—whether in support or opposition—with the CPP.

The final component of congruity is the degree of attitudinal harmony between the students and the political elite. Table 5, covering student opinion on national goals, Party ideology, and foreign policy, reveals foreign policy as the area of greatest attitudinal congruence (although agreement was low on the statements concerning American foreign policy toward Africa and the receipt of foreign aid). Congruence on matters of internal ideology, on the other hand, was low. The one-party state received little support;[40] nor did the students approve the government's attitudes toward trade unions and the opposition United Party.

Although 67 per cent of the students regarded Nkrumah as charismatic, this did not necessarily imply acceptance or support. Student definitions of Nkrumaism reflected ambivalence toward the leader and his ideology; only 13 per cent used affirmative terms in defining Nkrumaism, 19 per cent were negative, and 53 per cent were largely neutral, while—perhaps an additional indicator of ambivalence—15 per cent declined, or said they did not know how, to define the term. Student attitudes toward politicians also tended to be more negative than positive.

It is apparent that attitudinal congruence between students and the CPP was considerably lower on questions of domestic policy. While students evidenced some sympathy for general Party goals, they did not transfer this support to Party leaders. Moreover, recruitment patterns for the students' careerist orientations were quite different from those of the CPP, where intellectuals were mistrusted and the most desirable positions were filled on the basis of personalistic criteria and at the whim of Kwame Nkrumah. Although congruence with civil service and the teaching profession was higher, these elites also suffered from political pressure and attack, a factor that scarcely contributed to student sympathy for the CPP.

To summarize, the nature of the educational system, the gov-

TABLE 5

ATTITUDINAL CONGRUENCE: AGREEMENT OF UNIVERSITY OF GHANA
STUDENTS WITH THE CONVENTION PEOPLE'S PARTY, 1963

	Percentage of Students Supporting CPP position	
High Congruence		
The nations of West Africa have attained political independence but economic independence is yet to come.	96.1	(198)
Ghana's neutralist position in international politics is desirable.	83.5	(172)
African Socialism is not the same as "scientific socialism" practiced in Eastern countries.	82.5	(170)
Neutralism is the best policy for developing nations.	81.1	(167)
The European common market will impede economic growth in Africa.	73.3	(151)
A "United States of Africa" is desirable.	72.3	(149)

	Percentage of Students Opposing CPP position	
Low Congruence		
Trade unions should be independent of government control.[a]	93.2	(192)
Competing political parties are the lifeblood of democracy.[a]	86.9	(179)
A one-party system for Ghana is desirable.	80.1	(165)
The one-party system reflects African traditions.	74.3	(153)
American foreign policy toward Africa is neocolonialist.	55.8	(115)
The United Party is subversive.	53.9	(111)
Foreign aid is a threat to African independence.	53.9	(111)

	Percentage of Students	
	Supporting	Opposing
Areas of Ambivalence	CPP Position	CPP Position
Socialism is inevitable.	43.2 (89)	48.1 (99)
Socialism is preferable to capitalism.	46.1 (95)	39.8 (82)
	(N=206)	

[a] The CPP would have disagreed with these statements and agreed with
all the others. Absolute figures are in parentheses.

ernment's propensity to sanction and the students' perceived sanctionability, and the lack of congruity between students and the
political elite combined to discourage student political activity.
An educational pyramid that narrowed sharply at the higher levels
and the availability of relatively high-income, high-status careers
outside of politics combined to remove the prospect of "intellectual
unemployment" as a reason for student activism. Another potential
source of active opposition—attitudinal incongruity between stu-

dents and the political elite—was rendered inoperative by a highly deterrent sanction function. Generally only the CPP members and sympathizers at Legon were politically active, particularly after 1964. The majority neither supported the Party, nor—with the exception of the ill-fated leaders of the National Union of Ghana Students— dared to oppose it openly. For the most part, the students avoided politics. Thus, although the perceptual level of politicization was high, the behavioral level for all but Party members was low.

Reactions to the Coup d'État

When the fighting began at Flagstaff House in Accra before dawn on February 24, 1966, the sonorous booming of mortar fire interspersed with gun shots could be heard at the University of Legon, seven miles away. There was no certainty of what was happening until 6:00 A.M., when Colonel E. K. Kotoka announced over Radio Ghana that a coup was in process. By 7:00 A.M., students had begun to celebrate, although there was still no assurance that the attempt would be successful. By the afternoon, fears of failure were allayed and the jubilation grew. The students marched en masse through the campus, rang bells, ignored classes, and shouted their support for the newly formed National Liberation Council (NLC).

On that first day, the majority accepted the coup and joined the celebration. Another group was more cautious, "waiting to see" which side would win, reluctant to make what would have been a costly mistake had the coup failed. The Party activists on campus made up a third group. Many of them at first refused to believe the news. Several actually began issuing warnings and taking down the names of celebrating students. The demonstrators soon turned on them, and the Party activists' primary concern thereafter was for their own safety.

A prominent Ghanaian lecturer described the changed atmosphere at the University in these terms:

> You probably may *not* be able to imagine the air of freedom we are now breathing at Legon. The suffocation is now gone. Indeed, in the first few days of the coup discipline nearly broke down at Legon—and at the other sister University at Kumasi. The students sought to vent the spleen of their anger on Nkrumah's activists among them and several of them had to run away for some time. It was difficult restraining them from tearing their erstwhile tormentors literally into pieces.[41]

There was relatively little violence at the University, although several CPP activists were beaten and one had his room completely sacked. The Party's headquarters at the University was raided, and a fight broke out between demonstrators and CPP members who were caught trying to destroy possibly incriminating files.[42] Army officials arrived at the university the day after the coup and arrested the few Party activists who had not already left the campus.

On the third day after the coup, almost all the students, clad in academic gowns, went into Accra to demonstrate their support for the NLC—an act of fidelity Nkrumah had always hoped the students would commit for his benefit. The day before, a letter had been sent to the new rulers on behalf of the "Governments of all Halls" thanking them "for the successful overthrow of the old, corrupt, and tyrannical regime of Kwame Nkrumah."

The coup generated high spirits at Legon. The students' spontaneous approval appeared largely expressive of pent-up sentiments toward the old government. It was difficult to assess the full implications of the coup in the first few days. NLC pronouncements were vague and the campus was permeated by rumors. A rumor that Nkrumah (who was out of the country when the coup struck) had landed in northern Ghana and was marching toward Accra caused considerable apprehension. Even when such tales proved untrue they were not entirely discounted, for Nkrumah, broadcasting from Guinea, did promise to return and "liberate" the country.

If students and staff had been alienated from national politics and politicians during the Nkrumah era, the change in rulers reversed the situation. The immediate reaction of the majority of the Legon community was to accept and support the new political elite. One student interviewed described the new atmosphere at Legon as "a complete purification of the polluted air the intellectual was forced to inhale during the Nkrumah era." The NLC was careful to take advantage of its initial popularity by making goodwill gestures toward Legon. Several members of the Council accepted invitations to address various residence halls. In speeches outlining the political and social aims of the "revolution," they pledged the NLC to restore the University's academic freedom and integrity.

Silence had been the rule for the staff of the University since 1961, although a few members (such as William Abraham, Professor of Philosophy and later Pro Vice Chancellor) had been coopted by the CPP and a few others (including B. D. G. Folson, Acting Head of the Department of Political Science) had publicly questioned the Nkrumah government. Now, like the students, they exuded a new vitality.

Changes in Elite Congruity

Ghanaian students take many of their cues from faculty members and it is necessary therefore to describe the new activism among the Legon staff before we consider changes in student–political elite congruity.

Within days after the coup, a group of seventeen senior staff members created a Legon Committee on National Reconstruction (LCNR) to help demolish the Nkrumah myth and to assist the NLC in every way possible. On July 8, the LCNR published the first issue of the *Legon Observer,* a fortnightly publication endeavoring to be "an independent journal of opinion."[43]

The significance of the journal is considerable. Most of the Ghanaian press remains government-owned and, to a considerable extent, government-controlled. The *Legon Observer* has been highly critical of some Council policies, such as the release of certain CPP detainees, the decree permitting arrests without warrants, and "government by civil servants." Through the pages of the *Legon Observer,* the academic community has joined in the discussion of national issues and thereby created a new participatory role in politics for University intellectuals.

The University staff also took part in a series of lectures, sponsored by the Institute of Public Education, on the general theme, "What Went Wrong in Ghana, 1951–66." As the NLC turned to the task of administration, faculty members were appointed to important advisory bodies, including the Political Committee (now defunct) and the National Advisory Committee. Many of the other members of these committees were former United Party officials whose support of, if not ties with, Legon had always been strong. Legon faculty also joined delegations sent abroad to explain NLC policies and solicit support for the new government. Whatever civilian government might succeed the Council's military-police rule, it would almost certainly include a number of faculty members from the University of Ghana.

In the first year after the coup, few Legon faculty members showed much concern over the possibility of jeopardizing the University's independence through too close an integration of academe and politics. Some expatriate observers feared that the mood at Legon had shifted so quickly after the coup that traditional concerns over academic freedom and autonomy were obscured. On one occasion, after an address by K. A. Busia to a University audience, an expatriate faculty member asked why certain lecturers had been summarily dismissed from their posts after the coup. Pro Vice Chancellor Kwapong labeled the question "rubbish" and ruled it "out of order."[44] The facts of the alleged deportations are in doubt and, as the incident shows, the University administration did not welcome questions regarding them.

In 1966, student attitudes toward the new political milieu had not yet solidified. Most of the students had had no experience with any government but Nkrumah's; they were uncertain about the limits and expectations of political behavior under a freer system.

In this transition period, student–political elite congruity was based on attitudinal rather than structural factors. NLC recruitment patterns did not emphasize academic criteria. With the sole exception of Colonel A. A. Afrifa, who had completed secondary school (but did not graduate) and two years at Sandhurst, the level of education of NLC members was low. Two members had received secondary school certificates, three had attended secondary school but not to the certificate level, and the remaining two had only a primary school education. Again with the exception of the thirty-one-year old Afrifa, Council members had served from nineteen to twenty-seven years in the army or the police; most had little other occupational experience.

From the beginning most students generally agreed with the decisions of the NLC and sympathized with the Council in its task of rebuilding the economy and reshaping the polity. For the most part, students realized that running a government was a new experience for the army-police regime and that it would take some time for the new leaders to learn the ins and outs of administration. They also appreciated the NLC's abstention from direct involvement in University affairs.

Factors contributing to student support for the new regime included the popularity of the young, charismatic Colonel Afrifa, the political activities of faculty members, and campus ties with former United Party leaders (representing the old traditionalist-intelligentsia coalition that had opposed Nkrumah), who exercised some political power under the NLC. Despite these factors, students were still ambiguous about their potential political roles and unclear in their political views. They tended to agree with most of the Council's general positions, particularly with the idea that it was necessary to create order and stability before the restoration of constitutional government. Thus, 44 per cent of the students felt that elections should be postponed for three or more years.[45] Given the students' verbal commitment to liberal democratic ideals and the fact that the alternative to elections was arbitrary and unrepresentative authority, this response is surprising. The students were probably expressing the general anxiety that CPP factions might be the strongest political force in any immediate election, as well as their distrust of "politicians."

Although students were not particularly concerned to see an early restoration of civilian rule, the 1966 data suggest they did hold opinions about some dimensions of a future government.

Not surprisingly, 98 per cent of the respondents were of the opinion that Ghana needed a new generation of political leaders; yet their views of the kind of leadership required were mixed. One might expect an elitist image of leadership, but the data do not entirely support this expectation. Sixty-one per cent felt that highly educated people were best equipped to solve political problems, and 24 per cent believed that illiterates should not be allowed to vote;[46] yet only 35 per cent felt that political power should be in the hands of a small group of competent people. Multiple correlations of these items do not reveal any internally consistent pattern of elitist values. Although one might infer a certain antidemocratic bias from these responses, as well as from the response to the statement that it would be better to have strong leaders instead of so many speeches (66 per cent agreed), interviews indicated that first and foremost in the students' minds was the need for "good" and "competent" men "able" to solve Ghana's immediate problems.

In considering student attitudes toward leadership, we must bear in mind that the concept of leadership has been somewhat ambiguous in Ghana, partly as a result of the conflict among traditional norms, which emphasized ascriptively attained position; the personalistic system developed by Nkrumah, which demanded obedience to a charismatic leader; and the achievement criteria stressed, for example, in the civil service. Nevertheless, there was a tendency among the students to defer to established authority, however derived (but usually based on status considerations), and not to question its legitimacy. The long-term effects of the coup on this orientation are not clear.

If the students were unsure about the qualities of leadership needed in the new Ghana, they were more definite about the shape of future party politics. During the Nkrumah era students had opposed the creation of a one-party state, and consensus on this issue in 1966 was strong. Seventy-six per cent disagreed with the proposition that the one-party state reflects African traditions,

89 per cent did not believe that a one-party state would be best for
Ghana in the future, and 79 per cent were of the opinion that competition between political parties is the lifeblood of democracy.

In a developing nation where the entrepreneurial class is composed largely of farmers and small-market merchants, government
responsibility for economic development is necessarily great. It is
not surprising, therefore, that most of the students endorsed
basic tenets of welfare-state socialism. Seventy-six per cent agreed
with the proposition that the government should provide work for
all who need it, and 77 per cent felt that the government not only
should supervise the economic life of the country but should own
the basic industries as well. The students also held a favorable image
of the role of foreign capital in development, even though this was
somewhat incongruent with socialist ideology. Eighty-two per cent
felt that foreign capital brought more benefits than evils to Ghana,
and 8 per cent stated that it brought only benefits.

Students expressed some ambiguity, if not conservatism, on items
dealing with the pace and stringency of planned development.
While 76 per cent agreed with the proposition that it is never wise
to introduce changes rapidly in government or the economic order,
47 per cent agreed that the government should introduce a program
of rapid economic development even if this results in great sacrifices for the population in the early stages. Approximately 30 per
cent agreed with both items.

Although the students clearly envisioned an extensive economic
role for government, their orientation toward "socialism" is somewhat obscured by the disrepute into which the term has fallen since
the coup. Thus, only 21 per cent of the students considered themselves socialists, but 33 per cent viewed socialism as inevitable.
Forty-three per cent agreed that the means of production should
be controlled by the workers. Forty-eight per cent said that, given
a choice between capitalism and socialism, they would prefer socialism.

These attitudes and beliefs were congruent with NLC policy in
1966: a commitment to create a welfare state, a mixed economy, and
eventually a democratic polity. But student debate on issues had
just begun. Only in December 1966 did the revived National Union
of Ghana Students adopt a series of constitutional proposals for
submission to the Constitution Commission of the NLC.

On the other hand, there are areas in which students have been
critical of the new government almost from the beginning. Many
students shared the opinion that the NLC was "too soft" with former

CPP officials and said as much to visiting representatives of the Council. Yet responses were divided on a question probing for attitudes of vengeance. To the proposition that "every vestige of Nkrumaism must be rooted out no matter who is affected," 54 per cent agreed and 42 per cent disagreed. Nor was there a consensus on the type of action the NLC should take against former CPP supporters—continued imprisonment, criminal trials, confiscation of property, bans on political participation, or other reprisals. Students were also critical of police participation in the NLC, both because of the reputation of the police for petty corruption during the Nkrumah era and because of their minimal role in the actual coup d'état.

Finally, some of the issues on which students voiced criticism reflected their preoccupation with status trappings. They were quite critical, for example, of the temporary decision of Ghana Airways to stop accepting Ghanaian currency from passengers on international flights; they criticized the practice of "illiterates" and chiefs of sending congratulatory messages and gifts to the NLC. Others were angered when a Junior Common Room Council decided to "sacrifice" a day's breakfast in order to present food to the NLC. Students objected to these practices as too reminiscent of the Nkrumah era. Ironically, students expressed only limited and mixed reactions to two NLC decrees allowing the government to take "rumor-mongers" into custody without warrant and to hold them for twenty-eight days or such other period as the Attorney General might determine.[47]

A year after the coup, student-elite congruity remained largely undefined. Initial sympathy and gratitude had created a high degree of agreement over national goals and the solution of pressing fiscal problems. The structural discrepancy in backgrounds, however, could affect this attitudinal congruity were the NLC to follow the example of military elites in other countries and demonstrate the political style associated with military rule: command rather than persuasion and bargaining. On the other hand, the faculty's new role as government consultants had added luster to the intellectual elite, and students would undoubtedly find identification with this elite politically more profitable and perhaps emotionally more satisfying than under the Nkrumah government. To the extent that students could maintain their current identification with the NLC or transfer it without conflict to the now politically efficacious intelligentsia, their level of behavioral politicization could be expected to increase.

The Sanction Function After the Coup

In its use of sanctions, the NLC differed strikingly from the CPP regime. Punitive measures were directed by the new political authorities largely against ex-CPP leaders and in a rather gentle fashion. The position of the Council was clearly stated by its Chairman, General Ankrah, on June 3, 1966:

> This is the time for us to foster the spirit of national unity and conciliation, especially in our attitude toward former members of the disbanded Convention People's Party. It should be made clear that the Armed Forces and the Police Service did not depose Nkrumah only to perpetuate his wicked and obnoxious policies which brought so much sorrow and misery to many Ghanaian homes. We have no intention of imposing another rule of terror, fear and oppression on our fellow citizens. What is more, we are not prepared to resort to indiscriminate acts of vengeance against those who were associated with the discredited party. This would be a travesty of the very purpose of the Revolution. . . . We have made it abundantly clear that after thorough investigations all those suspected of having committed any criminal offenses will be put to trial, and dealt with according to law. . . . The Council's policy should not be mistaken for weakness.[48]

Despite a ban on all political activity, the threat of heavy sanctions for the ill-defined offense of "rumor-mongering," and the creation of Military Tribunals with power to try civilians, the NLC's use of sanctions was moderate in most respects. Those who hoarded goods were subject to army raids, certain CPP officials were "restored to protective custody" after alleged plots against the Council were discovered, and a large number of chiefs installed by the CPP were unseated. Yet there was an obvious sense of increased freedom in Ghana, evident in the openness of public debate and in the quiet but real political organizing which the Council chose to ignore. The *Legon Observer* published remarks critical of the NLC and, at times, of specific Council policies, such as the decrees on rumor-mongering.[49] A sense of congruity with the NLC and general approval of its record lessened perceptions of sanctionability among all Ghanaians, and among members of the Legon community in particular. Yet the balance of freedom remained precarious. On January 8, 1968, 29 persons associated with the *Legon Observer* were tried for contempt before the Accra High Court as a result of an article criticizing the judiciary for delays in hearing cases. Their conviction, plus the NLC's removal of four newspaper editors, illustrated the regime's schizophrenia regarding the exercise of freedom during its tenure. These incidents marked the first major clash between the government and the intellectuals.

Because they felt they had been unjustly treated by the Nkrumah government, students at the University of Ghana considered themselves among the prime beneficiaries of the coup. Nevertheless, after the initial enthusiastic demonstrations, the students were relatively cautious in their behavior toward the new regime. They did not engage in activity on or off campus that might be interpreted by the NLC as violating any kind of norm or providing grounds for the imposition of sanctions. Thus, at least at the end of the academic year 1965–66, students generally had resumed their former role as nonparticipants in politics.

Within a purely university context, however, there were indications that student attitudes might be changing and that preoccupation with sanctionability had given way to concern for defining student prerogatives and rights in campus affairs. Acquiescence seemed, in part, to be receding before new attitudes that could prefigure the development of student activism. But the revitalization of student organizations had not been dramatic, nor had militant new political groups emerged.

The primary evidence of attitudinal change comes from incidents such as the one at Kumasi University, in which students demanded the removal of the Vice Chancellor. On August 1, 1966, he was released from his duties, although the student protest was not the sole cause for his dismissal. Incidents at Legon, dating from a warning in March 1966 by the Pro Vice Chancellor against indiscipline, involved student-faculty conflicts over material prerogatives and questions of principle, which were significant departures from the students' former deference to authority. In two cases, approximately 400 and 1,000 students, respectively, demonstrated to protest University actions.[50]

High attitudinal congruity and a low propensity to impose sanctions had at least created supportive orientations among students toward the NLC. The Council had in no way threatened students at the University of Ghana or intervened in their affairs. In this new climate, the example of the Legon faculty was a potential stimulus to the development of student activism. Another critical factor in the future relationship between students and the political elite will be the ability of the latter to meet the students' high expectations on matters of status and career.

Politicization and Legitimacy

Politicization has been defined by Daniel Goldrich as a continuum of individual awareness and involvement in the world of politics and government.[51] Politicization involves two dimensions: (1) the perceptual awareness of government and its relevance to one's own life, and (2) behavioral involvement in political activity. Political roles may vary from the perceptually unrelated and inactive to the perceptually related, highly participant.

Our discussion of the Nkrumah and post-coup periods in terms of the three variables relevant to student politicization has suggested that the level of behavioral politicization among students was low during the Nkrumah period and had not yet been definitely established in the year following the coup. However, perceptual politicization among Legon students had been high in both periods. Students were and are well aware of government and its relevance to their lives. They are also relatively well informed about current events and personalities.[52]

Politicization was measured by similar items in the 1963 and 1966 surveys. Comparison of the two samples indicates little change in interest in politics, although in 1963 students rated their own interest as being higher than that of others, while the opposite was the case in 1966. In 1966, students spent less time discussing politics and were less inclined to participate in politics or to run for public office if they had the opportunity. One might have expected the opposite findings, given the change in regime, the removal of threats, and the greater attitudinal congruity between campus and government. The explanation lies in a number of factors. For some students, the coup reduced the salience of politics simply by removing fear. Other students admitted reacting to the revelations of misdeeds during the Nkrumah era with increasing cynicism, feeling that if Ghana could just rid herself of "politics" there would be fewer difficulties. However, opinions in this area were ambiguous, in part because the sample was drawn only four months after the coup. Certainly the new regime had not had time to imbue the term "politics" with non-Nkrumaist meaning.

The items in Table 6 were combined to derive an index of politicization.[53] The effectiveness of the sanction function in modifying behavioral levels of politicization in 1963 is demonstrated in Table 7. In terms of the index, which includes both perceptual and behavioral items, students who were CPP members, or who intended to join the Party, were more highly politicized than students

TABLE 6

STUDENT POLITICIZATION, 1963 AND 1966
(In Per Cent)

	1963	1966
Estimation of own interest in politics		
Actively interested	18.9 (39)	17.2 (36)
Very interested	34.0 (70)	33.5 (70)
Somewhat interested	39.3 (81)	36.8 (77)
Indifferent	5.8 (12)	8.6 (18)
Not interested	1.9 (4)	3.8 (8)
Time spent per week discussing politics		
One hour or less	11.2 (23)	35.9 (75)
Two hours	20.9 (43)	19.1 (40)
Three hours	18.5 (38)	13.4 (28)
Four hours	9.2 (19)	9.1 (19)
Five or six hours	9.2 (19)	12.4 (26)
Seven or eight hours	5.8 (12)	4.3 (9)
Nine or more hours	12.1 (25)	3.8 (8)
No answer and no data	13.1 (27)	1.9 (4)
Intention to participate in politics after *graduation from university*		
Yes	18.9 (39)	17.7 (37)
No	42.2 (87)	60.8 (127)
Don't know	38.4 (79)	21.1 (44)
No answer	0.5 (1)	0.5 (1)
Candidate for public office if *the opportunity arose*		
Yes	52.9 (109)	36.8 (77)
No	22.3 (46)	38.3 (80)
Don't know	19.9 (41)	23.0 (48)
No answer	4.9 (10) (N=206)	1.9 (4)
Political roles (1966 only)		
Would like to be a parliamentary candidate		13.9 (29)
Prefer to confine political activity to local level		1.9 (4)
Participate in politics only indirectly (as advisor)		56.5 (118)
Stay out of politics entirely		26.3 (55)
No answer		1.4 (3) (N=209)

categorized for their nonmembership or ambivalence.[54] However, examination of correlations with the individual items denoting politicization reveals that non-Party students were perceptually as politicized as the Party group. The distribution on "high interest in politics," in fact, is bimodal: 58 per cent of the Party students,

48 per cent of the Ambivalents, and 53 per cent of the non-Party students. Time spent discussing politics was also not correlated with Party membership. It was on questions dealing with future participation in politics (i.e., the behavioral aspect) that Party membership showed a significant positive correlation with politicization. The sanctionability of those who in effect rejected the Party dictated acquiescent and inactive roles and avoidance of the risks of oppositional activity. Thus the politicization index as a whole is skewed in favor of those who supported the CPP.

TABLE 7

POLITICIZATION AND PARTY POSITION, 1963
(In Per Cent)

| Politicization | PARTY POSITION | | |
	Party	Ambivalent	Non-Party
High	49.2 (29)	23.3 (14)	25.3 (22)
Medium	33.9 (20)	43.3 (26)	32.3 (28)
Low	16.9 (10)	33.3 (20)	42.5 (37)
	(N=59)	(N=60)	(N=87)

Less authoritarian political systems than Nkrumah's Ghana allow for an alignment or congruence between perceptual and behavioral politicization whether students support or oppose the government. Since the coup, there is evidence suggesting that perceptual and behavioral politicization are moving into this "expected relationship," i.e., that the highly politicized are not differentiated by perceptual and behavioral components and they expect to have greater influence in government and politics than other students.

Attitudes about legitimacy are an important dimension of perceptual and behavioral politicization. We assume, other things being equal, that the character of an individual's political activity will be related to the direction and intensity of his legitimacy orientations, but will also be affected by the nature of the political system. In open political systems, the highly politicized might either support or reject political authorities or the political regime. Although oppositional activity was largely impossible under Nkrumah, this does not mean attitudes were controlled. Attitudinal congruity has already been discussed (see Table 5), but not in relation to legitimacy orientations or evaluations of the regime.

In 1963, 43 per cent of the students agreed that a majority of

Ghanaians supported the CPP (34 per cent disagreed), but only 27 per cent thought the government represented the "will of the people."[55] As Table 8 indicates, even Party members did not respond with high estimates of the regime's legitimacy.

TABLE 8

PARTY POSITION AND LEGITIMACY ORIENTATIONS, 1963
(In Per Cent)

Orientations	PARTY POSITION		
	Party	Ambivalent	Non-Party
The CPP has the support of the majority of the Ghanaians.			
Agree	59.3	46.7	29.9
Disagree	13.6	28.3	52.9
Don't know	20.3	21.7	16.1
No answer	6.8	3.3	1.1
The Government represents the will of the people.			
Agree	49.2	23.3	14.9
Disagree	32.2	48.3	74.8
Don't know	18.6	26.7	9.2
No answer	—	1.7	1.1
	(N=59)	(N=60)	(N=87)

Conversely, 96 per cent of the 1966 sample felt that the NLC had the support of the majority of Ghanaians,[56] and 93 per cent personally approved of the Council's actions and policies. A small number of students distinguished between military rule and the NLC. Thus, 15 per cent of the students polled felt that *military rule* did not have the support of the majority of Ghanaians, but of these thirty-one individuals, twenty-eight believed the *NLC* had majority support. Whether distinctions between military rule and the NLC are maintained or increase remains to be seen.[57]

Legitimacy orientations reflect the effects of the sanction function on behavioral politicization. Further evidence of this linkage comes from student evaluations of civil liberties and the abilities of politicians. If non-Party membership in 1963 was an indication of incongruity with the political elite and of nonsupportive legitimacy orientations, and if students perceived themselves as highly vulnerable to sanctions, we would expect them to have rated low both the protection of civil liberties and the abilities of politicians. Asked to rate the protection of civil liberties as "excellent," "good," "satisfactory," "fair," or "poor" in 1963, 76 per cent of the students responded "fair" or "poor," including 51 per cent of the Party group and 90 per cent of the non-Party group. In 1966, only 13 per cent used these latter two ratings. The proportion labeling the protection of civil liberties as "good" or "excellent" had jumped from 5 per cent in 1963 to 54 per cent after the coup.

Student assessments of politicians were largely negative in both periods. The ability of the average Ghanaian politician was rated as "poor" or "fair" by 81 per cent of the students in 1963 and by 75 per cent after the coup. Students viewed politicians in light of their own experience with the Nkrumah regime. Whether such images will change may depend upon the restoration of civilian government.

Conclusion

The political attitudes and behavior of University of Ghana students have been affected by the three variables considered in this chapter: the educational system, elite congruity, and the sanction function. Although Legon students were and remain perceptually related to politics, their level of behavioral politicization has been low. An elitist system of education, in and of itself, tends to predispose students toward political inactivity. Solely on the basis of the educational structure, we would not expect Legon students in the near future to attain the relatively high levels of politicization common among a good many students in mass and more heterogeneous educational institutions, for example, in India, Indonesia, and Japan.

In Ghana, before the coup, both structural and attitudinal congruity between students and the political elite was low, but could not be translated into oppositional behavior because of the high sanction function. A few students, for idealistic and opportunistic reasons, did join the CPP and were politically active. For the majority, the only feasible options were ambivalence or opposition expressed through withdrawal, particularly after the crackdown at Legon in early 1964. Under the National Liberation Council, on the other hand, attitudinal congruence seemed relatively high and students perceived the NLC's propensity to impose sanctions as low. Like their predecessors under Nkrumah, students at Legon in 1966 were relatively well informed about politics and well aware of the relevance of government to their personal lives. If openness in the University and the political system increases, oppositional as well as supportive roles will be possible for the students.

Now, as in the Nkrumaist past, students are the objects of considerable attention. They hold a certain tangible influence in society that may very well be forged into political power. In the past, students seldom made demands upon the political system; their political behavior centered on reactions to events and pressures initiated by others and was never very extensive. Now there are indications that student political activity has increased. Since the coup, there have been numerous riots in secondary schools and protests in the universities, which portend the rise of a new generation of students not afraid to question authority or to make their wishes known. At Legon, students have challenged University actions and directed a few barbed comments against NLC policies they find too reminiscent of the Nkrumaist era. At the very least, the coup represented a symbolic break with that past and the students know they will have a part in shaping new alternatives.

NOTES

1. The 1963 data are based on a questionnaire distributed to 236 students in two political science classes at the University of Ghana and filled out during class periods. Thirty of the questionnaires were disqualified by the respondent's nationality or unusable for other reasons. The resulting sample *N* is 206, which represents 17 per cent of all Ghanaian students at the University during the academic year 1962–63.

The 1966 data are based on two questionnaires administered simultaneously by paid research assistants to a representative student sample. No student filled out more than one questionnaire; approximately 80 per cent were completed and returned. The total number of respondents was 376, or 20 per cent of the 1,879 Ghanaian students at the University. Those responding to questions about politicization and political attitudes, which were asked on one of the two questionnaires, numbered 209. To test the representative quality of our survey, we obtained data on 400 randomly selected students from application forms in the Registrar's files, and both sets of data were checked against aggregate statistics on enrollment by faculty, age, and home residence. Our samples compared well on these dimensions.

2. For the application of the structure of the educational system to mobility in the United States and the United Kingdom, see Ralph Turner, "Sponsored and Contest Mobility and the School System," *American Sociological Review,* XXV (1960), 855–67.

3. Seymour Martin Lipset, "University Students and Politics in Underdeveloped Countries," *Comparative Education Review,* X, No. 2 (June 1966), 149.

4. Calculated from absolute figures in Republic of Ghana, *1962 Statistical Year Book* (Accra: Government Printing Department, 1964); Research and Statistics Division Ministry of Education, *Statistics* (mimeo.; Accra, n.d.); *Facts and Figures* (mimeo.; University of Ghana, Legon, March 1966). Enrollment between 1950 and 1964–65 rose from 211,994 to 1,040,414 primary school pupils; 59,960 to 257,625 middle school pupils; 6,162 to 33,071 sec-

ondary school students; and 108 to 2,442 university students. The greatest proportional expansion occurred in the primary schools.

5. Cited in the *Report of the Commission on University Education, December 1960–January 1961* (Accra: Ministry of Information, 1961), p. 19. A later analysis of manpower needs suggests that the output of the educational system above the level of middle schools will be absorbed, if the projections of Ghana's Seven-Year Development Plan were accurate. (Walter Birmingham, I. Neustadt, and E. N. Omaboe, *A Study of Contemporary Ghana*, Vol. II: *Some Aspects of Social Structure* [Evanston: Northwestern University Press, 1967], pp. 233–34.)

6. It should be noted, however, that the median age of students at the University of Ghana was 24–25 years.

7. On the development of education in Ghana, see Philip Foster, *Education and Social Change in Ghana* (Chicago: University of Chicago Press, 1965), and Margaret G. Kelly, "The Ghanaian Intelligentsia" (unpublished Ph.D. dissertation, University of Chicago, 1959).

8. For a readable portrayal of these and other British academic practices, see C. P. Snow, *The Masters* (New York: Charles Scribner's, 1960). Eric Ashby characterizes them as "fripperies" but grants that the totality of the imported academic pattern was more than a veneer. (Eric Ashby, *Universities: British, Indian, African: A Study in the Ecology of Higher Education* [Cambridge, Mass.: Harvard University Press, 1966], p. 234.)

9. K. E. de Graft-Johnson, "Students in Ghana: An Incipient Elite" (unpublished paper, Institute of International Studies, University of California at Berkeley, 1963).

10. In 1960–61, Africans accounted for 28 per cent of the teaching and senior administrative staff. In 1965–66, Africans made up 62 per cent of the teaching and senior administrative staff, but only 47 per cent of the teaching staff alone.

11. In 1965–66, the Faculties of Arts, Law, and Social Sciences accounted for 1,238 of the undergraduate students, compared with 325 in Science, Agriculture, and Medicine.

12. One indicator of the scope of government participation in Ghanaian life is the total number of employees in the public sector. The public sector accounted for 225,009, or 62 per cent of the total of 365,215 employees reported for 1962. (Republic of Ghana, *1962 Statistical Year Book*, p. 87.) One must remember, however, that much of the nation's agriculture and trade is carried on by single-owner establishments with no reported employed help.

13. The trend is even more marked when students discriminate between "now" and "later." Jahoda found in his 1953 sample that distinguishing between the employment students expected immediately after graduation and what they hoped for "twenty years later" resulted in a sharp decline in the number of students planning on secondary teaching or educational administration (from 39.1 per cent to 13.6 per cent) and an increase in those looking forward to university teaching (from 3.3 per cent to 8.2 per cent). (Gustav Jahoda, "Social Background of a West African Student Population: II," *British Journal of Sociology*, VI [1955], 74.)

14. For a theoretical discussion of sanctions in the American political context, see Robert E. Agger, Daniel Goldrich, and Bert E. Swanson, *The Rulers and the Ruled* (New York: John Wiley, 1964), chap. iii.

15. An alternative formulation would be an adaptation of Merton's typology

of conformity, innovation, ritualism, retreatism, and rebellion. See Robert K. Merton, *Social Theory and Social Structure* (rev. ed.; Glencoe: The Free Press, 1957), chap. iv.

16. See Dennis Austin, *Politics in Ghana: 1946–1960* (New York: Oxford University Press, 1964); Henry Bretton, *The Rise and Fall of Kwame Nkrumah* (New York: Frederick A. Praeger, 1967); David J. Finlay, "Ghana and the Politics of Ideological Justification," in David J. Finlay, Ole R. Holsti, and Richard R. Fagen, *Enemies in Politics* (Chicago: Rand McNally, 1967), chap. iii.

17. Kwame Nkrumah, *Speech on the Tenth Anniversary of the C.P.P.* (Accra: Government Printer, 1959), pp. 24–25.

18. The Party press wrote: "It is mainly because the sympathies of the earliest generations of teachers in Legon were reactionary that Legon has had a tradition of reaction." ("Our Universities: Legon (5)," *The Spark*, November 22, 1963, p. 5.)

19. "The Political Role of Youth," *Ghanaian Times*, October 25, 1962, p. 5.

20. Nkrumah, *op. cit.*, pp. 24–25.

21. The Chief Justice, Sir Arku Korsah, had been dismissed after the Special Court he headed acquitted three men charged with treason in connection with an attempt on Nkrumah's life in 1962.

22. The warning was issued by S. G. Ikoku from the Ideological Institute. (*Ghanaian Times*, October 24, 1964.)

23. Bill Wordie, "The Ghanaian Student and National Politics," *Legonite* (Lent 1963), p. 17.

24. A. R. C. Fleischer, "Editorial: Press Attack on Legon," *Legonite* (Lent 1963), p. 5.

25. On the plans to make Legon a "CPP University," see Alex Kwapong, "Vice-Chancellor's Address to Congregation 26th March, 1966," *Legonite*, III, No. 2 (Lent 1966), 11–12.

26. It should also be mentioned that an option open to students in other societies—that of leaving the country to seek a more compatible political climate—scarcely existed for Ghanaian students because of stringent government control over the movement of citizens.

27. K. E. de Graft-Johnson, "The Evolution of Elites in Ghana," in P. C. Lloyd (ed.), *The New Elites of Tropical Africa* (New York: Oxford University Press, for the International African Institute, 1966), p. 112.

28. Literally, "Osagyefo" means "warrior-savior," i.e., one who turns prospective defeat into victory. In a column in the *Evening News*, Nkrumah was referred to as "His Messianic Dedication" and, occasionally, "the Redeemer."

29. Tibor Szamuely, formerly a lecturer at the Ideological Institute, has characterized the nature of Nkrumaism in his introduction to Colonel A. A. Afrifa's *The Ghana Coup* (New York: Humanities Press, 1966), pp. 11–30, as a modern totalitarian system closer in practice to the right than its progressive trappings and socialist declarations would indicate. According to Szamuely, the content of Nkrumaist doctrine was constantly changing, until it resembled a "doctrinal patchwork quilt" more than a unified ideology. See also David E. Apter, *Ghana In Transition* (New York: Atheneum, 1963), p. 207.

30. Kwame Nkrumah, *Flower of Learning* (Accra: Ministry of Information and Broadcasting, 1961), p. 1.

31. Austin, *op. cit.*, p. 12.

32. *Ibid.*, p. 416.

33. Even "traditional tribal elites" are represented at Legon. A sub-sample (N=167) of the 1966 survey was asked to list the traditional titles held by members of their immediate family. Twenty-eight per cent mentioned one or more titles.

34. The reverse trend in percentages of mothers with no education reflects the rapid expansion of educational opportunity for women at the elementary and middle school levels. The proportion of women at the University during this period increased from 2.8 per cent in 1953–54 to 12.6 per cent in 1965–66.

35. In 1953, Jahoda found that over one-half of his sample had experienced temporary or permanent difficulties of adjustment upon returning home during vacations. Jahoda, "Social Background of a West African Student Population: II," pp. 74–78.

36. The major exception to this generalization is in the area of Party membership. The 1963 survey found that of the fifty-nine students who were Party members or intended to join, 64 per cent had fathers who were also Party members. Of the eighty-seven students who were not members and did not intend to join, 65 per cent had fathers who were also nonmembers.

37. A survey of thirty secondary school headmasters in 1965 revealed that a majority were classifiable as cooperating with the CPP, while others feared the consequences of not doing so. Only a small minority either challenged the authority of the Party's Young Pioneer Movement officials or tolerated them while retaining their own jurisdiction. See Charles A. Ballard, Jr., "The Young Pioneer Movement" (unpublished paper, Institute of African Studies, University of Ghana, 1966).

38. Aristide R. Zolberg, *Creating Political Order* (Chicago: Rand McNally, 1966), p. 120.

39. Kwame Nkrumah, *I Speak of Freedom* (New York: Frederick A. Praeger, 1961), p. 173, quoted in Zolberg, *op. cit.*, p. 120.

40. Even among the fifty-nine students who were Party members or intended to join, only 27.1 per cent felt that the one-party system reflected African traditions, and only slightly more (30.6 per cent) felt it was the best system for Ghana.

41. Personal letter to one of the authors. Enthusiasm among the students ran too high for the University administration, for on March 2 the Pro Vice Chancellor, Alex Kwapong, called a meeting of the entire student body and admonished the students to cease harassing former CPP elements among them. Indiscipline, he warned, would not be tolerated.

42. One document, snatched from the hands of a CPP activist, was reportedly a list of names of students and lecturers to be detained in the future; this report fanned student anger.

43. Editorial, "We Make Our Bow," *The Legon Observer,* I, No. 1 (July 8, 1966), 1.

44. The question concerned the alleged deportation of two Russian lecturers. Others have pointed out that the Russians were not deported but, instead, withdrawn by the Soviet Embassy. On the other hand, Arthur Howarth, Dean of the School of Public Administration, was in fact deported by the NLC, one reason certainly being his support of Nkrumah.

Students were not excited by these events. One wrote of the expatriate questioner that

Ozanne's question was irrelevant. Busia is not the NLC and therefore does not know positively the motives for sacking Ozanne's friends from Ghana.

If Ozanne had been less emotional, he would perhaps have framed the question in such a way that would call upon the Speaker to give his opinion on the issue in view of his [Busia's] point that Tolerance was one of the fundamental requirements of Democracy. But he did not and therefore was guilty of two cardinal crimes in an academic institution: Deviation and Irrelevance.

Lord Green (pseud.), "Shame, Shame on You," *The Voice* (Accra), III, No. 16 (March 25, 1966), 1–3. But other students also criticized the way Kwapong had handled the incident.

45. Asked, "How soon do you think national elections should be held?," the students answered as follows (in per cent; absolute numbers are in parentheses):

3–18 months	26.3	(55)
2 years	21.1	(44)
3–6 years	39.7	(83)
More than 6 years	3.8	(8)
No time specified or no answer	9.1	(19)
	100.0	(209)

46. This is somewhat surprising, considering that 31 per cent of the students' fathers and 52 per cent of their mothers were illiterate. There was no statistical correlation between parental level of education and response to this question.

47. Later, however, at the December Congress of the National Union of Ghana Students, the decrees were described as "extremely dangerous and capable of being misused." The Union called for their repeal.

48. Lieutenant-General J. A. Ankrah, *First 100 Days* (Accra-Tema: State Publishing Corporation, 1966), p. 9.

49. See the editorial, "Rumors and Our New Rulers," *The Legon Observer*, I, No. 8 (October 14, 1966), 1–2.

50. One controversy involved the use of a room for television viewing. For using space belonging to the Senior Common Room (reserved for faculty members), several students were dismissed from the University. In protest, a general meeting of the student body was called by student leaders. At this meeting, dozens of Akuafo Hall students announced their refusal to sign a "loyalty pledge" in which the University authorities had asked them to promise to be "obedient in the future." The students simply left the space for their signatures blank or put down their room numbers instead. Afterwards, authorities reissued the pledge forms and threatened to expel any students of Akuafo Hall who refused to sign. Only one student refused.

The other demonstration took the form of a food strike in which approximately 400 students in Commonwealth Hall refused to eat one meal in protest against the expulsion of a student several weeks earlier because of a violent argument he had had with a dining hall steward. The students felt that the penalty of a twenty-eight day expulsion, which automatically meant that the student in question would have lost the entire academic year, was too severe. More important, they felt the penalty had been imposed by University officials to punish the student for his activities as a student leader.

51. Daniel Goldrich, *Sons of the Establishment: Elite Youth in Panama and Costa Rica* (Chicago: Rand McNally, 1966), pp. 5–15.

52. In both the 1963 and the 1966 surveys, students were asked to identify national and international figures and to demonstrate knowledge of recent events in Ghanaian politics. Over 90 per cent correctly named the following: the Soviet Premier (1966); the Secretary General of the United Nations (1963 and 1966); the Secretary General of the Organization of African Unity (1966); the Ghanaian Foreign Minister (1963); the Chief Justice dismissed over treason trials (1966); the Chairman of the National Economic Committee of Ghana (1966); and the date of Ghanaian independence (1963 and 1966).

The local press is not renowned for its quality; students in both 1963 and 1966 indicated a wide range of reading in other news sources, particularly *The Times* (London), *West Africa*, and *Time* magazine.

53. There were no significant differences in socio-economic background between the more and less politicized, which lends support to the contention that politically significant class lines do not exist in Ghana. See, for example, the discussion by K. E. de Graft-Johnson, "The Evolution of Elites in Ghana." There was, however, some relation between academic major and expected career on the one hand and politicization on the other. The more highly politicized tended to include a larger proportion of students planning careers in the professions, particularly law, and, in the 1966 sample, students in the Faculties of Arts, Social Sciences, and Law.

54. Party members are those who were currently members (45) or intended to join (14). Ambivalents are non-Party members who were uncertain of their intention to join or remain outside (60). Non-Party are those who were certain of their intention not to join (87).

55. This should be viewed against the 89.1 per cent vote for Nkrumah in Ghana's 1960 plebiscite. See Austin, *Politics in Ghana: 1946–60*, pp. 387–95.

56. The same question asked in 1963 was asked again in 1966, with "NLC" replacing "CPP." A "don't know" response category offered in 1963 was not available on the 1966 questionnaire, but the loss in comparability is minor.

57. In a survey conducted at Legon in February 1967, M. Peil and E. O. Odotei found that about one-fifth of the students felt the army should not be running the country. Nearly half of the students questioned thought that the army should have no role in government once civilian rule is restored. Fourteen per cent of the sample felt that the army should continue as a watchdog "to see that the new rulers do not abuse their power." "Return to Civilian Rule," *Legon Observer*, II, No. 12 (July 9–22, 1967), 7–9.

4. SOUTH AFRICA

MARTIN LEGASSICK
JOHN SHINGLER

South African students live in a unique environment. Crucial to any insight into their political attitudes and actions is an understanding of the main features of this environment: deep cleavage, rapid change, and bitter conflict. Extreme economic inequality, unrelenting political persecution, the color bar in every walk of life—all combine to make up a festering, impacted universe that every student leader must sooner or later confront, within his society and within himself.

The Divided Society

The central division in South Africa is between white and nonwhite, a color bar being drawn firmly and clearly through the social fabric to distinguish the two castes. The ratio of nonwhites to whites is approximately four to one, while net national income is distributed across the caste line in roughly the reverse proportions.[1] In 1962–63, annual per capita income of whites was $1,747, whereas the corresponding figure for nonwhites was $103; this seventeenfold gap has probably since increased.[2] Whites vote; nonwhites do not, or, where they do, wield no influence on the central government, which shapes South Africa's future. There is today no aspect of life

The authors acknowledge with thanks the cooperation of the National Union of South African Students head office, which provided some of the material on which this chapter has been based. They would also like to thank the many NUSAS officials who participated in discussions or commented on drafts of this chapter, as well as Talbot College, University of Western Ontario and McGill University for typing assistance.

in South Africa—from manufacturing to movie-going and making love—that is not either the exclusive preserve of whites or compartmentalized by color.[3] Since the advent of the present Nationalist government in 1948, opposition to this meticulously structured system of oppression has been effectively suppressed through the use of various instruments of control and punishment, including banning (restrictions on freedom of movement, association, expression), banishment to remote areas, imprisonment, torture, and execution.

The white caste includes three groups, two major and one minor. Politically dominant are the Afrikaners. Today comprising over 60 per cent of the white population[4] and speaking their own language, Afrikaans, they are the descendants of Dutch, French, and German settlers of the seventeenth and eighteenth centuries. The English-speaking South Africans are more recent arrivals, their immigration having begun only in the early nineteenth century. Increasing bilingualism, intermarriage, and social mixing have reduced the distance between the English and Afrikaner groups somewhat, but the English are still overrepresented in the upper reaches of the socio-economic ladder, while Afrikaners tend to occupy the middle and lower rungs. Among the few whites of neither Afrikaner nor English origin, the most interesting politically are the Jews, who have by and large been assimilated into the English stream while preserving their traditional religion and sense of identity.

The nonwhite caste is largely African, but includes Coloureds and Indians. The Africans—among them the Nguni (including the historically important Xhosa and Zulu peoples), the Sotho, the Shangaan-Tonga, and numerous minor groups—have undergone profound cultural and political change: loyalties and demands, particularly those of the younger generation, have shifted from traditional systems to new structures and symbols, including those of African nationalism. The Coloureds, though predominantly Afrikaans-speaking and closely tied to the culture of the whites, also suffer discrimination. The small Indian minority copes more adequately with discriminatory measures, because of the relative wealth of a few of their members and the resilience of their own culture.

Control of the state in South Africa is firmly in the hands of the Nationalist Party, the major political instrument of the Afrikaners. Afrikaner political culture is ethnocentric and authoritarian, reflecting the Afrikaner people's self-image as a neo-Calvinist white elect, racially superior to all nonwhite peoples and uncorrupted by the liberalism that is presumed to have undermined the North Atlantic community. This peculiar brand of nationalism—bitter, embattled, xenophobic—is an expression of the Afrikaners' vulnerable position in South Africa's social hierarchy.[5] The Afrikaners have been squeezed between two major forces in South African society. On the one hand, they were for years discriminated against in economic and social life by the English, who effectively denied them access to channels of upward mobility. At the same time, they faced the specter of rising African demands, including threats against the major economic and political supports of Afrikanerdom: the color bar in the labor market and the virtually all-white franchise.

In their efforts to strengthen what has been called the "granite wall" between the white and nonwhite castes, the Afrikaner Nationalists have successfully implemented their policy of apartheid (literally, separateness) through a spectrum of vigorously enforced segregatory laws. The challenge of English socio-economic hegemony has also been met; more and more Afrikaners have breached or bypassed the old, English-made barriers to economic influence and social status.

Because of their relatively advantageous social and economic position within the white caste, and also because of normative restraints built into their political culture, the English have not as a group sought or supported segregation to the same extent as the Afrikaner community. Their political culture, derived from nineteenth-century British liberalism, is essentially meliorist, concerned with civil liberties, the rule of law, and parliamentary democracy (but less concerned with full equality, social justice, or economic democracy), indebted to Locke and Mill (but not the Fabians).[6] Contemporary South African liberalism is expressed in varying degrees across a wide spectrum. The official opposition United Party, which has declined in strength since 1948, has lost most vestiges of its liberalism to the Progressive Party, which has a single Parliamentary member. Outside Parliament, liberal thought is represented in the scholarly Institute of Race Relations, Black Sash women's movement, and other voluntary civic-minded organizations, as well as in the Liberal Party itself.

The history of nonwhites in South Africa is a history of suffering and struggle. From the last violent African resistance in 1906 until World War II, most African spokesmen attempted to alleviate the position of their people by petitions and pleading. These African political leaders, with a tradition of almost one hundred years of socialization into British political culture—acquiring the goals, values, and symbols of liberal parliamentary democracy, learning as lawyers and teachers to use legal means of redress and reform—

pinned their hopes on the illusory influence of a liberal minority within the white caste. In the 1940's and 1950's, a new generation of leaders framed a Program of Action (adopted by the African National Congress in 1949) , which was implemented in the Defiance Campaign of 1952 and the strikes and boycotts of subsequent years: largely ignoring the liberal white minority,[7] the new strategy involved mobilizing the African people in vehement protest and nonviolent resistance. This extraparliamentary opposition was rigorously suppressed by the government, and in 1960 the African National Congress (ANC) and the Pan-Africanist Congress (PAC) , the two major African nationalist movements, were banned after police had shot demonstrators at Sharpeville and Langa.

In the early 1960's, four sabotage movements emerged. *Umkhonto we Sizwe* (the Spear of the Nation) had close ANC ties; *Poqo* (Alone) was linked with the PAC. *Yu Chi Chan* was founded and supported by Coloureds connected with the Trotskyist-influenced Non-European Unity Movement (NEUM). The African Resistance Movement (ARM) consisted largely of young white radicals, some of them associated with the National Union of South African Students (NUSAS) and the Liberal Party. By 1964, all four groups had been suppressed.[8]

Although white values and norms are crossing the color line in a process of "Westernization" facilitated by the economic interdependence resulting from industrialization, there is no discernible trend toward the emergence of any trans-racially shared sense of national identity. On the white side of the caste line, Afrikaners and English share a stronger sense of mutual belonging than was the case fifty or even twenty years ago. As the liberal white minority has grown smaller, more impotent, and more isolated, apartheid has become a virtually unquestioned element of the white consensus. On the nonwhite side, African nationalism is rising, exacerbating the impotent middle position of the Coloured and Indian minorities.

The Divided University

The university everywhere performs two discrete and often contradictory socializing functions. It embraces and transmits both the values of a largely Western academic culture and the values of the society of which it is a part. In any society there is an inevitable tension in the performance of these two functions. On the one hand, the university claims the right to criticize and remain unfettered by society's norms. On the other, society demands conformity with its conventions, while the state requires acquiescence to its laws and recognition of its formal institutions as the proper agencies of change. In South Africa, the contradiction between these two conceptions of the university has given rise to sharp and bitter conflict.

The ethnic cleavages of South African society have been reflected in, and perpetuated by, the universities themselves. Students have been segregated according to their particular ethnic group (see Table 1) and trained according to that group's supposedly unique needs and traditions. If we compare the percentage representation of each group in the full-time university student population to its representation in the general population, we can clearly see the inequality of higher educational opportunity in South Africa. In 1966, whites were 19 per cent of the total population, but 91 per cent of the student body. Asians (virtually all Indians) were 3 per cent of the total population and 4 per cent of the student body. Africans were by far the most under-represented: sixty-eight per cent of the nation, they were only 3 per cent of the university.[9] Caste barriers raised against higher education for nonwhites remain almost unpenetrated. In 1937, 5.5 of every 1,000 whites were university students. Thirty years later, the comparable figure for nonwhites was 0.25.[10] The dominant white community—even, to a considerable degree, its English component—supports the continuation of the status quo in education.

There are three groups of universities in South Africa: white Afrikaans-medium, white English-medium, and nonwhite. Most of the white universities have long histories.[11] By 1920, the English-medium University of Cape Town (UCT) and University of the Witwatersrand (Wits) and the Afrikaans-language University of Stellenbosch were in existence; the Universities of Natal, Rhodes (English-medium), the Orange Free State (UOFS), Potchefstroom, and Pretoria (Afrikaans-medium) later attained independent status after a period as subsidiary colleges of the dual-medium University of South Africa, an examining body only. A dual-medium University of Port Elizabeth opened in 1965 (here, in contrast to the other white universities, the government has a degree of control over crucial appointments), and in 1966 legislation was passed to establish a Rand Afrikaans University in Johannesburg.

Nonwhite higher education dates from 1916, with the founding of the South African Native College (later Fort Hare University College). The University of Natal began classes for nonwhites ("non-Europeans") in Durban (UN.NE) in 1936, maintaining separate campuses for whites in Durban (UN.D) and in Pietermaritzburg

TABLE 1

UNIVERSITY SEGREGATION IN SOUTH AFRICA, 1966[a]

COMPOSITION OF STUDENT BODY
(In Per Cent)

| Institution | Whites | Nonwhites | | | Total Enrollment of Student Body |
		Asians[b]	Coloureds	Africans	
University of:					
Pretoria	100	—	—	—	10,800
Stellenbosch	100	—	—	—	6,636
Natal (UN.D,UN.P)[c]	100	—	—	—	4,653
The Orange Free State	100	—	—	—	2,914
Potchefstroom	100	—	—	—	2,648
Port Elizabeth	100	—	—	—	574
Rhodes	98	2	—	—	1,678
The Witwatersrand	98	2	[d]	[d]	7,650
Cape Town	94	2	4	[e]	6,392
Natal (UN.NE)[f]	—	70	6	24	589
University College:					
for Indians	—	100	—	—	1,384
of the Western Cape	—	—	100	—	477
of the North	—	—	—	100	460
of Fort Hare	—	—	[g]	100	402
of Zululand	—	—	—	100	299
	N=43,321	N=2,137	N=788	N=1,310	47,556

[a] This table is based on enrollment figures given in Muriel Horrell (compiler), *A Survey of Race Relations in South Africa, 1966* (Johannesburg: South African Institute of Race Relations [SAIRR], 1967), p. 268, but covers only those universities that actually hold classes; the 17,401 students (14,263 whites, 1,616 Africans including 250 from outside South Africa, 1,024 Asians, and 498 Coloureds) taking the correspondence courses of the University of South Africa are consequently not included.

[b] The ratio of Indians to Chinese in the population at large is 99:1. The ratio of Indian to Chinese students is probably not significantly different.

[c] White campuses in Durban and Pietermaritzburg.

[d] Twelve Coloureds and six Africans were enrolled in the University of Witwatersrand and are included in the numerical totals.

[e] Three Africans were enrolled in the University of Cape Town and are included in the numerical totals.

[f] Nonwhite (non-European) campus in Durban.

[g] One Coloured was enrolled in the University College of Fort Hare and is included in the numerical totals.

(UN.P) . In 1959, under the Extension of University Education Act, "tribal colleges" were established in the Northern Transvaal for Sotho students, in Zululand for Zulu students, in the Western Cape for Coloureds, and in Durban for Indians. Fort Hare was transformed into a "tribal college" for Xhosa students under the Fort Hare University College Transfer Act the same year. Nonwhite South Africans also attended Pius XII University College in Basutoland, sometimes known as the Catholic University College. Founded in 1945, this institution became the University of Botswana, Lesotho, and Swaziland in 1963. Until 1959, instruction at colleges for nonwhites was, as it has remained at Pius XII, in English. At the "tribal colleges," Afrikaans and English are now both used, though the intention at the African colleges is for the vernacular to be the eventual medium.

With the exception of the "tribal colleges," the universities of South Africa are governed by University Councils and are not government-controlled, although they receive government subsidies to a high and increasing degree.[12] Government backbenchers have often regarded these subsidies as justifying government interference in the universities. In each Council, equal representation is normally given to government appointees, academic staff, and alumni. The balance of seats is usually held by various local bodies and benefactors, who thus have a strong influence on university policy when government and university clash. The Council appoints a Principal with executive powers, and delegates authority over defined academic matters to the University Senate, a senior faculty body.

The "tribal colleges," on the other hand, are under direct government control. At each college, a Rector is appointed by the Minister of Bantu Education. A University Council (white) and an Advisory Council (nonwhite) , with only such powers as the Minister may care to delegate, are appointed by the President of the Republic, who also designates their chairmen. The government hopes to complete the segregation of these colleges by gradually transforming them into entirely nonwhite-administered, nonwhite-taught institutions.

English-medium higher education in South Africa is almost, but not quite, inaccessible to children of the nonwhite caste. The Universities of the Witwatersrand and Cape Town, the "open" universities, located in large cosmopolitan communities, have claimed they do not use race as a criterion of student admission, though an investigating commission found in 1955 that in certain faculties at Wits there was limited admission, or no admission, of nonwhites.

The low and decreasing proportions of nonwhites at these two universities are mainly the result of government intimidation—since 1959 every nonwhite wishing to attend either university must obtain special ministerial permission and the channeling of nonwhite high school graduates toward the tribal colleges and into University of South Africa correspondence courses.[13] Wits and UCT student sports and social activities are segregated. The University of Natal provides separate and inferior facilities for nonwhites, and admits only nonwhites to its Medical School.[14]

Outlooks and orientations in the Afrikaner universities vary from the relative liberalism of Stellenbosch, situated in the more tolerant, cosmopolitan atmosphere of the Western Cape, to the harsh dogmatism of the Potchefstroom University for Christian Higher Education. Potchefstroom is the only white university, aside from the proposed Rand Afrikaans University, whose founding legislation does not include a "conscience clause," the proviso that forbids the administration of any religious test to staff or students as a condition for acceptance.

Since they came to power, the Nationalists have attacked the "open" universities, both because the few nonwhites at them blurred the clean lines of apartheid and because the "liberal" doctrines of the English-medium universities were regarded as dangerously "un–South African." Students and faculty members at UCT and Wits took the lead in opposing the passage of the university apartheid laws of 1959 that established the segregated "tribal colleges."[15] English-medium university administrators also opposed this legislation, but their steadfastness varied, being strongest at UCT—where T. B. Davie, Principal until 1955, flatly maintained that the University had a right to decide "who should teach in it, what should be taught, how it should be taught, and to whom"— and weakest at the University of Natal.

At the same time, the University Councils at Wits and UCT resisted, and have continued to resist, any attempts to desegregate student life at their universities. They have done so out of fear that social contacts between white and nonwhite might be used by the government to arouse white public opinion against the "openness" of their student admission policies.[16] At UCT, for example, J. P. Duminy, Principal from 1958, conducted a seven-year battle with student leaders over mixed dances, which culminated in a refusal by the student body to hold any official dances on campus at all.[17] On this issue, the University Councils attempted to maintain the "customs and conventions" of the white South African community, while student leaders demanded equal treatment for all participants in university life, and in so doing, defended internationally accepted notions of what a university should be.

Until recently the University Councils at the English-medium universities have been prepared to defend the right of students and teachers to hold and express their views, even when these were repugnant to most of the white community. There were signs of a retreat from this position, admittedly in an extreme case, when Wits took disciplinary action against students found guilty of sabotage, although the UCT authorities left the task of punishment to the courts.[18] In 1966–67, the students' representative councils of UCT and UN.D came into conflict with their administrations, and there are signs that the growing pressures of government and the white community have forced the Councils to curtail the powers of student government and limit the extent of student dissidence.

Faculty members are more inclined to take stands on political issues than administrators, but have far less power within the university. In general, the faculties at English-medium and Afrikaans-medium universities form homogeneous groups, both ethnically and in their political attitudes. The faculties of the Afrikaans-language universities are almost all Afrikaners, educated in South Africa or the Netherlands or West Germany; by and large, they support the Nationalist regime. Academic staff members at the English-medium universities are almost entirely English, and many of them have obtained higher degrees in Britain. In the early years, the English-language universities had to recruit heavily in Britain; those who came to South Africa carried their liberal values with them and promoted the traditions of freedom of expression and conscience that still characterize the English-medium universities, particularly Wits and UCT. English-speaking professors and instructors also tend to be critical of the Nationalist government. A sprinkling of nonwhite faculty members was distributed among Wits, UCT, UN.NE, and Fort Hare, although most of them have now left South Africa. Since 1960, the exodus of faculty from English-medium universities to posts overseas has weakened the liberality and lowered the academic standards of those institutions. Until 1959, instruction at the two existing universities for nonwhites, UN.NE and Fort Hare, was given entirely by English-speaking academics. Today, the "tribal college" system is staffed almost completely by Afrikaner teachers, the regime apparently hoping they will exert a less corrosive influence on the minds in their care.

English- and Afrikaans-speaking faculty members have different ideas of what a university should be. The former largely endorse the role prescribed by Western academic values, and would in general agree with Professor I. Gordon, Dean of the Faculty of Medicine at Natal, that university apartheid is "repugnant to the traditions of the universities of the free world since the Middle Ages."[19] Faculty members at the English-medium universities played an important role during the 1950's and early 1960's, not only in combating university apartheid measures, but in helping to organize the Liberal Party, the Progressive Party, and various ad hoc protest groups.

Afrikaners do not share the traditional Western view of the university; in general, they believe the university should promote "the moulding of people in God's image so that they become fully equipped for every good work." Education should be "Christian" ("based on Holy Scripture [as] expressed in the Articles of Faith of our three Afrikaans Churches") and "national" (defined as "love for everything that is our own").[20] To the Afrikaner Nationalist, the English concept of "academic freedom" is anathema. In February 1966, Minister of the Interior J. de Klerk (former Minister of Education, Arts, and Science), warned that the government might have to intervene "to ensure freedom of thought" on the UCT campus.

Afrikaner academics, however, conform rather less to these norms than do their fellow ethnic-group members outside the university. This is especially true of those associated with the South African Bureau of Racial Affairs, influential at Stellenbosch, which attempts to provide a liberal-theoretical underpinning to apartheid. On a number of occasions, faculty members have instigated minor revolts against government policy, and in the case of their protest at the formulation of the university apartheid legislation, were responsible for delaying its enactment by at least a year.[21] But this dissidence has never become widespread, and the pressures of Afrikanerdom have forced the "rebels" to recant or become impotent outcasts.

Students are influenced by their university environments in different ways and to differing degrees. Most white students enter the university straight from secondary school. They are thus younger (median age, nineteen and a half) and socially less experienced than nonwhite university students. The latter, on the average three to four years older than their white counterparts, include many who have had to seek employment or otherwise fend for themselves before entering the university. Opportunities for contact with life off the campus also vary. At Wits and UCT, and to a lesser degree at UN.D, there are large day-student communities that remain in close contact with the outside world. Students at most Afrikaans-medium and nonwhite institutions, however, as well as at Rhodes and UN.P, live in highly supervised residence halls that encourage a narrow social outlook. Finally, there are intrauniversity differences in environmental influence. At all the English-language universities, for example, arts faculty students are noticeably more liberal than those in the science faculties.

The South African university community, then, is bitterly divided. The divisions are both vertical, between English-medium and Afrikaans-medium, white and nonwhite universities, and horizontal, between administration, academic staff, and students. The horizontal divisions have been most marked at the nonwhite universities and least at the white Afrikaans-medium institutions. The English-medium universities occupy an intermediate position, with faculty members often caught in the cross fire between students and administration.

The vertical, society-based divisions in South African higher education have been subject to only muted criticism in the universities, which have never taken a stand against apartheid per se and have thus evaded the central issues of the South African polity. The English-medium universities have protested the violation of their autonomy, but this concern for their own institutional rights has not been matched by concern that the nonwhites participate fully in university life, or by a desire to correct the racial imbalance of educational opportunity. The Afrikaans-medium institutions, by ignoring or denying the cherished principle of autonomy, have isolated themselves from the English-medium universities and from the world university community.

The Divided Students: Attitudes

In South Africa's divided society, ethnicity conditions virtually every dimension of variability—left-right, participant-nonparticipant, and so on—on which student political attitudes and behavior might be measured. The image of the university as a tranquil island of enlightenment in a color-obsessed society is wholly false: ethnicity is in fact central to university life and to student politics.[22]

Each of the three main sectors of the South African student population—Afrikaner, English, and nonwhite—has its own pattern of political perceptions and attitudes. Afrikaner students identify almost to a man with the politically dominant Afrikaners. In the past, the Afrikaner student movement played some part in securing political power for the Afrikaner community; now these students are content to support the status quo their predecessors helped establish. Although more Afrikaner than English students hold intense and rigid political views, the Afrikaners do not express their views in political action as frequently as the English. Those who are active see their main task as exposing and opposing any "threat" to white supremacy and Afrikaner political control: Communism, liberalism, Negrophilia, and other such "alien" influences. A minuscule minority of Afrikaner students are opposed to apartheid, but they are of no relevance in South African political life.

The vast majority of white English-speaking students are uninvolved in political activity and shun political commitment of any kind. This pattern of withdrawal or "privatism" has been perceptively analyzed by Kurt Danziger in an attitudinal study comparing white (predominantly English-speaking) students with nonwhite students:

> The white group concentrates its choices in the sphere of purely personal satisfactions, the nonwhite group tends to put wider social interests first. . . . In the case of less privileged groups, social and individual goals tend to coincide, whereas in dominant social groups, conflict between public duty and individual interest tends to occur. . . . When [whites] do declare themselves to be willing to make sacrifices for an end other than their private satisfaction, this end tends to assume a conveniently abstract and nebulous character . . . assuaging the guilt that arises from the conflict between social ideals and private interest. . . . The pursuit of private satisfactions, however, is not only the result of the expectation of positive gains in that direction . . . it is also conditioned by fear of the consequences to the individual of participation in socio-political action. . . . The socially oriented individual is therefore compelled to face the possibility of political persecution. . . . The privatistic individual escapes this, but . . . may then develop less rational fears than are characteristic for his social isolation.[23]

In Danziger's study, of 196 white university students responding to the question, "What two things would you like to have that you don't now have?," 65 per cent mentioned various personal qualities and achievements and none mentioned political goals. Of the 97 nonwhite university student respondents, 63 per cent cited political goals while only 16 per cent mentioned personal qualities and achievements.[24] Complementary evidence was later obtained in a study by J. W. Mann, whose nonwhite student respondents were inclined toward community service and upheld democratic values, while the white (almost entirely English-speaking) students he questioned displayed the "privatist" syndrome of apolitical, personal concerns and were comparatively less attached to democratic values.[25]

Table 2 contrasts the attitudes of white and nonwhite students toward various statements about persons, society, and politics. The sample is too small to serve as a base for generalizations, but the findings are nonetheless suggestive. If the differences in beliefs seem great, it should be noted that the white respondents were all enrolled in an English-medium university. A comparison of Afrikaners and nonwhites would have revealed even greater divergences.

TABLE 2

WHITE AND NONWHITE STUDENTS' ATTITUDES[a]

Statement	Percentage of Nonwhites Agreeing	Percentage of Whites Agreeing
1. There are no substantial innate differences in mental ability between whites and nonwhites.	98	68
2. A "multiracial" society should be governed by the will of the majority.	83	45
3. White and nonwhite ought to be free to inter-marry.	78	50
4. Our society requires practical men rather than thinkers.	74	25
5. In South Africa, the future offers no possibility of progress.	59	20
6. Whites will never understand the mind of the nonwhite.	26	15
	(N=54)	(N=40)

[a] Adapted from Leonard Bloom, A. C. de Crespigny, and J. E. Spence, "An Inter-disciplinary Study of the Social, Moral, and Political Attitudes of White and Non-white South African University Students," *Journal of Social Psychology*, LIV (1961), 8-9. The respondents were 94 students in political science. Of the 54 nonwhites (Africans, Coloureds, and Indians), 29 were at Fort Hare (all male and almost all African) and 25 at UN.NE (predominantly male and predominantly Indian). Of the 40 whites (almost all English and roughly half male and half female), 21 were at UN.P and 19 at UN.D. The students were asked to identify each statement as "True" or "False" or to answer "Don't Know." The percentages above indicate the proportions within each caste answering "True." The "Don't Know" responses are either nonexistent or negligible, except in three cases where they exceeded 10 per cent: Statement 2, whites (20 per cent); Statement 3, whites (13 per cent); and Statement 6, nonwhites (11 per cent).

The high nonwhite agreement that whites and nonwhites are intellectually equal, that the majority should govern, and that whites and nonwhites should be free to marry is not surprising; it does show, however, how completely illegitimate the Nationalist regime, which rejects all three propositions, must be in the eyes of these students. Nor is there any reason to believe that their nonwhite colleagues elsewhere in South Africa do not also reject white racist ideology. This is hardly surprising. More striking, perhaps, is the fact that 59 per cent of the nonwhites sampled could not see any possibility of progress in South Africa's future. These students, one might surmise, interpreted "the future" to mean "under the present regime." Perhaps it is not reading too much into too little to suggest that if the future, as an extension of the oppressive status quo of apartheid, offers no possibility of (peaceful) progress, those whose lives are blocked in the racist present are likely to envision a radically different alternative future. Almost the same proportion—58 per cent—of another sample of nonwhite students said they expected large-scale violence and bloodshed in South Africa; 54 per cent of the whites surveyed concurred.[26]

Although support for the social order is of course proportionally far more common among white than among nonwhite students, one must distinguish between Afrikaner and English orientations within the white student community. Danziger found that in describing "white civilization" (a phrase he equated with "the ruling pattern of social relationships" in South Africa), the Afrikaner students showed "an extremely rigid tendency always to accept only favorable characteristics and to reject only unfavorable characteristics," while English students did accept some unfavorable and reject some favorable characterizations.[27] In studies over the past thirty years, I. D. MacCrone, T. F. Pettigrew, and Pierre van den Berghe all found considerably more prejudice against nonwhites among Afrikaner than among English students.[28]

In their political affiliations, the two groups diverge even more sharply: most Afrikaner students support the Nationalist Party, while most of the English students at least tacitly support the white parliamentary opposition parties. A small number of white English-speaking students have been associated with the Liberal Party, the Congress of Democrats (until banned, the white radical affiliate of the Congress Alliance), or the underground Communist Party. Others would call themselves independent liberals or radicals. For the most part, those white students who reject the ideology of white supremacy have reached this position during their university years. Others, already socialized by liberal or radical parents, become even more militant.

The English-medium universities, by emphasizing original thought and freedom of expression, introduce students to norms that cut deeply into—or, in the case of children of liberal or radical parents, extend—earlier patterns of socialization. This liberalizing function of higher education is not performed to the same degree by the technical colleges. The latter schools tend to induct students into instrumental, specialized roles of economic production that are unlikely to stimulate any deep questioning of the political order on the part of those who fill them. Danziger, for example, found that while only 31 per cent of the university students in his white sample judged "white civilization" favorably, 68 per cent of the technical college students did so. Of the university students, 32 per cent were unfavorable; of the technical students, only 14 per cent.[29] Within the English-speaking student community, it is from among those who are unfavorable to, or at least to some degree critical of, apartheid that most student activists are drawn.

Nonwhite students come to the university with more political knowledge and experience than most white students. Many have been politically active in secondary school. Until the repressive educational measures of 1959, at least, they were also active at the university. A 1955 report on Fort Hare referred to the students' "obsession with the struggle for liberation and with politics generally."[30] Political discussions and activity took place on and off the campus, permeating student life. Nonpolitical issues such as poor food and academic grievances, nonpolitical occasions such as the annual graduation ritual and other university ceremonies, were used by the students to advance their struggle against apartheid. This intense involvement seems to have continued at Fort Hare and UN.NE after 1959, but information on the tribal colleges—where student activity is clandestine, isolated, and exclusivist—is too sparse to support a general assessment.[31] At the "open" universities, on the other hand, nonwhite students have been tiny minorities, gracelessly tolerated but never fully accepted; this treatment has created considerable resentment among them. Nonwhites have been associated politically with the African National Congress, with groups clustered around the Non-European Unity Movement, or with the Pan-Africanist Congress. Since 1960, some nonwhite students have been convicted of sabotage, carried out independently or through the *Umkhonto we Sizwe*.

Some social scientists have tried to explain the intensity of student political activity in developing nations on the grounds that other extracurricular outlets for energy do not exist.[32] In South Africa, nonwhite student opposition and unrest should be seen instead as the natural reaction of individuals belonging to ethnic groups that are oppressed and denied opportunities for upward mobility. It is in the basic differences of outlook between whites and nonwhites shown in Table 1 that explanations of the latter's behavior must be sought, or in the alienation, mistrust, and hatred that mark African student images of other groups in South African society. In the van den Berghe study, when asked to characterize Afrikaners, African students most often described them as "oppressive" and "prejudiced." They saw the English-speaking whites as "hypocritical" and "cunning." White Jews were characterized as "money conscious" and "good in business," while Indians were perceived to be "good in business" and "dishonest." Coloureds were described as "color conscious" and "alcoholic," while rural Africans were rejected as "backward" and "subservient." After these projections of a hostile, inhospitable world, how did the students characterize themselves? Unfortunately, the question was not asked. But urban Africans, the one group to which they as students in a major city belonged, were described as "progressive" and "violent."[33]

The Divided Students: Organizations and Activity

What of the organizational forms of student action? Student government at each campus is centered in a Students' Representative Council (SRC), usually composed of between thirteen and seventeen members elected annually by the students; election turnouts are generally less than half the student body. At the tribal colleges, however, the SRC's have for the most part gone out of existence. The SRC's are, formally at least, nonpolitical bodies, focusing on matters of student welfare and recreation.

Almost every university has a student newspaper, usually a weekly, as well as numerous extracurricular societies and clubs reflecting the interests of the student body. Branches of the youth movements of political parties can be found at Afrikaner and nonwhite universities—the Nationalist Party's *Nasionale Jeugbond* (National Youth League) at the former, the ANC Youth League or perhaps a youth affiliate of the NEUM at the latter—although opposition youth wings have been clandestine at the nonwhite universities since the government banned the ANC and the PAC in

1960. The English-medium universities do not permit branches of political parties on campus; instead, students may belong to clubs such as the Liberal Society and the Human Rights Society at Wits or the Radical Society and the Modern World Society at UCT, or to off-campus political youth groups.

Student groups in South Africa are today ethnically based in membership, leadership, and outlook, but this fragmentation was not always so severe. The oldest organization, the National Union of South African Students (NUSAS), was founded in 1924, fourteen years after the political unification of South Africa, at a time when the fissiparous intrawhite trends of the nineteenth century had not yet reappeared. Its aims, within the context of the white community, were integrative, syndical, and nonpartisan. By promoting bicultural cooperation between Afrikaner and English students, NUSAS hoped to forge a new generation of South Africans that would repudiate a century of Anglo-Boer conflict. But the dream could not hide the reality: Afrikaner students opposed the comparatively liberal, internationalist tone of NUSAS policies, while the NUSAS leaders, with their faith in social harmony and cautious "native policy," could not accommodate the rising expectations of nonwhite students. A reluctance to admit nonwhites, specifically those at Fort Hare, or to take a clear-cut position on white-nonwhite relations inside or outside NUSAS, reflected the compromise orientation and meliorist attitudes of the white liberal minority leading NUSAS at the time.

The subsequent history of NUSAS, and of South African student politics in general, is one of widening constituency rifts: ethnic fragmentation and ideological polarization. The first, numerically most important loss was the disaffiliation from NUSAS of the Afrikaans-medium university centers in the 1930's, which formed their own Afrikaner National Student League, the *Afrikaanse Nasionale Studentebond* (ANSB), in a manifestation of reborn Afrikaner separatism. Since then, NUSAS has represented mainly the English-medium universities, although increases in nonwhite membership after 1945 did broaden its scope somewhat.

The Afrikaanse Studentebond. The Afrikaans-medium universities' split with NUSAS occurred ostensibly over the question of admitting a nonwhite center (Fort Hare) into NUSAS, but the deeper reasons can be seen in the Afrikaners' charge that the "national" in the NUSAS name "conveys nothing national in the Afrikaans sense."[34] The resignation statements of the Afrikaners showed the Anglophobia, Negrophobia, and scarcely disguised anti-

Semitism characteristic of Afrikaner nationalism at the time. The Afrikaner organization, the ANSB, developed strong Nazi overtones and subsequently declined with the defeat of the German Third Reich. A new Afrikaner Student League, the *Afrikaanse Studentebond* (ASB), was formed in 1948, shortly before the Nationalist Party's electoral victory, through the amalgamation of the old ANSB and the Federation of White South African Students. The ASB differed little in constitution or membership from the ANSB—one of its aims was (and still is) "to maintain white Christendom against Communism"[35]—but it did attempt to make Afrikaner nationalism respectable and to heal the breach that had split the Afrikaner community into pro-Nazi and pro-Allied factions during World War II.

In the mid-1960's, the ASB had a membership of about 28,000; it has been the largest student organization in South Africa since the 1950's, when it overtook NUSAS in size. Like NUSAS, it is a federation of constituent student bodies, which are represented at an annual policy-making Congress through their Students' Representative Councils. Representation is based on the number of students at each center, giving the University of Pretoria, which is almost twice as large as any other center, a dominant position. The ASB has a permanent office in Bloemfontein; its policies are influenced and implemented by a powerful, elected Executive. The ASB is considerably more monolithic in its members' attitudes than NUSAS and also more authoritarian in structure. These features help explain the absence of wide-ranging controversy and public give-and-take at ASB conferences.

Without exception, those who are active in the ASB support the Nationalist Party. However, differences of opinion within the organization do exist: as in the Nationalist Party itself, there is a constant tension between the avowed white supremacists and those who stress the separate (but implicitly unequal) development of the nonwhite communities. This division cuts across differences of opinion about the role of the ASB: whether it should continue to be a vehicle for the propagation of Afrikaner nationalism or confine itself to representing the syndical interests of Afrikaner students. The leadership has remained in the hands of those who are both militant nationalists and white supremacists, though concessions have occasionally been made to advocates of a less tough-minded policy on white-nonwhite relations.

From its inception the ASB favored completely segregated universities, and by 1949 it had decided to support apartheid as "the only solution retaining European political supremacy and avoiding the bloodshed consequent on equality."[36] In the mid-1950's, the supporters of separate development apparently acquired some influence: the ASB awarded a scholarship to an African high school teacher to study at Fort Hare, and an African spoke (in favor of apartheid) at the ASB Congress in 1955.[37] When the government's draft legislation on university apartheid was published in 1957, the ASB Congress voted a resolution favoring separate development for the universities on the condition that facilities would be made available "which are effective for the purposes of an equal academic standard." This marked a step away from the ASB's previous opposition to any higher education for nonwhites and, in the context of the times, indicated mild criticism of the government.[38] But in the same period—the mid-1950's—the ASB also condemned liberalism, criticized Catholicism, and called on Afrikaners to have more children and to reduce the influence of African domestics on their upbringing.[39]

Political differences in the ASB coincide with a north-south distinction; the rigid ethnocentrists tend to come from Pretoria University, Potchefstroom University, and the Transvaal training colleges in the north, while students at the University of the Orange Free State in the central region and, especially, Stellenbosch University in the extreme south are more flexible in attitude. It was Pretoria University students who sent a telegram to the University of Mississippi at the time of the James Meredith affair, in 1962, supporting "your battle for white civilization," and who, in a purportedly anti-Communist march in 1965, demonstrated against the British and American Embassies' practice of giving interracial parties.[40] Stellenbosch University is in an area (Cape province) where the Nationalist Party has traditionally been comparatively moderate and is the only Afrikaans-medium university that maintains regular contact with an English-language university (UCT). On several occasions (1953–54, 1958–59, 1961, 1966), Stellenbosch students or their leaders have rebelled against the ideological rigidity of the ASB, once even attempting to form a rival student federation for white English- and Afrikaans-speaking students.[41] These brief instances of opposition have usually reflected factional disputes on the broader Afrikaner political scene. The hard-core conservatives, however, have remained in command of the ASB.

The white Afrikaans-medium universities all have their own student newspapers. In addition, the ASB publishes *Die Voorlaier* (*The Leader*). But apart from thus communicating their views,

Afrikaner students do not engage in political action—demonstrations, rallies, and so on—as often as do English or nonwhite students. Afrikaner students have occasionally taken part in ASB-approved activities, including demonstrations against Soviet intervention in Hungary, in support of university apartheid, and against supposed left-wing influences in South Africa. They have also tried to break up antigovernment demonstrations, especially those organized by the Black Sash.[42] But on such occasions, the students are more likely to be organized by the *Nasionale Jeugbond* than by the ASB or by local SRC's.

The relationships between the ASB, the *Nasionale Jeugbond,* and the Nationalist Party itself are not easily unraveled. Officially, the ASB "has no connection with any political party,"[43] although it has always supported Nationalist Party principles. The ASB has perhaps deviated from Nationalist policy slightly more than the *Jeugbond,* which has sometimes, as in Stellenbosch in 1954, acted within the ASB framework to bring a straying center back into line. Candidates for SRC offices at Afrikaner universities often cite positions held in the Nationalist Party or the *Jeugbond* as proof of qualification for office: this would be inconceivable, no matter what party was involved, at the English-medium universities. Unfortunately, no details are available on leadership recruitment into the Nationalist Party through either the ASB or the *Jeugbond;* ironically, some of the present South African cabinet ministers were members of NUSAS rather than of the Afrikaner nationalist youth or student organizations before World War II.[44]

In the mid-1950's, the ASB made a bid for international student recognition, sending representatives to several meetings of the International Student Conference (ISC). Although a larger organization than NUSAS, the ASB was unable to obtain delegate status because it was not open to nonwhite students. The failure to gain admission into the international student community helped to stimulate the rethinking in the ASB that led to the internal crisis of 1958–59 involving dissidents at Stellenbosch; it also led the ASB to protest certain government actions, such as the confiscation of the passport of an NUSAS official who planned to attend the Fifth ISC, and the banning of an ISC publication. The ASB protest brought remedial action in the latter case.[45]

In the national arena, the ASB has been unremittingly hostile to NUSAS, declaring that "the aims of NUSAS will be fought in every possible way."[46] ASB accusations that the NUSAS is leftist, anti-Afrikaner, extremist, anti-Christian, undemocratic, and even guilty of "high treason" have brought threats of legal action by the NUSAS Executive.[47] At the same time, realizing that many students within NUSAS do not support the Union's official policy in favor of nonracialism, the ASB has concentrated its efforts on appealing to these students, both individually and through the more conservative NUSAS centers. Afrikaner student leaders have hoped—so far in vain—to form a comparable *English Studentebond* and perhaps a comparable nonwhite group that could federate with the ASB at the Executive level.[48]

All ASB attempts to develop contacts with NUSAS and with the English-medium universities have foundered, largely over the question of who should represent the various centers at meetings with the ASB. Afrikaner delegates were usually unwilling for nonwhites to be present at all, and always refused to meet non-white delegates representing the "open" universities. Since the ASB, which represents the majority of South African students, could only have advanced its aims by establishing closer contacts with NUSAS, this elevation of procedural matters into matters of principle indicates how ideologically rigid and tactically inflexible Afrikaner student politics are. After attending a NUSAS Congress in 1958, an Afrikaner student observer from Stellenbosch declared that "NUSAS is in fact controlled by Jews who believe in social and even biological integration," while the UOFS observer announced that his SRC was not prepared to reaffiliate unless the Afrikaner SRC's were given a two-thirds majority in the NUSAS Assembly.[49] Throughout the 1950's, such contacts as were maintained between NUSAS and the ASB were strictly formal, aimed at enhancing the intracaste image of the two groups as "cooperative" and thereby assuaging certain elements in their own constituencies. The leaders realized that differences of principle made reconciliation impossible. In 1962, ASB and NUSAS resolved to have no further contacts.[50] However, should NUSAS take a conservative turn in the future, a rapprochement between the two organizations would be likely.

The National Union of South African Students. In the mid-1930's, after the Afrikaner university centers disaffiliated from NUSAS and while the ASB moved to the right, NUSAS moved in an antifascist, leftward direction. The National Union of South African Students, then and throughout World War II, was a relatively small organization with few resources—other than verbal skills—for participation in politics. In the postwar period, however, steps were taken to develop a broader base and a more flexible structure. Nonwhite centers, such as Fort Hare and the Hewat Training College for Coloureds, were admitted into NUSAS in 1945. In the early 1950's, NUSAS became a federation of SRC's, each with the right to disassociate itself from policy resolutions passed at the annual NUSAS Student Assembly.[51] This provision for autonomous constituent commitment facilitated the continued participation of dissident conservative or apolitical English-medium centers, though not always of nonwhite centers.

The policy-making Student Assembly, to which each SRC or NUSAS branch sends delegates in proportion to the number of NUSAS members, forms part of the annual Congress. In 1965, the larger NUSAS centers changed their enrollment system from one of "automatic" individual membership, under which students have the option of resigning individually, to one of center enrollment, whereby a vote of the SRC determines the affiliation of the whole student body. This was done to prevent erosion of membership by the resignation from centers of large conservative minorities. Where the SRC does not wish to affiliate with the NUSAS, or is prevented from doing so by the university authorities, an individual membership branch can be established.

NUSAS policy is carried out, and emergency situations dealt with, by two bodies: the NUSAS Executive and a Standing Committee of SRC Presidents. The Executive has between eight and twenty members and is elected by the Assembly. Executive members and the SRC Presidents keep in regular touch, by visits, correspondence, and telephone, with the Head Office in Cape Town, where the President (full-time since 1958) and Vice President (full-time since 1963) work.

The national Executive, the SRC Presidents, and the chief local NUSAS office-holders form the Union's leadership, which is almost entirely white. Ethnically, the leadership has been largely Jewish. Jewish students are politically more active than their English counterparts. They are also considerably less prejudiced against nonwhites.[52] As a small minority within the white caste, subject to discrimination by Afrikaners, the Jews have perhaps been able to link personal and political concerns more easily than their more "privatist" English fellow students. The NUSAS leadership has also included a minority of Christians, many of whom have become politically active upon realizing the contradiction between Christian practice and Christian principle in South Africa; they have often found participation in NUSAS a secularizing experience.

The Executive reflects both a regional and an ideological spread, but the dominant figures in NUSAS have usually come from the largest English-medium centers: Wits and UCT. With the core support of Wits or UCT, or the training colleges, the Executive can usually build and wield a majority in the Assembly. The prospective recruit to NUSAS leadership generally becomes known in a local campus group, although not necessarily one that is politically active. By his own efforts, or with the help of the incumbent leadership, he may find himself attending a NUSAS Congress or being nominated for an SRC position or to the editorship of a student newspaper. As his involvement deepens, the socialization process advances, and he is brought more into line with NUSAS thinking, or with the thinking of the faction in NUSAS to which he has become attached. The NUSAS Congress, in particular, has sometimes produced dramatic shifts in the attitudes of individuals, usually in a more liberal direction.

In ideological terms, there have been several white leadership groups in NUSAS: the left, the conservatives, the apoliticals, the "old liberals," and the "new radicals." We will discuss these groups —as well as the small nonwhite element—and their strategies in the context of NUSAS' history, constituency, and aims, and in the broader framework of South African society and politics.

In the late 1940's and early 1950's, two coalitions—white leftist and nonwhite students on one side, white conservative and apolitical students on the other—clashed within NUSAS, leaving the organization's leadership to mediate between them. Two important events—the Nationalist Party victory in 1948 and the ANC's adoption in 1949 of the Program of Action—intensified the demands of the white left, which had controlled NUSAS a few years earlier, and of the nonwhites newly enrolled in the Union. The nonwhites saw the Nationalist triumph as a final failure of meliorist liberalism, while the white left viewed it as a victory for the fascism that had just been defeated in Europe. Both groups believed that NUSAS should oppose the new government and struggle for "political and social equality for all men in South Africa." They argued that NUSAS, in alliance with other organizations and particularly with African nationalist movements, should undertake political action to "make some change in the structure of South African society."[53] The coalition of white leftists and nonwhites, a substantial minority in NUSAS at the time, also favored the continuation of NUSAS' affiliation with the pro-Communist International Union of Students and the abandonment of all contacts with the ASB. The failure of NUSAS to satisfy these demands led several important nonwhite centers (Fort Hare, Hewat, and UN.NE) to resign, but the white left persisted until 1955, when it lost control of its stronghold, the SRC at Wits.

In short, the radicals demanded that NUSAS act as an intellectual vanguard stimulating revolutionary change. They placed primary importance on the political role of student organizations and subordinated consideration of the "representativity" of the membership of the organization to the belief that they should represent the interests of a larger, oppressed group in society (the nonwhite), with whom and for whom they should act. The concept was incompatible with the organizational changes instituted in the early 1950's, whereby NUSAS became a flexible federation of constituent SRC's, changes that were firmly upheld by the large white constituency of conservative and apolitical students represented through the SRC's.

White conservative and apolitical student leaders wanted NUSAS to limit its concerns to student welfare and other matters directly affecting students. "Students," said one of them, "are interested in practical benefits and not in unfulfilled ideals."[54] They complained of too many political campaigns initiated by NUSAS and too much criticism by NUSAS of university authorities. These students were uninterested in international affairs and eager for reconciliation with Afrikaans-speaking students, but they disapproved of the ASB because it was "political" (they tolerated the ISC because it claimed to be nonpolitical).

The conservatives saw NUSAS as a nationally representative student union within a legitimate political system. They believed the organization should play a syndical role, articulating student interests and demands and bargaining for them on behalf of its members. But this conception—central to British political thought since Locke—assumed the legitimacy of established procedures and existing political structures. Of this legitimacy, many NUSAS members were in doubt; nor did the Union, after about 1953, even represent the majority of South African students.

The NUSAS leaders could endorse neither position. Although reared in the Lockean tradition, they believed that syndicalism could operate only within a democratic political system. Furthermore, as liberals in outlook and frequently in party affiliation, the leaders of the Union rejected the illiberalism of the "vanguardist" approach, and responded with moderating formulae that avoided the central issue. NUSAS, they said, should be an open forum, for "the coming together of students of different racial origins and varying outlooks to discuss their common student problems has done, and can do, much to further interracial understanding, tolerance, and cooperation."[55] But a forum, if it is not to become a battlefield, must have a commonly accepted framework of debate. The liberal principles on which the NUSAS leadership wished to base criticism of government policy were satisfactory to neither the right nor the left: the leadership opposed the Nationalist government because it interfered with the freedom of voluntary association and with free competition in the "marketplace of ideas." They believed that government should play a "caretaker" role and that reasoned dialogue, not coercion, could resolve conflicts. This was the basis for their opposition to state intervention in the universities and to segregated education.

As an ideology of opposition, positing a civil libertarian ideal that was, and remains, anathema to a fundamentally illiberal regime, liberalism was the natural language of South Africa's white voice of conscience. But it was not a blueprint for action, in a situation that increasingly demanded action. A revolutionary program demanded less concern for legality and more acceptance of collective action, but the tactics and alliances involved were unacceptable to the NUSAS leaders, who continued the frustrating effort to create a liberal future by liberal means. In the early 1950's, they found themselves in a precarious position in the organization. Nonwhite centers disaffiliated and the white radical left exerted pressure; the apolitical right was equally dissatisfied; only the smaller nonwhite centers—Pius XII University College and the Bantu Normal College—gave the leadership consistent support.

In the mid-1950's, the situation changed for all the groups in NUSAS. The decline of the left, following its defeat in the Wits SRC, eliminated one extreme position within the Union; at the same time, increasingly widespread and blatant government intervention in the universities brought many advocates of the conservative extreme toward a centrist position, made an apolitical stance less tenable than ever, and led the nonwhite centers to return to NUSAS in the interests of forming a "common front" against university apartheid.

Government intervention in the 1950's took four forms: specific threats to segregate the universities; administrative discrimination against nonwhite students (prohibiting them from attending certain universities, refusing to issue them passports); educational apartheid legislation (to strengthen government control, to ensure ethnic separation, to imbue the curriculum with racist content);

and, finally, general legislation that codified, extended, and intensified discrimination, segregation, and authoritarian controls in all walks of life. Some of these measures—censorship of textbooks, for example—directly affected white students, who found it increasingly difficult to distinguish between political matters and matters affecting "students as such." The government's onslaught demonstrated both the impotence of meliorist liberalism and the need for transracial solidarity in NUSAS. Thus was made possible a new political role for NUSAS, a role that could be endorsed by a broad range of white students and in which they could cooperate with nonwhites—although the issues that inspired the latter were regarded as peripheral by the former, and vice versa.

Meanwhile, the NUSAS leadership had acquired important new experience in student politics and a broader range of political ideas, through increased contact with the International Student Conference—NUSAS was granted delegate status in the ISC in 1956 —and through the association of many NUSAS members with the Liberal Party. The formation of the Liberal Party, and also of the Congress of Democrats, both founded in 1953, increased the self-confidence of both liberals and radicals. In the Congress of Democrats, the white student left found the platform it had once had in NUSAS, while NUSAS leaders began increasingly to form a militant youth wing in the Liberal Party, where they pressed for political action on such matters as universal franchise and welfare state measures.

In 1957, the student syndicalism of the whites and the political aspirations of the nonwhites were unified in a NUSAS Assembly resolution declaring that a democratic education is possible only in a democratic society and that such a society should be based on the Universal Declaration of Human Rights, which would henceforth be the basic document underlying all NUSAS policy.[56] These principles, under which the organization still operates, framed a distinctive brand of NUSAS radicalism that flourished in the subsequent decade and was implemented by a new generation of NUSAS leaders distinctly more militant than their predecessors. Many of these "new radicals," like the white student left before them, became active in South African opposition politics after leaving the organization; a few even engaged in sabotage, an activity that would have been unthinkable for the 1947–57 NUSAS leadership.

By approving the 1957 resolution, NUSAS condemned apartheid *as such* for the first time and committed itself to goals that lay outside the dominant white consensus in South African society. The Union had explicitly abandoned a syndical approach, yet it had no clearly defined new role, except for the unsatisfactory model proposed by the earlier nonwhite-left coalition. For these Marxist and African nationalist student leaders there was no contradiction between means and ends: the struggle was one of national liberation, with revolutionary objectives attainable only by revolutionary means. If the proclaimed objectives of NUSAS were now similar to those of the left, the Union's flexible structure and apolitical-conservative membership precluded a revolutionary role, and the leadership still preferred to retain the existing structure and constituency, preferring protest, however outspoken, within the system, to revolutionary action, illiberal by its very nature, outside and against the system.

NUSAS has never adopted the techniques of nonviolent resistance—strikes, boycotts, and civil disobedience—although students at constituent centers, particularly the nonwhite centers, have occasionally done so on their own initiative.[57] Still less has NUSAS had the will or the capacity to engage in violent protest. The Union's most militant forms of action have been sober, orderly marches.

In terms of numbers mobilized, the most successful campaign launched by NUSAS was that against university apartheid in 1957–59, which involved approximately half the English-speaking white student population in marches and enlisted the cooperation of faculty members, university authorities, and citizens' committees in South Africa, as well as of student and university organizations around the world. This massive participation—which did not, however, prevent the government from implementing its plans—can be explained on two grounds: university apartheid was a matter that directly affected both the individual student and the university community as a whole. Official university support legitimized the campaign in the eyes of many students who would otherwise have been reluctant to incur the disapproval of university authorities.[58]

By 1960, the government had banned the major African nationalist organizations. NUSAS did not wish to suffer the same fate. Although its verbal criticism grew stronger in tone and broader in scope—South African society was "totalitarian," "in a state of siege" —the Union could not recapture the fervor and unanimity of 1957–59. Marches were organized, but not well attended; cooperation with ad hoc protest bodies continued, but was largely ineffective. NUSAS became neither a forum for debate nor a vanguard for action, but a voice of conscience. This role was politically marginal, but the leaders of NUSAS were at least aware of their organizational impotence.

The Union also sought to provide, necessarily on a limited scale, nonracial educational alternatives and political leadership training to white and nonwhite students. NUSAS' educational initiatives included university correspondence courses, overseas scholarships and loans for nonwhite students, and educational materials for political prisoners. A national leadership training seminar, discussion groups, the organization of an annual Day of Academic and Human Freedom, and the yearly Congress served as agencies of political socialization and recruitment.

Despite its nonrevolutionary role, the inadequacy of its resources, and its unwillingness to cooperate as an organization with extra-legal groups (for fear of jeopardizing its status as the most radical legal organization opposing apartheid in South Africa), NUSAS was subjected to continuing harassment by government officials. Since the early 1950's, Nationalist Party spokesmen had denounced NUSAS for its liberal, nonracial views. Nonwhite students had been intimidated into steering clear of the Union, and Special Branch informers had been exposed on white campuses. After 1963, the vitriol thickened and repression increased. Nationalist leaders—notably B. J. Vorster, then Minister of Justice and now Prime Minister of the Republic—condemned the Union at public meetings and over the radio, appealed to white parents to prevent their sons from joining, instigated students to organize splinter groups, arrested NUSAS leaders, and raided the Union's head office. To make the campaign credible, the government attributed to NUSAS revolutionary aims that the Union's policies and criticism implied but did not in fact entail.[59]

Two incidents enhanced the credibility of the government's picture of NUSAS as a dangerous and treasonable body, although neither, significantly, was initiated by the organization itself. At a Pan-African Student Seminar in Dar-es-Salaam in January 1964, attended by student organizations from East, Central, and Southern Africa, NUSAS came under severe criticism for retaining its apolitical-conservative membership and for failing to engage in revolutionary action measuring up to its radical language: the African delegates claimed, in fact, that NUSAS was not representative of the aspirations of the majority of the *people* of South Africa. This represented a complete reversal of the previously friendly relations between NUSAS and other African unions. The NUSAS representative walked out of the seminar, and both at the time and in later correspondence with the NUSAS President he described NUSAS as a part of the "liberation movement" in South Africa. This remark, and the representative's recommendations on radicalizing the Union's structure, were leaked to the South African press after they had been discussed at an NUSAS seminar; although they did not represent NUSAS policy, they were so labeled by the government and used to smear the organization.

If the "liberation movement" comprised those organizations with revolutionary political programs, NUSAS was indeed not a part of it. But within two months of the disclosure of the seminar discussions, a number of students, among them former NUSAS leaders, were arrested and charged with sabotage. It emerged at their trials that the organization involved was the African Resistance Movement (ARM), formed in 1960–61. ARM had been responsible for destroying electricity pylons and sabotaging railway lines in the Cape and Witwatersrand areas. Adrian Leftwich, President of the NUSAS in 1961–62, was one of the Cape leaders; turning state's evidence, he escaped imprisonment. Neville Rubin, President in 1958–59, was also implicated but had left the country; Hugh Lewin, a former Vice President for International Affairs, was sentenced to seven years' imprisonment in Johannesburg. A score of other students, some of whom fled the country, were implicated or sentenced; one of them, David de Keller, was arrested while attending the 1964 NUSAS Congress. The activities of ARM had been directed against property rather than life, although after the first series of arrests John Harris (a former local official of NUSAS) exploded a bomb in the Johannesburg railway station and was executed for murder. ARM's activities were halted by these arrests, known as the "July raids" of 1964.

A large part of the impetus for ARM originated in the frustration felt by NUSAS leaders, a frustration caused by the gap between their aspirations and their achievements, between the liberal-based meliorist policies they had to execute and their revolutionary dreams of overthrowing the seemingly immovable white power structure. At his trial, Alan Brooks, a former NUSAS activist, justified his turn to violence, saying: "The failure of the campaign [against the segregation of the universities] planted the seeds of the inadequacy of constitutional methods in opposing government policy."[60]

The ultimate aims of ARM, if there were any, do not emerge from the reports of the trials. At the stage at which it was crushed it involved no incumbent NUSAS officials, and it is unlikely that these officeholders would have compromised their organization in this way. But the ARM arrests and trials allowed the government to heap substantial guilt-by-association on NUSAS and to intensify its campaign of vilification against the Union. The government appeared unwilling to ban NUSAS outright, and, by the exertion of almost monolithic control through skillful political manipulation, the leaders managed to weather the storm. The public outcry aroused by the disclosure of discussions in NUSAS after the Dar-es-Salaam meeting, by the sight of young white radicals engaged in violence, and by the government's campaign against the Union, set a limit on the radicalization of NUSAS that the organization will not now pass. Recent protest marches—in 1966 over the banning of NUSAS President Ian Robertson, and in 1967 when Dr. Raymond Hoffenberg, a respected liberal professor at UCT, was banned—indicate that the voice of conscience has not died. But that these protests should occur only when measures are taken against white liberals, and that the banning, imprisonment, detention without trial, and torture of thousands of nonwhites have not aroused the same response, indicate the limitations under which NUSAS still operates.

Its official statements and constitutional purposes notwithstanding, NUSAS has for most of its history been a student organization for English-speaking whites. For various reasons—above all the radicalizing effects of government intervention in the universities— NUSAS has been dominated by liberal and, more recently, radical elements from this constituency. It is questionable whether this orientation can be maintained in the face of new generations of white students, unattracted to politics, conditioned by the status quo, and accepting the legitimacy of the apartheid system established over the last twenty years.[61] Nor can the leadership take comfort in the greater involvement of nonwhites in NUSAS in the decade since 1957, for these new members have joined as much from a lack of other legal outlets for expression as from any positive commitment to NUSAS. In any event, NUSAS will almost certainly not be involved in promoting any truly radical—i.e., revolutionary— future change in South Africa.

Nonwhite Student Politics. Nonwhite student political activity in South Africa is chronically underreported and underdocumented in comparison with the activities of white students. For this reason, the wholly erroneous impression may be gained that white students have been more active politically than nonwhites.

An adequate study of nonwhite student politics would require research inside South Africa—personal interviews, in particular—that the authors have been unable to undertake. Four aspects of nonwhite student activity can, however, be briefly examined: nonwhites in NUSAS, nonwhite student organizations, nonwhites at the tribal colleges, and nonwhites in exile.

While Afrikaner and English students are sufficiently numerous to form organizations with substantial finances and personnel, nonwhite students are numerically few (see Table 1), geographically and socially segregated, and extremely limited as to resources. Nonwhite student organizations have been ineffective and have remained secondary to the politically active nationalist movements and their youth wings.

Among nonwhites, there is overwhelming support for a thoroughly political role for students. Nonwhites also tend to employ more militant tactics than those used by white students, although these actions (strikes, boycotts) are more often directed against conditions within the university—unfair regulations, bad food, discriminatory practices, authoritarian or paternalistic treatment by university officials—than against the system of apartheid as such. Unlike NUSAS and the ASB, nonwhite student organizations often attempt to recruit secondary school pupils as members. Nonwhite secondary school students are politically conscious and active: protests similar to those at nonwhite universities have often occurred in the secondary schools, resulting in expulsions or even the closing of the schools concerned. The students involved are usually African, although in 1966 there was substantial unrest at Indian secondary schools in the Witwatersrand area, partly in protest against the celebration of Republic Day.[62]

Until 1945, nonwhite students were extremely few in number and quite isolated from the politics of white students. Their activity was not, however, insignificant: nonwhite students at Fort Hare, for example, were instrumental in forming the ANC Youth League in the early 1940's. In 1945, NUSAS voted to admit nonwhite centers. NUSAS offered social status, material rewards, and tactical advantages in disseminating nonwhite views, but participation in a white-dominated organization unable to satisfy nonwhite aspirations could be interpreted in nonwhite eyes as a betrayal of the nationalist struggle and as the defection of an elite from its people.

Despite this ambivalence, nonwhite centers have been represented at NUSAS Assemblies continually since 1945; in 1966, there were more nonwhite delegates than ever before. A few nonwhites filled important, influential positions in the NUSAS Executive and played a significant role in policy formation, particularly in the early 1960's.[63] As we have noted, nonwhite enthusiasm for NUSAS was greatest during the "common front" against university apartheid in 1957–59; at other times, nonwhite centers have disaffiliated, participated halfheartedly and critically, or been precluded from membership by university authorities.

African nationalism, not NUSAS, has been the major influence on African student politics. The African student leaders of the 1950's and 1960's acquired their political consciousness in the period when deferential delegations had given way to strikes, boycotts, and other forms of militant nonviolence. Their predecessors, the student generation of the 1940's at Fort Hare, had not only developed this new strategy and secured its implementation by the ANC, but many of them, like Nelson Mandela and Oliver Tambo, were now leaders of the African nationalist movement. From 1948, these African leaders faced not a benign tutor but an aggressive opponent: the Nationalist government, which sought to roll back all the incremental advances of the past hundred years, swiftly and mercilessly silenced its critics and rejected, as did the African leaders in their turn, gradualist values. The African student leaders of the 1950's and 1960's were participants in the battles of that period, when the more monolithic, ruthless, and experienced force of Afrikaner nationalism inflicted a series of defeats on the African nationalist movement, leaving as African gains only a more widespread and determined political awareness. These student leaders gained experience from the miscalculations and mistakes of their elders, and were participants in, indeed probably among the warmest supporters of, the final decision to resort to violence.

It was in this context, in the aftermath of a 1961 student strike called to protest South Africa's newly declared status as a Republic, that two specifically African student organizations were formed: the African Students' Association (ASA) and the African Students' Union of South Africa (ASUSA). They were the first student groups since the ASB to be founded on an exclusivist ethnic base.[64] Tied to the ANC and the PAC, respectively, ASA and ASUSA were in one sense "front" organizations for these banned African nationalist movements. In another sense, they reflected the emerging emphasis among African leaders on purely African cadres, symbols, and goals.

ASA was not intended as an alternative to NUSAS, and in fact there was some cooperation between the two organizations. ASUSA, however, was consistently hostile to NUSAS. ASUSA enjoyed support at Pius XII University College in Basutoland and at the tribal colleges in the Northern Transvaal and Zululand, while ASA dominated Fort Hare and UN.NE. The memberships of ASA and ASUSA were extremely small and their funds negligible. The government soon prevented African student leaders from engaging in overt political activity at the colleges; this repression, together with the absence of any significant nonwhite constituency at the "open" universities, severely limited the capacity for action of these organizations. The two groups were harassed by the government, particularly in the form of police persecution of their officers; today they no longer exist inside the country, although ASA survives in exile.

The central reason for the failure of ASA and ASUSA was not merely government intimidation; there were simply not enough African university students in South Africa to sustain such organizations. Politicians seeking to mobilize significant political support on a large scale had to rely on newly urbanized workers and disaffected peasants. The student community could provide a cadre of leaders, nothing more, and often not even that. ASA and ASUSA were fated under these circumstances to be small, fragile groups of minor political potential.

Nor is it likely that African nationalist student organizations will have any greater impact in the foreseeable future. The number of African students, as a proportion of the over-all African population, is unlikely to increase fast enough to give them status as a significant minority in any form of direct, mass action. The location of the tribal colleges established in 1959—remote from the politically pivotal areas of the country—and the close surveillance of students at these institutions also appear to preclude such a role.

A major source of future African student participation in politics may be the high schools. The African secondary school population is expanding rapidly. The schools are located largely in the major cities, where the students are subject not only to the daily oppressions and frustrations of urban life, but also to potentially radicalizing influences from their peers, their teachers, and from the urban university student community. Even these nonwhite secondary students, however, are more likely to be mobilized into party youth wings than in student organizations.

Student groups have also been formed under the auspices of other nonwhite political movements, notably the Congress Alliance and the NEUM. Most hostile toward NUSAS were the largely Coloured student supporters of the NEUM. Pro-NEUM students engineered—or at least gained increased nonwhite support because of—the disaffiliation from NUSAS of Fort Hare, UN.NE, and Hewat in the early 1950's.[65] In 1957, the first NEUM student organization was formed, the Peninsula Students' Union (CPSU); it gained substantial strength among Coloured students at UCT and at Western Cape secondary schools and training colleges. This was nominally expanded by the creation of a Progressive National Students' Organization a few years later, but its main bases have remained in the Western Cape and, to a lesser extent, among Indian students in Natal (the Durban Students' Union). In the radical NEUM tradition, members of these organizations have been vociferous, argumentative intellectuals who have regarded almost any legal political action as "collaboration with the oppressor." The NEUM attitude toward NUSAS was expressed in a resolution of disaffiliation submitted to the SRC of UN.NE in 1961 and only narrowly defeated:

> NUSAS has not really changed but only changed its tactics to further the politics and interests of Imperialism-Liberalism. . . .
>
> NUSAS, an offshoot of Liberalism in the student section, seeks to moderate the militancy of nonwhite students and thereby hopes to prevent a national and united struggle of the oppressed people. . . .
>
> NUSAS, by refusing to ally itself with the Liberatory Movement, reveals its utter contempt for the struggles and conditions of the oppressed people.[66]

The CPSU denounced the campaign against university apartheid, rejecting "academic nonsegregation" and "university autonomy" as liberal slogans that did not probe deeply or widely enough into the structure of apartheid or launch a sufficiently militant assault on Nationalist policy. In such instances, NEUM-affiliated groups were often important in sophisticating ideas within NUSAS: such criticism, for example, stimulated NUSAS to define and redefine the terms on which a university could claim autonomy.[67]

Should NUSAS be banned, dissolve itself, or fall into more conservative hands, the sole potential for student opposition to the South African regime will shift to the students at the tribal colleges, and to students in exile. (Certainly the few white liberal or radical students who would remain inside South Africa could not sustain themselves without the support of a national organization). The numbers of exile students are at least as great as those at the tribal colleges. Most of them already feel that NUSAS, inside or outside the country, cannot represent them, and the time may come when the embryonic student groupings that exist in Britain, the United States, and some countries in Europe, may form a national student movement on the model adopted by overseas students from Iran and Algeria.

Two of the dilemmas faced by the leaders of NUSAS have already been outlined: their inability to accept either a purely syndical or a purely revolutionary role for the organization, and the contradiction between their revolutionary goals and the means they were able to employ to implement them.

A third dilemma, unique to the NUSAS leadership, reflected their position as white critics of white supremacy. As whites, they were inextricably part of the very system they criticized. In effect, to support the goals of NUSAS was to support, at least by implication, the demise of a political and social structure that secured them their status and within which they operated, and to promote, at least indirectly, changes that might end by inflicting loss and suffering, perhaps indiscriminately, on the white community. And yet, because they were not committed to action commensurate with their goals (as were their more left-wing white colleagues), they were open to charges by nonwhites of hypocrisy, timidity, and squeamishness, and even of objective support of the existing system. Theirs was the same dilemma that plagued Camus in Algeria, and which he was able to resolve only by remaining silent.

Furthermore, although the leaders of NUSAS rejected the obsessively ethnic basis and operation of the social order in South Africa, they could not escape the fact that the movements to change that order were themselves ethnically oriented, in membership and strategy, if not in goals. With its multiracial composition and its nonracial goals, NUSAS differed not only from the society as a whole and from its antagonists in that society, but even from the only groups that could have been its allies.

Elements of the same conflict could be seen in the recruitment of nonwhite office-holders in NUSAS. Despite its multiracial membership, NUSAS was essentially white-populated, white-financed, white-led, and white-controlled, although its policies ran counter to the nationally dominant white consensus. Nonwhites, as delegates and office-holders, did play a role, but were for the most part overshadowed by their white counterparts, and in some instances were callously used and manipulated as symbols of NUSAS' integrated nonracialism. There were several remarkable exceptions, as we have noted, especially in the early 1960's, but critics of NUSAS could remind even these few nonwhite leaders that they had been elected with white support and could thus imply that they had forsaken their origins. It is noteworthy that NUSAS has never had a non-white President. The one African who was strongly urged to run refused to do so on the grounds that an African President would harm NUSAS at white conservative centers and would facilitate a ban on the organization.

How, it might be asked, could NUSAS continue to recruit leadership in the face of such dilemmas and of such a gap between aspiration and achievement? There are two reasons. In the first place, the white students who joined the organization were drawn deeper and deeper into the world of NUSAS by the very alienation from their society that their involvement stimulated, until they were unable to live in the society except on the basis of some overt form of opposition. In the second place, students in NUSAS, and especially those who became leaders, were, or became, highly neurotic. A common saying both among NUSAS leaders and their detractors was that involvement in the political life of NUSAS was a form of therapy for the participants. It offered them an opportunity to express passionately felt rage against the social order; it also offered them a sense of involvement and accomplishment, a community of similarly alienated friends, and the hope of obliterating guilt through action.

Upon graduation, or upon leaving NUSAS, the leaders of the organization had to seek new ways of resolving their dilemmas. A minority turned to sabotage; others began professional careers, enduring a decline in political influence and, in many cases, a rising sense of frustration. The majority went into voluntary exile in Britain, Canada, and the United States; generally they studied for higher degrees, and, almost without exception, they have not returned to South Africa.

Conclusion

Because of the caste structure, the ethnic fragmentation, and the systematic coercion that characterize South African society and politics, the emergence of a unified multiracial national student movement—essentially a fully realized NUSAS—appears to be out of the question. Nor for that matter is *any* student organization in South Africa likely to affect government policy, let alone bring about basic changes in the system.

Student organizations in South Africa will, however, continue to play socializing roles for different ethnic and ideological groups. Among the whites, the ASB will continue to transmit the ideas and spirit of Afrikaner nationalism to successive generations of Afrikaner students. But should it limit itself to this task alone, it will stagnate, for Afrikaner nationalism is already being submerged by a more inclusive white South African nationalism. Thus, if cracks should appear in the ASB monolith, they may reflect renewed debate about relations with English-speaking white students.

The multiracialism of NUSAS has been sharply curtailed by the legislation of 1959 and will be negated by laws now enacted to outlaw multiracial organizations outright. For the time being, however, NUSAS remains an important liberalizing, if not radicalizing, agency of political socialization for young English-speaking whites. It has also served as a bridge between whites and nonwhites. Finally, NUSAS may simply continue to offer community to those who would otherwise be left quite alone in an implacably hostile environment. But it will be unable to perform any of these functions in the absence of a sympathetic subculture in white society; signs that the caste line is strengthening and that the intracaste distinctions between Afrikaner and English are increasingly blurred can only be read with apprehension by NUSAS leaders.

Finally, nonwhite student organizations, at the tribal colleges, in the secondary schools, or in exile—however small, ineffectual, and short-lived they may be—will play their part in the socialization of a new generation of nonwhite leaders. Insofar as the mass arrests and repression of the early 1960's have broken the continuity of African leadership, the training and experience in political debate and action that nonwhite student groups can provide will bear particular significance. Indeed, the attitudes, perspectives, and policies that African, Coloured, and Indian students are formulating today will shape the strategy of the freedom struggle in South Africa for the next generation.

NOTES

1. The population ratio has been calculated from estimates for 1966 issued by the South African Bureau of Statistics; cited in Muriel Horrell (compiler), *A Survey of Race Relations in South Africa, 1966* (Johannesburg: South African Institute of Race Relations [SAIRR], 1967), p. 122. For the percentage distribution of national income between the white and nonwhite castes, see *ibid.*, p. 210, and Muriel Horrell (compiler), *A Survey of Race Relations in South Africa, 1964* (Johannesburg: SAIRR, 1965), p. 231. Also see the statistical information in D. Hobart Houghton, *The South African Economy* (New York: Oxford University Press, 1964), p. 238.

2. Calculated (at the conversion rate of U.S. $1.40 to the South African

rand) from figures, based on data from the Standard Bank of South Africa, in Horrell, *Survey, 1964*, p. 231. On the likelihood that the intercaste gap in per capita income is widening, see Muriel Horrell (compiler), *A Survey of Race Relations in South Africa, 1965* (Johannesburg: SAIRR, 1966), p. 208.

3. See Muriel Horrell, *Legislation and Race Relations* (rev. ed.; Johannesburg: SAIRR, 1966).

4. The 1960 Census recorded that nearly 60 per cent of the white population was Afrikaans-speaking. (*Population Census*, September 6, 1960, Sample Tabulation No. 1 [Pretoria: Government Printer, RP No. 62/1963], p. 24.) On the Afrikaner population, see also Sheila Patterson, *The Last Trek: A Study of the Boer People and the Afrikaner Nation* (London: Routledge and Kegan Paul, 1957), pp. 67–71, and Leonard M. Thompson, *Politics in the Republic of South Africa* (Boston: Little, Brown, 1966), pp. 30–35.

5. On the relationship between Afrikaner social status and political orientations, see Patterson, *op. cit.*, especially pp. 133–75; Stanley Trapido, "Political Institutions and Afrikaner Social Structures in the Republic of South Africa," *American Political Science Review*, LVII, No. 1 (March 1963), 75–87. Also see Leonard M. Thompson, "The South African Dilemma," in Louis Hartz (ed.), *The Founding of New Societies* (New York: Harcourt, Brace and World, 1964), pp. 178–218; I. D. MacCrone, *Race Attitudes in South Africa* (London: Oxford University Press, 1937).

6. See, for example, the credo of a leading South African liberal, Leo Marquard, in his *Liberalism in South Africa* (Johannesburg: SAIRR, 1965).

7. Communist and left-wing whites, however, as well as Coloureds, Indians, and nonracial trade unions, cooperated with the African National Congress within the framework of the Congress Alliance.

8. For the history of extra-parliamentary opposition, see, among others, Leo Kuper, *Passive Resistance in South Africa* (New Haven: Yale University Press, 1960), especially pp. 27–46; Edward Roux, *Time Longer Than Rope* (Madison: University of Wisconsin Press, 1964); Mary Benson, *South Africa: The Struggle for a Birthright* (Middlesex: Penguin Books, 1966); Muriel Horrell, *Action, Reaction and Counteraction* (Johannesburg: SAIRR, 1963); and the annual volumes of the *Survey of Race Relations in South Africa*, compiled by Muriel Horrell. Of the sabotage organizations, *Yu Chi Chan* never engaged in actual violence, while *Umkhonto we Sizwe* has been reconstituted as an army of trained guerrillas, at present mostly outside of the Republic.

9. Student body percentages were calculated from the numerical totals in Table 1, general population percentages from Horrell, *Survey, 1966*, p. 122. The Asian category includes a numerically insignificant Chinese element (roughly 1 per cent of all Asians in the general population).

10. E. G. Pells, *300 Years of Education in South Africa* (Cape Town: Juta, 1954), p. 120; "Enrollment at S.A. Universities and University Colleges" (mimeo.; National Union of South African Students, February 20, 1967).

11. For the history of higher education in South Africa, see Ernest G. Malherbe, *Education in South Africa (1652–1922)* (Cape Town: Juta, 1925); M. E. McKerron, *A History of Education in South Africa* (Pretoria: Van Schaik, 1934), pp. 84–98; Pells, *op. cit.*, especially chap. xii. On higher education for nonwhites in the 1950's and 1960's, see Muriel Horrell, *A Decade of Bantu Education* (Johannesburg: SAIRR, 1964), pp. 138–52.

12. In 1963, the state subsidy varied at different universities from 63 per cent to 80 per cent, with an average of 71 per cent. (*Annual Report*, De-

partment of Education, Arts and Science [Pretoria: Government Printer, 1963].)
Most of the remaining funds come from student fees, while endowments and
donations constitute a final source.

13. Nonwhite enrollment at Wits has declined from 6 per cent (1952), to
3 per cent (1963), to 2 per cent (1967). Nonwhite enrollment at UCT rose
from 5 per cent to 8 per cent in the period 1952–63, declining to 6 per cent
in 1966. Nonwhites were not admitted to the Dentistry or Fine Arts Faculties at Wits and there was, at both Wits and UCT, limited admission in Engineering and Medicine. See "South Africa," *RIC Yearbook* (Leiden: Coordinating Secretariat of National Unions of Students, 1955–56). Presumably,
university authorities believed that nonwhites would not be given the opportunity to pursue careers in these fields. In 1966, Africans constituted 0.06 per
cent of all the students at these "open" universities.

14. The same staff teaches separate classes of whites and nonwhites, sometimes giving the same lecture four times in one day. For two different views
of the Natal system, see E. G. Malherbe in *Die Burger* (Cape Town), February 20, 1957, and V. Junod in *Cape Times* (Cape Town), January 7, 1957.

15. The campaign against university apartheid has been discussed at length
in numerous articles and books. See A. M. Macdonald, *A Contribution to a
Bibliography on University Apartheid* (Cape Town: University of Cape Town,
School of Librarianship, 1959); Gwendolen Carter, *The Politics of Inequality*
(New York: Frederick A. Praeger, 1962), pp. 110–12, 261 ff.; Horrell, *A
Decade of Bantu Education*, pp. 121–38; Thompson, *Politics in the Republic
of South Africa*, pp. 107–8, 148–49. Also see Martin Legassick, *NUSAS: Ethnic Cleavage and Ethnic Integration in South African Universities* (Occasional Papers, African Studies Center, University of California, Los Angeles,
1967).

16. A certain paternalism, however, has also been evident in the attitudes
toward nonwhites shown by administrators at the "open" universities. H. R.
Raikes, Principal of Wits, for example, believed that Africans should be allowed "to enjoy Western European culture fully and eventually to become full
citizens" and found "the other alternatives—continuance of [the] 'master-race'
policy or an overrapid development—both . . . unsatisfactory." *The Star* (Johannesburg), July 5, 1951.

17. See Legassick, *op. cit.*, on this issue. Valuable information on the attitude of nonwhite UCT students to social segregation is contained in *The
Guardian* (Cape Town), June 14, 1951; *Cape Times*, October 9, 1952; *House
of Assembly Debates (Hansard)*, No. 82 (1953), columns 2567–2667 *passim*.

18. See *Cape Times*, December 11, 1964; *Cape Argus* (Cape Town), December 10, 1964; *The Star* (weekly ed.), April 3, 1965.

19. *Rand Daily Mail* (Johannesburg), August 22, 1958.

20. A. L. Behr and R. G. Macmillan, *Education in South Africa* (Pretoria:
Van Schaik, 1966), p. 57.

21. For example, see the South African press, May 17–21, 23, 26, 1955;
New Age (Cape Town), March 7, 1957; *Pretoria News*, March 11, 1957;
Sunday Times (Johannesburg), May 26, 1957; *Press Digest* (Johannesburg),
1961, pp. 175, 398–99, 408–9, 420, 438, 448.

22. Indicative of the salience of ethnicity for South African students are
the findings of Pierre van den Berghe in a survey of university, college, and
advanced-vocational students in Durban. Van den Berghe found that of the
346 who answered the question, "What different groups would you say there

are in South Africa?," 93 per cent mentioned ethnic groups. Interestingly, only 14 per cent of the respondents distinguished between English and Afrikaners; among the white students, where one might expect this intracaste division to be most salient, less than one-fourth mentioned it. Van den Berghe's full sample of 374 students was 37 per cent Indian, 33 per cent white, 27 per cent African, and 3 per cent Coloured. See his "Race Attitudes in Durban, South Africa," *Journal of Social Psychology*, LVII (1962), 57.

23. Kurt Danziger, "Value Differences among South African Students," *Journal of Abnormal and Social Psychology*, LVII (1958), 342–43. Danziger questioned 195 university and college students: 125 whites, 43 Africans, and 37 Indians. Of the whites, only 21 were Afrikaans-speaking. When asked "What are the two worst things that could happen to you during your lifetime?" (open-ended), responses classified under "physical misfortune, ill health" ranked first in frequency for both whites and nonwhites. At the next level of frequency, the answers diverged sharply: second most frequent among the whites were answers classified as "loss or lack of love," a category that ranked next to last in frequency among nonwhites. (One would expect the white sample to contain a higher proportion of female students than the nonwhite sample, which might account for the relative frequency of answers such as "not getting married," "being unhappily married," and "being unable to love anybody." Unfortunately, Danziger does not offer any information on the sex of his respondents.) Second most frequent among nonwhites were answers classified under "political persecution," the category ranking last in frequency among whites.

24. Calculated from figures in *ibid.*, p. 342. The other response categories used were "familial goals" (31 per cent of the whites, 5 per cent of the nonwhites) and "educational opportunities" (4 per cent of the whites, 15 per cent of the nonwhites). The question was open-ended.

25. Mann's sample comprised 79 UN.D students, 30 whites (of whom only one spoke Afrikaans), and 49 nonwhites (31 Indians, 12 Africans, and 6 Coloureds). See J. W. Mann, "Race-linked Values in South Africa," *Journal of Social Psychology*, LVIII (1962), 31–41.

26. Van den Berghe, *op. cit.*, p. 71.

27. Danziger, *op. cit.*, pp. 340, 342.

28. See the findings of I. D. MacCrone, based on biennial surveys of Wits students in the period 1934–44, in his "Race Attitudes: An Analysis and Interpretation," in Ellen Hellmann (ed.), *Handbook on Race Relations in South Africa* (London: Oxford University Press, 1949), pp. 690–97. For the results of Thomas F. Pettigrew's 1956 survey of University of Natal students, see his "Social Distance Attitudes of South African Students," *Social Forces*, No. 38 (October 1959–May 1960), pp. 246–53. Finally, see van den Berghe, *op. cit.*, p. 70.

29. Calculated from figures in Danziger, *op. cit.*, p. 341. The technical students also showed much less ambiguity toward "white civilization" than the university students. Only 18 per cent of the technical students' responses could be classified as "intermediate" (i.e., roughly even mixtures of favorable and unfavorable judgments), whereas this was the most populated response category among university students, with 38 per cent. Seventy-two university and 34 technical college students answered the question.

30. *Report of the Fort Hare Commission* (Lovedale: Lovedale Press, 1955).

31. On Fort Hare student activity, see Winston Nagan, "Fort Hare Record," *The New African*, IV, No. 5 (July 1965), 101–3.

32. See Seymour Martin Lipset, "University Students and Politics in Under-developed Countries," *Minerva,* III, No. 1 (Autumn 1964), 45–47.

33. Van den Berghe, *op. cit.,* pp. 59–60. The first stereotype in each pair was the one most frequently given, while the second was the next most commonly used. The question was open-ended.

34. Neville Rubin, *History of the Relations between NUSAS, the Afrikaanse Studentebond, and the Afrikaans University Centres* (Cape Town: NUSAS, 1960), p. 5. On the split, see *ibid.,* pp. 2–10, and Legassick, *op. cit.*

35. *Rand Daily Mail,* August 16, 1948.

36. *Ibid.* Also see *Die Transvaler* (Johannesburg), August 1, 1949. The ASB resolution read, in part;

> The Native problem . . . can be solved with the goodwill of the whole popu-lation of South Africa. The problem is that of two races [white and black], both of which have the right of existence. This existence can only be pre-served if the two races develop as different identities in their own territories. This difference in race . . . is not created by man, but . . . made by God.

This conception of apartheid, which was government policy at the time, involves a black "race" developing separately, and is less sophisticated than the present rationalization, in which the separate "tribes" or "nations" of the Xhosa, Zulu, etc., each have their own "identity." Neither theory, of course, can be con-sistently justified in historical or cultural terms.

37. *Die Transvaler,* January 21, April 5, and April 8, 1955.

38. *Die Burger,* April 17, 1957; "NUSAS Assembly Minutes" (mimeo.; NU-SAS, 1952), pp. 28–29.

39. *Die Volksblad* (Bloemfontein), April 5, 1956; *Southern Cross* (UCT), April 11, 1956.

40. *Press Digest,* 1962, p. 403; *The Star,* April 8, 1965; *Rand Daily Mail,* April 9, 1965. In 1959, however, Liberal Party and United Party groups were reported in existence at Pretoria University. See *Press Digest,* 1959, p. 191; *ibid.,* 1961, p. 212.

41. See *Die Burger,* August 24–26, September 14, December 8, 1954, April 18, 1959; *Cape Argus,* March 24, 1959; *Die Transvaler,* March 31, 1959; *Press Digest,* 1959, pp. 157, 190. See "NUSAS Assembly Minutes," 1960, p. 15, for a statement by Foreign Minister Eric Louw aimed at preventing Stellenbosch students from cooperating with NUSAS. Also see "NUSAS President's Report" (mimeo.; NUSAS, 1958), p. 19.

42. See, for example, the comments by Helen Suzman, M.P., a Progressive Party member and a lone critic of apartheid in the House of Assembly, in *Hansard,* 1964, col. 7757.

43. *Rand Daily Mail,* August 16, 1948.

44. Minister of the Interior J. de Klerk, for example, was a founder of NUSAS. See *Hansard,* 1964, col. 5988. For the educational backgrounds of candidates in the 1953 general election, see Carter, *op. cit.,* pp. 176–78. For the education of members of the 1963 cabinet, see Thompson, *Politics in the Republic of South Africa,* pp. 114–20.

45. *Die Transvaler,* April 4, 1956; "NUSAS Assembly Minutes," 1959, p. 17; Legassick, *op. cit.* Publications of the ISC have since been returned to the censor's list.

46. *Die Transvaler,* August 8, 1950.

47. See "NUSAS Assembly Minutes," 1952, p. 26; 1957, p. 15; 1958, p. 14; 1959, pp. 12, 19–20; *Cape Times,* July 3, 1957.

48. See *Die Transvaler,* August 8, 1950, and September 17, 1962; *The Star,*

October 4, 1950; "NUSAS Assembly Minutes," 1961, p. 21. The ASB did attempt to set up branches at the English-language centers for Afrikaner students only. These branches were generally refused recognition, and hence facilities, by the local SRC's because they were not open to all students. When Conservative Students' Associations were formed in 1963, the ASB did not regard them favorably because they sought to enroll both English-speaking and Afrikaans-speaking students.

49. "NUSAS Assembly Minutes," 1959, pp. 12, 14.

50. *Ibid.*, 1962, p. 24. For further details on ASB-NUSAS relations, see Rubin, *op. cit.*, and Legassick, *op. cit.*

51. See "NUSAS Assembly Minutes," 1952, p. 11; 1953, p. 9.

52. For accumulated evidence on this point, see MacCrone, Pettigrew, and van den Berghe, as cited in n. 28.

53. The two phrases quoted are from a motion submitted jointly by a white and a nonwhite delegate to the 1951 NUSAS Assembly. "NUSAS Assembly Minutes," 1951, pp. 19, 21. The motion lost by a wide margin (19 to 2), but similar resolutions between 1952 and 1955 were closely contested.

54. *Ibid.*, 1953, p. 138; 1954, p. 92, Annexure 9; 1955, Annexure 3.

55. *Cape Argus*, July 26, 1949, reported in *Press Digest*, 1949, p. 340. Also see, for example, the remarks by Philip Tobias, President of NUSAS 1948–51, in *Rand Daily Mail*, August 9, 1950.

56. Resolution 122/57, "NUSAS Assembly Minutes," 1957, p. 34; Legassick, *op. cit.*

57. In 1952, some 250 Wits students marched in support of the ANC's Defiance Campaign; in 1956 white students demonstrated in support of the Hungarian uprising. These were almost the only student marches prior to the campaign against university apartheid in 1957–59. In the latter campaign, the NUSAS Assembly voted to demonstrate only if all other methods failed. ("NUSAS Assembly Minutes," 1954, Annexure 2.) More recently, protest fasts have occurred at UN.D and at Rhodes University. (*Ibid.*, 1963, pp. 38, 44; *Evening Post* [Port Elizabeth], May 20, 1965.)

58. For evidence of this reticence, see "NUSAS Assembly Minutes," 1952, p. 22; 1953, p. 17; 1955, Annexure 3.

59. See Legassick, *op. cit.*

60. Addendum to *Report of the Special Committee on the Politics of Apartheid of the Government of South Africa* (United Nations Document A/5825/Add 1, December 10, 1964), p. 53.

61. Rhodes and UN.D reverted to the "students as such" position in the early 1960's. On the full resurgence of conservatism at UN.D, see "NUSAS Assembly Minutes," 1961, pp. 12–15. On more recent events, see John Armour, "As the Pace Gets Hotter," *The New African*, IV, No. 4 (June 1965), 94; David le Roux, "Bridging South Africa's Youth Gap," *The New African*, IV, No. 6 (August 1965), 128–29.

62. On nonwhite university student protests, see Leo Kuper, *An African Bourgeoisie* (New Haven: Yale University Press, 1965), pp. 143–66; Winston Nagan, *op. cit.* On nonwhite protests in the secondary schools, see the references in Legassick, *op. cit.*

63. The most influential and best-known of the nonwhites in NUSAS were probably Thami Mhlambiso, Vice President in 1961–62, and Seretse Choabi, Fort Hare President in the early 1960's.

64. The South African Union of Democratic Students (SAUDS) had been

a nonracial Congress Alliance affiliate in the early 1950's, the Sons of Young Africa (SOYA) was a pro-NEUM youth organization, open to Coloureds and Indians though at one time strong among Africans at Fort Hare. One proximate cause for the formation of purely African student groups at this time (1961) may have been the inability of the nonracial NUSAS to help those African students who had been expelled for taking part in a 1961 strike at Fort Hare against the declaration of the Republic of South Africa.

65. "NUSAS Assembly Minutes," 1953, p. 12; *Fort Hare Commission Report*, p. 12.

66. "An Open Letter to the Catholic University College [Pius XII], Basutoland" (mimeo.; CPSU, June 8, 1959). See also "CPSU News Bulletin" (mimeo.; CPSU, October 1961).

67. "NUSAS Assembly Minutes," 1957, Annexure 5; 1958, p. 25 and Annexure 7.

5. CHINA

BRUCE D. LARKIN

In 1966–67, millions of Chinese college and secondary school students were caught up in a struggle convulsing the national political life. How is this Red Guard movement best understood? Was its appearance a momentary aberration, an event without roots in Chinese society, of only passing significance? Or did it reveal forces of enduring importance in Chinese political life? Specifically, is the student movement an autonomous force in Chinese politics?

This is hazardous terrain. Political life typically involves a hidden side: dimensions of planning and intrigue that are not readily accessible to observers. In China, these have been nurtured by a tradition of secret societies, by the Chinese Communist Party's years of clandestinity and guerrilla warfare, and by political incentives to guard one's thoughts. The problem in studying China is compounded by the paucity of reliable information about even the less sensitive aspects of Chinese social and political life.

Under these conditions, we cannot pretend to achieve a convincing causal analysis of student political behavior in China. We can, however, identify patterns of concern and action in phenomena—such as the Red Guard movement—that otherwise seem abrupt and inexplicable.

We shall begin with the historical context, highlighting major instances of student political action in China from the May 4th incident of 1919 to the "Hundred Flowers" episode of 1957. A second section will focus on the Red Guard movement of 1966–67. In a third section, we shall suggest five thematic contrasts that illuminate China's student political tradition. In a brief conclusion, our

I am indebted to members and fellows of Cowell College, the University of California at Santa Cruz, for encouraging me in this work.

146

analysis of the events of 1966 will be considered in both historical and thematic perspective.

Students and Politics in Historical Context

Students and Politics to 1949. China's modern student movement can be dated from May 4, 1919. On that date, more than 3,000 students demonstrated in Peking against the decision of the Paris Peace Conference to grant former German territories in China's Shantung province to Japan rather than return them to China. Barred from entering the foreign diplomatic legation quarter in Peking, the students attacked a Chinese official who had signed a note agreeing to Japan's territorial demands. Martial law was declared in the area around the legation quarter, and a number of students were arrested.

Had the students not moved immediately to organize themselves for sustained activity, the May 4th incident might have been soon forgotten. But on the morning of May 5, student representatives from colleges and universities in Peking met and established the Student Union of the Middle (Secondary) Schools and Institutions of Higher Learning in Peking, the first group of its type. A month later, the drive for organization led to the creation of the Student Union of the Republic of China to coordinate student activities throughout the nation.[1]

As a defense of Chinese territorial integrity, the May 4th Movement succeeded: the Japanese did not take Shantung. But the movement also reflected rising student interest in vernacular education, the adaptation of Western political institutions, the emancipation of women, and other programs of national reform. For a time after the May 4th incident, the program of external vigilance combined with internal reform appeared to unite student opinion; but as the students became increasingly engaged in political party activities in the years 1920–23, they began to feel the divisive effects of partisan involvement. By 1924, both the Kuomintang (KMT) and the Chinese Communist Party (CCP) were recruiting students as members. Henceforth the government listed student unions as political factions.[2]

Meanwhile, Chinese "work-and-study students" who had flocked to France in the aftermath of World War I were also involved in party organization and recruitment.[3] While the CCP was being organized in China in 1920–21, a group of students in France formed the Young China Communist Party (1921). On returning to China, several of these student leaders became important CCP figures; nearly half a century later, three of their number—Premier Chou En-lai, Foreign Minister Ch'en I, and CCP General Secretary Teng Hsiao-p'ing—would find themselves embroiled in the Great Proletarian Cultural Revolution.

The next major instance of student political expression in China took place in 1925. On May 30, 1925, students distributed handbills and harangued passers-by on the streets of Shanghai to protest the killing of a Chinese labor leader by a Japanese foreman in a Japanese-owned cotton mill in the city. Some students were arrested. When a crowd gathered at the police station to demand their release, the British police inspector gave the order to fire; thirteen Chinese were killed and a number of others wounded. In the surge of antiforeign feeling provoked by these events, Shanghai was paralyzed by a strike of 200,000 workers.

The May 30th incident and the movement it engendered swung many more students over to a radically nationalist, anti-imperialist position, such as that embodied in the KMT's call for national unity against domestic warlords and foreign imperialists.[4] But student commitment to the Nationalists (KMT) was undermined by increasing tensions between Communists and Nationalists, tensions that culminated in Chiang Kai-shek's massive anti-Communist purge of April 1927. The CCP was gravely hurt. Chiang occupied Peking in June 1928 and initiated a ten-year period of nominal national unity under a KMT government in Nanking.

In 1931 and again in 1935, the student movement was aroused by Japanese encroachments on China. In mid-September 1931, Japan moved against Chinese forces in Manchuria, seizing the strategic city of Mukden. The students responded immediately. In Shanghai, Nanking, and Peiping (as Peking was called in 1928–49), they quickly organized extralegal Resist Japan National Salvation Associations. But Chiang's government preferred a policy of inaction and accommodation that disillusioned many students. The Association in Shanghai declared a week-long strike in defiance of government restrictions.[5]

Designed largely to exact an effective response to Japan from the Nanking government, the students' agitation in 1931 did not succeed. Though they numbered in the thousands, student demonstrators failed to achieve cohesion in a nationwide organization; the Nanking government pursued a policy of appeasement well into the 1930's.

In 1935, the Japanese renewed their pressure on North China. Students feared Chiang's regime would submit to a Japanese plan to create a "North China Autonomous Region," designed to consolidate Japanese control in a large area including Peiping. On December 9, students tried to deliver a petition to the Nanking government's representative in Peiping; they urged opposition to the "autonomy" scheme and demanded action to unite China against foreign incursions.[6] Unsuccessful in their efforts to deliver the petition, some of their number battered by the police, the students organized a large-scale student strike. A few days later, on December 16, more than 7,000 students from twenty-eight institutions demonstrated in Peiping despite determined army and police attempts to quell their march. Although the students' initiative eventually petered out, the Japanese did shelve their "autonomy" proposals.

The December 9th Movement marked an important step forward in the radicalization of Chinese students. In John Israel's view,

A generation of students who had been cajoled and coerced [by the Nanking government] into manifest acquiescence suddenly appeared in the streets by the thousands to demand a halt to enemy aggression. . . . Developments after December Ninth gravitated toward the left, following the pattern of all nationwide protests since the May Thirtieth Movement. No popular nationalist drive ever retained its spontaneity more than a few weeks. Once the amateur nonpartisan leaders had spent their passion, the professionals were able to turn movements to their own advantage by organization, propaganda, and behind-the-scenes manipulation. To the rank and file, demonstrations and strikes were vehicles for expressing patriotism; only revolutionaries had a vested interest in mass movements as such. . . . Except for the CCP, the KMT was the only group with sufficient leadership and expertise to mobilize students, but by 1935 the KMT's unpopular foreign policy and its negative attitude toward student politics had all but destroyed its chances to be a serious contender.[7]

Students posed problems to both the KMT and CCP during the two parties' nominal cooperation in the anti-Japanese "united front." At its base in Yenan, the CCP endeavored to absorb students and intellectuals who brought themselves to the Party but were often ideologically heterodox. Mao's "Talks at the Yenan Forum on Literature and Art," widely redistributed during the Great Proletarian Cultural Revolution in 1966, sought to bend party members to an orthodox style of analysis and work.[8] Where the KMT writ ran, students were subject to increasing surveillance and the universities pressed toward orthodoxy.[9] When Japan fell, students in KMT areas saw less and less reason to moderate their criticism of the ineffective Nationalist government. The KMT's suppression of dissent only encouraged antigovernment action by a growing number of interlinked, sophisticated student organizations. A Western observer wrote from Peiping in March 1948 that "students are the most vocal opposition group in China today."[10]

The students could not, however, create an alternative to the regime. The one force that combined effective physical power with a claim to legitimacy and an intent to rule was the Communist Party. Students realized that a disintegration of KMT rule would bring the CCP to power. The Communists, in turn, understood that their success would depend in part on the intensity and persistence of student protests against the Kuomintang. Mao Tse-tung hailed the student movement against Chiang's regime as the "second front" —after the fighting front of the People's Liberation Army—in the struggle against "the reactionary Chiang Kai-shek government."[11] Presenting itself as the champion of civil liberties and social justice, the CCP met with considerable success in its efforts to gain support among members of the intelligentsia, including students.[12]

Consolidation. Although student disaffection had weakened the Kuomintang's legitimacy, the decisive Communist victories were won on Mao's "first front": Communist military successes dominated events in late 1948 and brought the greater part of China under CCP control in 1949. But military success was not a substitute for political victory in these "liberated areas." Failure to govern might prove the undoing of the CCP, just as it had foreshadowed the KMT's defeat; political necessity demanded administrative performance.

Although students were not enlisted in the actual shaping of CCP policy, they were recruited to assist in its execution. University and middle school students over the age of eighteen were sped through political training courses and dispatched to newly won areas to work as cadres in propaganda and administration.[13] Other students joined the exodus from the mainland. China's university population dropped sharply.[14]

Chinese students were given an attractive, indeed a compelling, new option to join with the Communist Party in total commitment to a new China, a China swept clean of the manifold evils of the past. In one sense, this commitment—and the tasks of persuasion and organization it entailed—was profoundly political. But it simultaneously involved the denial of opposition to the Party and thus drastically contracted the scope of politics. In this double sense, politicization of the students implied their depoliticization.

For the new Communist government, student commitment served a threefold purpose. The government acquired needed personnel, bolstered its claim to widespread support, and was able more easily to introduce extensive educational changes aimed at harnessing the universities in the service of its goals.[15]

The shape of the future for China's universities had already been drawn in institutions established by the CCP in "liberated areas" before 1949. Rudimentary by any academic standard, but highly sophisticated in the pedagogy of political education, these institutions trained thousands of army officers and prospective cadres. In one school, all students were required to complete a three- to six-month basic political "orientation" course; those chosen to continue their training were directed not toward intellectual attainment but toward skills required to secure the Party's social, political, and military objectives.[16]

Immediately after the installation of the Government of the Chinese People's Republic in Peking, on October 1, 1949, the student-to-cadre process was vastly expanded. In 1950, in the capital city alone, an estimated total of more than 200,000 students were graduated from six-month political education courses at the People's Revolutionary College and other institutions.[17] Other notions—that universities should be institutions of scholarly inquiry or that they should be modeled along Soviet lines as specialized technical training centers—were also in the air. But the wartime concept of education—a stripped-down utilitarian conception stressing political work—remained uppermost in the minds of many CCP leaders. It would be celebrated again with partisan fervor in the turmoil of "cultural revolution" more than twenty-five years later.[18]

The newly established government gained political control over higher education in three steps. First, private foreign-supported institutions, such as Yenching University in Peking, were placed under government control and their resources reallocated. Second, technical and other institutions were reorganized to stress specialized practical studies—agriculture, metallurgy, and so forth—and the number of universities for general studies was reduced to seven.[19] The third and most far-reaching step was the launching of a movement to eradicate remnants of "bourgeois thinking" from the minds of university personnel. Early in 1952, this ideological campaign was wedded to a nationwide movement against waste, corruption, and "bureaucratism," yielding in the universities to a full-scale attack on political nonconformity.[20]

How did students respond to these political controls? For the most part they submitted; organized political expression was confined to the official youth and student associations, chiefly the China Young Communist League and the All-China Student Federation. Official reports attributed to students an active role in pressing thought reform on their teachers: "The students organized themselves into groups to interview the teachers, mobilize them, hold heart-to-heart talks with them, help them do away with their doubts, and sincerely assist them in their ideological reform."[21]

There is also evidence that student response lagged behind CCP hopes. For example, when Hunan University students were called on to participate in the agrarian reform movement in November 1951, they held back: "Some even doubted whether ideological reform was necessary for them or whether participation in the agrarian reform movement could reform one's ideology."[22] Of those who were willing to take part, some were motivated by curiosity, others by fear, and still others by a wish to command as cadres. Of some six hundred Amoy University Youth League members in 1952, to cite another case, a press report complained that fewer than ten were activists.[23]

But these signs of passivity and even (it may be assumed) discontent were not significant. Through a combination of earned legitimacy, organized loyalty, and coerced conformity, the CCP effectively precluded any outburst of student opposition until 1957. To make future heterodoxy less likely, it had effected institutional and ideological reforms tying the universities more closely to Party and State.

Two additional steps taken to alter the character of higher education in China are worth mentioning. In the early 1950's, about one year—it varied in the different fields of study—was shaved from the duration of higher education.[24] Though intended primarily to produce graduates more quickly, the move had the concomitant effect of rendering studenthood an even more transient role than it had been in the past and its occupants perhaps even more dependent on extra-university forces. (Proposals to shorten the term of study abounded in the turmoil of 1966, not without similar connotations.) A more direct attack on unwanted ideological views came in efforts to cut down the proportion of students of "bourgeois background" entering the universities, to "place all educational facilities at the disposal of workers and peasants."[25] For at least seven years after 1952, the proportion of students in higher education who were considered to be of worker and peasant origin steadily increased.[26]

But official criticism of the students' political shortcomings persisted.[27] In July 1955, Minister of Higher Education Yang Hsiu-feng, while acknowledging a considerable rise in the social consciousness of students, complained that

> there is a small number of students whose political quality is so inferior that useful personnel can hardly be made out of them. . . . Some students are seriously corroded by the bourgeois way of thinking. . . . They lead a decadent life and even band themselves together to form vagabond gangs to violate laws and discipline. . . . Some even form themselves into organizations. Reactionary cliques of this nature have been uncovered at the Futan University and the Chiaotung University in Shanghai.[28]

Yang insisted on a rigorous examination of the political ties of future students and an increased effort to enroll nonbourgeois youths into the schools.

Despite the awareness of inadequacies in its control of the universities, however, the CCP did not prevent the "Hundred Flowers" outburst of 1957. Indeed, the Party invited it.

The Hundred Flowers. The "Hundred Flowers" episode of 1957 followed public encouragement by the Party—and ultimately by Mao Tse-tung himself—of certain forms of expression and criticism.[29] The problem posed by the Party was this: How could the intelligentsia—students among them—be brought more enthusiastically into the process of economic construction? In February 1957, in a speech inviting the "blooming of a hundred flowers," the "contending of a hundred schools of thought," Mao acknowledged that small-scale student strikes had taken place during 1956. He identified two major causes of this unrest: "bureaucratism" in the leadership and insufficient ideological and political work among the students.[30] Free expression—within specified limits—would promote new attainments in the arts and sciences.[31] Mao probably also reasoned that national construction would suffer if the intelligentsia were not given a freer hand.

Attacks on "bureaucratism, subjectivism, and sectarianism" soon exceeded the Party's expectations. On May 19, 1957, the first *ta-tzu-pao* (large-character posters) were displayed on what became known as the "democratic wall" of Peking University, as students took up the "blooming and contending" that until then had been confined to other sectors of the intelligentsia. But the criticisms were too trenchant, too thoroughgoing; free comment was abruptly cut off. An "anti-rightist" campaign reached deep into the universities in the latter half of 1957, and in the Great Leap Forward of 1958, trust in "expertise" gave way to demands for political reliability and mass mobilization.

Three facets of the Hundred Flowers experience are worth noting: the content of student criticism, its organizational potential, and its final suppression by the Party. The content of student criticism is perhaps best indicated by quoting the critics themselves:

> I believe that public ownership is better than private ownership, but I hold that the socialism we now have is not genuine socialism . . . Genuine socialism should be very democratic, but ours is undemocratic.[32]
>
> A man is judged not by his virtues and abilities, but by whether or not he is a Party member or a [Communist Youth] League member.[33]
>
> We want Party leadership, but we are resolutely opposed to the Party alone making decisions and implementing them.[34]
>
> Socialism belongs to the people, not only to the Party members.[35]
>
> Give the people the freedom to shout "long live," but also give them real freedom to form assemblies and societies. . . . Reduce the administrative apparatus. . . . Abolish Party dictatorship. . . . Let the professors run the universities.[36]
>
> I think *Chinese Youth* [a youth publication] could blaze a new trail by publishing some of the typical and representative Impressionist and Dadaist works, as well as English and American modern short stories. . . .[37]

Seemingly unlimited Party claims, the weight of bureaucratic controls, the personality cult of Stalin (and, by implication, of Mao), the confines of cultural orthodoxy—these were the students' prime targets. Yet by and large their critiques were advanced from avowedly Marxist-Leninist positions. The critics implied that Party practices were worth reforming. And some must have imagined, out of naïveté or a belief that the Party was benign, that their modest efforts would accomplish reforms.

The students did not limit themselves to verbal dissent; they also tried to organize. At Peking University, a Hundred Flowers Society was formed; one of its leading figures, T'an T'ien-jung, was subsequently denounced as the "chieftain of the rightist students" at that institution and accused of proposing to organize a political party.[38] The publications *Public Square* and *The Relay Baton of Peking University,* according to later Chinese criticism, were put out by members of this group to further their organizational work in Peking and nearby Tientsin. In Wuhan University, far from the Peking-Tientsin region, several third-year students reportedly established a *Flame Newspaper* that criticized the Party's control over the University. The Wuhan students were said to have been in close touch with a leading student critic in Peking, Lin Hsi-ling of the People's University.[39]

But as Lin Hsi-ling complained, and as René Goldman—then a student in Peking—later confirmed, the Party's control of communications severely inhibited interuniversity coordination on a regional, as well as a national, scale.[40] Student attempts to organize outside the official youth and student hierarchy were small in scale, of limited effect, and quickly contained by the CCP.

The only announced executions in the wake of the Hundred Flowers criticism were those of three middle school students who had led a riot in Hanyang. But a thousand senior Party officials were transferred to work in universities and middle schools.[41] At Peking University, a new eight-hour-a-week course in political study was instituted in all departments in the autumn of 1957; some eight hundred "rightists" were identified—about 10 per cent of the student body—and either sent away for "reform through labor" or placed under Party supervision. The "rectification" campaign did not end at Peking University until January 1958.[42]

China then experienced the violent movements of the Great Leap Forward in 1958 and the grave economic difficulties of 1959–60. Efforts to consolidate the economy in 1961 involved some recognition of apolitical "virtues and abilities"—as Lin Hsi-ling had demanded in 1957—but Mao's theme of "politics in command" dominated the ensuing years. There doubtless persisted among students in this period many of the same concerns that had been voiced in 1957: dissatisfaction over politically determined job-placement criteria, unsureness about the place of expertise in the university, and resentment against the rigidity of Party bureaucrats and Youth League cadres. But the student community did not figure as a spontaneous force in Chinese politics again until 1966.

The Red Guards. China's Great Proletarian Cultural Revolution, of which the Red Guard movement became a part, can be traced to any number of origins.[43] Prominent among them are Mao's deepening distrust of an entrenched Party bureaucracy; the free-floating enmity and frustration of thousands of intellectually disadvantaged young "Reds" in educational institutions still not wholly purged of apolitical "expert" values; Mao's anxiety that "revisionism" and even *embourgeoisement* might turn China's youth from their true path as a revolutionary successor generation; an ongoing struggle for power at the top that may already have shown itself in Mao's displacement by Liu Shao-ch'i as President of the People's Republic in 1958; the lesson of 1957 that discontented intellectual flowers may yield bitter fruit unless uprooted; and the sharpening of incompatible plans to overcome Chinese weakness in a hazardous and threatening world.

In the brief history of the Red Guard movement, two stages should be distinguished. Although there are indications of earlier ferment, the Red Guards first appeared as an organized force at the Tsinghua University middle school in Peking in May 1966. Red Guard units soon sprang up in middle schools and universities throughout the country, denouncing "bourgeois, revisionist" educational administrators and teachers, curricular programs that divorced students from the practical realities of life, and university admission and job placement policies that favored academically qualified middle school graduates over the "politically qualified" sons of workers, soldiers, and peasants.[44] During this first stage, schools and colleges constituted the arena of student action.

The students' assault soon implicated the Peking Municipal Party Committee and its Chairman, P'eng Chen, but not until August did the second stage—when the arena of action expanded to include the Party bureaucracy—become readily discernible. A plenary session of the CCP Central Committee (August 1–12) endorsed the developing "cultural revolution," and on August 18 the first of a series of massive Red Guard rallies was held in Peking. The students' declamatory and, increasingly, physical action now thrust up through the educational establishment against "those Party persons in authority who are taking the capitalist path," a reference to President Liu Shao-ch'i and others reportedly associated with him. The students' contribution to the ensuing holocaust—amply described elsewhere (see Note 43)—reached its emotional zenith in 1966; it declined in vigor the following year, but in late 1967 the larger questions of long-term Party control and the succession to Mao still hung in the balance.

We can now briefly assess these events through the alternative lenses of a few of the interpretations suggested earlier.

It is clear that Mao did fear a stagnation of revolutionary spirit among China's educated youth. As the *Peking Review* put it in 1964:

Raised with special authority by Chairman Mao Tse-tung, this question [of "bringing up heirs for the revolution"] ... is a question, in the final analysis, of how to ensure that the revolution, won by the older generation at the cost of such sacrifices, will be carried victoriously to the end . . . that our sons and grandsons and their successors will continue to advance, generation after generation, along the Marxist-Leninist, and not the revisionist path. . . .[45]

Several reasons for Mao's concern can be advanced. The students of the 1960's had benefited from the status quo that Mao and his comrades in arms had fought to establish. For this younger generation, the "Long March" of the 1930's and the revolutionary struggle of the 1940's were only vicariously experienced history. The much-vaunted austerity, dedication, and egalitarianism of the "spirit of Yenan" (Mao's wartime headquarters) must have seemed remote to these students as they trained in classrooms and laboratories for elite careers.

The organization designed to keep the younger generation's revolutionary fervor and Maoist loyalty alive—the China Young Communist League (CYCL)—had become more of a routine mass feeder mechanism for the Party than a revolutionary vanguard for the youth. In 1965, some 8 million young people aged fifteen through twenty-five were recruited into the CYCL, and 600,000 League members were in turn accepted into the Party.[46] This drastic expansion in League membership in 1965 may have been dictated in part by the demands for revolutionary reinvigoration expressed at the Ninth CYCL Congress in June 1964.[47] If so, the intended effect was achieved, but not in the direction expected by CYCL leaders. In 1966, the League bureaucracy—swollen, unwieldy, and Party-controlled—was completely bypassed by the Red Guards, many of whom had doubtless joined the League in the massive infusion of new and "redder" blood the previous year.

Politicization had eroded objective tests of competence. Criteria of admission, retention, and placement were often unclear, and when clear were often disputed. Egalitarian doctrine, the desirability of being a student, and the shortage of middle school and university places converged to produce deep disagreements about the mission of the educational system.

In such a climate, attacks on narrow academic criteria and elitist definitions of competence flourished, and the Red Guards drew heavily from those of worker and peasant backgrounds who stood to be disadvantaged by demands for performance.

The Great Proletarian Cultural Revolution also embraced deep divisions within the CCP leadership. In their massive display of support for Mao, the Red Guards may have intimidated persons who sought to undercut, if not actually oust, the Party Chairman.[48]

But the Red Guard movement cannot be viewed simply as an instrument of intra-Party struggle. In fact, splits within the Party probably gave the Red Guards considerable freedom of action, so much so that the movement eventually had to be slowed down to prevent its centrifugal disintegration into sheer anarchy.

Were the Red Guards a creature of Mao Tse-tung and Defense Minister Lin Piao, organized and controlled from above? Or did they possess their own internal engine fueled with elements of *student* choice, spontaneity, and commitment? If intrinsic initiative were absent, we would simply write off Chinese students as an autonomous political force in 1966. In fact, while the record shows strong leadership from the center and official encouragement of Red Guard organizations, it also reveals apparently unsanctioned acts and strenuous efforts by the center to impose constraints.

Anna Louise Strong, an American long resident in China, asserts that the Red Guards "began as a movement of left-wing students to protect themselves against 'reactionary' school authorities" and were not at first considered "legal." The first Red Guard unit, formed sometime late in May 1966 at the middle school attached to Tsinghua University in Peking, initially worked "under cover," emerging into the open only on June 6.[49]

According to Strong, students at

> several other schools were also organizing at about the same time under various names: Red Guards, Red Eagles, Red Banners, Red Flag. Often there were several organizations in the same school with different names and somewhat different ideas. They all tried to promote the "Cultural Revolution" and the study of Mao's works, so in general they tried to unite. Differences, however, still exist in methods and even in ideas. At first none of the organizations was recognized by the school authorities, who sometimes even tried to suppress them.[50]

Despite her partisan viewpoint, Strong's account may be substantially accurate. But a Central Committee circular of May 16 anticipating "new and fierce struggle . . . on the ideological front" inspired a *ta-tzu-pao* at Peking University attacking the University's President and Party Committee Secretary, Lu P'ing.[51] On June 1, the poster's contents were broadcast over the radio and the *People's Daily* attacked "bourgeois 'scholars' and 'authorities' " for trying to "win over the masses, the youth and the generations yet unborn." Whether individual Red Guard units were created on explicit orders from above is a moot question, but their organizers did enjoy official support. Nor could the movement have grown to such vast proportions without material, as well as moral, backing from key leaders, including Mao and Lin Piao.[52]

According to a sanctioned account, student action from below was important in ousting the "work team" sent to Peking University by the Central Committee on June 4 to channel the students' fervor. Leading Party figures visited the University on four successive days in July, investigating the controversy, and the work team was disbanded; the students organized their own cultural revolution committee.[53] The Mao-Lin faction subsequently attributed the work team to its intra-Party enemies, charging that such teams had "directed the spearhead of struggle against the revolutionary Left instead of the handful of persons in the Party who are in authority and are taking the capitalist road."[54] Nonetheless, even if student attacks on the work team were prompted by high Maoist militants in conscious struggle against Liu Shao-ch'i, the fact remains that the work team could not cope with the most radical students.[55]

On August 8, the CCP Central Committee drew up a statement—called the "Sixteen Points"—inveighing against violence, against forcing a minority to submit, and against failing to distinguish "ordinary bourgeois academic ideas" from serious deviations. Noting that "contention between different views is unavoidable, necessary and beneficial" and urging the students not to fear disorder, the Committee nevertheless insisted that students not take the law into their own hands.[56]

Chiang Ch'ing later acknowledged that "new problems cropped up" a few days after the first Red Guard rally of August 18. Without identifying these problems, she implied that the Cultural Revolution Group of the Central Committee had followed, rather than led, the Red Guards:

> We immediately gathered the facts and investigated and were therefore able to keep up with the constantly developing revolutionary situation. This is what I have described as striving to follow Mao Tse-tung's thought closely on the one hand, and striving to catch up with the spirit of daring and courage, the revolutionary rebel spirit, of the young revolutionaries on the other.[57]

Free-wheeling Red Guard behavior elicited new words of caution from Chou En-lai, who took a stern view of activities that might interfere with economic production:

> In order to facilitate the normal progress of industrial and agricultural production, the Red Guards and revolutionary students from the universities, colleges and middle schools are now *not* to go to the factories

and enterprises and to Party, government and public organizations of county level and below, and people's communes in the rural areas to establish revolutionary ties. . . . Factories and rural areas cannot take time off like the schools and stop production to make revolution. Revolutionary students should respect the masses of workers and peasants, trust them and have confidence in their being fully able to successfully make revolution on their own.[58]

Other steps were taken to manage the students. A Red Guard Liaison Center was established on August 27 as a result of advice given by Chou En-lai to a meeting of 2,000 Red Guard representatives from throughout Peking, but it did not have executive authority.[59] Attached to the Red Guards, too, were "revolutionary teachers." But the CCP Central Committee's decision that "all college students and representatives of middle school students in the other parts of the country shall come to Peking group after group at different times"[60] forced the most extraordinary measure: some 100,000 men from the People's Liberation Army were assigned to monitor the influx to Peking. By an official account, these army guides "were with the revolutionary youngsters all the time and lavished great care on them, living, eating and studying with them." Their object, however, was not merely educational, but to keep order.[61]

Getting the Red Guards to go home, or at least to leave Peking, proved a more difficult problem. Chou En-lai urged the students to work in the countryside and to learn from the peasants; Lin Piao encouraged "traveling on foot"—which would not tax the transportation system.[62] The fourth in the series of Red Guard rallies, on October 18, was already a perfunctory affair. Later rallies seemed designed more to satisfy Red Guard wishes to see the CCP leadership —and Mao above all—than to accomplish any clear political purpose. On October 31, all Red Guard travel was suspended for five days and the students' future movements placed under army control, reportedly because of student interference with scheduled rail operations.[63] Efforts to flush the visitors from Peking were intensified. A double rally held on November 25–26, 1966, was explicitly designated "the last one until next spring when the weather will become warm again."[64] Cold weather complicated the problems of housing and caring for the young pilgrims in Peking and provided a rationale for their dispersal.

Within its constraints, the Red Guard movement became a nationwide mass movement. Its members crisscrossed the country, probably amazing the very CCP leaders who had encouraged them.[65]

Their number, enthusiasm, and chaotic organization had freed the students from more than limited Party control.

The case for autonomy and spontaneity should not be overstated. The Party certainly took steps to open and maintain channels of "advice" to Red Guard units. Red Guard maintenance, travel, and press activities required provision of food, mass transport, and paper and printing equipment on a large scale, services that were obtainable only with official sanction. And on matters of central political concern, the Red Guards were rent by factions; where they most nearly appeared to have one voice, they merely echoed Mao's words and Mao-approved edicts. The chief focus of spontaneity lay in local struggles, limited because local. A second was travel and "exchanging revolutionary experiences," limited because largely apolitical. Nevertheless, millions of youths shared an exhilarating common experience and proclaimed their dedication to a new society.

What of the impact of the Red Guards on the Chinese economy and polity? In the economic sphere, one should not wholly discount the "rationality" of Maoist thought. The notion that economic development can be accelerated by an input of revolutionary fervor and frugality makes some sense—particularly in a labor-intensive economy—if institutional mechanisms of incremental advance are not simultaneously sacrificed. Education, especially technical training, is one such mechanism. Emptying the schools for an academic year in 1966–67 will have its cost, although the Party did at least recognize the critical role of technical education and, to an extent, sought to protect students in science and technology from the disruptive influences of "cultural revolution."[66]

Nor have cost-benefit considerations been systematically expunged from economic planning and organization in Communist China; there was more aberration than innovation in the Great Leap Forward.[67] Disruptive political violence and other side effects of the "cultural revolution" may depress the Chinese economy, but the impact of the Red Guards per se on long-term economic progress will probably center on the problem of manpower utilization. Even here, the mere act of raising a fist against "revisionism," under a benevolent Maoist sun, need not and probably will not guarantee the unskilled and incompetent among the Red Guards entry into China's managerial establishment.

A closely related problem is that of specialization. In China in 1966–67, despite years of emphasis on revolutionary versatility and role substitution—the proletarianization of intellectuals and the uplifting of proletarians, the unity of mental and manual labor, the fusion of theory with practice—educated men remained in a separate, differentially rewarded social category. In a society of egalitarian mass involvement, universities were still selective, status-bestowing institutions. Many of them, particularly those in the social sciences and the humanities, were hardly recognizable as universities in the Western sense. Yet the boundary around China's expert subculture, though it be breached, made porous, and redrawn, will never completely disappear. Some degree of specialization in role and function will remain a permanent fact of life in China, as in any other modernizing nation.

It is on China's political culture and her view of external realities that the Red Guards may leave a far deeper mark. The Red Guards acted out a scenario that could be expressed in a handful of highly stereotyped roles and propositions. Despite the calls to "investigation and study" in the *Quotations from Chairman Mao Tse-tung*[68]—the famous "little red book"—Red Guard positions were reductionist in the extreme, relying heavily on a few rigid distinctions. The simplistic style of this kind of thinking, if not its content, may well persist into the future, stunting China's political imagination.

In its view of the world beyond China's borders, the Red Guard movement was, on the whole, Sinocentric and selectively xenophobic —a position most concretely expressed in Red Guard assaults on foreign embassies and diplomatic personnel. The central charge against Mao's enemies was the charge of "revisionism," a label pinned squarely on the Soviet Union. To the specter of Soviet power was added the massive, mounting U.S. military involvement in Viet-Nam; one can hardly blame the Chinese for viewing the systematic aerial reduction of North Viet-Nam as an ominous portent. It was probably partly with this perceived double threat in mind that the Red Guard movement was touted as a "reserve force" of the People's Liberation Army.

Both internal and external politics, for the CCP, revolve around distrust, tension, and struggle. Red Guards have had an intensive lesson in all three, to the probable detriment of Chinese unity and of international community as well.

Students and Politics in Thematic Context

We now turn from our analysis of China's student political history to explore five thematic polarities—implicit and sometimes explicit in the preceding discussion—that have framed the expectations of students in China and in part fired their political commitments: youth vs. elders, modernity vs. tradition, red vs. expert, pure vs. impure, and national identity vs. foreign incursion.

Youth vs. Elders. The five Confucian relationships include two that involve the deference of young to elder: the relationships of son to father and of younger brother to elder brother. Until the nineteenth century, students generally conformed to the Confucian code of behavior unquestioningly. But after World War I, Peking University and other institutions underwent a period of cultural florescence. Students, professors, and administrators severely criticized the Confucian tradition and, as the carrier of that tradition, the older generation as well.

In 1936, Olga Lang obtained survey data on the attitudes of 1,700 students—1,164 in colleges, 536 in middle schools—in China. Cross-pressured by the traditional value of filial respect and their own assertive independence, 40 per cent of the college students sampled declined to answer a question asking whether they had ever disapproved of their parents' behavior. Forty-three per cent vigorously criticized their parents, directing the brunt of their attack against the father's political views, variously described as "reactionary," "conservative," "feudal," and "against the trend of the times." Seventeen per cent found no fault with their parents; only two out of the 1,164 students gave the classic Confucian reply: "Children should not criticize their parents."[69]

Interestingly, the proportion of male students in Lang's sample holding "purely negative attitudes toward their fathers" was *not* larger among students professing a radical political position—equated by Lang with support for the Communist Party—than among those with "conservative and moderately democratic political views." A radical stance was instead associated with lower-class origin and with the atmosphere of the college. The student's family income level and the probability that he held radical political views were inversely related. Among students in non-Christian institutions, radical views were more frequently expressed than those of any other political coloration, but ranked next to last in frequency among students at Christian colleges. Finally, those studying in North China—where the Japanese threat was most immediately felt—included "many more" radicals than did their colleagues in the central and southern regions.[70]

Yet, although disapproval of one's parents was not a cause of radical political commitment, once the young people adopted radical ideas, which usually happened during their college years or in the higher grades of high school, their relations to their families changed. Their views encountered strong opposition from their parents because the young people advocated a new political and economic system which threatened the privileged position of the father. Furthermore, the whole ideology of Communism was a flagrant contradiction of the old Chinese tradition. The radical youths were more critical of the old Chinese family system than other youths; they . . . did not dislike their parents more than the other students, but they criticized them more often and more openly.[71]

In China, radical politics implied solidarities inconsistent with a family-centered outlook. Once adopted, radical political opinions exacerbated intergenerational tension, which in turn probably only hardened the original opinions, at least until the student became independent of his father and thus escaped the latter's intervention.

From 1949 onward, the radical position was raised to orthodoxy and institutionalized. Viewing filial loyalties as inherently competitive with its own claims to allegiance, the CCP sought to undo the primacy of father-son relationships. Children of "bourgeois" families—as many students and young intellectuals were classified—were encouraged to denounce their fathers as a self-cleansing sign of their total surrender to the Party. Robert Lifton has described the denunciation of the father, as an individual and a representative of the discredited past, as "the ultimate symbolic act in the thought reform of young Chinese. . . . [M]any found it to be extremely painful."[72]

In the Yenan period and again in the Great Proletarian Cultural Revolution, Mao Tse-tung endeavored to identify the CCP as a party of youth. Youth were not considered spontaneously or instinctively revolutionary; they were to be carefully molded and trained. Once they had been educated politically, they could play a "vanguard" role.[73] To the proportionally few students for whom this role was open, Party work offered a sense of personal worth and accomplishment that replaced and outweighed traditional family and career satisfactions. But—as Mao realized—generational succession is an unending process, and the loyalties of the unborn cannot be committed.

Modernity vs. Tradition. The tension between modern and traditional values was an important stimulus to the student movement in its early years. For young intellectuals on the eve of the May 4 outburst of 1919, the contrast was starkly posed, as in this excerpt from an article written by the editor of *New Youth,* a monthly that circulated widely among students, in defense of the magazine and its reformist views:

> In order to support Mr. Democracy, we are obliged to oppose Confucianism, the code of rituals, chastity, traditional ethics, old politics; and in order to support Mr. Science, we are compelled to oppose traditional arts, traditional religion; and in order to support Mr. Democracy and Mr. Science, we just have to oppose the so-called national heritage and old literature.[74]

Governments in pre-Communist China, to the extent that they remained attached to traditional practices, were even more vulnerable to the student criticism and hostility that followed the May 4th incident of 1919 and the May 30th incident of 1925. Nor, in the 1930's, did Chiang Kai-shek's "New Life" movement stressing proper conduct in the traditional mode make much headway among Chinese students, who were attracted in larger and larger numbers to the radically modernist conceptions of Communism.[75]

Since 1949, modernization has become (and will remain) a primary social, economic, and bureaucratic value, for each major contender in the Communist polity has a stake in its implementation. The economic managers must promote modernization to achieve their stated goals. The military must modernize (e.g., perfect a nuclear capacity) to protect the state against technologically advanced enemies. The Party must foster modernization to avoid jeopardizing its legitimacy, which stems in part from material performance.

But although all politically effective persons in China are committed to modernization, some strategies stress political reliability and mass mobilization, while others focus on expertise and cumulative advance. The most interesting strategies intermix these emphases in complex and subtle ways. Nonetheless, it is useful to picture a clash between "reds" and "experts," in which the role of the university is invariably a subject of dispute.

Red vs. Expert. For the government, this polarity raises the vital question: What balance shall be struck between political training and professional education? For the student, the question is equally critical: What balance should I strike between political zeal and academic effort to fulfill my own expectations in life? The answer to the first, public question determines for many students the answer to the second, private dilemma.

Beginning in 1949, the CCP consolidated its position and moved slowly toward greater, but still qualified, emphasis on political reliability and a corresponding devaluation of academic and professional excellence. Increasingly, students resented being taught by newly graduated lecturers who lacked academic preparation or ability. The President of Peking University said during the Hundred Flowers period that red but inexpert teachers could not command student confidence.[76]

In the "anti-rightist" campaign that followed the Hundred Flowers, and during the Great Leap Forward of 1958, the scales tipped decisively in favor of political reliability. The CCP virtually committed itself to the view that mass political consciousness alone, ignited and unleashed against objective conditions of underdevelopment, could rocket the nation forward to modernity. Higher educational institutions continued to function, but only after students had "voluntarily" spent much of the term in "productive labor," such as stoking backyard steel furnaces.

The balance did not shift again until 1961, when bad harvests and the dislocations of the Great Leap forced a retreat.[77] In effect, the Party sought both redness and expertise. The crosscurrents appeared in Hu Yao-pang's speech to the China Young Communist League in 1964: he warned youth to be ever vigilant against incipient revisionism, but at the same time urged the CYCL to "develop students' initiative and ability for independent thought in the course of their studies."[78] Called upon to do two very different and demanding things at once, students were under great pressure.

Fearful of unfavorable placement, uncertain whether he had given both expertise and redness their due, the student might try to escape being judged. Criticism in 1957 was from the "right," in 1966 from the "left," but the two cases have this in common: In both instances students acted as the school year came to a close, when their futures were most uncertain. Once the "anti-rightist" reaction of 1957 was under way, once the Red Guard movement of 1966 was formalized and given freedom of movement, opportunism dictated that the student take the most "revolutionary" position as his own. The movements gathered strength, both as they began and as they took form, from students who feared the consequences of inaction.

Pure vs. Impure

In all situations of ideological totalism, the experiential world is sharply divided into the pure and the impure, into the absolutely good and the absolutely evil. The good and the pure are of course those ideas, feelings, and actions which are consistent with the totalist ideology and policy; anything else is apt to be relegated to the bad and the impure. Nothing human is immune from the flood of stern moral judgments. . . . Once an individual person has experienced the totalist polarization of good and evil, he has great difficulty in regaining a more balanced inner sensitivity to the complexities of human morality. For there is no emotional bondage greater than that of the man whose entire guilt potential—neurotic and existential—has become the property of ideological totalists.[79]

The Chinese student movement carried a purist strain long before 1949. A Western observer of the May 4th Movement reported that students spurned politics because of "the hopelessness of the political muddle, with corrupt officials and provincial military governors in real control."[80] The typical father attacked by the students whom Olga Lang queried in 1936 drew fire not only because his politics were old-fashioned, but because his private life was also weighed and found wanting. He abused his paternal authority. He was "immoral," "corrupt," "lazy," "egotistic," "too cautious." He often gambled, smoked opium, frequented brothels.[81] And Hu Wei-han, a former Nanking student leader who enlisted during World War II in a special student military unit, found himself "deeply disturbed by the enormous corruption and inefficiency regarding payrolls, allocation of weapons, and training arrangements."[82] In each instance students tested the real world by a purist standard, found it impure, and aired their disgust.

The CCP put itself forward as the judge of purity. It defined what was impure, and it extended grace to those who overcame corruption. It set in motion forms of mutual support and multiple scrutiny that wedded the individual to political processes. But it also ran a risk. Once committed to purism, a student could find impurities not only within himself or his colleagues, but also within the party leadership or in the society at large. Perhaps this is what led Lin Hsi-ling to voice some of her most trenchant criticisms in 1957. From her own purist standard, professedly based on a Marxist-Leninist world view, she asked the central question: *Who* defines purity? If you disagree with the party leadership, she complained, your words will be attacked as counterrevolutionary.[83] Others chose the same time to denounce special privilege among Party cadres.[84] But Lin voiced most clearly the purists' dilemma: "If we are satisfied with the existing society, there will be no further development."[85]

Mao could have uttered those words. Red Guard attacks on "revisionism" are directed at the stagnation that Mao perceives in orderly process. In its place, he would put revolutionary motion, a continuing agitation. As any Red Guard could read in his little red book:

> Dust will accumulate if a room is not cleaned regularly; our faces will get dirty if they are not washed regularly. Our comrades' minds and our Party's work may also collect dust, and also need sweeping and washing. The proverb "Running water is never stale and a door-hinge is never worm-eaten" means that constant motion prevents the inroads of germs and other organisms.[86]

Of course, Mao's intent was very different from that of Lin Hsi-ling, but they shared an ultimate purist standard. Both sought purity through action and change. To the extent that the CCP leadership could persuade China's youth that it had the key to purification, it could develop their emotions into a powerful force for protection against critics. Youth could be enlisted in action that was revolutionary in appearance but which acknowledged the old leadership. But were the CCP to lose this key, it risked becoming a target of those same emotions.

Chinese Identity vs. Foreign Incursion. In 1919, 1925, 1931, and 1935, fear for the territorial integrity and identity of China was the chief impetus to the student movement. Students turned to the CCP during World War II in large part because the Party seemed a truer champion of China against Japan than did the KMT. In each case, the students sought a return to China's one-time strength, now recast in the image of a modern nation-state. However politically ineffective students may have been, they have dramatized the demands of nationalism in modern China.

The re-establishment of a unified and assertive Chinese state deprived the student community of its unique place in nationalist expression. But the nationalist theme returned with the Red Guards. As we have noted, they were touted as a "reserve" for the People's Liberation Army. Against whom? Against the Soviet Union and the United States, two states hostile to China's emergence as a world power and most able to inflict terrible damage upon her.

The presence or absence of a foreign threat does not determine, in some mechanical way, whether or not a large-scale student movement will develop. But it is fair to conclude that Chinese students will support a movement more readily if they believe it will act to defend China's national identity against some imminent assault. National survival is a purist imperative, not merely one among several choices.

Conclusion

The Red Guard's strength and independence had several roots. Underlying the student mobilization was a history of student intervention in politics, a history of which students and Party leaders both were conscious.[87] Onto this backdrop there converged in 1966 some of the most powerful stimuli to student mobilization. The Mao-Lin faction's encouragement fostered student opportunism, cementing a powerful interplay of motives.

Some striking parallels between events of 1966 and those decades earlier may indicate conscious imitation, or suggest that environment and circumstance conduced to certain forms of action. For example, in late 1931 more than 23,000 students, incensed over Japan's advance into Manchuria, converged on Nanking to demand a more forceful government stand against the invader. They disrupted rail traffic, demanding free transportation and intimidating railroad personnel.[88] Similar reports of commandeered trains and rail disruption were published in 1966. Management of the Nanking petitioners was routinized, usually centering on an appearance by Chiang Kai-shek.[89] One group of students from Shanghai whom Chiang refused to see gathered before government offices, refusing to leave until he appeared.[90] In 1966, 1,000 chanting Red Guards assembled across from the State Council offices under a banner proclaiming: "We Demand that Chou En-lai Receive Us Immediately!" Security police closed iron gates leading to the office complex, but the students staged a sitdown strike, insisting on their demand.[91]

By December 1931, the government decided students had to be barred from coming to the capital, but it quickly reversed itself. A U.S. diplomat observed that students were more easily controlled at close range than in distant railroad stations.[92] Ultimately the students were marched to trains and expelled from Peking; trains carrying new demonstrators were prevented from entering the capital. Finally, there is also precedent for students going into the countryside.[93]

Student organization has an element of tradition, romanticized in post-1949 Chinese internal propaganda. There exist models for organization within schools and for coordinating action among schools, and ample precedent exists for enlisting middle school students into movements with university students. Peking—and Peking University—is the symbolic center, setting a pattern to be copied elsewhere.

Students have mobilized in large numbers only when real issues have been at stake—and only when they believed they could alter the course of Chinese political life. Though students have been subjected to ideological reform within the schools and have performed labor under the close guidance of Party authorities, there has been no precedent for mass student action *except* when students thought they held the initiative and were their own masters. Mao Tse-tung and Lin Piao, to the extent that they foresaw and encouraged a student role in 1966, realized that it would have to involve much spontaneous student energy and tap an autonomous will to commitment.

But there is also a history of political management of the tension between student spontaneity and government control. Students were typically appeased and outwaited, until their unity was broken. If political devices could not vent threatening and intolerable pressures, the government could turn to force; the army was in reserve. This is not to say that in 1966 the Mao-Lin faction felt threatened by students—though placing transport under army command and closing Peking to outsiders were forceful acts—but that it could encourage and capitalize upon student action while harboring uncertainty about that action's ultimate thrust. The People's Liberation Army guaranteed a margin of permissible error.

Youth, modernity, purism, and nationalism are the four banners of the Chinese student movement. Of the thematic poles we have discussed, youth and modernity are consistent but rarely dramatic in their impetus to the student movement. Nationalism, by contrast, catalyzed the pre-1949 movements. Purism, ever present but accentuated by the doctrinal style of Maoist thought, was the central feature in 1957 and 1966, though to different ends. In fact, all five thematic polarities—including the peculiarly Maoist antagonism between "red" and "expert"—contributed to the electric tensions of 1966. The problem of generational succession was crucial for Mao. To the Red Guard students, Mao's vision was a promise of rewards, through politics, that they felt had been denied them in classrooms and offices by an older, bureaucratized generation. In their assault on vestiges of "bourgeois thinking" and classical tradition, in their use of Mao's aphorisms to wash and sweep the mind and house of China, in their exaltation of political over intellectual values, these students were not only "modern" but rigidly futurist, not merely "pure" but fanatically purist, not only "red" but the reddest of all. Finally, the Red Guards also believed they were acting to defend China's revolutionary identity from external threats.

Just as 1919 and 1935 formed part of the lore of Chinese students in 1966, so the massive action of 1966 will be remembered decades hence. Patterns of political action have been created; millions will remember their Red Guard participation as a profound personal experience. Later generations of Chinese students may glorify or denounce the Red Guard movement, but they will not be indifferent to its sources or to its massive energies.

The lore of the past, a widespread purist and nationalist animus, and opportunism: when these three elements reinforce one another, the student movement can intervene significantly in politics. The tie between students and politics in China is the belief that students have a special mission, a special role to play, derived in part from history and partly from myth. As long as the belief remains—and it has proved durable indeed—the tie will not be broken.

NOTES

1. See Chow Tse-tsung, *The May Fourth Movement* (Cambridge, Mass.: Harvard University Press, 1960), pp. 99–123. For bibliographic references, see Chow Tse-tsung, *Research Guide to "The May Fourth Movement"* (Cambridge, Mass.: Harvard University Press, 1963).

2. Chow Tse-tsung, *The May Fourth Movement*, pp. 164, 264–65.

3. The "work-and-study students" were poor, working in France in hopes of financing their education there. Of the roughly 1,600 in this category in France in 1920—less than half actually enrolled in educational institutions—many were already quite politicized. Perhaps in part because they lived in conditions of proletarian poverty—more than 1,700 of all the Chinese students in France were on relief in 1920—these "student workers" were more attracted to radical political alternatives than their economically better-off counterparts in the United States. The student leaders in France were conscious of the economic contrast and confident they would become political leaders in China. In their weekly journal, *Lu Ou* (*Study in Europe*), they wrote, "Please wait and see to whom our country will belong." See Chow Tse-tsung, *The May Fourth Movement*, pp. 26–31, 35–40, 249.

4. Kiang Wen-han, *The Chinese Student Movement* (New York: King's Crown, 1948), pp. 84–85, 95.

5. For a detailed treatment of these and related events, see John Israel, *Student Nationalism in China, 1927–1937* (Stanford: Stanford University Press, for the Hoover Institution, 1966), chap. iii.

6. The students' demands included (a) opposition to "autonomy," (b) open conduct of foreign relations, (c) an end to arbitrary arrests, (d) protection of territorial integrity, (e) an end to the civil war between KMT and CCP forces, and (f) freedom of speech, press, assembly, and organization. (*Ibid.*, p. 119.) On the December 9th Movement, also see Chiang Nan-hsiang, *et al.*, *The Roar of a Nation: Reminiscences of the December 9th Student Movement*

(Peking: Foreign Languages Press, 1963); Hubert Freyn, *Prelude to War: The Chinese Student Rebellion of 1935–1936* (Shanghai, 1939); Jessie G. Lutz, "December 9, 1935: Student Nationalism and the China Christian Colleges," *The Journal of Asian Studies*, XXVI, No. 4 (August 1967), 627–48; John Israel, "The December 9th Movement: A Case Study in Chinese Communist Historiography," *The China Quarterly*, No. 23 (July-September 1965), 140–69.

7. Israel, *Student Nationalism*, p. 152.

8. See Boyd Compton, *Mao's China: Party Reform Documents, 1942–44* (Seattle: University of Washington Press, 1952). Also see Mao Tse-tung, "The Orientation of the Youth Movement" (May 4, 1939), *Selected Works* (Peking: Foreign Languages Press, 1965), II, 241–49, and "Talks at the Yenan Forum on Literature and Art," *ibid.*, III, 69–98.

9. Theodore H. White and Annalee Jacoby, *Thunder Out of China* (New York: William Sloane, 1946), pp. 60, 107–11.

10. A. Doak Barnett, *China on the Eve of Communist Takeover* (New York: Frederick A. Praeger, 1963), p. 43.

11. Mao Tse-tung, "The Chiang Kai-shek Government is Besieged by the Whole People" (May 30, 1947), *Selected Works of Mao Tse-tung*, IV, 135. Mao cited China's student political tradition—the May 4th and December 9th Movements—as proof that "the upsurge of the [anti-KMT] student movement will inevitably promote an upsurge of the whole people's movement." (*Ibid.*, p. 136.) A brief CCP account of the "patriotic student movement" and its activities between December 1946 and the Communists' accession to power appears as an editor's note in *ibid.*, pp. 138–39.

12. See John K. Fairbank, *The United States and China* (Cambridge, Mass.: Harvard University Press, 1959), p. 204.

13. S. B. Thomas, "Recent Educational Policy in Communist China," in Michael Lindsay, *Notes on Educational Problems in Communist China* (New York: Institute of Pacific Relations, 1950), Supplements, pp. 182, 189.

14. The KMT claimed 155,036 were enrolled in higher education in 1947–48; CCP figures for 1949–50 assert 116,500. The two estimates are not strictly comparable, but do at least roughly indicate the drop. Leo A. Orleans, *Professional Manpower and Education in Communist China* (Washington, D.C.: National Science Foundation, 1961), pp. 68–69. The CCP attributed the decline to the enlistment of students in revolutionary work. Ma Hsü-lun, *Jen-min Jih-pao* (JMJP, the CCP's *People's Daily* in Peking), September 24, 1952, p. 2, cited in Chung Shih, *Higher Education in Communist China* (Hong Kong: Union Research Institute, 1953), p. 67.

15. Nine of the 585 members of the Chinese People's Political Consultative Conference, the highest interim legislative body, were students. (*1950 Jen-min Shou-ts'e* [Shanghai: Ta Kung Pao, 1950], p. B24.) On the willingness of students and intellectuals to believe that the CCP offered a new opportunity for China, see A. Doak Barnett, *Communist China: The Early Years, 1949–55* (New York: Frederick A. Praeger, 1964), p. 11.

16. Lindsay, *op. cit.*, Appendix I, p. 66; Marion Menzies and William Paget, "Communist Educational Policies in Certain North China Rural Areas in 1948," in *ibid.*, Supplements, p. 160. On a trip through the border regions ("liberated areas") of North China in 1947–48, Menzies and Paget were told by their Communist hosts that in the previous ten years over 30,000 students had graduated from Lien Ta (North China Associated University) alone, but this figure includes many who took only the "orientation" course. Of the

University's 705 "graduates" in 1946, the two observers were told, over half were then employed in "military" (278) or "mass" (100) service. (*Ibid.*, p. 161.) The educational process centered in "mutual-study" groups, which were carefully balanced by geographic and class origin to maximize their politically integrative potential and used a kind of buddy system to speed and control their members' progress:

> The mutual-study group, of about ten individuals, is formed by the university authorities soon after the students arrive. We learned that it is done this way, rather than by the students themselves upon the basis of individual preference, in order to have each group as heterogeneous as possible. Thus, students from the Border Regions are placed with newly-arrived students from outside, and those from peasant or worker families are placed with those from upper-class families. This group studies together; there is a constant interchange of ideas, criticism, suggestion and persuasion among its members, and between the group and professors. Learning is almost exclusively a group, social process. The group is composed of individuals in pairs; a good student "adopts" a poor one, helps him with his studies, and, if he is not industrious, encourages him to study harder.

Academic achievement accounted for only one-fifth of the student's final grade. (*Ibid.*, p. 168.)

17. Barnett, *Communist China*, p. 42.

18. In the heat of student mobilization during July 1966, the example of the Chinese People's Anti-Japanese Military and Political College (K'angta)—headed by Lin Piao, it functioned from 1936 to 1945—was a subject of much public comment. "We must carry on and spread K'angta's glorious tradition," wrote the *People's Daily*, "run all schools and colleges in the country on really Kangta lines, train large numbers of successors of the proletarian revolutionary cause." (JMJP, August 1, 1966, p. 2, cited in *Peking Review*, No. 32 [August 5, 1966], p. 14.)

19. Chung Shih, *op. cit.*, p. 47.

20. Barnett, *Communist China*, pp. 132–33.

21. A Chinese press report, cited in *ibid.*, p. 132.

22. *Ch'ang-chiang Jih-pao* (*The Yangtze River Daily*), January 9, 1952; cited in Chung Shih, *op. cit.*, p. 132.

23. *Fukien Jih-pao* (*Fukien Daily*), October 18, 1952; cited in *ibid.*

24. Orleans, *op. cit.*, p. 57. Some lengthening followed in 1955.

25. Ma Hsü-lun, "Successes of People's Education," *Culture, Education and Health in New China* (Peking: Foreign Languages Press, 1952); reprinted in part in Stewart Fraser (ed.), *Chinese Communist Education* (New York: John Wiley, 1965), p. 133.

26. René Goldman, in "Peking University Today," *The China Quarterly*, No. 7 (July-September 1961), p. 101, estimated the percentage of students of worker and peasant origin at Peking University as nineteen in 1954, thirty-five in 1958, and over seventy in 1959. Figures on the changing class composition of students in 1951–58 published in *Ten Great Years* (Peking: State Statistical Bureau, 1960), p. 200, indicate that students of worker and peasant origin increased in this period from roughly one-fifth to one-half in higher education and from one-half to three-fourths in the secondary schools.

27. See, for example, Chang Chung-lin (Director of Planning, Ministry of Higher Education), "Strive to Improve the Low Quality of Higher Education," JMJP, June 30, 1955; translated in the *Survey of the China Mainland*

Press (SCMP) (U.S. Consulate General, Hong Kong), No. 1088 (July 14, 1955), and reprinted in part in Fraser, *op. cit.*, p. 213.

28. Yang Hsiu-feng, speech to a plenary session of the First National People's Congress; translated in *Current Background* (U.S. Consulate General, Hong Kong), No. 351 (August 29, 1955), and reprinted in part in Fraser, *op. cit.*, p. 218.

29. On student involvement in the Hundred Flowers episode, two collections of documents are particularly useful: Roderick MacFarquhar, *The Hundred Flowers Campaign and the Chinese Intellectuals* (New York: Frederick A. Praeger, 1960), chap. viii, "Students," pp. 130–73; Dennis J. Doolin, *Communist China: The Politics of Student Opposition* (Stanford: Hoover Institution, 1964).

30. Mao Tse-tung, *On the Correct Handling of Contradictions Among the People* (Peking: Foreign Languages Press, 1960), a speech delivered on February 27, 1957, to the Eleventh Session (Enlarged) of the Supreme State Conference, p. 59. This published version of Mao's speech includes a number of *ex post facto* additions, but the portions to which we are referring may well be from the original text. For more detailed information on the student unrest and its probable causes, see the report of Reuter's Peking correspondent in MacFarquhar, *op. cit.*, pp. 22–23.

31. Mao Tse-tung, *On the Correct Handling of Contradictions*, pp. 48–49:
The policy of letting a hundred flowers bloom and a hundred schools of thought contend is designed to promote the flourishing of the progress of science; it is designed to enable a socialist culture to thrive in our land. . . . We think that it is harmful to the growth of art and science if administrative measures are used to impose one particular style of art or school of thought and to ban another.

32. From a speech by Lin Hsi-ling at a debate held May 23, 1957, at Peking University; translated and published in Doolin, *op. cit.*, p. 27.

33. From a speech by Lin Hsi-ling at a debate held May 30, 1957, at People's University, Peking; in *ibid.*, p. 31.

34. From a *ta-tzu-pao*, "Democracy? Party Rule?," by "Heaven, Water, Heart" (pseud.), at Normal University, Peking, June 6, 1957; in *ibid.*, p. 50.

35. Lin Hsi-ling speech, May 30, 1957; in *ibid.*, p. 38.

36. From an unsigned *ta-tzu-pao*, Tsinghua University, Peking, June 2, 1957; in *ibid.*, p. 66.

37. Fang Yu-chung (General Secretary, Communist Youth League, Hopei, Peking Middle Schools), *Chinese Youth*, No. 11 (June 1, 1957); cited in MacFarquhar, *op. cit.*, p. 138.

38. New China News Agency (NCNA), July 12, 1957, and *Chung-kuo Ch'ing-nien Pao* (*China Youth Newspaper*), August 9, 1957; cited in *ibid.*, p. 136.

39. NCNA, June 30, July 12, 1957, and JMJP, August 17, 1957; cited in *ibid.*, pp. 134, 142–45.

40. Lin Hsi-ling speech, May 23, 1957, in Doolin, *op. cit.*, p. 28; René Goldman, "The Rectification Campaign at Peking University: May–June 1957," *The China Quarterly*, No. 12 (October-December 1962), p. 152.

41. MacFarquhar, *op. cit.*, p. 264. Two hundred were assigned to top positions such as university or middle school president or vice president.

42. Goldman, "The Rectification Campaign," pp. 150, 153.

43. The literature on the Great Proletarian Cultural Revolution and the

Red Guards, already vast, is rapidly growing; the following references are only a sampling of the material available in English. On preliminaries, see Doris Rich, "Who Will Carry On?: The Search for Red Heirs," *Current Scene* (Hong Kong), III, No. 12 (February 1, 1965); Donald J. Munro, "Dissent in Communist China: The Current Anti-Intellectual Campaign in Perspective," *Current Scene*, IV, No. 11 (June 1, 1966); and E. Stuart Kirby (ed.), *Youth in China* (Hong Kong: Dragonfly Books, 1965). On the 1966 upheaval itself, see Ellis Joffe, "China in Mid-1966: 'Cultural Revolution' or Struggle for Power?," *The China Quarterly*, No. 27 (July-September 1966), pp. 123–31; "Foreign Expert," "Eyewitness of the Cultural Revolution," *The China Quarterly*, No. 28 (October-December 1966), pp. 1–7; for an orthodox overview by a CIA analyst, see Philip Bridgham, "Mao's 'Cultural Revolution': Origin and Development," *The China Quarterly*, No. 29 (January-March 1967), pp. 1–35; John Israel, "The Red Guards in Historical Perspective: Continuity and Change in the Chinese Youth Movement," *The China Quarterly*, No. 30 (April-June 1967), pp. 1–32, is especially useful; Franz Schurmann, "What is Happening in China?," *The New York Review of Books*, October 20, 1966, and the exchange of letters between Schurmann and Joseph Levenson in the January 12, 1967, issue; the editorial, "War on the Old World: The Red Guards in China," *Current Scene*, IV, No. 16 (September 5, 1966); Maurice Kelly, "The Making of a Proletarian Intellectual: Higher Education and 'Cultural Revolution' in China," *Current Scene*, IV, No. 19 (October 21, 1966); C. T. Hu, "The Chinese University: Target of the Cultural Revolution," *Saturday Review*, L, No. 33 (August 19, 1967), 52–54, 68–70. For foreign press coverage, particularly of the *ta-tzu-pao*, see U.S. Embassy, Tokyo, *Daily Summary of Japanese Press* and *Summary of Selected Japanese Magazines;* and David Oancia's reports to *The Toronto Globe and Mail*, sometimes also published in *The New York Times*. For the Chinese press, see *Survey of the China Mainland Press* (SCMP) and *Selections from China Mainland Magazines*. *Peking Review* is another useful source. For a chronology of events, see the running "Quarterly Chronicle and Documentation," in *The China Quarterly*.

44. According to a report in *Eastern Horizon*, a Hong Kong monthly disseminating views favorable to the People's Republic, students from worker-peasant families made up as little as 20 per cent of the annual matriculation at Peking University in the years immediately prior to 1966. In 1964–65, of those entering the Physics Faculty—where academic standards were presumably relatively high—only 4 per cent had worker-peasant backgrounds. Lu P'ing, the University's President and also Secretary of its Party Committee, had, according to this report, discriminated against students of worker-peasant origin both academically and by recommending them for jobs as secondary school teachers—often, one may assume, in rural areas—rather than as university instructors or candidates for further study and research. In 1962, no students from worker-peasant families were given staff positions at the University or sent to "higher research institutes," while of the forty-two who dropped out of the University that year, thirty-three were of worker-peasant origin. Lu P'ing derided these academically more poorly equipped students, calling them "simpletons with overdeveloped limbs" and "rough porcelain on which you can't do fine engraving." Lu P'ing—still according to the report —even ordered the removal of Mao's quotations from the walls of the University; in the Faculty of Philosophy, only 5 per cent of class time was devoted to studying Mao's works. For these reasons, seven Philosophy Faculty

staff members, named in the article, posted the first *ta-tzu-pao* at the University on May 25, 1966. A. Jackson-Thomas, K. Janaka, and A. Manheim (all foreigners resident in Peking), "How It All Started in Peking University," *Eastern Horizon,* VI, No. 5 (May 1967), 23–26.

One does not have to accept the validity of these charges to believe that they were an important motivating factor in the subsequent student campaign. For parallel evidence, see JMJP, August 15, 1966; translated in SCMP, No. 3767 (August 24, 1966), pp. 14–15, and cited in Israel, "The Red Guards in Historical Perspective," p. 7.

45. "Bringing Up Heirs for the Revolution," *Peking Review,* No. 30 (July 24, 1964), p. 19.

46. NCNA, May 3, 1966; cited in *The China Quarterly,* No. 27 (July–September 1966), p. 216.

47. See, for example, Hu Yao-pang's report to the Congress on behalf of the outgoing CYCL Central Committee, "For the Revolutionization of our Youth!," in *Peking Review,* No. 28 (July 10, 1964), pp. 8–22.

48. There are indications that Mao failed to win acceptance of views pressed on an unannounced meeting of the CCP Central Committee in September 1965 and that criticisms of the Vice Mayor of Peking, Wu Han, in November 1965 were the first probing thrusts of a Maoist counterattack. (Cf. Bridgham, *op. cit.,* pp. 15–18.) Charges were made in 1967 that Mao's enemies had planned his overthrow early in 1966. (*The New York Times,* April 18, 1967, and Reuters.) Certainly the severity of these accusations supports the conclusion that Mao's continued leadership was under determined assault by other forces within the CCP.

49. Anna Louise Strong, *National Guardian* (New York), October 15, 1966, pp. 6–7. Her report on events at Tsinghua is based on a discussion with Red Guards in Peking in September 1966. Her account almost surely enjoys official Chinese sanction.

50. *Ibid.,* p. 6.

51. "Circular of Central Committee of Chinese Communist Party (May 16, 1966)," *Peking Review,* No. 21 (May 19, 1967). For the text of the *ta-tzu-pao,* see *Peking Review,* No. 37 (September 9, 1966), pp. 19–20, and JMJP, June 2, 1966. On the origins of the *ta-tzu-pao,* see Nieh Yuan-tzu, *et al.,* JMJP, May 19, 1967, p. 4.

52. Another observer concluded that "it now seems that the Red Guards were not a key element in a carefully prepared long-range plan, but rather began in June as an improvised replacement for a Party apparatus found to be more resistant and unresponsive than expected." The editorial, "A Year of Revolution: Mao Tse-tung and the 'Anti-Party' Struggle," *Current Scene,* VI, No. 22 (December 10, 1965), 5.

53. Jackson-Thomas, *et al., op. cit.,* pp. 26–28. See also Agence France-Presse, August 1, 1966; cited in "War on the Old World," p. 6.

54. *Hung-ch'i (Red Flag),* No. 15 (1966); editorial, in *Peking Review,* No. 51 (December 16, 1966), p. 6. Cf. Chiang Ch'ing's remarks of November 28, in *Peking Review,* No. 50 (December 9, 1966), pp. 7–8 and Israel, "The Red Guards in Historical Perspective," p. 9.

55. According to an Agence France-Presse report of August 10, 1966, Premier Chou En-lai, CCP General Secretary Teng Hsiao-p'ing, and Mao's wife Chiang Ch'ing spoke at Peking University and Tsinghua University during the first week of August in an effort to restrain excesses of the "cultural revolution" at those institutions. (Cited in "War on the Old World," p. 6.)

56. "Decision of the Central Committee of the Chinese Communist Party Concerning the Great Proletarian Cultural Revolution" (the "16 Points"), Point 7:

In the course of the movement, with the exception of cases of active counter-revolutionaries where there is clear evidence of crimes such as murder, arson, poisoning, sabotage or theft of state secrets, which should be handled in accordance with the law, no measures should be taken against students at universities, colleges, middle schools and primary schools because of problems that arise in the movement. To prevent the struggle from being diverted from its main objective, it is not allowed, whatever the pretext, to incite the masses to struggle against each other or the students to do likewise. Even proven Rightists should be dealt with on the merits of each case at a later stage of the movement. (*Peking Review*, No. 33 [August 12, 1966], p. 9.)

Point 6 also urged restraint:

The method to be used in debates is to present the facts, reason things out, and persuade through reasoning. Any method of forcing a minority holding different views to submit is impermissible. The minority should be protected, because sometimes the truth is with the minority. . . . When there is a debate, it should be conducted by reasoning, not by coercion or force. (*Ibid.*)

57. Chiang Ch'ing, speech of November 28, 1966, excerpted and paraphrased in *Peking Review*, No. 50 (December 9, 1966), p. 8.

58. *Peking Review*, No. 39 (September 23, 1966), p. 12. Italics added.

59. Strong, *op. cit.*, p. 6. She reported that as late as September 1966 there was no single organization in Peking competent to plan or command Red Guard activities on a citywide basis; organizational consolidation had taken place only at the level of the capital's eight districts, and even then only to a limited degree.

60. Chou En-lai, speech to the second Red Guard rally, August 31, 1966, *Peking Review*, No. 37 (September 9, 1966), p. 12.

61. Chou En-lai told an assembly of army "reception workers" on December 19, 1966:

You have helped train the revolutionary young fighters. It must have been very intense, heavy and meticulous work, making them feel at home and then seeing them off. . . . At the peak, there were more than 3 million revolutionary students and teachers in Peking and yet order was very good. (*Peking Review*, No. 1 [January 1, 1967], pp. 4–5.)

62. *Peking Review*, No. 39 (September 23, 1966), p. 12, and No. 46 (November 11, 1966), pp. 10–11.

63. *The New York Times*, November 3, 1966.

64. *Peking Review*, No. 49 (November 2, 1966), p. 6.

65. One report has it that Chou En-lai was astounded to find the original estimate of 200,000 visitors to Peking far exceeded. (Israel, "The Red Guards in Historical Perspective," p. 18, citing *Yomiuri*, January 15, 1967; translated in *Daily Summary of Japanese Press*, January 17, 1967, p. 13.) Officially, some 11 million were said to have attended the string of Red Guard rallies.

66. See Point 12 of the "16 Points," *Peking Review*, No. 33 (August 12, 1966).

67. See, for example, Dwight H. Perkins, "Incentives and Profits in Chinese

Industry: The Challenge of Economics to Ideology's Machine," *Current Scene,* IV, No. 10 (May 15, 1966).

68. Mao Tse-tung, *Quotations from Chairman Mao Tse-tung* (Peking: Foreign Languages Press, 1966), pp. 230–36, 304–12.

69. Percentages were calculated from figures in Olga Lang, *Chinese Family and Society* (New Haven: Yale University Press, 1946), pp. 285–86. The 1,164 students in her sample represented approximately 2.5 per cent of all students enrolled in higher education in China in 1936. (*Ibid.,* p. 270.)

70. *Ibid.,* pp. 316–18.

71. *Ibid.,* p. 320.

72. Robert Jay Lifton, *Thought Reform and the Psychology of Totalism: A Study of "Brainwashing" in China* (New York: W. W. Norton, 1961), p. 267. For specific cases, see *ibid.,* pp. 267–70, and Fraser, *op. cit.,* pp. 136–40.

73. Mao Tse-tung, "The Orientation of the Youth Movement," p. 248.

74. Ch'en Tu-hsiu, "Our Answers to the Charges Against the Magazine," *New Youth,* VI, No. 1 (January 15, 1919); translated and cited in Kiang Wen-han, *op. cit.,* p. 25.

75. John K. Fairbank, Edwin O. Reischauer, and Albert M. Craig, *East Asia: The Modern Transformation* (Boston: Houghton Mifflin, 1965), p. 713.

76. Goldman, "The Rectification Campaign," pp. 142–43.

77. Foreign Minister Ch'en I called on foreign language students to master their studies, justifying competence in language as a "tool for political struggle." (*Kuang-ming Jih-pao [The Enlightenment Daily],* March 19, 1962; translated in SCMP 2713, p. 1.) The talk was originally published in the *Teaching and Study of Foreign Languages Quarterly,* No. 1 (1962).

78. Hu Yao-pang, *op. cit.,* p. 17.

79. Lifton, *op. cit.,* pp. 423–25.

80. John Dewey, who lectured at Peking University in the winter of 1919; cited in Chow Tse-tsung, *The May Fourth Movement,* p. 224.

81. Lang, *op. cit.,* p. 286.

82. Lifton, *op. cit.,* p. 284.

83. Lin Hsi-ling speech, May 30, 1957, in Doolin, *op. cit.,* pp. 40–41.

84. Cf. Goldman, "The Rectification Campaign," p. 146. Also see, in Doolin, *op. cit.,* p. 63:

What does it mean when the Communists say they suffer so that the people may not suffer and that they let the people enjoy things before they do the same? What do they mean when they speak of suffering now in order to have a happy life later? These are lies. We ask: Is Chairman Mao, who enjoys the best things in life and passes the summer at Chinwangtao and spends his vacations at Yü-ch'üan-shan, having a hard time?

85. Lin Hsi-ling speech, May 30, 1957, in Doolin, *op. cit.,* p. 37.

86. Mao Tse-tung, *Quotations,* pp. 259–60, or pp. 223–24 of the Chinese edition.

87. May 4 continues to be celebrated as the anniversary of the May 4th incident. (See JMJP, May 4, 1967, p. 1, and May 4, 1966, p. 4.) When Lin Hsi-ling spoke at Peking University on May 23, 1957, she began her remarks by noting that Peking University inherits the traditions of the May 4th Movement. (Doolin, *op. cit.,* p. 23.) Press reports mentioned the May 4th tradition both during the height of the Hundred Flowers period and, in a somewhat different vein, after it was controlled. *Kuang-ming Jih-pao,* May 26, 1957: "The students themselves considered that in opening up the 'Democratic Wall'

and publishing large-character newspapers they were not hindering their studies, but they thought that this was carrying on the democratic traditions of Peking University at the time of the May 4th Movement." (Cited in MacFarquhar, *op. cit.*, p. 133; see *ibid.*, also, pp. 142, 169.) A set of stories of the December 9th Movement (1935) was published as recently as 1961: *I-erh chiu hui-i-lu* (Peking: Chung-kuo Ching-nien Ch'u-pan She, 1961). They are available in English as *The Roar of a Nation,* with differences noted by John Israel in "The December 9th Movement," pp. 140–69, especially pp. 159–64.

88. Israel, *Student Nationalism,* pp. 58, 72.

89. *Ibid.,* pp. 60–61:

After a group had been fed and lodged under close surveillance, its leaders would be summoned to the Kuomintang's Ministry of Propaganda for an intimate talk about government plans to resist Japan, and secret party resolutions would be produced as evidence of sincerity. High-level party and government officials would speak to the assembled students, who would afterwards be shepherded to the government offices to present their petition; Chiang Kai-shek would usually appear to say a few words. If they behaved very well, they might be treated to a pilgrimage to Sun Yat-sen's tomb before being escorted to a train waiting to take them home.

90. *Ibid.,* pp. 61–62.

91. David Oancia, in *The New York Times,* November 9, 1965.

92. Israel, *Student Nationalism,* p. 70.

93. After the December 1935 events, students undertook propaganda work in the villages, which was in many respects akin to that proposed for the Red Guards, save that in 1966 students were urged to learn from the peasants. See Wang Nien-chi, "Off to the Countryside," in *The Roar of a Nation,* pp. 109–29, and Israel, *Student Nationalism,* pp. 134–38.

6. INDONESIA

HARSJA W. BACHTIAR

In 1966–67, under the banner of the Action Command of Indonesian Students *(Kesatuan Aksi Mahasiswa Indonesia,* or KAMI),[1] a formidable number of university students participated in possibly the most fundamental and certainly one of the most dramatic upheavals the world's fifth most populous state has experienced since it became independent on August 17, 1945. It would therefore be of considerable interest to trace the role of these students in the course of events set in motion by the abortive coup d'état in Djakarta on the night of September 30, 1965. This chapter, then, is a preliminary endeavor to describe and analyze the political activities of Indonesian students, and of KAMI in particular, in their proper historical and social contexts.

Students in Colonial Indonesia

Before Indonesia became independent, the university student community in what was then the Dutch East Indies was quite small and its indigenous sector even smaller. The Dutch did not establish an institution of higher education in the colony until 1920. In that year a Higher Technical School was founded in Bandung, West Java, primarily on the initiative of private Dutch business interests. Twenty-eight students were enrolled in the school's first academic year, only two of them Indonesians.[2]

A Higher Law School was established in 1924 and a Higher Med-

An earlier version of this chapter was submitted to an international conference on students and politics, sponsored by the Center for International Affairs, Harvard University, and the University of Puerto Rico, held in San Juan, Puerto Rico, March 28–31, 1966. The author is much indebted to Professor Seymour Martin Lipset for introducing him to the study of student politics.

ical School in 1927 in the capital city of Batavia (now Djakarta).
In 1940, the long-awaited Faculty of Letters and Philosophy was
also formed in Djakarta. A year later, these four institutions of
higher learning—now called faculties in anticipation of their transformation into one university—were increased to five with the addition of a Faculty of Agriculture, established temporarily in Djakarta
pending its final location in nearby Bogor.

On the eve of World War II, Indonesians were still an absolute
minority among university students (who were largely of European
and Chinese descent) in their own native land.[3] In standards, staff,
and medium of instruction, these institutions were essentially
Dutch.[4]

Although Dutch became the language of the new Western-
educated Indonesian intelligentsia, students were captivated by the
idea of establishing Malay as the language of all Indonesians. In
1928, the delegates to a national youth congress held in Batavia
under the leadership of student political activists unanimously
adopted a resolution to this effect. The Indonesian language
(bahasa Indonesia) was to become one of the strongest forces in the
unification of an ethnically, culturally, linguistically, and geographically diverse and dispersed population.

Precisely because they were few in number and a minority in the
university community, students in colonial Indonesia were fairly
homogeneous politically and greatly concerned with the fate of
their people. They were acutely conscious of the ill effects of Dutch
colonialism, for most had suffered personally from them. In the
Dutch-dominated cities, Indonesian youths could not avoid becoming aware of the racial discrimination inherent in any colonial
society. They were driven to seek lodgings in areas of the town separated from the neighborhoods where the Dutch maintained their
houses and mansions. Like their indigenous fellow citizens, Indonesian students were called *"inlanders"* ("natives") by the Dutch,
frequently with derogative intent. Every day they could read in the
Dutch newspapers that they were essentially an inferior people.
Furthermore, a sizable number among them came from the lower
classes, despite the elitist character of higher education in the
colony.[5]

What the students lacked in numbers they made up in organization and awareness. In discussion groups and youth congresses,
in newspapers and journals, they condemned the Dutch for oppress-
ing the native population, accused the indigenous local elites of

obstructing progress, and urged their fellow countrymen to awaken and build a new society in an independent Indonesia.

The few Indonesians who studied in Holland, a free and democratic country, became even more conscious of the great disparity between colonizer and colonized. In the early 1920's, they consolidated their strength by transforming the existing Indonesian student organization into a militant body: the Indonesian Association *(Perhimpoenan Indonesia)*.[6] Its members were among the first to promote the idea of independence and national unity. They proudly named their organizational journal *Indonesia Merdeka (Free Indonesia)*.

When the League Against Colonial Suppression and Imperialism convened an international congress in Brussels in 1927, *Perhimpoenan Indonesia* sent a five-member delegation under the leadership of twenty-five year old Mohammad Hatta, a student of economics in Rotterdam. Nearly two decades later, Hatta would proclaim (with Sukarno) the independence of Indonesia and become the nation's first Vice President. In Brussels, he was elected to the Presidium of the Congress. Another student, Nazir Pamontjak, later Indonesian Ambassador in Paris, delivered a fiery speech against Dutch colonial oppression. The Congress voted a resolution supporting the Indonesian independence movement.[7] Through participation in such activities, the student leaders also established close ties with other nationalists, men like Jawaharlal Nehru and Léopold Senghor. When they returned to Indonesia, many members of *Perhimpoenan Indonesia* became leaders in nationalist study clubs, political parties, and trade unions.

While native Indonesians committed their energies to these endeavors, students of Chinese descent abstained from nationalist activity. Instead, they associated themselves with the Republic of China or with the dominant Dutch elite. In 1936, Chinese students formed their own exclusive association, *Ta Hsioh Hsioh Sing Hui* (University Student Association).[8] Their politically passive stance during the formative years of the Indonesian nation was to add to the difficulties they later faced as members of an economically pivotal, culturally unassimilated minority in Indonesian society.

In 1942, with the defeat of the Dutch colonial government by the invading Japanese armed forces, all institutions of higher education in Indonesia were closed down. Later, the Japanese occupational government reopened the Faculty of Medicine in Djakarta and the Faculty of Technology in Bandung. Since Dutch members of the teaching staff were classified by the Japanese as enemies, and therefore unemployable, Indonesians were appointed as professors and lecturers to teach at these institutions. The language of instruction became Indonesian, whose scientific vocabulary expanded rapidly in consequence. These important changes in university education heightened the students' sense of national identity. At the same time, student resentment against the occupation grew. Students at the Higher Medical School were particularly active, maintaining close contact with the anti-Japanese underground and helping to prepare the way for Indonesia's declaration of independence on August 17, 1945.

After the Japanese surrender, the Dutch tried to regain control of their ex-colony. They managed to recapture Djakarta after the fledgling government of the Republic of Indonesia had withdrawn to the ancient city of Jogjakarta in Central Java. A great many students also evacuated Djakarta to join the revolutionary government in its struggle against the Dutch or to continue their studies in nationalist-held areas. Institutions of higher education were eventually re-established under republican auspices in and near Jogjakarta.[9]

On January 21, 1946, the Dutch created a "temporary university" to attract Indonesian students to their side. On March 10, 1947, they named it the "University of Indonesia," but only nine native Indonesians (compared to 103 Dutch and 98 Chinese students) enrolled for the first academic year.[10] After hostilities ended in 1949, with the formal Dutch cession of sovereignty, the students of Chinese origin at the University enjoyed a considerable academic advantage over the Indonesians, who returned to Djakarta to enroll after having interrupted their studies to fight against the Dutch.

In 1947, the University of Indonesia comprised Faculties of Medicine, Law, Literature and Philosophy, and Agriculture (in Djakarta) ; Technology and Exact Sciences (Bandung) ; Veterinary Science (Bogor); Medicine (Surabaja); and Economics (Makassar). Virtually all the professors and lecturers were Dutch, and instruction was given in the Dutch language. Student extracurricular activities were patterned after those in Holland, and student publications— which advertised dances and *kroeg* (drinking) meetings—were almost devoid of political content. With a few exceptions—e.g., a boycott of lectures by nationalist students at the Higher Technical School in Bandung to protest a Dutch military offensive against the Republic in December 1948—students at the Dutch-controlled University were politically inactive during this period.

Matters were entirely different in areas controlled by the revolutionary government. The republican capital of Jogjakarta and the surrounding towns were crowded with supporters of the nationalist cause. Here the students pursued their studies under teachers who were frequently called away on missions for the embattled Republic. Many students were also called to take arms against the Dutch or to serve the revolutionary government in other ways. Those competent in foreign languages (especially English), for example, were recruited as translators, interpreters, and radio broadcasters.

The higher schools in republican-held territory were merged into a university in Jogjakarta, inaugurated on December 19, 1949.[11] Gadjah Mada University—named after a famed empire-builder of the fourteenth-century Madjapahit kingdom—rightfully claimed to be the only revolutionary university in Indonesia. The traditionally high status that professors had enjoyed in the Dutch academic system, combined with the hierarchically oriented Javanese culture of the host sultanate of Jogjakarta, lent a rather conservative color to student-teacher relations at the new university. But all classes were taught in Indonesian (interspersed with Javanese and English terms) and the University's atmosphere and aspirations were vigorously nationalist.

Expansion of the University Student Community

The "nationalization" of the University of Indonesia, which was undertaken after the colonial era belatedly drew to a close in December 1949, proved a difficult task. By 1955, the teaching staff was still less than one-third Indonesian and the University, in standards and curriculum, was for all practical purposes still a Dutch institution.[12]

During the Dutch occupation of Djakarta (1946–50), the republican government had clandestinely operated a senior high school in the city. Graduates from this and other nationalist-run schools, as well as many students from Gadjah Mada University who moved to Djakarta in search of better educational facilities, found themselves at a disadvantage at the University of Indonesia because of their insufficient knowledge of Dutch. Gradually, however, foreign instructors were replaced by Indonesians. Eventually, all instruction at the University of Indonesia was in the national language, although foreign professors were permitted to lecture in English (rather than Dutch). The students were regarded as a mature, highly select group, and the University did not attempt to exercise control over their pace of study. The University was designed, in short, as a training center for future members of the national elite.

In the early 1950's, student associations in Indonesia showed little interest in political matters. Extracurricular activities were focused on sports, entertainment, and the like. Many politically interested students went overseas on scholarships, studying in such countries as Holland, England, the United States, and Japan. A few leaders of student associations at the University of Indonesia and Gadjah Mada University also traveled abroad, representing their members at international conferences.

Independent Indonesia avoided taking sides in the Cold War, and therefore became the object of much attention, in various forms, from foreign governments. At the same time, the economic situation of the country was satisfactory. Students who lived on government scholarships had enough funds to meet expenses for board and lodging. There was little to complain about.

When the government returned to Djakarta, Gadjah Mada University lost many of its prominent professors and had difficulty finding replacements. The University became dependent on instructors at institutions of higher education in Djakarta, Bogor, Bandung, and Surabaja, who flew each month to Jogjakarta to hold classes. The resident professors became more provincial in outlook, giving lectures that had become petrified in their subject matter and clinging to Gadjah Mada's reputation as the one and only revolutionary university in the country.[13] Nevertheless, the number of students— from all parts of the archipelago—rapidly increased. Enrollment rose from 387 in 1946–47 to 15,714 in 1961–62.[14] Many were attracted to Gadjah Mada by its culturally congenial atmosphere as a national university in a native Indonesian town. Also, Jogjakarta was (and remains) a less expensive place to live than the capital city of Djakarta.[15]

During the colonial era, all institutions of higher education were located in Java. After independence, people in all parts of the country began to demand the establishment of universities in their own regions to accommodate the growing number of high-school graduates who wanted to continue their studies but could not afford advanced academic training in Java. The people were also aware of the shortage of university-trained personnel in the regions and of the painful fact that young men sent to the universities in Java often failed to return home upon graduation, preferring to work in the much more developed towns of Java.[16] Regional prestige was also involved.

The government accordingly developed and implemented an ambitious program to provide each province with at least one state university. At present, there are institutions of higher education in all provincial capitals and in some other towns as well.[17]

All Indonesian universities, although academically autonomous, are under the administrative jurisdiction of the Department of Education and Culture. The government also maintains institutions of higher education under the jurisdiction of other ministries. Students enrolled at these service academies, although frequently not considered so by outsiders, believe themselves no different from university students since the same academic degrees are offered by these institutions. Many participate actively in university student activities, including political activities.[18]

The state universities, especially those located in such large urban centers as Djakarta and Bandung, have been unable to accommodate the rapidly expanding number of high school graduates wishing to continue their studies. This unpromising situation has stimulated religious groups, political parties, wealthy parents, and members of the academic profession to establish private institutions to help meet the rising demand for higher education. Djakarta alone now has more than ten private universities of varying size, quality, and orientation.[19]

In the light of this expansion, what is the present numerical strength of the student community in Indonesia? Estimates vary widely—37,760 (1960), 29,095 (1963), 50,000 (1963), and 100,000 (1964)—and none can be considered accurate. More reliably, the Department of Higher Education and Science reported a student enrollment of 279,624 for 1965.[20] Part of the variation stems from whether or not one's definition of a "university student" includes students in the service academies. The official 1965 figure of 279,624 includes those enrolled in the service academies as well as those in private universities. It is, however, rather difficult to keep track of enrollments at the new private universities that have sprung up in towns all over the archipelago.

Social Cleavages and Student Organizations

Social cleavages in the student community are essentially a reflection of cleavages evident in Indonesian society as a whole.[21]

There is, first, the cleavage between students with a secular outlook and those who are religiously oriented. A great many of the latter are deeply concerned about the erosion of their religion by social forces giving primacy to the attainment of material goals.[22] In February 1947, university students of the Islamic faith established in Jogjakarta what later developed into the largest Islamic student organization in Indonesia, the Islamic Student Association (*Himpunan Mahasiswa Islam,* or HMI). HMI recruited its members primarily among students of lower-middle-class origin, with a rather large proportion coming from regions outside Java. It represents the modern sectors of the religiously oriented Islamic student community. In its early years, HMI was closely associated with the *Masjumi,* one of the largest political parties in the country until an unsympathetic government forced its dissolution in 1960. The *Masjumi* was dominated by politicians with academic backgrounds who could easily develop rapport with HMI students—unlike, for example, the equally large Islamic *Nahdatul Ulama* party, which was led by more orthodox religious leaders without university training.

In 1955, HMI's membership was estimated at 2,505.[23] By 1967, the figure had risen to a reported 100,000. HMI members have a strong sense of being future leaders of the Islamic community, which encompasses the overwhelming majority of the Indonesian population.

As a student association closely linked with a major component of the Indonesian cultural system—the constellation of modernistic Islamic values—the political significance of HMI increased considerably with the creation of new universities. The rapid growth of Indonesia's student population also enlarged the size and geographic scope of the other major student organizations. Especially after the political campaigns preceding the 1955 general election, political parties, aware of the importance of support from future members of the professional elite, took an active interest in organizing and recruiting the student community.

When the *Nahdatul Ulama,* presently the largest party in Indonesia, could not bring HMI under its wing, it organized its own Indonesian Movement of Islamic Students (*Pergerakan Mahasiswa Islam Indonesia,* or PMII). PMII members tend to be of rural origin and native to the island of Java. They are more conservative and parochial in outlook and less influenced by Western cultural values than HMI students. A significant part of the PMII, including its leadership, is recruited from the various State Institutes of Islamic Religion.

Two other political parties based on Islam have their own, smaller student associations. The *Partai Sarekat Islam Indonesia* (PSII) has its *Sarekat Mahasiswa Muslimin Indonesia* (SEMMI). The

Persatuan Tarbijah Islamijah (PERTI), a smaller party, recruits its younger leaders through its *Gerakan Mahasiswa Islam Indonesia* (GERMAHII).[24]

Another Islamic student association is the *Ikatan Mahasiswa Muhammadijah* (IMM), affiliated with a relatively old, nonpolitical, and widely respected organization, the *Muhammadijah,* which since the 1910's has done a great deal to improve the education, health, and social welfare of the Islamic community in Indonesia. The *Muhammadijah* also maintains its own university.

The Islamic student associations have been quite concerned about the challenge of secularist elements in the student community and, more recently, over the ascendancy of its militant, antireligious Communist sector. Although during their formative years the Islamic student groups did not express much resentment against the still organizationally weak Christian students, this situation changed somewhat when the Christian student associations became strong enough to assert their own will in politics.

Among the Christian student organizations are the Protestant Indonesian Movement of Christian Students *(Gerakan Mahasiswa Kristen Indonesia,* or GMKI) and the Union of Roman Catholic Students of the Republic of Indonesia *(Perhimpunan Mahasiswa Katholik Republik Indonesia,* or PMKRI). The largely Christian Batak, Menadonese, and Ambonese ethnic groups—apart from the Javanese, who are well represented in all student associations—are heavily represented in the GMKI. Like the HMI, the PMKRI was established during the period of revolutionary conflict in 1947. A sizable number of its estimated 17,000 members are of Chinese descent and not all members of the PMKRI are Catholics.

Nationalistic students, eager to develop a "genuinely Indonesian" student tradition in the face of a Western cultural penetration they deeply resented, became a fertile source of members for the student association of the Indonesian National Party (PNI), the Indonesian National Student Movement *(Gerakan Mahasiswa Nasional Indonesia,* or GMNI). GMNI maintained close relations with the leaders of the parent party (themselves former student activists) and enthusiastically supported all activities it thought might add to the glory of the Indonesian state. It particularly extolled Sukarno, who had worked closely with leaders of the PNI since the mid-1920's, as the "Great Leader of the Revolution."

Although in its ideology GMNI emphasizes its orientation toward the common man—expressed in its ideological vocabulary as *marhaenism*—in reality the PNI maintains a paternalistic relationship with its student affiliate, heavily influenced, one suspects, by the feudal tradition of the Javanese people, the main social base of both the party and the student organization.[25]

Another nationalistic student organization was the *Gerakan Mahasiswa Indonesia* (GERMINDO), affiliated with the leftist-oriented Indonesian Party (PARTINDO). Also nationalistic but without left-wing overtones was the *Mahasiswa Pantjasila* (MA-PANTJAS), affiliated since 1961 with the military-dominated, anti-Communist Union of the Supporters of Indonesian Independence (IPKI).

Much more egalitarian in its basic values, and in this respect similar to the religious student organizations, was the secularly oriented Communist Concentration of Indonesian Student Movements *(Consentrasi Gerakan Mahasiswa Indonesia,* or CGMI). Its members, from urban lower-class and peasant backgrounds, initially belonged to local student groups opposing the Dutch-inherited elitist values that dominated the student community in the major university towns and cities. In November 1956, these local associations merged to form the CGMI, which later on became affiliated with the Indonesian Communist Party (PKI).

In its first year of existence, CGMI reported a membership of about 1,180 students. But the organization grew rapidly. In 1960, it claimed 7,000 members; in 1963, 17,000; and in mid-1964, about 32,000 members.[26]

CGMI was used by the PKI to spread Communist influence among the students.[27] It was also used by university graduates who had received their academic degrees in the Soviet Union, Eastern Europe, or China; in CGMI, they found support for their efforts to gain or maintain positions as instructors in the state universities. The professors who controlled appointments and promotions at these universities were largely oriented toward Western Europe and the United States, and were not at all enthusiastic about accepting graduates trained in Communist countries.[28]

Predictably, the Communist CGMI soon came into conflict with the Islamic HMI. On September 13, 1965, CGMI made the Presidium of the internationally recognized Federation of Indonesian Student Associations *(Perserikatan Perhimpunan Mahasiswa Indonesia,* or PPMI) issue a statement demanding the dissolution of HMI as a "counter-revolutionary" organization linked to the illegal *Masjumi* party and associated with the American CIA.[29]

In many university communities, CGMI worked to gain political dominance at the expense of HMI. In September 1965, under pressure from the CGMI, the Rector of the private National University in Djakarta ordered HMI to cease all its activities within the University. In Bogor, the Rector of the state Institute of Agriculture expelled four HMI activists.[30] CGMI also sent a delegation jointly with GMNI to meet with Subandrio, the First Deputy Prime Minister, to demand that the central government dissolve HMI. GERMINDO, the student association affiliated with the radical left-wing PARTINDO, expressed its full support of this demand.[31]

In the evening of September 29, 1965, D. N. Aidit, Chairman of the Central Committee of the Indonesian Communist Party, spoke at the opening of the Third Congress of CGMI, held in Djakarta and attended by the President of the Republic. Aidit tauntingly dared his student audience: "The CGMI must eliminate the HMI! Otherwise, it is better for its male members just to wear frocks!"[32] This was an open declaration of war.

The Attempted Coup of September 1965 and the Formation of KAMI

Brought under systematic attack by well-organized and aggressively militant members of the CGMI; vilified and condemned to destruction by the powerful PKI; rejected, if not undermined, by the largest Islamic political party in the country; and living under a government unable to forget that HMI had been closely associated with a party (*Masjumi*) whose leaders a few years earlier had supported a large-scale rebellion—the HMI students suddenly found their desperate situation radically changed by an unsuccessful coup d'état.

Early in the morning of Friday, October 1, 1965, two days after the Communist Party's leader had openly incited the CGMI students to eliminate HMI, a coup d'état took place. Six high army generals, including the Commander in Chief of the Army, were seized in their homes and brutally murdered by members of an insurgent group calling itself the "September 30th Movement." The group was led by a lieutenant colonel of the presidential palace guard, and received active support from some segments of the PKI, including its Chairman, D. N. Aidit.

At the time, President Sukarno was in the company of some of the insurgents at the Halim Perdana Kusuma air force base near Djakarta. Some of the participants in the short-lived uprising had received military training from Air Force instructors at the base where, that morning, the bodies of the murdered generals had been dumped in a well. The President's presence at the air force base later provoked questions, still unanswered, concerning his role in the attempted coup.

The situation in the capital city of Djakarta, however, was brought swiftly under control by Major General Suharto, who emerged from relative obscurity to become a national hero. The brutal murder of the generals and others, and the evident involvement of the Communist Party in the killings, provided the long-awaited legitimization for a determined assault against the extreme left. Those who were opposed to the Communists but had been under severe restraints—for the central government, under the personal leadership of President Sukarno, enthusiastically endorsed the Communists as an essential element in the Indonesian nation—now felt free to launch their attack openly.

The Islamic student groups, acutely conscious of the effects of ideological conflict upon their personal lives, organized themselves to destroy the centers of Communist activity. About 5,000 students participated in a rally on October 5 demanding that the President ban the PKI. Three days later, HMI students, joined by other anti-Communist groups, burned down the PKI headquarters and ransacked and burned the home of D. N. Aidit; in the following days, they also burned down the central offices of the Communist Movement of Indonesian Women (GERWANI), the People's Youth (*Pemuda Rakjat*), and the All-Indonesian Central Organization of Trade Unions (SOBSI).

Within the Indonesian student community, political activists engaged in feverish maneuvers to mobilize as many students as possible in support of their cause. In a series of meetings and a shower of declarations, petitions, and exhortations, leaders of the anti-Communist Islamic student associations such as HMI and PMII, leaders of the Roman Catholic PMKRI, and leaders of the federation of the normally nonpolitical local student organizations (SOMAL) urged the Presidium of the Federation of Indonesian Student Associations (PPMI) to convene an extraordinary congress.[33] The purpose of the congress was to condemn the Communist efforts to control the country, change the political orientation of PPMI, and eliminate elements sympathetic to the Communist cause.

Other student leaders, relying on the support they expected to get from the still powerful PNI, from PARTINDO, and even from the President himself, put up strong resistance. The leaders of

GMNI, the PNI student association, argued vehemently that the
students should refrain from any political action and await the
political solution promised earlier by the President.

At the invitation of the Minister of Higher Education and
Science, Major General Sjarif Thajeb, leaders of the various student associations (excepting CGMI, PERHIMI, and GERMINDO)
held a meeting at the Minister's home on October 25, 1965. In the
presence of Minister Thajeb, the students engaged in a heated discussion. More than the future of PPMI was at stake. The leaders
of GMNI were well aware that their own position within the student community was closely linked with the existence of PPMI
and with their political dominance of the organization. After a
vigorous exchange of arguments, Minister Thajeb proposed the
establishment of a new student organization, to be called the
Action Command of Indonesian Students (KAMI).[34] His proposal was accepted. Thus, on October 25, 1965, KAMI came into
existence and, within a few months, emerged as the politically
most powerful student organization in the country. Upon its
establishment, a Presidium was immediately installed, comprising
leaders of five major student organizations: PMII, SOMAL,
PMKRI, MAPANTJAS, and GMNI.[35] The leaders of GMNI,
however, refused to participate in an organization where they
would clearly be in a minority.

The PPMI held its Sixth Congress, which also proved to be its
last, on December 29, 1965. The federation decided to dissolve
itself because "it considered that it no longer reflected the life
and aspirations of progressive-revolutionary Indonesian students
and could no longer be justified politically, organically, or psychologically."[36]

KAMI and the Political Transformation of Indonesia

Before the attempted coup, the President had been acclaimed
as the "Great Leader of the Revolution" whom every true Indonesian had to obey if the revolution were to be successful. The
Communist Party had been depicted together with nationalism
and religion, as one of three essential pillars of the nation (NA-
SAKOM). The general public had also been indoctrinated to
regard the newly independent neighbor state of Malaysia as a
British "imperialist tool."

These ideas could not be eliminated and replaced in an orderly
manner through the proper channels of communication: the latter were still under the control of those who had promoted such

values. The President was still the most powerful leader in the nation. The military leadership, while more than favorably disposed toward anti-Communist activities, could not by itself bring about major changes in the prevailing system of values except by providing information heavily implicating the PKI in activities considered destructive to the nation.

Student demonstrations provided the ideal means to circumvent government-controlled channels of communication and rapidly bring about changes in public opinion. The ideas that Communism was public enemy number one, that Communist China was no longer a close friend but a menace to the security of the state, and that there was corruption and inefficiency in the upper levels of the national government were introduced on the streets of Djakarta. The lively student marches through the capital city were witnessed by many who had been dissatisfied in previous years but who, trying to be good Indonesians, still subscribed to the old values. In a relatively short time, most of the population in Djakarta and many other areas became acquainted with the rebellious students' new ideas, which were given prominence in the emerging anti-Communist press. Without press coverage and support, the student demonstrations would have been much less effective.

The students also received substantial support from certain sectors of the military leadership. The well-equipped Indonesian Army did not prevent the unarmed students from demonstrating in the streets, although it could easily have done so. The armed forces were not sufficiently unified to enable the military leadership to act against the legitimate authority of the land. Consequently, individual military elements agreeing with KAMI provided aid whenever they could. Transportation and loudspeakers were sometimes supplied to the students and permission to demonstrate was nearly always granted. The students could also count on some Army protection when they were attacked by armed groups—including segments of the military itself—hostile to the new anti-Communist student movement.

Leaders of some of the political parties gave the students financial aid, tactical advice, encouragement, and moral support. The powerful Islamic *Nahdatul Ulama* party did not actively support the central government, despite its formal participation in it. This abstention partly incapacitated the government in its attempts to bring the rebelling students under control. Aid given by the military tended to attract greater attention than that given by the politicians, not so much because it was more effective but because the military, easily distinguishable by their uniforms and equipment, tended to be much more conspicuous. In fact, informal meetings of politicians and students in private homes may have generated politically more significant actions than those directly affected by the aid of the military.

However, KAMI did not lack opposition. There was, first of all, the President himself. In a radio speech on October 23, 1965, two days before KAMI was born, Sukarno had threatened to order the Army to "shoot and kill" anyone continuing to demonstrate or caught destroying Communist homes and property in defiance of his twice-repeated orders to refrain from such activities.[37] He said he needed a quiet atmosphere to help him reach a political solution to the crisis. The President was eager to preserve his idea of NASAKOM.

Relations between students and the central government were aggravated by the clumsy action of Third Deputy Prime Minister Chaerul Saleh, who as Coordinating Minister of the Compartment of Development attempted to bridge the wide gap between official and black-market prices by raising the price of gasoline from 4 to 250 rupiahs per liter.[38] Most students—who rented private rooms and were constantly affected by price fluctuations—suffered severely from the increase in the price of gasoline. The bus fare to and from the university was so high that the ordinary student was barely able to attend lectures.

In its first days, KAMI faced basic organizational problems that had to be solved before effective action could begin. The number of participating member associations increased considerably after KAMI's establishment on October 25. A series of working sessions were held to consolidate the students' strength. Leaders of the following student associations took part: the Islamic HMI, PMII, SEMMI, IMM, and GERMAHII; the Catholic PMKRI and the Protestant GMKI; the radical nationalist GMNI and MAPANTJAS; the local SOMAL and GMD; the socialist *Pelopor Mahasiswa Sosialis Indonesia* (PELMASI); and the student press association, *Ikatan Pers Mahasiswa Indonesia* (IPMI). The participants reached agreement on the basic principles and program of KAMI and on the general concept of an Indonesian "national union of students," and adopted a number of resolutions.[39]

KAMI's Three Demands

On January 10, 1966, the students' accelerating action culminated in the formulation of the "Three Demands of the Indonesian

People," the *Trituntutan Rakjat* (*Tritura*): (1) to dissolve the PKI, (2) to replace the existing Cabinet, and (3) to lower the prices of goods.[40] These three demands, constituting KAMI's fighting program, were first proclaimed at a massive student rally held in front of the Faculty of Medicine of the University of Indonesia. Support from sympathetic sections of the military was expressed at the rally by Colonel Sarwo Edhie, Commander of the Army's crack commando regiment (RPKAD), who consistently sided with the new student movement throughout its evolution.

The KAMI leaders called a student boycott of classes and led their followers in a demonstration to protest the higher transportation fares. The demonstrating students marched to the State Secretariat, located near the presidential palace, where, after waiting for hours, they were received by Chaerul Saleh. The Third Deputy Prime Minister brushed the student demands aside as inconsequential. His attitude gave birth to a phrase that rapidly became popular among the residents of the capital: *"menteri goblok"* ("stupid ministers").

The students often interrupted their demonstrations to pray together in the street. Conducted according to the religious practices of the participating student, collective prayer was both a source of spiritual strength and a way of emphasizing values distinctly contrary to those of the secular extreme left.

Leaders of KAMI not only carried out "naked action." They also strengthened their ties with anti-Communist members of the Indonesian national intelligentsia and senior officers of the Army. In cooperation with the Faculty of Economics at the University of Indonesia, KAMI organized a week-long Economic and Financial Seminar, principally as a demonstration of solidarity among members of KAMI, the anti-Communist intellectuals, and the leadership of the Army, and as a public expression of the urgent need to drastically overhaul the national economy.[41] The seminar participants, who included General A. H. Nasution and Adam Malik (later, head of the national legislature and Foreign Minister, respectively), presented themselves as a counter-elite challenging the competence and legitimacy of the elite led by President Sukarno. At these and other meetings, many members of the teaching staffs of the University of Indonesia and the Bandung Institute of Technology maintained close advisory relationships with the new student movement.

On January 11, the day after the *Tritura* was announced to the public, the students took to the streets again. This time, they painted their demands wherever they found space to write and to put up posters criticizing the government for the rising cost of living. At strategic locations in Djakarta, students brought traffic to a standstill. They raised their fists, with two fingers extended, shouting "Two hundred! Two hundred!," in protest against the recent rise in public municipal bus fares, from 200 to 1,000 rupiahs. The students' cries were acclaimed by the populace. On the third day of their demonstrations against rising prices, students went on a "Long March" from the University of Indonesia to Senajan, outside Djakarta, where members of Parliament were meeting. The students urged the latter to act as genuine popular representatives serving the interests of the people.

On January 13, the municipal government yielded to the demand for lower public bus fares, announcing their reduction to the original price of 200 rupiahs. This concrete result increased the students' self-confidence and prestige. They had become effective agents of change.

But the price of gasoline remained the same. On January 14, KAMI students broke into the offices of *Pertamin,* the state oil company, in Djakarta's harbor area, and forced the director to sign a decree lowering the price of gasoline from 1,000 rupiahs to 250 rupiahs a liter. The students then actually manned a number of service stations in the capital to enforce the lower price.

The President and KAMI

On January 15, President Sukarno, acknowledging the students' influential position, invited representatives of KAMI to attend a plenary session of the cabinet at his palace in Bogor. The President intended to give the students a personal account of the nation's economic difficulties. But instead of dispatching a small delegation, students from Djakarta, Bogor, and Bandung converged en masse at the palace. Students from Djakarta arrived in a convoy of seventy trucks. The Presidential Tjakrabirawa guard, already in disrepute because of their exclusiveness and their involvement in the "September 30 Movement," fired shots in the air to prevent the students from breaking into the palace.

At the cabinet meeting, the President reported the results of a fact-finding mission he had appointed to assess the extent of the casualties that had occurred in the disturbances following the attempted coup. In the regions surveyed by the mission—East and Central Java, Bali, and North Sumatra—78,000 persons were known to have perished. To the students, he said: "I am really sad and I almost cry because you call my Ministers stupid. We have condemned the Communist way and slogans, but now you are using them yourselves and yours are even worse."[42]

Two days later, the Djakarta military command placed a ban on all demonstrations within its area of jurisdiction; it justified the step on the grounds that the demonstrations against rising prices had been exploited by both "imperialists and Communists."[43] This attempt to prohibit protests failed. The next day, in explicit defiance of the ban, the students staged another demonstration against price increases.

The President tried to use persuasion to bring the students under control. He received a delegation of KAMI leaders in his palace and told them he could well understand their demands but could not approve their methods. The student leaders assured the President they had never criticized or questioned him; they only felt that some of his assistants had made serious mistakes. Before leaving the palace, the delegation pledged full support for President Sukarno.[44]

Members of GERMINDO, the student association of a party (PARTINDO) that KAMI regarded as an ally of the Communists, did not remain quiet. On January 19, 1966, they organized a rally in front of their own headquarters, extolling President Sukarno as the "Great Leader of the Revolution." The students declared their unfaltering allegiance to the President as their only effective protector in the struggle for existence.

The President first responded to these crosscurrents of student opinion by approving proposals to halve the price of gasoline and by appointing a committee to find ways to control the price of rice and of other essential goods. But in a speech in Djakarta on January 20, he struck back at KAMI. He warned the students, who had come to the Presidential Palace expecting to hear him discuss new economic measures, that neocolonialist and imperialist powers were lending support to their demonstrations. In the presence of his cabinet ministers and a crowd of about 5,000 people, he severely criticized the students of Djakarta for staging demonstrations against his ministers and called upon the people to stand behind him in confronting his enemies.

KAMI students were in the minority at the rally. Other students took it upon themselves to defend what they regarded as the honor of the President. A wild free-for-all broke out. A number of students, including several girls, were injured before security troops arrived to quell the clash. KAMI leaders immediately issued a statement

denouncing the extreme left wing of the Indonesian National
Party (PNI), led by Ministers Ali Sastroamidjojo and Surachman,
as instigators of "terror tactics."[45]

The students suspended their protests for about two weeks to
permit the celebration of the religious holidays. On February 2,
KAMI, arguing that no improvements were yet visible in the state
of the nation, resumed its activities by boycotting classes again. Still
the "Three Demands of the People"—to dissolve the Communist
Party, replace the Cabinet, and lower prices—remained unsatisfied.
Again the students took to the streets. This time they demonstrated
in front of the Embassies of the United States and of Communist
China, criticizing both countries for interfering in the internal
affairs of the nation.[46]

Meanwhile, students opposed to KAMI sought guidance from the
President. On February 15 at his palace in Djakarta, Sukarno received delegates from GERMINDO, the *Perhimpunan Mahasiswa
Indonesia* (PMI), the *Madjelis Mahasiswa Indonesia* (MMI), and
the private Bung Karno University. The President expressed his
great concern for the revolution, which, he said, had lately showed
signs of being drawn to the right. He criticized "certain groups of
students" for falling under the influence of "neocolonialists, colonialists, and imperialists." He urged the students to join in the formation of a Sukarno Front, "not for my sake but for the sake of the
Revolution."[47]

On February 16, KAMI changed its tactics. Its members went
back to class in order to give the central government time to act to
improve the general situation.

The opponents of KAMI consolidated their strength. The central
government was purged of elements sympathetic to the demands
for a more rational, responsible, and effective government. In a
radio broadcast to the nation on February 21, the President announced the dismissal of General A. H. Nasution, Minister of the
Armed Forces, and a number of other ministers.[48] With the ouster
of General Nasution, who had been in the forefront of the campaign for major political and economic change, KAMI lost one of
its chief supporters in the government.

The surprised KAMI students reacted with a mass rally held near
the Presidential Palace in Djakarta on February 23. The students
pledged their support for the dismissed General Nasution and their
aversion for First Deputy Prime Minister Subandrio, whom they
held responsible for the sorry state of affairs in the country and
whose foreign policy they condemned as a disastrous adventure.

At the same time, about three hundred left-wing nationalistic *Gerakan Mahasiswa Nasional Indonesia* (GMNI) students tried to storm the American Embassy. They climbed over the Embassy fence, covered Embassy cars with placards, and tore down the American flag, shouting, "Go home, Yankees!" and "To hell with Green!" (U.S. Ambassador Marshall Green, in Washington at the time). The students believed the Ambassador was pulling the strings behind what they regarded as demonstrations against Sukarno. Policemen dispersed the mob by firing into the air.[49]

Death of a Student, Birth of a Martyr: The Struggle Continues

Desperately trying to prevent the politicians of the Sukarno era from consolidating their position, the students set out to forestall the installation of new ministers scheduled for February 24. Early in the morning of the 24th, hundreds of KAMI members, together with high school students organized under the banners of their own organization, the Action Command of Indonesian High School Youth *(Kesatuan Aksi Pemuda Peladjar Indonesia,* or KAPPI), blocked access to the presidential palace by flattening the tires of cars and trucks in the surrounding streets. The fourteen new ministers had to be flown by helicopter to the palace, where the President duly accepted them into his cabinet.

In the ensuing confrontation between the demonstrators and the presidential guards, two students were killed. One was a fourth-year medical student of the University of Indonesia, Arif Rachman Hakim of West Sumatra. The government denied that any fatalities had occurred.

February 25 became a day of public sympathy for the new student movement. The body of Arif Rachman was borne, in solemn funeral procession, from the University of Indonesia to a cemetery in Kebajoran, a suburb of Djakarta. Along the five-mile route, people watched respectfully and served refreshments to the members of the procession to express their sympathy. The special correspondent for *The Times* (London) reported, "I saw more than 50,000 at the cemetery and tens of thousands more turned out for hours in the blazing equatorial sun to line the route."[50] The military showed their solidarity with the students of KAMI through the presence of a platoon of troops from the Djakarta military garrison, which fired a last salute at the funeral, and with wreaths from high officers, including Lieutenant General Suharto.

The very same day, Sukarno issued a presidential decree banning all student demonstrations and ordering the dissolution of KAMI.

Over government-controlled Radio Djakarta, it was announced that henceforth no assembly of more than five persons would be allowed and that strong action would be taken against anyone disobeying the President's order. The curfew in the capital city was extended to run from 9 P.M. to 6 A.M. The militant KAMI branch in Bandung immediately declared its refusal to recognize the presidential ban.[51]

President Sukarno strongly encouraged the GMNI students in their actions against KAMI in defense of what both regarded as the honor of the nation. On February 28, Sukarno appeared at a mass rally sponsored by the youth organization of the Indonesian National Party (PNI), the *Gerakan Siswa Nasional Indonesia* (GSNI). In his speech, the President told an audience of about 15,000 militant supporters of the PNI that the Revolution was wavering, that some people were trying to force it to the right, but that "our Revolution will soon return to its original leftist rails." The President called on the GMNI students to unite and restore the Revolution to its proper course.[52]

It was here that Subandrio made an ominous speech, later to be held against him. He charged "rightists" and "neocolonialist agents" with endangering the revolution and threatening the President. These "rightists forces" should be destroyed, he exhorted; "we are finished" if they win. "If they use terror," he shouted, "we will strike back with counter-terror!"[53]

After the rally, the aroused GMNI students, their ranks swollen with members of the youth and labor organizations of the PNI, marched to the University of Indonesia, which they had come to identify as the headquarters of the "anti-revolutionary rightist" student movement. The main road leading to the University soon filled with people armed with a great variety of weapons and intent on destroying the University. The few members of KAMI who happened to be on the University grounds, not expecting such a massive attack, hurriedly requested protection. The Djakarta military garrison promptly sent troops and armored cars to break up the confrontation.

Meanwhile, members of KAMI were pasting posters on the windshields of passing cars to spread the word that KAMI would continue its struggle until the "Three Demands of the People"— "Dissolve the PKI!," "Change the Cabinet!," "Lower Commodity Prices!"—were met.

The University of Indonesia had become a small but mighty bastion. Hundreds, perhaps thousands, of students gathered on the

University grounds, ignoring the presidential ban. The police and troops stood guard, but permitted the students to enter and leave the grounds. The students rode through the streets of Djakarta in a truck convoy, and hanged in effigy Minister Subandrio.

On March 3, in a special decree signed by the acting Minister of Higher Education and Science, Johannes Leimena, the University of Indonesia was ordered closed until further notice. The University was soon occupied by troops, who did not prevent the students from continuing their activities. With the help of students from the Bandung Institute of Technology, students at the University of Indonesia were able to broadcast the "message of the people's suffering" through their clandestine Radio Ampera and tell their version of events to the public, which naturally heard nothing about KAMI's activities over the government-controlled Radio Republik Indonesia. Radio Ampera broadcast its news commentaries at 7 P.M., when the government's news program also went on the air. The students' transmitters also proved useful in sending messages to students in various parts of the city, facilitating preparations for collective action.[54]

On March 4, about 3,000 members of KAMI gathered at the University of Indonesia to establish a semi-military organization to defend their university, their activities, and themselves against the established political elite. In the presence of the mother of the first student killed, members of KAMI established the "Arif Rachman Hakim Ampera Regiment," dividing themselves into seven battalions, each named for one of the first seven military victims of the attempted coup d'état. A KAMI spokesman reported that students of forty-two institutions of higher education had expressed their readiness to join the new regiment.[55]

The following day, several thousand students left the University grounds for another street demonstration. They marched to the office of First Deputy Prime Minister Subandrio, carrying his effigy—in the form of a dog wearing spectacles, labeled "Dog of Peking," in reference to the close ties with the Chinese government the bespectacled Minister had promoted.

KAMI began to receive political support from a rapidly increasing number of groups. Newspapers published reports and editorials favorable to KAMI. In Bandung, a group of 179 university graduates, the majority of them instructors at the Bandung Institute of Technology, established their own action command, the *Kesatuan Aksi Sardjana Indonesia* (KASI), organized specifically to support

KAMI's struggle. Similar organizations, consisting primarily of instructors and graduates of the University of Indonesia, were set up in Djakarta.

On March 7, 1966, about 3,000 high school pupils belonging to the militant KAPPI attacked the offices of the Ministry of Basic Education and demanded the ouster of the allegedly Communist-sympathizing Minister Sumardjo. They swarmed into the building, triumphantly declaring it the property of KAPPI.[56]

This and other actions by the slogan-chanting youngsters of KAPPI had a great impact on the general public. KAPPI leaders were able to mobilize a seemingly limitless number of young people. Since a great many were years younger than the university students, members of KAPPI received considerably more public sympathy. Their activities, consciously conducted to support their "elder brothers," gave the latter impetus and inspiration. When the government banned the university students' activities, KAPPI staged a massive demonstration of support at the University of Indonesia, where the key KAMI members were contemplating their apparent defeat. Members of KAPPI and KAMI met and embraced one another; the meeting inspired the university students to continue the struggle despite the ban imposed upon them.[57] Support for KAMI from the adult sectors of the population came through a firm pledge of support issued by the Pantjasila Front, the organization which incorporated, at least nominally, most of the anti-Communist political organizations.

On March 10, KAMI students assaulted the Consulate General of the Chinese People's Republic in Djakarta. The students crashed the gate with a truck and swarmed in, carrying iron bars, clubs, daggers, and stones, "striking at everybody and everything in sight and thoroughly smashing up all the rooms," as the Chinese Foreign Ministry's note of protest to the Indonesian Embassy in Peking put it.[58]

President Sukarno tried to counteract KAMI's activities by inviting leaders of the major political parties to his palace for a meeting with members of the cabinet's presidium. A six-hour discussion on the political situation ensued. At the end, the participants were requested to sign a statement declaring that "they do not approve of the means used by students, pupils and youths in launching their actions which, directly or indirectly, endanger the continuation of the Indonesian Revolution and the authority of Bung Karno [President Sukarno]," and that "they fully realize the graveness of the present situation and the existence of subversive activities by neo-colonialists, colonialists and imperialists." The leaders of the nine political parties present agreed to sign the statement.[59] Outside the palace, however, some of the signatories, mindful of the political dangers involved, repudiated the statement and declared they were not at all against the students.

Outcome: The Extreme Left Defeated

March 11, 1966, turned out to be a landmark in Indonesian history. On that day, KAMI students again blocked the streets around the palace in Djakarta to forestall a meeting of the cabinet. Again the ministers were flown by helicopter to the palace, where the President, aware of sharp political differences among them, told them flatly to follow his commands or resign. Meanwhile, six battallions of the Siliwangi Division from Bandung took up positions on the outskirts of the capital. When the President was notified of this threatening deployment of troops, he immediately left the palace by helicopter for his residence in Bogor, in the company of his two chief aides, Ministers Subandrio and Chaerul Saleh.

A military delegation, sent by Lieutenant General Suharto, soon appeared at the presidential palace in Bogor. The emissaries explained to Sukarno that Suharto needed broad authority to enable him to re-establish order in the country, that without such authority much more violence would certainly occur. The President conceded and signed a decree delegating extensive authority to Suharto to "take any step considered necessary to ensure the security, calm and stability of the government machinery and the process of the Revolution and to guarantee the personal safety of the President."[60]

The decree, duly made known to the nation, was considered a major victory by all who were engaged in the campaign against the Communists. The peaceful transfer of extensive power from the President to the General had to a large extent been made possible by the general public endorsement of the new ideas introduced in Djakarta by the students of KAMI and KAPPI. Their slogans and shouting, their posters and pamphlets had prepared the capital's citizenry for important high-level political changes.

The next day, KAMI students saw the fulfillment of one of their three main demands. "The Indonesian Communist Party," read the Presidential decree, signed by Lieutenant General Suharto, "is hereby declared banned throughout the sovereign territory of the Republic of Indonesia."[61] In a victorious show of force, the Army's para-commandos (RPKAD), under the leadership of Colonel Sarwo Edhie, the students' ally, marched through the streets of Djakarta accompanied by thousands of jubilant students, and Suharto was soon showered with pledges of support. A massive rally was held in Djakarta by the Pantjasila Front, which encompassed all legal political parties, trade unions, and other mass organizations, to "express gratitude to the President for putting his trust in General Suharto."[62]

KAMI's political influence should not, however, be overestimated. The Communists' inability to maintain their political position after the September 30 coup attempt should be attributed not to KAMI itself but primarily to the physical elimination of tens of thousands of Communists by religiously oriented people, previously threatened and now enraged, in rural areas and small towns. The infamous massacres carried out by members of *Pemuda Ansor,* the youth association of the powerful Islamic *Nahdatul Ulama* party, greatly weakened the social base on which the PKI had built its political power and permitted university students in the cities and towns to attain their goals with much less difficulty than would otherwise have been the case.

In any event, the banning of the Communist Party was only one of the students' three demands. The *Tritura* also included a call for changes in the cabinet. Having already prepared a list of twenty-four ministers they wanted removed,[63] KAMI students themselves took the initiative of purging the cabinet. They kidnaped a number of ministers, took them to the University of Indonesia, where they were confined and interrogated in the office of the Dean of the Faculty of Medicine, and then handed them over to the military authorities. Early in the morning of March 18, Lieutenant General Suharto announced that Subandrio, Chaerul Saleh, and thirteen other ministers had been taken into custody "to ensure that these ministers would not fall victim to unbridled action by certain groups."[64] These radical measures paved the way for a series of changes in cabinet membership that gradually excluded all known Communist sympathizers and supporters of Sukarno's policies.

The students' actions also led to the discovery of information damaging to the position of the President himself. The supporters of the new movement toward a "New Order" in Indonesia capitalized on these disclosures and demanded that the Provisional People's Consultative Assembly (MPRS), as the appropriate legal body, should be convened in special session to discuss the position of the President. It took the supporters of the "New Order" one year to complete preparations for the removal of the President in accordance with the provisions of the 1945 Constitution, which they wanted to revive as the legal basis of the republic. On March 12, 1967, the Assembly unanimously decided to deprive Sukarno of all his official titles and to appoint Suharto as Acting President of the

Republic. Thus ended an era, colorful in style but so damaging to the general state of the nation that it had sown the seeds of its own ultimate demise.

Conclusion

Following the downfall of Sukarno, students became more conspicuously visible outside the confines of the university than at any time in their nation's history. In major cities, they could be easily identified by their distinctively colored and emblazoned jackets, each indicating its owner's university affiliation, or by their special military drill uniforms, issued by the army within the framework of its program for national defense. Whether they were actually demonstrating to press their demands or merely strolling the streets, the students' presence was ubiquitous and unmistakable.

Students were visible in other ways as well. Their slogans could be seen everywhere, their volume and tone a measure of the intensity of student sentiments. Among the many newspapers sold in the streets, the student press—especially *Harian KAMI (KAMI Daily,* or *OUR Daily)* and *Mahasiswa Indonesia (The Indonesian Student)*— gained an important place. These publications were widely read for the sharply critical thrust of their reporting and discussion of public affairs. The radio waves too were invaded by student voices, broadcast through a host of transmitters.

In recognition of their political power and achievement, the students were given legislative berths; thirteen KAMI leaders from Djakarta represented the students in Parliament. These delegates, however, did not maintain their seats without opposition, for many students regarded representation in Parliament as a misconception of the proper role of students in politics. Outside Djakarta, these legislative newcomers were criticized for representing only the students in the capital city. The fact that special material benefits were accorded to members of Parliament further weakened the image and position of these delegates in the eyes of their fellow students.

Does KAMI today constitute a unified student movement? In seeking an answer to this question, several factors must be considered. At no time has KAMI been more than a federation of autonomous student associations, despite the many attempts to forge its constituency into one unified national body. Differences in basic values and ideology persist, as do the ties with political parties that most of its member organizations maintain. KAMI therefore cannot escape close and continuing involvement in adult party politics.

There is, however, an "independent" element in the university community trying to defend the principle of political neutrality in academic life. Drawing much of its support from among the adherents of the formerly nonpolitically oriented local organizations incorporated in SOMAL, this group stresses loyalty to the Alma Mater above any political partisanship. This widening sector of campus opinion has naturally come into conflict with the party-affiliated segments of the university community.

Strains also exist between the capital and the regions. The leadership is monopolized by Djakarta, where "national political organizations and personalities are more on the minds of students and are also more available as the foci of thought, agitation and demonstration."[65] Each regional unit of KAMI has its own political complexion, reflecting current local patterns of power that need not conform to the balance of forces in the national capital. Furthermore, within each area, particularly prominent institutions tend to dominate the student political scene—e.g., the University of Indonesia in Djakarta, the Bandung Institute of Technology in Bandung, and Gadjah Mada University in Jogjakarta—a fact that can cause resentment among students on less favored campuses.

Finally, the student movement in Indonesia has fostered its own elite, an elite that has grown increasingly distinct from the student community at large. This elite is recognized as a prime beneficiary of inequalities in the distribution of gains in the developing "New Order," while most of the students see no substantial improvement in their own living conditions.

It seems clear, then, that KAMI is far from a unified student movement. Nevertheless, KAMI continues to express a vision of students as a moral force in society opposed to whatever it regards as destructive of the "New Order." Whether this ideal dominates the thinking and activities of the students or whether it is subordinated to the parochial interests of particular groups will depend very much on the presence or absence of common sentiment with respect to a particular target, whether a government considered ineffective or a military establishment considered too dominant.

NOTES

1. In Indonesian, *kami* means "we" in an exclusive sense (as opposed to "they").

2. S. L. van der Wal (ed.), *Het Onderwijsbeleid in Nederlandsch-Indië 1900–1940* (Groningen: J. P. Wolters, 1963), p. 700.

3. In 1939–40, 157 Indonesians, 83 Europeans, and 78 Chinese entered institutions of higher education in the Indies. *Ibid.*

4. In his reevaluation of colonial education in Indonesia, I. J. Brugmans argued that many Indonesians encountered great obstacles (apart from the obvious financial ones) in their endeavors to acquire advanced academic training because these Higher Schools were rooted in alien (Western) academic soil. Only after 1914 did the colonial government operate Dutch-language elementary schools for Indonesians. Of every 100 Indonesians who entered the Western educational system, only 2 survived the official seven years of elementary and 6 of secondary schooling to continue their studies at a higher level. However, Indonesians did not want the academic standards lowered, for in that event they would be unable to compete with Dutch university graduates trained in Holland. See Brugmans, "Onderwijspolitiek," in H. Baudet and I. J. Brugmans (eds.), *Balans van Beleid* (Assen: Van Gorcum, 1961), pp. 158–63.

5. In the various ethnic societies in Indonesia, where for centuries hereditary ruling classes had dominated the social, political, and cultural scene, there was little interest in the newly introduced medical profession, then largely directed toward public health. As a result, ambitious young men of lower social origins were able to enroll in the Higher Medical School, where they naturally became more concerned over existing conditions in the larger society than their fellow students of more aristocratic background in the Higher Law School.

The few Indonesian students at the Higher Technical School were not from upper-class families. Sukarno, for example, who enrolled in 1921 to become one of the first eight Indonesian students in higher education in the country, was the son of a small-town schoolteacher. See Bernhard Dahm, *Sukarnos Kampf um Indonesiens Unabhängigkeit* (Frankfurt am Main: Alfred Metzner Verlag, 1966), pp. 17, 33; and Cindy Adams, *Sukarno* (Indianapolis: Bobbs-Merrill, 1965), pp. 1–60.

6. For an account of the development of *Perhimpoenan Indonesia*, see Mohammad Hatta's courtroom defense, "Indonesie Vrij" ("Free Indonesia"), at the trial of the association in The Hague, March 1928, in his *Verspreide Geschriften* (Djakarta: C. P. J. van der Peet, 1952), pp. 209–308.

7. See Mohammad Hatta, "Het Brusselse Congres Tegen Imperialisme en Koloniale Onderdrukking en onze buitenlandse propaganda," published in *Indonesia Merdeka* in 1927 and reprinted in *Verspreide Geschriften*, pp. 175–81.

8. Not until 1957 did the association adopt an Indonesian name: the Indonesian Student Association (*Perhimpunan Mahasiswa Indonesia*, or PERHIMI). Donald E. Willmott, *The National Status of Chinese in Indonesia, 1900–1958* (Ithaca: Modern Indonesia Project, Cornell University, 1961), p. 105. In October 1965, the central government outlawed PERHIMI as a pro-Communist organization.

9. See Sardjito, "Gadjah Mada State University," *Institute of International Education News Bulletin*, XXXII (December 1956), 7–11, 43.

10. *Het Indisch Nieuws* (The Hague), II, No. 6 (February 9, 1946), 10–11.

11. Sardjito, *op. cit.*, p. 10.

12. Embassy of Indonesia in Washington, D.C., *Report on Indonesia*, IV, No. 13 (February 27, 1953), 5–6; and J. M. van der Kroef, "Higher Education in Indonesia," *Journal of Higher Education*, XXVI, No. 7 (October 1955), 377.

13. Joseph Fischer has written a number of studies of Gadjah Mada University: "The Student Population of a Southeast Asian University: An Indonesian Example," *International Journal of Comparative Sociology*, II, No. 2 (September 1961), 224–33; "The University Student in South and Southeast

Asia," *Minerva*, II, No. 1 (Autumn 1963), 39–53; "Universities and the Political Process in Southeast Asia," *Pacific Affairs*, XXXV, No. 1 (Spring 1963), 3–15; "Indonesia," in James S. Coleman (ed.), *Education and Political Development* (Princeton: Princeton University Press, 1964), pp. 92–122; and *Universities in Southeast Asia: An Essay on Comparison and Development* (Columbus: Ohio State University Press, 1964).

As for Fischer's observation that Gadjah Mada University is the country's most "national" university because "from its inception it has always attracted students from all of the major Indonesian islands" ("Student Population," p. 226), it should be stressed that this is also true of the University of Indonesia. Since the first institutions of higher education were established in the 1920's, the student body in every faculty has included students from various regions. And it is not true that Mohammad Hatta and General A. H. Nasution are South Sumatrans, "who had traditionally migrated to Java," nor that "the most Islamicized groups—the Atjehnese, orthodox Minangkabau and coastal Malay traders—have not in the past sought university education to the same degree as other Sumatrans." (*Ibid.*, p. 229.) In 1918, students from these particular ethnic groups, together with Batak students from North Sumatra, already had their own student association in Djakarta, dominated by Minangkabau students. Named *Jong Sumatra* (Young Sumatra), this organization published its own monthly journal. The religiously devout Mohammad Hatta is of Minangkabau origin, as are quite a number of other prominent Western-educated national leaders. General Nasution is a Mandailing Batak of North Sumatra.

14. See Tables 9 and 10 in Fischer, *Universities in Southeast Asia*, pp. 113–14.

15. The diversity of social backgrounds represented at Gadjah Mada reflects these attractions. Fischer ("The Student Population of a Southeast Asian University," p. 232) has given the following distribution of parental occupations in a sample of 858 University graduates (1952–60):

Father's Occupation	University Graduates Per Cent	Number
Higher government	11	(95)
Professional	4	(35)
Teachers	18	(155)
Police and military	2	(20)
Self and privately employed	16	(135)
Pension and lower government	33	(280)
Village officials	4	(35)
Artisans and skilled labor	1	(11)
Farmers	11	(92)
	100	(858)

The arrangement of the categories has been changed to conform roughly to the prevailing social hierarchy. The percentages of students whose parental occupation was classified as "higher government" or "professional," the highest ranking social categories, are much smaller for the new students who enrolled for the academic year 1960–61, being, respectively, 6 per cent and 3 per cent. See Table 1 in *ibid.*, p. 233.

16. Fischer reported that during the period 1952–60, more than half of the non-Java graduates of Gadjah Mada University did not return to their home islands. ("Indonesia," p. 119.) A survey taken by two student associations in 1960 showed that among Gadjah Mada alumni from the island of Sumatra,

about 70 per cent found employment with the central government in Java and most indicated they did not wish to return to their family homes. See Fischer, "Universities and the Political Process," p. 8.

17. This rapid expansion contradicts Fischer's pessimistic observation, made in 1963, that broadening the university base is a "decade or more away, and Indonesians as yet appear not to have taken political note of the fact that a half dozen cities and two universities virtually monopolize the only channels of highest social mobility." ("Indonesia," p. 95.) Apart from the fact that the military organization, the religious community, and the existing political party system also provide effective channels of highest social mobility, students are also studying at the following state universities (location and year of establishment in parentheses): Padjadjaran (Bandung, 1957), Diponegoro (Semarang, 1961), Djenderal Sudirman (Purwokerto, 1963), Airlangga (Surabaja, 1954), Djember (Djember, 1964), Brawidjaja (Malang, 1963), Udajana (Den Pasar, 1962), Teluk Betung (Teluk Betung, 1965), Sriwidjaja (Palembang, 1960), Andalas (Padang, 1956), Riau (Pakan Baru, 1962), Djambi (Telanaipura, 1963), North Sumatera (Medan, 1957), Sjah Kuala (Banda Atjeh, 1961), Dwikora (Pontianak, 1963), Palangkaraja (Palangkaraja, 1963), Lambung Mangkurat (Bandjarmasin, 1960), Mataram (Samarinda, 1962), Hasanuddin (Makassar, 1956), Sam Ratulangi (Manado, 1961), Pattimura (Ambon, 1962), and Tjenderawasih (Sukarnapura, 1962), and the following state institutes: Bandung Institute of Technology (1959), Surabaja Institute of Technology (1960), Bogor Institute of Agriculture (1963), and a score of Institutes of Teachers' Training and Pedagogy, namely in Djakarta, Bandung, Malang, Jogjakarta, Surabaja, Makasar, Medan, Semarang, Manado, and Padang.

18. Prominent among these institutions of higher education are the State Institutes of Islamic Religion (IAIN), the Protestant Higher Theological School, and the Roman Catholic Higher Seminary, all under the administrative jurisdiction of the Ministry of Religion. The IAIN have branches in a number of towns and are an important source of membership for the Islamic student associations.

The special academies, maintained by the various ministries and primarily located in Djakarta and Bandung, include the Police Academy, Academy of Taxation, Academy of Journalism, Academy of Textiles, Academy of Public Works and Energy, Academy of Postal Service, Telephone and Telegraph, and a number of other such service schools. T. H. Silcock reports the existence of twenty-eight such academies, established to train civil servants beyond the senior high school level, in his *Southeast Asian University: A Comparative Account of Some Developmental Problems* (Durham: Duke University Press, 1964), p. 54. In 1965, Djakarta had 35, Bogor 4, Bandung 14, Semarang 1, Magelang 1, Jogjakarta 14, Surabaja 2, Malang 3, Den Pasar 1, Makasar 3, Manado 1, Padang 1, and Palembang 1 such academies.

Cadets of the military academies tend to disassociate themselves from the "civilian" university student community, perhaps with the exception of student officers of the Military Academy of Law, whose academic training is in many respects similar to that of the Faculty of Law at the University of Indonesia.

19. According to Fischer, "with the exception of a Lutheran college in Medan, Sumatra, and an Islamic university in Jogjakarta, Java, there are no private universities in Indonesia." (*Universities in Southeast Asia*, pp. 65–66.) When Fischer wrote this in 1963, Djakarta alone had the following private universities: the National University (est. 1949), the Indonesian Christian

University (est. 1953), the Muhammadijah University, the Indonesian Islamic University, the Krisnadwipajana University, the Ibn Chaldun University, the "Seventeenth of August" University, the Res Publica University, the Tarumanegara University, the Bung Karno University, the Atma Djaja University, the Kartini University, and some others. The city of Bandung already had: the Parahiangan University (est. 1953), the Merdeka University, the Pasundan University, the Ganesha University, the Nahdatul Ulama University, and the Sawerigading University.

20. Bachtiar Rifai *et. al.* (eds.), *Perguruan Tinggi di Indonesia* (Djakarta: Departemen Perguruan Tinggi dan Ilmu Pengetahuan, 1965), p. 349. The first four figures were obtained from, respectively, the *Statistical Pocketbook of Indonesia 1963* (Djakarta: Biro Pusat Statistik, 1963), p. 31; Embassy of Indonesia, Washington, D.C., "The Year in Review," *Report on Indonesia*, XI, No. 3 (January 1962), 9; Fischer, "Indonesia," p. 92; and Silcock, *op. cit.*, p. 59. Silcock explained that only 35,000 of the approximately 100,000 students were in government universities, and more than half of these were in the University of Indonesia and Gadjah Mada. The Department of Higher Education and Science, however, reported a larger enrollment at state universities than at private institutions, i.e., 158,682 at state universities and 82,589 at private universities for the year 1965.

21. A recent study, based on a sample of eighty university students and thirty-six high school students in Djakarta, concludes that the Indonesian family is not a primary agent of student political socialization. This finding is attributed to two factors: the instability of Indonesian families, where "separations and divorces occur with great frequency," and social change. See Steven Douglas, "Political Socialization in Indonesia" (unpublished Ph.D. dissertation, University of Illinois, 1966). Douglas suggests that cleavages within the student community are not the result of political orientations acquired from the students' parents. However, since his analysis of family structure is based on patterns described by Hildred Geertz in her study of lower- and middle-class families in a small East Java town, *The Javanese Family* (Glencoe: The Free Press, 1961), and not based on patterns manifested by the families of the 116 informants themselves, the finding is inconclusive. The ethnic diversity of Indonesia reflects a variety of family structures.

Our own observations as an Indonesian youth, and later as a university instructor, suggest that the family is indeed a primary agent of political socialization if the meaning attributed to "political orientations" is not limited to national political issues, official ideological statements, and what is popularly regarded as the "business of politicians." Curiously, no one has yet studied the relationship between the political orientations of members of the various student associations and their respective parents, a study that would certainly yield more relevant information about the role of the family as an agent of political socialization.

22. At Gadjah Mada University, Fischer noted a "completely secularist attitude [among] all university officials and most students, and [a] resulting absence of religious issues as sources of conflict." ("Universities and the Political Process," p. 9) "What is strikingly obvious at Gadjah Mada," he wrote elsewhere, "is the relative unimportance of Islam among university students," adding in a footnote that "there are very few student Islamic organizations on the Gadjah Mada campus." ("Student Population," p. 231.)

Gadjah Mada University does not consist of a single campus; at the time of

Fischer's research, there were at least four different centers of the University in Jogjakarta. The center Fischer seems to refer to was then dominated by GMNI, a secular nationalist student association; religiously oriented students were dominant in other centers. The latent political conflict between the two groups has since broken out into the open.

23. J. B. Amstutz, "The Indonesian Youth Movement, 1908–1955" (unpublished Ph.D. dissertation, Tufts University, Fletcher School of Law and Diplomacy, 1958), p. 357. Amstutz reported the existence of HMI branches in Djakarta, Bogor, Bandung, Jogjakarta, Surakarta and Surabaja (Java), Palembang, Padang and Medan (Sumatra), and Makassar (Celebes).

24. There are, in addition, a number of student associations not affiliated in any way with political parties; they include the *Gerakan Mahasiswa Djakarta* (GMD), *Perhimpunan Mahasiswa Djakarta* (PMD), *Gerakan Mahasiswa Surabaja* (GMS), *Ikatan Mahasiswa Djakarta* (IMADA), *Ikatan Mahasiswa Bandung* (IMABA), and *Musjawarah Mahasiswa Bogor* (MMB). With the rise of politically oriented mass student associations, many of these elitist student groups banded together to form their own federation, the Joint Secretariat of Local Student Associations (*Sekretariat Bersama Organisasi Mahasiswa Lokal*, or SOMAL).

25. More than other students, GMNI members manifest a cultural pattern known as *bapakism*. Douglas has described the term as symbolizing "the belief of Indonesians that proper family relationships are based on obedience to the father (*bapak*) and that relationships are carried over into behavior within social and political organizations." Analyzing the pattern in psychoanalytic terms, he noted "a striking parallel in Indonesia between authority relationships in political organizations and families." (See Douglas, *op. cit.*, pp. 39–44, 200.) Politicians like Sukarno consciously tried to transfer the father-son relationship to politics, envisioning the Indonesian people as one large family. But the various ethnic cultural patterns in Indonesia prescribe much more differentiated political roles. The attempt by nationalist leaders to project the father-son relationship into politics is to some degree, in fact, aimed at counteracting the influence on political style of the elaborate social hierarchy of the Javanese and other culturally feudal ethnic groups. The individualistic Battaks, on the other hand, mindful of the fact that none is willing to be subordinated to others, often call each other *ketua* (chairman).

26. See Donald Hindley, *The Communist Party of Indonesia* (Berkeley: University of California Press, 1964), pp. 196–97, and the report of the Antara News Agency (Djakarta), April 7, 1964. The rapid growth in CGMI membership reflects a phenomenon in developing countries that S. M. Lipset has noted: an increase in the proportion of university students coming from lower middle-class, village, and even peasant families. "Students from these backgrounds tend to be less sophisticated, less at ease in the languages of academic discourse. Despite what seems to be their great seriousness in the pursuit of a 'career' through attendance at university, they have more difficulties in settling down. Their pecuniary as well as cultural poverty places them under a great strain." See his "University Students and Politics in Underdeveloped Countries," *Minerva*, III, No. 1 (Autumn 1964), 47.

27. In his study, Douglas reported that a rather large proportion of his sample (34 per cent) preferred to read *Warta Bhakti, Bintang Timur*, and *Harian Rakjat*, newspapers of the extreme left. When asked to name the "best" economic system, 31 per cent mentioned mainland China, 18 per cent Japan,

9 per cent the Soviet Union, and none the United States. As to the "best" political system, 33 per cent were in favor of either Communist China or the Soviet Union, and only 1 per cent favored the United States. (Douglas, *op. cit.*, pp. 131, 184. His survey was conducted well before the events of October 1965.)

28. Douglas has written: "At the university level the political prejudices of teachers lean in the . . . 'conservative' direction. . . . Indonesian university professors tend to identify with the modern 'world culture,' which in their minds is associated with the United States and Western Europe." Many of these teachers had studied in the United States. "From 1956 through 1964 the Faculties of Medicine, Economics, and Agriculture at the University of Indonesia and the Bandung Institute of Technology . . . sent a total number of more than 750 staff members to the United States for training under AID and Ford Foundation programs." (Douglas, *op. cit.*, pp. 104–5.) For details about Indonesian-American interuniversity relations, see Bruce L. Smith, *Indonesian-American Cooperation in Higher Education* (East Lansing: Michigan State University, 1960).

29. *Suluh Indonesia* (Djakarta), September 13, 1965.

30. *Ibid.*, September 18, 1965.

31. *Ibid.*, September 20, 1965.

32. *Warta Bhakti* (Djakarta), September 30, 1965.

33. Rohali Sani, "Satu tahun usia K.A.M.I.: Perdjuangan Orde Baru belum selesai," *Mahasiswa Indonesia* (West Java ed.), No. 20 (Fifth Week, October 1966), p. 5. See also Djoni Sunarga Hardja Sumantri, "KAMI dilahirkan untuk menang," *Harian KAMI* (Djakarta), I, No. 99 (October 25, 1966), 2–3.

34. Major General Thajeb, a former Rector of the University of Indonesia, explained that he took the initiative in proposing the establishment of a unified-action command because he was greatly disturbed when he saw each student organization engaged in its own campaign against the Communists. A collective campaign under a unified leadership would be more effective. For the Minister's motivation, see *Harian KAMI*, I, No. 99 (October 25, 1966), 1, 3.

35. See Sani, *op. cit.* According to D. S. Hardja Sumantri, HMI, in a meeting with leaders of some other student associations held on October 24 to prepare for the meeting with Minister Thajeb, proposed the establishment of a new national student federation to replace the existing PPMI. Hardja Sumantri mentioned the participation of the following student associations in the meeting of October 25 at the Minister's house: HMI, GMNI, GMKI, PMKRI, PMII, SOMAL, SEMMI, MAPANTJAS, PELMASI, IMM, and GMD. (See Hardja Sumantri, *op. cit.*, p. 3.) It is rather curious that student groups as large as HMI and GMKI did not become members of KAMI's first Presidium.

36. *Youth and Freedom*, VII, No. 6 (1965), 22.

37. *The New York Times*, October 24, 1965.

38. Consulate General of Indonesia in New York, *News & Views*, No. 80 (November 30, 1965), 5.

39. *Angkatan Bersendjata* (Djakarta), December 17, 1965.

40. See especially the commemorative issue of *Harian KAMI*, January 10, 1967; *Sinar Harapan*, January 11, 1966; and *Api Pantjasila* (Djakarta), January 11, 1966.

41. For the papers presented to the seminar, see Kesatuan Aksi Mahasiswa Indonesia, Fakultas Ekonomi, Universitas Indonesia, *The Leader, The Man and The Gun: Seminar Ekonomi K.A.M.I., Djakarta, 10 s/d 20 Djanuari 1966*

(Djakarta: Jajasan Badan Penerbit, Fakultas Ekonomi, Universitas Indonesia, 1966).

42. *The New York Times,* January 16, 1966. Also see *News & Views,* No. 94 (January 19, 1966), pp. 1–2.

43. *Ibid.,* p. 6. See also *The Times* (London), January 18, 1966.

44. *News & Views,* No. 95 (January 20, 1966), p. 1.

45. *The New York Times,* January 22, 1966.

46. *Sinar Harapan* (Djakarta), October 26, 1966.

47. *News & Views,* No. 106 (February 18, 1966), p. 1.

48. *The New York Times, New York Herald Tribune, Boston Globe,* February 22, 1966; *The New York Times,* February 23, 1966.

49. *The Times* (London), *The New York Times,* February 24, 1966.

50. *The Times* (London), February 28, 1966. For details about Hakim's death, see the articles by Azwirman Noersal, Taufig Ismáil, Hakim Sarimuda, and Ismed Hadad in *Harian KAMI,* February 25, 1967.

51. Presidential Decree No. 041/KOGAM/66. See Rohali Sani, *op. cit.; Sinar Harapan,* October 26, 1966; *Berita Yudha* (Djakarta), October 27, 1966. The ban did not affect the actual existence of KAMI.

52. *Sinar Harapan,* February 28, 1966. See also *The New York Times* and *The Times* (London), March 1, 1966.

53. *G-30-S Dihadapan Mahmillub 3 Di Djakarta (Perkara Dr. Subandrio)* (Djakarta: Pusat Pendidikan Kehakiman A.D. 1967), pp. 286–292.

54. See *Harian KAMI,* January 10, 1967. The student radio station became quite popular, broadcasting information not released by any government agency. Its modern musical entertainment also attracted many listeners. By 1967, twenty student transmitters were reported in operation in Djakarta and fifty more in Bandung. Ismed Hadad, head of KAMI's central Information Bureau, suggested organizing the entire network into a National Radio of Indonesian Students, with each KAMI branch operating at least one station. See *Harian KAMI,* I, No. 112 (November 10, 1966), 2.

55. "Student Action in Indonesia," *Minerva,* IV, No. 3 (Spring 1966), 440. See also *Kompas,* May 7, 1966. KAMI also had an "Aris Margono Ampera Regiment" in Jogjakarta. This activity is not surprising. In the major cities for several years before the aborted coup of September 30, 1965, the Army had given paramilitary training to university students in anticipation of a Communist attempt to seize the government. Paramilitary training imposed in the framework of the campaigns to free West Irian (ex-Dutch New Guinea) and destroy Malaysia also served the students well. Prior association with soldiers and officers facilitated not only student paramilitary activity per se but political communication between the students and the military as well.

56. *The Times* (London), March 8, 1966.

57. Information concerning this meeting was kindly given by Ali Wardhana, Senior Lecturer at the Faculty of Economics of the University of Indonesia and economic assistant to General Suharto, and A. D. Siregar, Chairman of the Indonesian Federation of Muslim Trade Unions, who happened to witness the event.

58. *Peking Review,* IX, No. 12 (March 18, 1966), 5. In May 1966, KAMI moved its headquarters into the building, conveniently located near the University of Indonesia.

59. *Sinar Harapan*, March 11, 1966. Signing the statement were representatives of the PNI, PARTINDO, *Partai Katholik*, IPKI, *Nahdatul Ulama*, PSII, *Muhammadijah*, PERTI, and PARKINDO (the Indonesian Christian Party).

60. *Sinar Harapan*, March 12, 1960.

61. *Ibid.* See also *The New York Times*, March 13, 1966.

62. *Sinar Harapan*, March 15, 1966. See also *The New York Times*, March 16, 1966.

63. *Api Pantjasila*, March 17, 1966. See also *The Times* (London), March 15, 1966; and *Christian Science Monitor*, March 15 and 17, 1966.

64. *Sinar Harapan*, March 18, 1966. See also *The New York Times*, March 20, 1966.

65. Lipset, *op. cit.*, p. 41. KAMI's geographical expansion seems to have paralleled that of the Japanese *Zengakuren* student movement, where

leadership is taken by students of the leading universities . . . and [where] most participants belong to them. At the same time students in the minor leagues may feel that they must follow the example set by those in the major leagues in order to assure themselves that they are university students too. Thus the same type of movement spreads easily all over the country, and federation is readily accomplished under the leadership of the students in leading universities.

M. Shimbori, "Zengakuren: A Japanese Case Study of a Student Political Movement," *Sociology of Education*, XXXVII, No. 2 (1964), 232; cited by Lipset, *loc. cit.*

7. SOUTH VIET-NAM

DAVID MARR

To write with confidence about almost any aspect of contemporary South Viet-Nam is virtually an act of faith. Fast-moving developments, within and outside the country, often leave the patient researcher grasping sheaves of relatively irrelevant data. Because of the nature of the conflict and, perhaps more important, the revolution in mass media technology, emotions have been aroused around the world to a degree that greatly limits, if it does not preclude, serious scholarship. Concerned citizens are bombarded daily with estimates, summaries, interviews, photographs, predictions, and so on. The result, more often than not, is emotional and intellectual chaos.

In all of this, perhaps the political activities and attitudes of South Viet-Nam's university and high school students have been the least understood. This is not simply the result of insensitive reporting of an essentially alien situation. Rather, one could argue that among all the shifts of power, all the collapsing institutional façades, students and student political movements are the most fluid, the least subject to institutionalization—and thus the least susceptible to extended analysis at any point in time. Since mid-

This chapter is the product of two research trips to South Viet-Nam, the first in 1965 (for an M.A. thesis in Asian studies at the University of California, Berkeley) and the second in 1967. I would particularly like to thank the many Vietnamese students who willingly discussed all aspects of the situation and passed on many valuable written sources. Since social science research facilities are lacking in Viet-Nam, or at best sadly underdeveloped, as a result of prolonged war and colonial neglect, I have also been dependent on a wide range of teachers and officials, both Vietnamese and foreign. None are responsible for the opinions expressed here, but all deserve a note of appreciation for their kind introductions, personal notes, impressions, and unfailing politeness.

1963, South Viet-Nam's students have been an integral part of a seemingly permanent social and political crisis. This chapter is an attempt to analyze their position within that crisis environment.[1]

Some foreign observers, after comparing the physical perils of rural existence in Viet-Nam today with the relative security of urban living, have concluded that urban Vietnamese are somewhat detached from the surrounding tragedy, living in "oases" apart from the dismal, brutal impact of war. While this may still be true of some among the older generation, extensive interviewing of students and regular reading of student publications indicate that this is not a common posture among the young. Whereas by almost any measure South Viet-Nam may be considered an "underdeveloped" country, it does not follow that her political culture is equally underdeveloped. War and prolonged revolution have sensitized large segments of the population to the meaning of politics in its most basic form: the art of survival amid raw conflict. Urban Vietnamese, including students, have had to learn this art, picking their way through a kaleidoscopic range of possible associations, identities, and purposes.

The overriding impression, to an outsider at least, is one of many young, sensitive individuals caught up in, and brooding over, their country's predicament. Heirs to both Confucian and French intellectual traditions, politically alert students consider themselves members of the elite, bearing a distinct outlook and a heavy responsibility to serve as critics, judges and, it is hoped, as a spiritual vanguard of their troubled society. As we shall observe, one of youth's frustrations has been the gap between its self-conceived role on the one hand and, on the other, both its own capabilities and the limited role that other groups have been willing to allow it—especially in time of war.

In common with young intellectuals throughout much of the world today, South Viet-Nam's university and high school students are not at all satisfied with the apparent social values and political performance of their elders. Institutions such as the family, church, and school, through which young men and women have had to pass, have been gravely undermined by decades of turmoil and are no longer inculcating cultural norms suitable to contemporary conditions. Students often express the opinion that "youth" stands at the pivotal point of contemporary national thought and activity, unsullied by the corrupting influences of French colonial rule or by participation in the oppressive regime of Ngo Dinh Diem. Whether this is true or not, it gives some indication of the deep student dissatisfaction with the record of those who have preceded them. To the dismay of parents, teachers, and military officers, youth no longer always conducts itself with its seniors' status and sensitivities in mind.[2]

As students have developed outlooks broadly different from those of their parents and older relatives, they have naturally sought "outside" social and political affiliations superseding the traditional focus on relationships within the family hierarchy. But external relations in Vietnamese society are still largely fluid in nature, based on direct, quick benefits to the individuals concerned, and not conducive to broader, more stable patterns. Qualitatively speaking, this pursuit of truly lasting bonds beyond the family has so far met with little success, causing further personal insecurity and disorientation. The important exceptions to this rule—i.e., the minority who *have* found new ideological or religious commitment and visionary purpose—will bear examining in some detail below.

In this admittedly impressionistic account of student political attitudes and activities, we shall first sketch out the general student environment, emphasizing the contemporary university generation. We shall then move to a brief discussion of student political activities in recent years, particularly since 1963. Finally, we shall try to portray student political relationships and attitudes vis-à-vis certain crucial nonstudent segments of South Viet-Nam's power structure, including "orthodox political elements," the National Liberation Front (NLF), religious organizations, the military-bureaucratic apparatus, and the American military-civilian establishment in South Viet-Nam.

Education and the War

To narrow our focus for a moment: what is the position of Vietnamese students today in their immediate university and high school surroundings? As can well be imagined, the atmosphere of instability, the sense of shock over the killing or maiming of one's relatives and friends in continual warfare, the personal insecurity of clouded futures and uncertain occupations, schooling unsuited to the times, difficult living conditions, rising prices—all this has had a devastating effect on scholastic habits and standards. Some students are still spurred on by personal ambition or family pressure to secure diplomas for the sake of social prestige and potential economic rewards, but with most graduates being inducted into the armed services—perhaps "for the duration"—even these traditional stimuli have lost much of their meaning.

Those students who still try to take their education seriously are frustrated by antiquated curricula and a teaching staff that mostly resists radical change.[3] Some students would like to conduct serious investigations of the political, social, and economic problems facing contemporary Viet-Nam, but professors tend to cling to their tried-and-true formulas of formal lectures and required readings, seldom asking for imaginative research or even seminar papers. The paucity of primary material in the libraries is another obstacle to scholarship. Students also complain bitterly that the content of their courses has changed very little in the past decade, a time when Viet-Nam has been undergoing what may well be its greatest crisis in centuries. Almost all students oppose continued reliance on old French educational procedures, some of which are no longer in use even in France. Use of the French language in university textbooks and lectures is galling to young nationalists, since it forces them to begin studying French at an early age, just as their fathers did before them. No one has been able to initiate the massive translation program that might break this cycle. As a result of the American presence and the infusion of American culture, English is being used more each year. However, the mere substitution of English for French in the schools is hardly an acceptable solution for young intellectuals interested in their own unique national culture. Sustained political pressure in 1966 and 1967 finally induced the Ministry of Education to at least plan for the future compulsory use of the Vietnamese language in all university classes, but no one has explained how this is going to affect the many incoming American teachers, not to mention the remaining Europeans.

At present (1967) there are five universities in South Viet-Nam. Most important by virtue of size, location, and age is the University of Saigon, with a student enrollment of 24,102 in 1966.[4] The University of Hue, while much smaller (3,001), has often rivaled Saigon in political significance. In addition, there are the Universities of Dalat (1,303), Van Hanh (1,226), and the infant campus at Can Tho (948), opened in August 1966.[5] It is difficult to generalize about the position of students within such disparate educational environments. For example, like universities located in large cities in many other countries, the University of Saigon has no unified campus and no large concentrations of students living in dormitories or hostels. The majority live with their families, or with relatives or friends of the family, or rent apartments in various parts of Saigon and Cholon. With this diffuse pattern of living, the social and political importance of the five existing student hostels is out of all proportion to the small total number of students (500–600) residing in them.

In striking contrast is the University of Dalat, whose single campus is located outside of town in pleasant surroundings. Most Dalat students are away from their families for the first time. Newspapers arrive erratically, and road connections with Saigon are often interdicted. All this probably helps to account for the higher frequency of student interaction and the tightly knit associations found at Dalat. No figures are available, but it appears that Dalat has a higher percentage of students from upper-class families than do the other universities. Even this generalization may have to be modified, however, since the student body has quadrupled in three years and the University is changing from a small, cliquish institution, dominated by Catholic priests and the Ngo family, to a major campus dependent on state subsidies and obeying the government's academic statutes.

Somewhere in between these extremes lies the University of Hue. It follows a semiurban, scattered residential pattern, yet students tend to draw together tightly in opposition to outside forces. The little city of Hue, formerly the royal capital, still performs its traditional function as an educational and intellectual magnet for students, writers, artists, and monks from all central Viet-Nam. With the upsurge of Buddhist spiritual and organizational efforts, Hue has at times rivaled in political significance the cosmopolitan but disoriented urban complex of Saigon-Cholon. Hue's intensely nationalistic outlook, perhaps intertwined with simple provincialism and residual xenophobia, provides university and high school students with a hypersensitive political environment. Because this atmosphere tends to distract students (and some teachers) from the prosaic task of training for elite careers, conflicts with government-appointed administrators have been common and bitter. In 1966, the U.S. government became a direct party to the conflict by suddenly withdrawing all supplies and services of personnel previously granted Hue University—apparently in retaliation for the burning of the USIS Library during the Buddhist-led struggle against the Ky regime.

Van Hanh University was founded in Saigon in early 1964 on the initiative of young Buddhist leaders active in the anti-Diem movement. Created amid intense political and intellectual turmoil, Van Hanh still shows the strengths and weaknesses of that beginning. Yawning gaps remain in the teaching staff and the academic program; students apparently attend either out of faith in Van Hanh's future or because they cannot get into one of the older universities. Nevertheless, there is a certain zeal among students and faculty, a willingness to experiment, that is lacking elsewhere. Van Hanh remains administratively and financially subordinate to the Unified Buddhist Church of Viet-Nam (*Vien Hoa Dao*), and energetic young monks can be found in almost every school activity, but this has not kept students and some teachers from advancing independent political ideas.[6]

What can be said of Vietnamese teacher-student relationships in general? For an American observer, accustomed to at least occasional verbal interplay between student and teacher, the absence of such interaction in foreign universities is disconcerting. In Viet-Nam, we may place the historical blame for such a lack of communication on the French, for in precolonial times intensely personal, lasting relationships between Confucian master and loyal pupil were extremely common. Today, however, student dissatisfaction with older, stubbornly Francophile instructors is as much the result of the generation gap as it is of the colonial heritage. Particularly at the University of Saigon, where many teachers hold outside jobs and the student-faculty ratio is very high, the staff has little influence on student behavior. Yet there are students who do interact closely with some of the younger, more progressive teachers; the communications barrier can be circumvented. Such contacts have been even more evident at the University of Hue, while at Van Hanh teacher-student interplay and conviviality are the rule rather than the exception.

Although high school students are not of primary interest to us in the present chapter, it should at least be noted that their situation is quite different from that of the university students. Largely because of the demanding course of study in the high schools and the preoccupation with passing the difficult *baccalauréat* examinations, the number of consistently concerned and activist students at this level is much lower than in the universities. Nevertheless, masses of high school students do become politically engaged in moments of major conflict.

During 1965 and 1966, the military authorities, the police, and the Ministry of Education regained enough self-confidence to try to quell student opposition through the selective drafting of "troublemakers" and, in some cases, their outright imprisonment. Academic regulations have been tightened. No longer can students "hang around" in school for years, finishing at their own discretion. The authorities, of course, have argued that increasing pressure on students to work hard and to advance will substantially improve academic standards. But the fact that many teachers and school administrators have also been drafted, combined with the hyperpolitical atmosphere of continuing war and revolution, makes any academic improvement ephemeral. Each student body and university environment in Viet-Nam, being part of a more general social fragmentation and demoralization, and suffering from a musical-chairs routine of appointments and removals, will hardly see major improvements in academic standards until the larger problem of cleavage and conflict is resolved.

Student Politics Before and After Diem

We are too close to events in Viet-Nam to claim any sort of historical objectivity. Also, much of the basic data on student political activities remains within closed files or in the minds of still silent participants. What follows is merely an attempt to provide some perspective on the present situation, based largely on interviews with student activists and a reading of what little has been published on the subject.

Politics has been a part of modern higher education in Viet-Nam since the French initially established a School of Medicine in 1902. The School of Medicine was one of the earliest and best ways for young Vietnamese to penetrate French restrictions on modern educational advancement, perhaps even to the level of postgraduate training in Paris. Not surprisingly, the School produced a high proportion of doctors involved in politics. In 1907, in an attempt to offset the attractions of study abroad, particularly in Japan, the French granted a group of progressive scholar-gentry permission to set up the *Dong Kinh Nghia Thuc,* a tuition-free higher institution that taught and promoted broad socio-economic and cultural reform for almost one year before it was closed down and its leading teachers jailed as enemies of French colonial rule.[7] Governor General Albert Sarraut (1911–14 and 1917–19) worked seriously to develop a University of Indochina, but in 1925–26, growing nationalist sentiment again led to a confrontation. Many students were expelled, background investigations were made more thorough to keep out "undesirable" applicants, and the curriculum was once again purged of subversive elements. Largely as a result of such controls, the university campus (in Hanoi) remained outside the mainstream of Vietnamese political developments during the late 1930's and 1940's, although covert activity continued and many students gave up their studies for activist roles in the countryside.[8]

The 1954 Geneva settlement left the fledgling government in South Viet-Nam a host of problems, one of them the integration of refugee professors and students from the North into what had previously been only a secondary campus in Saigon—renamed the "National University of Viet-Nam." Friction soon developed between the leaders of the Saigon Student Union (SSU), who were predominantly southerners, and the refugee students.[9] The issue that sparked student debates, demonstrations, and occasional fighting was, broadly speaking, the attitude toward Communism. The intensely anti-Communist refugees carried the attack to the ideologically eclectic, more cosmopolitan southerners. While engaged in this dispute, the students enjoyed relative freedom of speech and action. They organized a National Student Union (*Tong-Hoi Sinh-Vien Quoc Gia*) with accredited membership in the International Student Conference (ISC). Organizations also grew up in the high schools, involving students and teachers in joint activities.[10]

But in the 1958–60 period the Diem regime began to carve out for itself a major role in youth and student affairs, first by infiltrating organizations with police informers and then by imposing government supervision of student elections at the universities. A Directorate of Youth and Sports organized a Republican Youth group (*Thanh Nien Cong Hoa*) as a source of mass political support for the regime. By 1960, the now heavily infiltrated student unions had little genuine support. Government repression increased in reaction to increasing political dissent and proto-NLF activism.[11] The decision of the Ninth ISC that same year to withdraw recognition from the National Student Union was based on doubts about its representative nature.[12]

By 1961, the expression of anti-Diem attitudes in periodicals or public meetings had become impossible. High school student organizations soon disintegrated or were absorbed into the Republican Youth. The barriers of distrust between students and government rose higher and higher. Student organizations could not be overtly maintained outside the approved spectrum of government interests, a fact that led some of the more embittered students to join one of several rapidly expanding NLF youth affiliates. Those who chose to make their way upward within the framework of the Diem regime soon lost influence and prestige with their peers, for they had become minor functionaries in the system rather than representatives of student aspirations and attitudes. Under Diem, student leaders could openly do little more, as one student put it, "than compete with nuns in their visits to homes for the aged, hospitals, and orphanages."[13] The regime's monopoly on all important political and social endeavors was unrelenting.

The basic elements of the crisis in 1963 that ended in the overthrow of President Diem are fairly well known in the West. The role of Buddhist students in these events is common knowledge.[14] Less well known is the degree to which secularly oriented urban youth and students were also drawn into the struggle, usually in loose cooperation with Buddhist youths. The secular students became active as individuals or in small groups, working covertly, initially with no thought of organizing en masse. Their organizational techniques were rudimentary; most had never before participated in covert planning, intelligence gathering, open agitation, and so on. Many were caught and jailed because of their ineptitude. But the remainder learned quickly. By October 1963, the students had learned how to shake off pursuing plainclothesmen, how to use girls for decoys and liaison, and how to best move packets of antigovernment leaflets from one place to another. By this time many Catholic students were disgusted with the regime and showed their sympathy with Diem's student opponents, for example, by allowing the latter to enter church buildings secretly to use mimeograph machines. With secret police roaming everywhere, Catholic church buildings were certainly among the least dangerous places to run off antigovernment broadsides.

The success of the military coup d'état of November 1–2, 1963, released deep political and psychological tensions that had been building up since at least 1960. In the days immediately following the coup, crowds ran freely in the streets, destroying anything symbolizing the Ngo family's rule—statues, pictures, stores, the inside of the National Palace and the National Assembly building, Vietnamese Special Forces installations—and fraternizing with the victorious soldiers and marines. Non-Communist political prisoners were released and paraded around Saigon, among them hundreds of youths jailed in the preceding months of antigovernment activism. The coup leaders jailed or placed under house arrest most high-level civilian supporters of the old regime. What to do with close military supporters of the Ngo family was a more difficult problem, one that would plague succeeding juntas in South Viet-Nam for more than a year. Pressure on the military to purge their ranks of members of Diem's *Can Lao* party came from Buddhist leaders, newly freed politicians, returning émigré politicians, and from most youth and student groups as well.

The new political climate had a euphoric effect on those youth and students sensitive to their environment and eager to overcome Viet-Nam's vast problems. One student later wrote:

> Unsatisfied aspirations overflowed like flood water. Youth were found everywhere demanding opportunities and means from their elders to benefit the people and country. We still remember the whole week of seminars in Thong Nhat Theater, one month after November 1, 1963; dozens of projects and plans for youth activities were sent to the Military Revolutionary Council. But the elders in the government at that time were so embarrassed and overcome that they could do nothing and therefore lost a very *precious* opportunity.[15]

The coup leaders' political inexperience—and factionalism within the Military Revolutionary Council (MRC)—slowed their response to these and other suggestions. They were too cautious and thus failed to capitalize on the broad support they enjoyed in the first months following the overthrow of Diem.

In any event, the euphoria did not last. Politically observant students were quick to sense the weaknesses within the MRC and quickly disillusioned over the prospects for radical change. Many turned to pessimism and a search for ways to live with, not to change, the status quo. The proud word revolution, so often on the lips of students just after the coup, was less and less frequently applied to the military regime in serious conversation. Once again, revolution became a term signifying future aspirations rather than present realities.

The first new student group to organize and make itself felt in Saigon after the November coup was the General Assembly of Student Delegates (*Hoi-Dong Chu-Tich Sinh-Vien Saigon*). Each faculty of the University of Saigon and other higher institutions sent from four to ten representatives to the Assembly and an elected Executive Committee (*Ban Chap Hanh*) soon became the nerve center of student political activism. The formula of representation by which each faculty sent delegates to the Assembly definitely favored the small faculties over the large ones. Disputes over this question brought the collapse of the Assembly and its Executive Committee in March 1964, but they were replaced not long afterward by the Saigon Student Union (*Tong-Hoi Sinh-Vien Saigon*), or SSU, in a somewhat uneasy organizational compromise. The Executive Committee of the new SSU was elected directly by the student body, not through faculty delegates, although several additional Committee members were appointed by the winning slate of candidates. To counterbalance the executive, the SSU Constitution provided for a Student Council (*Hoi-Dong Sinh-Vien*) charged with "guarding the principles of the Constitution" and composed of the student presidents of the fifteen faculties and advanced schools. Before long, the Student Council had elected five of its politically more active members to work as a Leading Council, thus setting the stage for a running battle between two groups of highly motivated activist leaders: the Leading Council and the Executive Committee.

Meanwhile, national political developments continued to hold the students' interest. In the late spring and summer of 1964, the SSU headquarters on Duy Tan Street in Saigon resembled a political campaign center. Members hurried in and out on assigned missions, reporters hovered about, important adult political figures awaited audiences with top student leaders, duplicating machines clattered out leaflets, and mass meetings jammed the main hall, while the sounds of high-pitched voices resounded through an imperfect public address system. A few students and intellectuals had mourned the loss of power on January 30, 1964, of Major General Duong Van Minh and his followers to Major General Nguyen Khanh, but they did not regret the simultaneous departure of Premier (former Vice President) Nguyen Ngoc Tho and his "technocrat cabinet." At first, the dynamic General Khanh appeared determined to impose tight controls over his colleagues in the MRC. He also developed a tentative alliance with elements of the *Dai Viet* party, a bourgeois nationalist group founded during World War II. By early April, however, the *Dai Viet* alliance was already on the rocks, one of its leaders (Ha Thuc Ky) having resigned under fire as Minister of Interior and another (Deputy Prime Minister Nguyen Ton Hoan) occupying an increasingly circumscribed position. From then on, General Khanh relied mostly on his military cronies, ruling by simple fiat. Khanh's dissolution of the Council of Notables—a civilian advisory body selected during General Minh's short tenure—and his closing of thirteen newspapers solidified intellectual discontent. The young SSU leaders were closely involved in the oppositionist moves leading to the political crisis of August-September 1964.

During the late summer of 1964, however, increasing tensions between the Executive Committee and the Leading Council threatened student unity in Saigon, always a fragile thing at best. The various groups began printing vituperative statements against one another in their weekly newspapers. Differences were exacerbated by outside political groups, including older party leaders, government officials, and religious organizations. Several prominent student leaders became the butt of much bitter comment because of apparent improvements in their material status. The SSU was fast losing its already tenuous position as a focus for specifically student interests. Buddhist leaders could induce several thousand students to demonstrate on short order. Catholic priests did likewise. Political parties controlled smaller blocs of students, and even supporters of General Khanh were able to persuade some students to wreck the SSU headquarters in August 1964. By October, the SSU was no longer a primary spokesman for Saigon student interests; by November, the Union was so fragmented that a conference called to solve the students' differences ended in the dissolution of both the Executive Committee and the Leading Council. For all practical purposes, the SSU was temporarily out of the political picture.

In Hue, organizational activity following the coup against Diem proceeded with more regularity and fewer internal contradictions, largely as a result of the dominant new influence of the Buddhist hierarchy. The army and the civil bureaucracy were under constant pressure to purge all *Can Lao* members. Thich (The Venerable) Tri Quang, easily the most powerful Buddhist leader in central Viet-Nam, had criticized Khanh's regime as early as February 1964, and his views were shared by most of the youth and student leadership in Hue. Colonel Nguyen Chanh Thi, Commanding Officer of the First Division (later, Major General in charge of I Corps), who had no love for General Khanh, was just as interested as the Buddhists in purging *Can Lao* members and knew he would have to develop good relations with Buddhist leaders to solidify his power base in central Viet-Nam. Hoang Van Giau, head of the Hue Student Union (HSU) at the time, enjoyed a close intellectual relationship with Thich Tri Quang and with other young monks. Students, young teachers, and a few monks together published a weekly journal, *Lap Truong* (*Viewpoint*), criticizing Khanh and calling for a determined, radical implementation of the "Revolution." *Lap Truong's* position also included an element of anti-Americanism and vague support for a policy of nonalignment in foreign affairs.

Soon a loose movement, also called *Lap Truong*, spread down the central Vietnamese coast. By early August 1964, Youth and Student Salvation Committees (*Uy Ban Sinh-Vien Thanh-Nien Hoc-Sinh Cuu Quoc*) had been formed in Hue, Da-Nang, Quang-

Tri, and a few other provincial towns; they publicly declared their intention to bring down General Khanh and his followers. Together with similar events in Saigon, demonstrations against Khanh's "dictatorship and personalism" broke out at various points in central Viet-Nam in late August. As a result, the Military Revolutionary Council was disbanded and Khanh began his slide into political oblivion.

Youth and student activities with regard to the regime of Tran Van Huong, who followed Khanh as Premier, were less clear-cut, partly because of the previously described student disunity in Saigon, but also because Huong provided much less of a target than Khanh. First of all, he was a civilian premier—one of the prime demands of the anti-Khanh demonstrators. Second, he showed sincerity and honesty in trying to reimpose discipline within the bureaucracy without a solid power base of his own to operate from. Finally, he was a recognized intellectual and as such enjoyed initial sympathy from his peers in Saigon. Although he belonged to no organized religion and emphasized many times that religious affiliation would not affect his government, he had many Catholic supporters; the religious problem helped bring about his rather quick demise.

It appears that the first demonstrations against Huong in Saigon grew out of his brusque rejection of Thich Tam Chau's "suggested list" of new cabinet members. Thich Tri Quang personally opposed antigovernment action at that time, but went along with Tam Chau in the interests of old friendship and Buddhist solidarity. The timing of the demonstrations irritated many Saigon youth and student leaders, who were then deeply involved in mobilizing volunteers and material for flood relief in central Viet-Nam. At first, the demonstrators were few and ineffective, but clear cases of police brutality—particularly by the hated Combat Police (*Canh-Sat Chien-Dau*), who specialized in riot control—soon led many non-Buddhist youths to join. The resulting atmosphere of crisis and excitement brought in still more demonstrators. SSU leaders moved to negotiate, but Premier Huong, a stern teacher in the Confucian mold, refused to receive them. The honor of climaxing the anti-Huong campaign fell to the militant Buddhist youth and students in Hue, who denounced the government in Saigon as American-made. They destroyed the interior of the USIS Library, attempted to burn down the building, and had already planned selective assaults on private American residences in Hue, when victory—the resignation of Huong and his regime—rendered further violence unnecessary.

What were the implications for the youth and student community of more than one year of intense political activism? In the cold terms of activist techniques and organizational control, student groups had come a long way from the naïveté and spontaneity of the struggle against Diem in 1963. Now, prior to any demonstration, careful planning sessions would be held through the night and perhaps several small "shock teams" (fifteen to twenty students) formed. In the ensuing demonstration or street fight, such teams, staying close together and strictly disciplined, would be committed to the struggle only at the right time and place. Normally a mass of middle school pupils and even younger children—not subject to leadership discipline—would screen the shock teams, creating a false appearance of aimless movement and senseless destruction.[16] By the end of 1964, some young activists, particularly middle school boys (thirteen to nineteen years old), had become real experts in street combat. Often a "command group" of two or three leaders would perch high on a wall and direct the shock teams below with hand signals. Techniques were developed for defense against advancing police cordons—for example, bicycles lined together (usually two bicycles high) and braced from behind, a particularly effective way to block gates and narrow street entrances.

But if their techniques had improved with experience, the students' sense of autonomous solidarity had largely drained away. It may never be possible to ascertain to what degree these young people were "bought" by various political parties, religious groups, and military cliques. In a way, the question is irrelevant, since the many ill-founded rumors that circulated concerning bribery of students were just as ruinous as any facts. By the end of 1964, most of the urban polity and a good portion of the urban youth believed the student activists' direct involvement in politics had soiled them with corruption and debased their revolutionary idealism. As one middle-aged merchant expressed it, "At least four top student leaders had gone into the struggle against Major General Khanh poor and came out of it with their families riding motor scooters." Since "the people had entered the struggle behind these student leaders," they emerged dismayed and cynical when they saw this traditional use of political power for family profit "among the one group [the students] that had stayed clean in the past ten years."[17]

Student Politics, 1965-67

Perhaps partly as a reaction to these stories of skulduggery and selfishness, there appeared to be a lull in student political activity through the early months of 1965. One group that did keep active, however, comprised the more militant young Catholic students, who joined in Colonel Pham Ngoc Thao's unsuccessful February 1965 coup attempt. In May they were more successful, helping to pressure Premier Phan Huy Quat out of office. Meanwhile, in March, new Student Union elections were held, both in Saigon and in Hue. The winning slate for the Executive Council of the SSU was immediately attacked by a variety of influential student leaders as unrepresentative and thus incapable of providing the unifying influence the students supposedly still desired. In Hue there was a change of names at the top of the HSU, but effective control could still be traced to the association of Buddhist University Students (*Sinh-Vien Phat-Tu*).

Most youth and student groups greeted Brigadier General Nguyen Cao Ky's appointment as premier with a skeptical wait-and-see attitude brought on by past experience and knowledge that the junta's success would depend more on the ability of its members to work together than on the attributes of Ky as an individual. Students in Hue still viewed with unconcealed hostility any high-ranking officer or official who was Catholic—in this case, Major General Nguyen Van Thieu, Armed Forces Commander and Chairman of the junta's National Leadership Committee (*Uy Ban Lanh Dao Quoc Gia*). In August 1965, student leaders in Hue were writing articles and organizing meetings against Thieu. In contrast, Saigon student leaders seemed to see the political situation more in terms of issues than of personalities; those who wanted to follow Hue in demanding Thieu's removal found little support. Some youth leaders even joined a group, organized by the Ministry of Youth and Sports, to "conduct war" on speculators and profiteers—mostly Chinese.

One key issue for students during the summer of 1965 was the set of "revolutionary proposals" made by Premier Ky in June—in particular, his plans for a fuller engagement of youth in both the war effort and the "social revolution" being carried out in rural and poor urban areas. Rumors abounded. According to one, universities would be closed and all students and professors mobilized. (There is evidence that such an idea was seriously considered by the junta in June, but soon dropped—perhaps partly on the advice of U.S. officials.) [18] A number of student leaders said privately that they would be willing to go, if all students were really to be involved and if the government had a concrete plan for using them to best advantage—i.e., not as mere "cannon fodder" but as social or political action cadres.

Then the government suggested drastically cutting the total number of university students by imposing strict quotas and entrance examinations on every faculty. Almost all student organizations strongly resisted this proposal on the probably accurate grounds that favoritism and pay-offs to officials would more than ever determine who could and could not enter the universities. Again, the government chose not to push this plan beyond the trial balloon stage.

Finally, the government announced it would tighten enforcement of existing draft laws, set up an experimental youth social action project in Saigon's eighth district and draft men in the thirty-four-to-thirty-seven-year age group, regardless of occupation or previous exemption. The third policy would have affected a number of university teachers, particularly assistant professors without tenure, including many of the younger instructors to whom students felt much closer than to the older-generation academicians. Several teachers indicated they might refuse the order and go to jail in protest. According to estimates, some faculties—especially in Hue— would have lost enough teachers to force a sharp curtailment of instruction.

Hue teachers were the first to react, the HSU and other student groups quickly aligning with them to hold protest meetings and publish declarations whose scope extended well beyond the draft issue. News of events in Hue spread to Saigon, and by August 19 various faculties in the capital were organizing meetings critical of the Ky regime. On August 22, Hue protesters raised the political temperature still higher by passing a declaration roundly denouncing mobilization plans as a waste of potential nationalist cadres and a technique to disperse the opposition, thus leading again to dictatorship. The students again demanded the removal of General Thieu, for allowing "foreigners to infringe on the nation's sovereignty and the people's right of self-determination."[19] The next day in Saigon, two government ministers attended a student meeting at the Faculty of Science and made conciliatory speeches. The more radical student leaders had intended to make August 25 (the first anniversary of a huge demonstration against General Khanh) the climax of their confrontation policy, but that same day Premier Ky announced a concession: men thirty-four to thirty-seven years old whose jobs were "essential to the nation"—including university instructors—would be "mobilized in position," i.e., not drafted.[20] Political tensions subsided, although student dissatisfaction remained on many other issues.

For the remainder of 1965, the military junta seems to have handled itself well, providing no immediate openings to its opponents. However, worsening inflation and social antagonisms, created by the tremendous multiplication of American personnel and expenditure, threatened the Saigon regime's entire urban position in a long-term sense. Apparently to improve relations with students, and perhaps to begin to salvage its image abroad, the government permitted student delegations to travel to the United States and to South Korea.

The first five months of 1966 saw the sharpest, most bitter political conflict among non-Communist elements since the crisis of 1963. Throughout 1965 student groups in Hue, working in closest alliance with the Buddhist hierarchy of central Viet-Nam, had been eager to confront the Saigon regime and, in particular, to eliminate General Thieu. Although the story is still incomplete, it appears that during January-February 1966, these student and religious leaders attempted to consolidate support among military men and civil servants in central Viet-Nam and thus prepare for a major new confrontation with the Saigon regime. But Premier Ky and his associates moved first. They purged Major General Nguyen Chanh Thi, then the head of I Corps in central Viet-Nam, who was friendly to the dissidents in Hue. The antigovernment forces rallied behind Thi. In retrospect, it seems that Premier Ky thus succeeded in forcing the pace of his opposition, leading them to take advanced, radical positions that had much backing in Hue and Da-Nang, but failed to generate sufficient support in the Mekong Delta or even among Saigon's Buddhist and student groups. In Saigon, what in 1964 had been truly a student movement was now publicly exposed as fragmented beyond recognition and incapable of generating mass support. By early June 1966, Premier Ky had smashed the opposition and jailed or summarily drafted hundreds of university and high school students. As a semi-independent element in Vietnamese politics, students were again out of the picture—for the time being, at least.

The Student Community and Five Clusters of Power

Having discussed the Vietnamese students' general environment and surveyed their recent political activities, we can now proceed to analyze their political role in context, i.e., in relation to five important nonstudent foci of political power. In the process, perhaps the contours of South Viet-Nam's student political culture will more clearly emerge from the surrounding fluidity of revolutionary change. The five clusters of power whose interaction with the student community we shall examine are orthodox political elements, the National Liberation Front, religious organizations, the military-bureaucratic apparatus, and the American establishment.

Orthodox Political Elements. By "orthodox political elements" we mean the upper bourgeois beneficiaries of prior sociopolitical arrangements in Viet-Nam, including most of those older Vietnamese who prospered under the French or under President Diem, or both, and are now trying to hold on to what they have. Historically, their generation is the product of the traditional system's early erosion under colonial pressure and the growth before World War II of a small, politically weak bourgeoisie.[21] Intellectually, they are the transitional generation, reflecting a patchwork quilt of residual Confucian scholar-official standards on the one hand and the values, ideologies, and collective self-images of modernity on the other.

It is ironic, although natural, that some individuals labeled "orthodox" or "traditional" by students today were, in their younger years, radical agents of change, part of the cutting edge of opposition to a highly conservative, almost immovable French colonial structure. The "Constitutionalists," for example, hounded the French for reform in the 1920's. Although they became rather anachronistic in the 1930's and early 1940's, wealth and social position allowed many of them (or their sons) a second political opportunity in the 1950's. Nationalist groups of more violent proclivities, such as the *Viet-Nam Quoc Dan Dang* (VNQDD), *Phuc Quoc,* and *Dong Minh Hoi*—facing up to repeated, complete failure from 1925 to 1945—generally moved to the left and the *Viet-Minh,* or to the right and political obscurity. From 1954 to 1960, those who chose the South found some solace in the Diem regime, but a series of confrontations in 1960–61 again found many of them in exile, in prison, or simply in apolitical withdrawal. But while they declined in political influence, these "orthodox" types seldom suffered a parallel loss of economic or social status. Even those who had their property confiscated by President Diem, for example, have managed to bounce back since his demise.

Whatever attention is paid to these aging, non-Communist, nationalist parties and cliques by students today is based on faint memories of the early anti-French struggle and not on any doctrinal agreement over what should be done now or in the future. Nor has past anti-French unity been transferable to the present in the crucial field of recruiting and training young cadres. Some party leaders have sought unity and student converts in anti-Communistic coalitions, but while they may agree that Communism must be defeated, they apparently cannot agree on positive programs of social, economic, and political revolution. "Oppose Communism, but favor what?" is a question that elicits from them either philosophic platitudes or bitter argument. One Vietnamese observer has concluded: "Nationalist attitudes are negative attitudes, strong only in opposition and destruction, but apparently weak in growth and construction. A Nationalist only knows how to say 'No' and finds it difficult to say 'Yes, we have. . . .'"[22]

One of the reasons for the students' disaffection with "orthodox" nationalists becomes apparent during discussions of the subject of revolution.[23] During the anti-French struggle, it became fashionable to use the term revolution in a rather easy, inflated manner. Yet, when confronted with actual revolution—with the torment, the mass excitement, and the bitter class conflict in certain areas of Viet-Nam in the period 1945–55—most bourgeois nationalists were repelled and eventually fled the scene. Only Communists and certain other Marxist nationalists could view the fratricidal aspects of the anticolonial struggle with any degree of equanimity. After 1955, non-Marxist nationalists in Saigon clung firmly to their revolutionary vocabulary, but the students gradually saw through their elders' rhetoric to the fundamentally conservative core beneath.

Working tacitly with the military junta, factions of the *Dai-Viet* and VNQDD have staked out bureaucratic positions in certain provinces and districts. The Constituent Assembly elected in September 1966 included a number of "orthodox" nationalists, and a survey of all presidential and upper house candidates for the September 1967 elections revealed a veritable onslaught of minor party representatives. During the crucial precampaign maneuvering of April-June 1967, some urban youth groups were interested enough to indicate support for one or more of these slates. A number of candidates realized the value of student cadres as a means of lending fervor and intellectual persuasiveness to their propaganda, but most were unwilling to give students a major voice in political strategy. And when the Ky regime pressured the Constituent Assembly into eliminating three presidential candidates who were quite popular among the various youth segments, involvement began to look much less attractive. In the end, most young people adopted a position of vague detachment, while a minority went into the August campaign actively pursuing one of two ends—support for Tran Van Huong and allied upper house slates or "energetic observation" of the proceedings to exert pressure for a "clean election"—usually including calls for the resignation from office of candidates Thieu and Ky.

Marxism and the NLF. In 1945–54, while many "orthodox" politicians were sitting out the conflict or collaborating with the French, the *Viet-Minh* led the bulk of the politicized Vietnamese to a stunning anticolonial victory. To understand contemporary student attitudes toward the National Liberation Front (NLF), we must first appreciate their attitudes toward the *Viet-Minh,* its spiritual if not organizational progenitor.

Marxism has exerted an appeal on Vietnamese students at least since 1925. Young Vietnamese in Paris and Canton enjoyed intimate contacts with radical movements and often smuggled reading materials back to their compatriots at home. From the 1930's on, the Indochinese Communist Party (ICP) gave high priority to the translation into Vietnamese of standard Marxist-Leninist works.[24] Marxist doctrine was particularly important after 1945 in marshaling intellectual support for the *Viet-Minh*'s long struggle.[25] Marxism provided an ideological rationale and Leninism a tight organizational framework for the extreme, emotional nationalism of the *Viet-Minh* cadres. Even among intellectuals not committed or antagonistic to the *Viet-Minh,* Marxist-Leninist concepts like "struggle," "contradiction," and "front" worked themselves into the common political vocabulary.

Marxist ideas have thus become deeply intertwined with nationalism (and related antiforeign feelings) and with a humanistic position against social injustice. Leninist techniques have enjoyed even greater popularity. Almost all activist students have developed an extremely high regard for propaganda as a political weapon and for cadre indoctrination and discipline as the key to political success, largely from their indirect observation of *Viet-Minh* and NLF techniques. Students in South Viet-Nam, whether "Communist," "non-Communist," or "anti-Communist," must in some degree and form determine their relationship to Marxism-Leninism.

Yet, beyond what they have heard from relatives and friends or observed themselves in recent years, urban students are not generally exposed to the more sophisticated aspects of original Marxist doctrine, not to mention the wealth of commentary that has developed over the years. Some lectures on Marxism are permitted in high schools and universities, but students feel the teachers know and care very little about the subject—especially if a student asks penetrating, perhaps embarrassing, questions. Marxist texts may be known by title, but only the most determined individuals will attempt to secure copies, either through NLF contacts or by buying expensive editions smuggled in from France. Such difficulties lead the student to rely mostly on random conversations, rumors, and scattered references in secondary sources. In practice, this often results in fervent advocacy of "isms"—"socialism," "social nationalism," "democratic socialism," "communalism," or some other interesting category—with only the barest knowledge of their theoretical and historical underpinnings.[26]

How does all this affect student attitudes toward and relationships with the NLF? A covert Liberation Student Union (LSU) does exist, claiming general representation of university, high school, and other students.[27] This organization appears to enjoy predominance only in NLF-controlled areas, but it may also have a considerable following in the high schools of certain provincial capitals where many students come from NLF areas or nurse specific socio-economic grievances against the regime. Inside the major urban centers, however, there is scant indication that the LSU has secured much of a following. This does *not* mean that urban youth lack contacts with the NLF: a few highly motivated cells probably exist in every school, but their liaison is with NLF political committees directly and not via the LSU. Many other students are influenced through friends or relatives in the NLF. Finally, an even larger number of politically active students hold *opinions* on social injustice—corruption in the national bureaucracy, the continuing need to struggle against foreign domination, and so forth—that happen to coincide with general NLF positions. Yet, in actually facing up to these social evils, in advocating *policies,* these same students still appear to be seeking alternatives to the NLF. The NLF in their eyes has not achieved the status enjoyed by the *Viet-Minh* after 1945. Nguyen Huu Tho is not Ho Chi Minh.

Rightist Catholic student groups spend most of their organizational energies denouncing Communism and working against those groups they consider Communist-infiltrated or Communist-dominated. Catholic refugees from the north regard Southern Vietnamese as too "sentimental and defeatist," too prone to talk about a "brother-versus-brother" war while—they say—the Communists are absorbed in the cold calculus of conquering land and people.[28] In contrast, many Buddhist students tend to emphasize what should be done about the *non*-Communist members of the NLF. While recognizing that the (Communist) People's Revolutionary Party (PRP) internally controls the sprawling NLF apparatus on the basis of general directives from Hanoi, the Buddhists believe that masses of lesser cadres and rank-and-file types could be "won back" —provided there were something worth coming back to. Hence their long-standing advocacy of radical social revolution at home and eventual nonalignment abroad.

Perhaps more numerous than strictly Catholic and Buddhist students are those who view both Marxism and the NLF from a secular vantage point. Observation of events over the period 1963– 67 has led them, often reluctantly, to the conclusion that all problems in South Viet-Nam somehow lead back to politics, or money, or both combined. From this it follows that any really serious rectification of South Viet-Nam's unhappy status must include a "clean sweep," a "total revolution" in personal and group behavior. Unfortunately, it is in specifying the political, economic, social, educational, and cultural aspects of this enforced revolution that disagreement and confusion predominate. Some seem transfixed by abstract models of an ideal society and more or less use these abstractions as a measure against which the regime in power can be roundly chastised. Applied effort bores them. Others use all the revolutionary terminology in rhythmic fashion, but when pressed to the wall reveal themselves at best as social tinkerers, mild reformists.

There remain a few, a decreasing few, who have tried and are still trying to help engineer in South Viet-Nam a final revolutionary crisis under alternative values and leadership to those posed by the NLF. While frankly admiring the proven organizational qualities of the Hanoi brand of Marxism-Leninism, they have refrained from joining the NLF, out of basic distrust and out of dismay at the demonstrated social results of its doctrine as applied in North Viet-Nam and China. Attempts at running their own secret organizations have not been particularly successful, leading these young men slowly to the conclusion that discipline and commitment without a doctrinal framework, without an internally consistent ideology, leads to fragmentation and demoralization. Here, however, they are unsure of themselves, lacking the background and the proper source materials to create such a doctrinal framework and afraid that external forces will deprive them of the time to theorize and experiment.[29] In 1967, there was no evidence of improvement in their chances for success. On the contrary, such an approach seemed destined to meet with increasing hostility from both sides in the conflict.

Buddhists and Catholics. The search for a coherent and useful conceptual framework is by no means limited to the study of Marxism or Marxist-related doctrines. Among the religious doctrines of South Viet-Nam, we shall discuss Catholicism and Buddhism, while readily admitting that a more comprehensive study of student interaction with organized religion would include the Cao Dai, Hoa Hao, and Protestant sects.

In recent years, leaders of both Catholic and Buddhist hierarchies, hoping to combine religious faith with modern social and political commitment, have placed great emphasis on developing ideas and programs for youth. Vietnamese Buddhism, although it underwent a quiet regeneration in the 1950's, found its greatest political strength in the anti-Diem struggle of 1963. The political attractions of organized Buddhism ever since have drawn their mystique and their appeal to youth from that momentous victory. In fact, young monks and the Buddhist youths who followed them made up the vanguard in 1963 and remain today at the heart of most Buddhist activism. Their plans have been broad and ambitious, but problems of finance, regional jealousy, policy differences, personality clashes and, most important of all, the corrosive effects of war have made progress a painful, erratic affair. The political reversals of 1966 have split and apparently demoralized the *Vien Hoa Dao* leadership. It is doubtful whether they can make any further progress against the frankly hostile, restrictive policies of the present regime.

On a national scale, the most important youth-centered group has been the Buddhist Family association *(Gia Dinh Phat Tu)*, commonly known in English as the "Buddhist Scouts" because it is patterned after the Scouting movement *(Phong Trao Huong Dao)*. The Buddhist Family operates under the Youth Commission of the *Vien Hoa Dao;* its organization fans out into the provinces in separate male and female branches.[30] The local Family (similar to a scout troop) concentrates on religious indoctrination, cultural improvement (music, theater, composition, art), and social activism (charitable work, the teaching of basic skills, first aid), as well as the standard camping and sports activities. Each Family seeks to create and nurture community spirit and a sense of mutual need and aid among Family members. In times of political conflict, Family units have participated as disciplined Buddhist demonstrators, bodyguards, collectors of intelligence, and as logistical auxiliaries. The military draft, however, has drained away much of the experienced leadership.

Reflecting the opposition to Diem in 1963, many high schools in Hue, Da-Nang, Saigon, and certain provincial capitals sprouted associations for the "protection of Buddhism." The *Vien Hoa Dao,* particularly in 1964, tried to transform these ad hoc groups into high school "Buddhist student unions," hoping to keep their memberships united and enthusiastic. But by 1965 many of these groups had apparently lost their vitality. Only at best do they now serve as communication links between the Youth Commission and individual high school students of Buddhist faith.

Such is not the case at the university level. Each campus has a Buddhist University Student association *(Sinh-Vien Phat-Tu)* that plays an important, albeit varying, role in student politics. Among University of Hue students in 1964, the Buddhist University Students (BUS) claimed 500 members in a student body of about 3,000 and tended to dominate the Hue Student Union. The BUS at the University of Saigon has also shown political muscle at several key junctures, but its growth has been slower and its impact less sustained. The BUS in Dalat is part of a larger Buddhist attempt to penetrate an area of traditional Catholic dominance, so far with limited success. It appears that each BUS association has been sustained more by political activism than by religious indoctrination or social welfare efforts. Many BUS members know more about day-to-day political alliances and tactics than they do about Buddhist doctrines or the realities of life among the common people. In view of the Buddhists' political defeats of 1966, one can speculate whether or not this stress on short-run political maneuvering, to the detriment of value indoctrination and popular contact, may have been the undoing of an apparently promising movement.

It is still difficult to generalize about contemporary Catholic youth and student groups, for events since Diem have confused organizational positions and attitudes considerably. With the fall of Diem, Catholicism lost its protective umbrella and was forced into a defensive posture, some Catholic groups losing political influence, many individual Catholics losing self-confidence, and all again painfully conscious of their minority status. Catholic students now are most fervent and categorical about the inappropriateness of religious affiliation as a device for national unity, for only Buddhism could hope to play such a role. While Catholic students as a whole seem badly split on political issues, certain groups among them have developed considerable internal unity, discipline, and organizational sophistication.

For example, the Student Confederation for Freedom and Democracy *(Tong Lien-Doan Sinh-Vien Hoc-Sinh Tu-Do Dan-Chu,* generally known as *Tu-Dan)* is a small but militant group of persons unified by their religious faith and memories of their families fleeing the North to settle in the refugee suburbs of Saigon. *Tu-Dan's* activist nucleus is probably only a few hundred students strong, but these students have a proven capability for mobilizing large masses of Catholic youth at crucial moments, as in the May 1965 demonstrations to force the resignation of Premier Phan Huy Quat. Their dominant political line is uncompromising anti-Communism and open hostility to the so-called clique of the Buddhist leader Thich Tri Quang, which they have placed beyond the pale as "Communist sympathizers."

Two of the hostels for University of Saigon students are operated and partially financed by Catholic monastic societies. The Renaissance Club *(Cau-Lac-Bo Phuc-Hung)* has a Dominican priest (of Vietnamese nationality) in charge and a number of Dominicans in residence, but most routine administration is handled by student committees. While political debate inside the Club is not encouraged and the name "Renaissance" cannot be used as a student political label, residents are free, even encouraged, to act on the outside. Indeed, many have occupied leadership positions in major student and youth organizations; others are well known writers on political and social issues. In contrast to the *Tu-Dan* activists, Renaissance members have generally maintained good relations with the *Vien Hoa Dao* and at times have tried to mediate conflicts between radical Catholic and radical Buddhist elements. The Alexandre de Rhodes Hostel *(Cu-Xa Dac-Lo)* is directed by a Jesuit priest (a Canadian) and has about ten Jesuits in residence, most of them active in China prior to 1950. Discipline here is quite strict compared to that of the Renaissance Club. Student residents appear to concentrate on their studies and enjoy the superior amenities of the Hostel, bothering less with the political ferment beyond its gates.

The Military Bureaucracy. The political instability of recent years, in the context of two decades of general social turmoil, has played a part in severely limiting the desires of young intellectuals to associate themselves with any leadership group holding state power in Saigon. The students' reluctance is understandable. To-day's collaborators have too often become tomorrow's political pariahs. South Viet-Nam lacks any truly legitimate government achieved either through the formalities of a traditional selection process or, as many student leaders have advocated, "via the people's hearts, due to the implementation of a revolution."[31] In addition, Vietnamese students share the more universal tendency of youth to follow a pure "ethic of absolute ends" that, more often than not, conflicts with the established adult elite's "ethic of responsibility."[32] Vietnamese students are in some degree the heirs of French tradi-tions in student politics, which emphasize declamatory, agitational, and revolutionary techniques and platforms. They have clashed bitterly with those who view the higher educational system mainly as a mechanism for career training and the implantation of author-itative ideals and institutions. Today—when everything is ques-tionable, nothing sacrosanct—students tend to sneer at any regime operating from old premises and old power relationships, while emotionally craving a dynamic, sweeping, even absolutist solution to their country's dilemma.

As we have already shown, student groups have been an im-portant force in the urban political game of musical chairs since 1963. They have also been party to the institutional tension and occasional conflict between the civil and military bureaucracies. During the period of early large-scale mobilization against the NLF (1961–62), the Ngo family (Diem, Nhu, Can, Thuc) and its as-sociates kept the civilian bureaucracy under tight control and maintained dominance over the military. As the counterguerrilla effort, operating from techniques and principles introduced by U.S. military "advisers," came to occupy the almost complete attention of both civil and military bureaucracies, it was inevitable that the military would rapidly increase its numbers, skills, and func-tional significance. The military coup d'état of November 1963 was the fruition of this development, as were the serious demoral-ization and disintegration of the civilian bureaucracy and the mili-tary's fumbling attempts to fill political roles for which they lacked experience. In such a situation, with adult elites and counter-elites so insecure and ineffectual, it is not surprising that student organizations had just enough spirit and momentum to gain con-siderable influence in urban politics.

Nevertheless, the students seem to lack either the continuity of leadership or the sense of strategy to turn immediate advantages into long-term gains. They are most effective when serving as the vanguard for more sophisticated leaders, or perhaps when reacting on their own to some sudden change in political fortunes. Their ability to stabilize and defend whatever they may have gained by such sharp, spirited thrusts is very limited.

The military leaders, providing they manage somehow to put the lid on their own fratricidal bickering, display roughly the reverse strengths and weaknesses. They seldom catch the fleeting opportunity, but their pyramidal structure, their monopoly on heavy weapons, and their abundant resources allow them considerable leeway when attempting to stabilize and defend a position. In March-April 1966, for example, Premier Ky may have fumbled and procrastinated in the early stages of his showdown with the Buddhist-student-bureaucratic coalition in central Viet-Nam, but his final physical blow was overwhelming.

In retrospect, it may appear that the military in South Viet-Nam have slowly encroached upon and absorbed the potential for independent action of first the civil bureaucracy, then the university and high school students (drafted, jailed, or neutralized politically), and finally the religious organizations. In view of the continuing armed struggle with the NLF and regular North Vietnamese units, there is naturally a tremendous impetus behind such expansion. But the struggle is also eminently political; no ruling elite without a political ideology or party apparatus is likely to achieve decisive victory. The military's lack of popular legitimacy makes it all the more vulnerable to attacks from relatively small but determined counter-elites—while other groups watch the proceedings with relative dispassion, since they have never come to identify with those in power. Students share with other civilian sectors a traditional contempt for "uncouth" generals and favor, at least in principle, a strictly professional, nonpolitical armed forces. Military leaders involved in politics, the students argue, tend to rule by fiat, threat, and imprisonment, seldom giving sufficient emphasis to mobilizing mass support or to patiently explaining and selling their policies to others.[33] Unless the generals can convince civilians of their ability at noncoercive politics, material reconstruction, and institutional development, these attitudes are unlikely to soften.

The September 1967 election of General Thieu as President of the "Second Republic" has apparently legitimized military rule in the eyes of Saigon's international friends. But what the election meant for South Viet-Nam's youth and for the population at large remained unclear at the time of writing. The political segments that were hostile to Thieu and to the military junta prior to the election remained just as hostile afterwards, and they were joined by some angry and ambitious losers. In the military, privileges and powers carefully maintained in balance since June 1965 were bound to be realigned by postelection governmental changes. Most importantly, if Generals Thieu and Ky were unable to work out a new division of power between them and thereby sparked some sort of showdown, major student groups could be expected to take quick advantage of the situation, along with the militant Buddhist opposition and many of the defeated candidates. General Thieu, however, is considered, even by his worst enemies, to be one of the most skillful backroom politicians ever to emerge in South Viet-Nam's armed forces. He is known to admire the South Korean "solution" of President Park Chung Hee, and he may yet work out some short-term settlement along similar lines.

The Americans. War, destruction, mass migration, political turmoil, economic chaos, the entry of hundreds of thousands of foreign soldiers—all this exerts unbelievable pressure on every level of society in South Viet-Nam. Even the most parochial of village dwellers has learned the elemental fact that politics—political allegiance—is intimately tied with the problems of daily survival. Thus it is not surprising to find that elements traditionally weak in consciousness of politics above the village level have developed definite, coherent attitudes.

This is particularly true with regard to foreign soldiers. Perhaps the most common feeling in the countryside is one of stifling impotence, seeing oneself as a mere pawn, a fragile willow branch in a great storm. For the average villager this may be a matter of watching in angry silence as first one force and then another tramps across his rice fields. One force, however, invariably includes foreigners, thus stirring deeply rooted feelings among a proud and sensitive people.

University students have formed a more complex picture of the American presence, but beneath their nuanced views is the same underlying core of bitterness regarding the apparent permanence of a vicious circle of death, degradation, and exploitation created largely by forces beyond their control. Even militantly anti-Communist students—who live by the notion of a "Free World" against "Communism," endorse American bombing of the North, and talk about total extermination of the *Viet-Cong*—still fear above all a general American "sell-out" of their interests. Buddhist students paint a word picture of two mighty fighting elephants (East and

West, China and the United States) trampling the grass (North and South Viet-Nam) beneath them. In this image, however, the "grass" assumes a passive, blameless position. More to the point is the picture provided by Dalat students of two small bantam roosters, clawing at each other in a battle to the death, egged on and supported by two huge overseers leaning into the ring.

Many students in South Viet-Nam, looking back over the past decade, are not at all convinced that the Americans have brought anything to counterinsurgency efforts beyond tricky gadgets and warmed-over French military ideas. In the cities, they watch while exclusively American installations sprout up on Vietnamese soil, surrounded by barbed wire, sandbags, massive concrete cylinders, and hard-eyed armed guards. There is sometimes a certain wry contempt for the vaunted technical superiority of the United States, whose mighty guns and scientific methods have come to naught when pitted against small, totally dedicated terrorist squads.

The inflationary effect of the American presence is often directly unsettling to students, since many come from middle class families with fixed incomes. Americans are also blamed for increased prostitution, street begging, black market activity, and the outlandish prices of taxi and pedicab rides, food, and the services of household servants. The students decry the emergence of an important new "parasite" class specializing in the provision of goods and services to Americans, but the final irony comes when economic troubles lead them (often under family pressure) to part-time or even full-time employment in the U.S. offices.[34]

Yet, after all this accumulated bitterness has come forth, most students will admit that in the first months of 1965 the *alternative* to large-scale U.S. intervention was probably a general collapse of the counterinsurgency effort, followed by urban panic. The reality, which many of them are only facing frankly after the fact, was either NLF victory or long-term American intervention. Some student leaders take heart in the situation, saying, for example: "Now, at last, America is willing to sacrifice American lives, whereas before you took the easy way of supplying material aid—of which the U.S. has an overabundance anyway."[35] Others, however, warn that a favorable military decision had better come quickly because the longer U.S. troops remain the greater will be the harm done to the people and the more intense will anti-American sentiments become.[36] One youth leader maintained that, historically, the most important advantage the Communist leadership of the *Viet-Minh* had after 1946 was that "to fight *against* the Communists meant to walk with the French and thus become a traitor."[37] If they wish to exert any kind of popular influence, non-Communist nationalists must above all avoid falling into this position again, but the continuing indispensability of American aid and intervention is making this harder all the time.

U.S. government relations with successive Saigon regimes are the subject of almost universal criticism among students. The statement, "The United States should allow Viet-Nam true independence in its choice of government and economic system," is a common opener to specific condemnation of American policies toward each regime in South Viet-Nam from 1955 to the present.[38] The CIA is generally thought to play a role in the success or failure of particular political factions and often to hedge its bet by backing more than one party to a struggle. If the Saigon regime acts contrary to U.S. policy, students expect it to be undermined by one or more of the many countermeasures available to U.S. officials: public expressions of disapproval (which encourage rival political groups to act), economic pressure, undercover manipulation, or even military action by readily available U.S. units. On the other hand, students see those regimes that follow U.S. policy guidance most closely as the most vulnerable to honorable nationalist opposition.

Conclusion

Analytically inclined Vietnamese students may conclude that the best they can hope for is a military breathing spell to provide precious time for young organized nationalists to develop a political alternative to the NLF on the one hand and to semipermanent U.S. dependency on the other. They associate such a hypothetical opportunity with the breathing spell that Diem enjoyed from 1955 to 1958 but failed to use properly. If a military cease-fire, tacit or negotiated, does develop, these students believe the NLF will immediately shift into an intensely political drive—meaning that young nationalist cadres will somehow have to be organized, trained, and (hopefully) gain experience in local political action *before* this stage of essentially nonmilitary competition occurs.[39]

As of September 1967, no politically significant element in South Viet-Nam, including the armed forces, had the right kind of cadres trained and experienced for this competition. With the political spectrum continuing to polarize to the left and right, student hopes for a genuinely independent movement gradually diminish, forcing more and more the distasteful choice between partisan extremes.

In the fall of 1967, the NLF publicized a program amplifying their famous "ten points" of 1960 and directing new attention to any and all groups willing to give top priority to a national struggle against U.S. intervention. If the war goes on in the present manner, this program is likely to attract Vietnamese youth and students who have up to now remained uncommitted. Their compatriots, who for reasons of religion, ideology, family loyalty, or self-interest just cannot commit themselves to the NLF, will then be left in an untenable position—forced to choose between exile (which is difficult to reach) and open alignment with the U.S. establishment. With political battle lines thus so sharply drawn, the war may become basically a question of which side is able to carry on the struggle one day longer than the other—in other words, a terrible, grinding test of psychological and physical endurance.

If, on the other hand, there are definite moves in 1968–69 toward a negotiated settlement, the future is likely to be much more fluid, much less predictable. The patterns of activity and attitudes of the past decade will suddenly seem anachronistic. In this context, youth will have a decided advantage over their elders, being less wedded to the past and more likely to move with the rhythm of a completely new social and political situation. With the possibility that blood, battle, and repeated family mourning can be transformed into only an ugly memory, hopes may well escalate day by day, and all parties to the negotiations may be forced to scale down their demands and accept the overriding desire—of so many Vietnamese people—for peace.

NOTES

1. Two research techniques accounted for most of the information in this study: informal interviewing of recognized student and youth leaders, and regular reading of student and youth publications. Other sources included conferences, debates, and seminars conducted by various formal and informal organizations. I have generally limited footnote citations to printed sources, with the exception of a few direct quotations from interviews.

2. This situation was perceptively discussed as early as 1958 by Father L. M. Parrel, "Thanh Nien Viet-Nam Ngay Nay" ("Vietnamese Youth Today"), *Bach Khoa*, No. 73, pp. 119–27, and No. 74, pp. 46–51; originally published in the *Bulletin de la Société des Missions Etrangères de Paris*, No. 119 (December 1958).

3. The problem of educational reform is a subject in itself, on which much critical comment has been published in South Viet-Nam in official reports, con-

ference minutes, and local journals and newspapers. For an example of the journalistic discussions, see *Sinh Vien* (*The Student*), published by the Saigon Student Union (SSU), particularly Nos. 5–9 (1965). For two recent education-reform proposals, see (U.S.) Higher Education Survey Team, "Preliminary Report on Public Universities of the Republic of Viet-Nam," submitted April 1967 and available from the Education Section, USAID/Saigon; and Nguyen Van Trung, "Dai-Hoc va Phat-Trien Quoc-Gia" ("The University and National Development"), SSU, Saigon, June 1967.

4. Some students enroll in two or even three faculties of a university and are counted each time, a fact that is not reflected in these figures provided by the Ministry of Education.

5. For further general information on the Universities of Saigon, Hue, and Dalat, see *Day Dai Hoc* (*Introducing the University*), compiled annually by the Young Catholic Student Association in Saigon.

6. Mr. Ho Huu Tuong, for example, a former "Trotskyite" jailed for years by the French and by President Diem, is a respected and outspoken Van Hanh faculty member. The Van Hanh Student Union has also taken positions different from those of the *Vien Hoa Dao* (Institute for the Propagation of the Faith) on several important occasions.

7. See Le Thanh Khoi, *Le Viet-Nam: Histoire et Civilisation* (Paris: Editions de Minuit, 1955); Nguyen Hien Le, *Dong Kinh Nghia Thuc* (published by the author, Saigon, 1956).

8. In 1934, a branch of the French National Union of Students (UNEF) was recognized in Hanoi and appears to have lasted until 1944. After 1944, the *Viet-Minh* were covertly represented on the campus. See Research and Information Commission, International Student Conference (ISC), "The Student Movement in South Viet-Nam," a mimeographed report to the tenth ISC, 1962.

9. Information from Mr. Hoang Ngoc Tue, Secretary-General of the SSU at that time.

10. Nguyen Huu Thai, "Student Movements in South Viet-Nam" (unpublished paper, Saigon, 1965).

11. Technically speaking, the NLF was not founded until December 20, 1960.

12. "The Student Movement in South Viet-Nam."

13. Nguyen Huu An, "Mot Thach Do Cho Thanh Nien Sinh Vien Hoc Sinh Viet-Nam" ("A Challenge to Vietnamese Youth and Students"), *Len Duong* (Saigon), Nos. 2–3 (May 1965[?]), p. 2.

14. A number of books in Vietnamese have appeared since 1963 attempting to document the crisis. See, for example, Tue Giac, *Viet-Nam Phat Giao Tranh Dau Su* (*History of the Buddhist Struggle in Viet-Nam*) (Saigon: Hoa Nghiem, 1964); Quoc Tue, *Cong Cuoc Tranh Dau Cua Phat Giao Viet-Nam* (*Vietnamese Buddhism's Task of Struggle*) (Saigon: 1964). For an interpretation from Hanoi, see M. N., "Vai Tro Cua Phat Giao Mien Nam Trong Cuoc Lat Do Che Do Doc Tai Ngo Dinh Diem" ("The Role of South Vietnamese Buddhism in Overthrowing the Dictatorial Regime of Ngo Dinh Diem"), *Nghien Cuu Lich Su*, No. 89 (August 1966).

15. Nguyen Huu An, *loc. cit.* Italics in original.

16. Most American reporters on the scene saw the aimlessness of the mass and missed the semimilitary character of the shock teams. This was also the impression of casual U.S. military observers, who saw in such demonstrations mere childish irresponsibility.

17. Informal discussion with Mr. Santasinh, a merchant, Saigon, July 5, 1965.

18. Interview with Mr. Arthur Bardos, head of the USIS Cultural Affairs Section, Saigon, August 22, 1965.

19. "Hue/Thua Thien Student Declaration of August 22," distributed in Hue as a broadside. Original in Vietnamese.

20. Premier Ky press statement, quoted in *Chinh Luan* (Saigon), August 27, 1965.

21. The development of an urban *bourgeoisie* in Indochina has naturally been of particular interest to Communist historians, given their requirements of historical periodization. One journal, *Nghien Cuu Lich Su* (Hanoi), has published scores of articles on this subject. For an independent Marxist interpretation, see J. Chesneaux, "Stages in the Development of the Vietnam National Movement, 1862–1940," *Past and Present* (London) (April 1955), pp. 63–75.

22. Nguyen Van Trung, *Hanh Trinh* (Saigon), I (October 1964), 15.

23. Stenographic notes on a discussion between Professor P. J. Honey and Vietnamese student leaders, Saigon, July 30, 1965.

24. Ho Chi Minh *et al.*, *A Heroic People: Memoirs from the Revolution* (Hanoi: Foreign Languages Publishing House, 1965), p. 101. See also Nguyen Duy Trinh *et al.*, *In the Enemy's Net: Memoirs from the Revolution* (Hanoi: Foreign Languages Publishing House, 1962).

25. Truong Chinh, *The August Revolution* and *The Resistance Will Win;* reproduced together as *Primer for Revolt* (New York: Frederick A. Praeger, 1963).

26. Only since late 1964 have articles appeared in Vietnamese intellectual journals on contemporary variants of socialism such as those in Algeria, Egypt, Cuba, Israel, and Yugoslavia. See, for example, *Hanh Trinh*, Nos. 3–4 and 5.

27. To Minh Trung, "Phong Trao Dau Tranh Chong My va Tay Sai cua Hoc Sinh Sinh Vien Mien Nam (1954–1965)" ("The Anti-American, Anti-Puppet Struggle Movement of South Vietnam's Students [1954–1965]"), *Nghien Cuu Lich Su* (Hanoi), January 1966, pp. 7–19.

28. Unsigned editorial in the daily newspaper *Thang Tien* (Saigon), July 9, 1965.

29. Of the many youth and student groups existing in 1965–67, perhaps the National Voluntary Service (NVS) (*Doan Thanh Nien Chi Nguyen Viet-Nam*) had advanced farthest in developing a coherent doctrine of this type. See David Marr, "A Study of Political Attitudes and Activities among Young Urban Intellectuals in South Viet-Nam" (unpublished M.A. thesis, University of California, Berkeley, 1965), pp. 102–8.

30. In 1965 the Buddhist Family claimed 96,000 members, the bulk of these in central Viet-Nam. It is doubtful that even the leadership can verify these figures, since the war has cut communication with many local Families (troops).

31. Speaker "S-3," minutes of the "Patriotism and Youth Day" discussions, Saigon, July 22, 1965.

32. Max Weber, *Essays in Sociology*, trans. and ed. H. H. Gerth and C. W. Mills (New York: Oxford University Press, 1946), pp. 126–27.

33. Chinh Yen, "Students and Military Leaders," *Tinh Thuong* (Saigon), No. 19 (July 1965). Original in Vietnamese.

34. Commentary on these developments can be found in the editorials and columns of almost any daily newspaper in Saigon (1965–67). See also *Hanh Trinh*, No. 6 (June 1965).

35. Conversation with the Vice Chairman of the Dalat Student Union, Dalat, July 30, 1965.

36. Conversation with the Chairman and Vice Chairman of the Hue Student Union, Hue, July 17, 1965.

37. Tran Ngoc Bau, Chairman of the National Voluntary Service (NVS), stenographic notes on Honey discussion, Saigon, July 30, 1965.

38. Nguyen Huu Thai, *op. cit.*

39. The NVS leadership in particular has operated on the basis of this assumption. It also turned up in the author's conversations with the Hue Student Union leadership in Hue, July 17, 1965.

8. BRAZIL

ROBERT O. MYHR

University students in Brazil have long been involved in the politics of the nation. In fact, Brazilians often speak of a "student tradition," that is, an accepted pattern of student behavior that has affected the political and social life of the nation.[1] This tradition has been an elitist one, for students in Brazil have come predominantly from the privileged economic and social classes. It has also been an uneven tradition. Student involvement in Brazilian politics in the past has occurred sporadically, with varying intensity in different parts of the nation at different times across several generations.

Young Brazilians were instrumental in early movements for independence. During the nineteenth century, students actively fought for the abolition of slavery and the establishment of the Republic. In the late 1930's, they sparked the slowly burning, democratic opposition to the mild dictatorship of President Getúlio Vargas. Following World War II, this traditional pattern of student political activism intensified. It was no longer sporadic, uncoordinated, and incidental; on the contrary, the university student sector became highly structured and politicized. Prior to the military take-over of the Brazilian government on April 1, 1964, the National Union of Students (*União Nacional dos Estudantes,* or UNE) had developed into a chief spokesman for the nationalistic, leftist forces of the nation, calling for radical solutions to Brazil's economic and social problems. In pressing for far-reaching changes

This chapter presents some of the findings of a larger study on the political role of university students in Brazil. The author gratefully acknowledges the financial support of the Fulbright program in Brazil, the Institute of Latin American Studies of Columbia University, and the University of Washington.

249

within the system, the students saw themselves as modern aboli-
tionists, republicans, and democrats in the best Brazilian tradition
of their predecessors.

The purpose of this chapter is to examine the established pattern of student political behavior in contemporary Brazil. First,
to provide a background for understanding student politics, we
shall describe the university environment and the students within
it. Second, we shall relate some of the more significant recent student action for political change in Brazil. Finally, we shall discuss
student political tactics and their impact on the political system.
The chapter will devote only passing attention to the political role
of the students within the university itself. It will concentrate
instead on their role in national politics. But it should be pointed
out that this division is quite arbitrary, for the issues in the university and those in the broader political spectrum often overlap.

The University: Context for Politics

University-level education is the highest rung on the Brazilian
educational ladder; few young Brazilians ever climb that high.
Before entering the university, students generally pass through two
lower levels of the educational system.[2] All Brazilian children supposedly attend four years of free and compulsory primary school,
as guaranteed by the federal Constitution. In fact, 5 to 10 per cent
of these children never set foot in a schoolhouse, and of those who
do, only about 12 per cent complete the first four years.

The young pupils then go through the two cycles of secondary
education, the *ginásio* (four years) and the *colégio* (three). The
secondary school may be either vocational or academic. Despite
the great need for vocational graduates, the more prestigious academic secondary schools draw four out of five students. In 1962,
65 per cent of these schools were privately operated and enrolled
70 per cent of the secondary student population; many of them
are run by the Roman Catholic Church.

The secondary level is a great bottleneck in the educational
system. Generally speaking, only the upper-class and the middle-
sector students make their way beyond this level. Entrance requires
a separate examination and the private schools are relatively expensive. In addition, pupils must provide their own books. These
expenses are very high for a poor family in Brazil. Many poorer
secondary students have to work full- or part-time and eventually
become discouraged or drop out of secondary school because it
interferes with their work or proves too expensive. For every 100

elementary school graduates, 60 enter the academic *ginásio;* 40 of these graduate. From this first cycle, only 4 enter the *colégio;* 1 of these 4 completes the second cycle and may seek university admission.

Entrance to the university requires a difficult special examination, the *vestibular.* Each faculty holds its own *vestibular* every year. This examination is a critical point in the career of a young Brazilian, for he must not only choose his professional faculty but also pass the *vestibular* to enter that faculty. If he fails, however, he may attempt the examination repeatedly until he passes or becomes discouraged.

These examinations tend to favor the students from the more privileged classes because they have usually had a better secondary preparation. Moreover, the *vestibulares* often require extra preparation through tutoring or an extra year of specialized classes. Competition is stiff, for there are far fewer places available than there are applicants. For example, the medical school of the University of Brazil in Rio admits about 200 students annually from the 2,000 who take the examination; the engineering faculty at the same institution accepts 600 out of some 3,000 applicants; and the University of São Paulo admits about 1 in 4 each year. In the smaller universities and independent faculties, there are fewer applicants, but the competition is still fairly intense. Once a student has gained admission, however, his education is free and his academic work within the faculty relatively easy.

The individual faculty has traditionally been and remains the basic institution of higher education in Brazil. Each faculty controls its own staff appointments, admissions, and curriculum. Although many are still entirely independent and private, several have been incorporated into the universities. However, they still remain as separate entities for the most part, and a student's academic, social, and political life still centers around his particular faculty. The Catholic University of Rio and the controversial new University of Brasília may provide exceptions to this general rule.

The Brazilian universities, then, have been superimposed on a traditional system of independent faculties. They are organized and administered under a federal law of 1931 as modified by the 1961 Law of Directives and Bases of Education. The law states that "the universities are constituted by the union under common administration, of five or more establishments of higher education."[3] The number of universities has greatly increased in the last ten years. In 1954 there were seventeen, in 1959 twenty-one, and in 1961 thirty-two. By 1964, there were a total of thirty-nine universities in Brazil. In addition to the federal universities, twelve were Roman Catholic, three were state-run, and one was private (Mackenzie University of São Paulo). All but five of these institutions were established after 1946. In addition, there were around four hundred unaffiliated and independent faculties. Except for nominal fees, education is free in the federal and state universities and faculties, but tuition is charged in the Catholic universities and Mackenzie University.

The universities and the independent faculties, including private institutions, are controlled by the federal government through the Ministry of Education and Culture, which determines their accreditation and allocates federal funds. The federal government has also established basic curricular requirements and rules for the selection of professors and administrators.

Each university is administered by a rector and a university council. The rector is chosen by the President of the Republic from a list of three names submitted by the university council. The council is made up of representatives from each faculty, one alumnus, and one student, who is usually president of the central directorate of students at the university. Each faculty, in turn, is headed by a director, a technical-administrative council, and a "congregation," a council of professors with perhaps one representative from the student body. The director of the faculty is also selected by the federal government from a list of three nominees prepared by the congregation. Although the private institutions do receive federal aid, they enjoy more freedom in choosing their professors and directors; in the organization of curriculum, however, they are entirely subject to government standards.

Federal control over university administration makes these institutions highly vulnerable to changes in regional and national politics. Pressure by politicians or influential intellectuals on the President or his Minister of Education can force the resignation of university officials.[4] In addition, since all of the universities and most of the faculties are dependent on federal funds, they are subject to political control over their operational expenses and specialized programs. The rectors and other university officials must take the political situation into account; they cannot withdraw from political realities or be completely independent in their ideas and programs. In this environment, higher education itself is highly political and students are extremely aware of the pressures that influence their own particular faculties.

The organization of the teaching staff adds to this political atmosphere. Within each faculty, the staff is arranged in a hierarchical pattern. On the lowest levels are the instructors and assistants; then come the associate and assistant professors, who are chosen through competitive examinations. Finally, at the head of each department within the faculty is the full professor, the *catedrático*. He has been selected after a special competition and holds lifetime tenure. Each department has only one *catedrático* and his power in his field is almost absolute within the faculty. He sets the tone for his subject and recommends all hiring and firing in the lesser academic ranks.

This system has led to abuses. The full professor can promote favorites and prevent others from rising in faculty rank. He may ignore his students and teaching duties for research or spend his time in consultant positions or in the private practice of his professional specialty. On the other hand, a professor of lower rank may use his popularity among students to enhance his position within the faculty even to the point where students may threaten to strike to defend his retention or promote his advancement.

The problems of the teaching staff are enhanced by the fact that most professors are underpaid and forced to hold one or more additional jobs. They move from one job to another, are late for classes, and sometimes never arrive at all. Moreover, they cannot remain at the university after classes to talk with students or to concentrate on the problems in the faculty, for they have too many other obligations.[5] As a result, the traditional system of formal lectures continues with little change; there is little experimentation with new curricula, seminars, or discussion courses. Yet the classes are remarkably informal. Students enter and leave the classroom at will, and they freely interrupt the professor to ask questions or make comments.

Generally speaking, study demands on the students in the non-scientific faculties are not great. Some students, working full-time, do not have time to study a great deal; others enroll in two different faculties at once. Examinations usually require the student to have done a little basic reading and to be able to regurgitate the general ideas given in the lectures. Cheating on examinations is not uncommon.[6] Although a few students fail a course from time to time, they need only repeat the examination or take the course again until they have passed it. Students rarely are forced to leave the university because of academic failure.

In this nonrigorous atmosphere, higher education follows its traditional pattern. Although there has been an infusion of new ideas in a few of the more famous faculties, old customs remain in force. University level education is still a mark of distinction for the elite and upwardly mobile groups in society, instead of providing the quality and quantity of highly trained professionals sorely needed for the economic and political modernization of Brazil.

The physical environment of Brazilian universities adds one further dimension to higher education in Brazil. Although some of the small independent faculties are located in the smaller cities, almost all the universities are in large cities or urban centers; there are no small college or university towns. Consequently, the large universities not only draw most of their students from the urban population, but also, through their students, may have a political effect on the masses concentrated in these urban centers. With a few exceptions, such as the University of Brasília, the universities do not have campuses, but rather a series of buildings housing various faculties spread out around the city. There is no central library for the university; instead, libraries—often duplicating each other's holdings—are located in each faculty. Many of the universities lack modern classrooms and laboratory facilities. Certain basic courses may be repeated in each of the faculties instead of being held jointly with other faculties within the university.

The university, then, has been little more than a grouping of a few faculties into one administrative unit. There is currently a trend toward expansion, modernization, and unification of the universities into "university cities" situated outside of the metropolitan areas, but some stand half-completed while others are still only elaborate plans.[7]

One observer has summed up the Brazilian university very well. He states that "with rare exceptions, the university does not represent a true community: both staff and students come to the university only for academic exercises and spend much of their energy elsewhere. There is almost no relationship between the students and the teaching and administrative staff. These are part-time students and part-time teachers in a part-time university."[8]

Brazilian university students are dissatisfied with their educational system. At the primary school level, they advocate a drastic increase in schools, teachers, teacher-training facilities, and books. Idealistic and humanitarian in outlook, they see the need for all Brazilian children, rich and poor, urban and rural, to have a primary school education.

The commitment of the university students to these reforms, however, remains mainly a verbal one. Few, if any, would voluntarily serve for a year or two as elementary school teachers in remote areas of the interior, nor would they spend several years working with children in the urban *favelas* (slums) on a strictly voluntary basis. They talk a great deal, but do little.[9]

To improve the secondary school situation and eliminate the financial barriers, students have called for the establishment of more free public schools, scholarships for poor but qualified pupils, government book subsidies, and inexpensive student restaurants. The bulk of student activity to improve secondary education in Brazil has been channeled through secondary student organizations similar to those found at the university level.[10] By means of student strikes, demonstrations, and group protest meetings, the high school students have voiced their demands for change in these schools. They have usually been supported in these actions by their university counterparts. But student activity to improve secondary education always seems to deteriorate into student politicking, rabble-rousing, and fun-making, to the loss of any truly goal-directed action for bettering the educational system. National politics, Communism, "imperialism," local student politics, soccer, and the opposite sex weigh more heavily in the minds of secondary student leaders than do educational reforms.

Student disenchantment with higher education is part of the Brazilian student tradition. Since the foundation of the faculties in the nineteenth century, students have protested against written tests, class attendance, short vacations, strict professors, and so on. "But," writes one Brazilian educator, "in more recent times these demonstrations ceased, and others have taken their place—in the opposite sense—in favor of instruction."[11] These include strikes against illegally nominated professors, demonstrations against examination frauds, and protests against overloaded classes. University students have also called for better secondary training for all students, more preparation for the *vestibular,* more seminars and smaller classes, new and modern lab facilities and libraries, and more government funds for higher education.[12] However, much of the students' attention has been focused on their own interests as opposed to the general interest of improving the faculties and universities. They have devoted a great deal of time and energy to obtaining inexpensive student restaurants, student meeting halls, and special student rates for plays, concerts, movies, and public transportation.

Most university student action to change higher education has been taken under the widely flung banner of university reform.[13] The university reform movement, which originated in Argentina in 1918, and then spread to the rest of Latin America, has never achieved full force in Brazil. Its first manifestations can be traced back to the late 1920's, when Professor Bruno Lobo campaigned for university reform in Rio and São Paulo. After the Vargas takeover, the movement made some headway in the Francisco Campos Law of 1931, under which students gained nominal representation on university councils and the right to organize in each faculty. In later years, however, university reform ceased to be an issue as students devoted their energies to combating the dictatorship. More recently, the movement has re-emerged as an important issue in university student politics.

Until the nature of the university changes and the quality of higher education improves, university reform will continue to unify students politically. It will remain an issue because students, as well as educators, recognize the need to reform and modernize Brazilian education. The university students will also use the educational reform issue as a basis for broader political activity. Consequently, the nature of Brazil's educational system and her university environment are important in understanding student political behavior in Brazil.

The Brazilian Student: Social Origins and Political Orientations

University enrollment has more than tripled in the postwar period. Total enrollment in 1948 was 38,000; in 1958, it was 84,500. By 1966, there were approximately 121,000 students in Brazilian higher education. The law faculties continue to attract the greatest number of students. They are followed closely by the faculties of philosophy, then by engineering, economics, and medicine, and finally by the faculties of dentistry, agriculture, architecture, and other disciplines. About one-fourth of the students are women, most of whom attend the faculties of philosophy.[14] About 10 per cent of the students are married; the percentage is significantly higher for men, especially those from the lower economic levels of society.[15] A large proportion of the students are enrolled in universities in the more developed states of Brazil. In 1962, 47 per cent were registered in Guanabara and São Paulo; these states plus Rio Grande do Sul, Minas Gerais, and Paraná accounted for 75 per cent of the students and 73 per cent of the teaching staff in higher education in Brazil that year.

University students in Brazil are slightly older than their counterparts in the United States. This difference can be explained by the fact that young Brazilians may spend a couple of years preparing for the *vestibular,* work for a few years before entering a faculty, or attend classes only part-time because they hold regular jobs. Scheman's survey of 1,250 Brazilian students taken in 1960 indicates a rather high average age of 25.9 years for all law students. However, a 1963 study of students in various faculties throughout the nation found 22 years to be the median age of the students. Another 1963 study—by the Institute of Social and Economic Studies (INESE) in São Paulo—showed that 97 per cent of the university students interviewed were under 30, and that 84 per cent were 25 or younger.[16] Female students are distinctly younger, on the average.

Brazilian university students are definitely an elite group from the middle and upper classes of Brazilian society. Almost all the students are upper class in their goals and attitudes or are definitely upwardly mobile. Invariably, though, students will tend to classify themselves as middle class, even if they come from relatively high or low positions on the social scale according to other criteria.[17] Extremely few students come from the lower classes, for the economic barrier to education is great, especially at the secondary school level. In 1960, according to Scheman, 68 per cent of Brazilian law school students had attended a private or parochial secondary school. Almost all of their fathers had some education, and 63 per cent of them had secondary- or university-level training. "Less than 1 per cent, 8 out of 1,250 students polled [in the Scheman study], stated that their fathers had no education. Since 46 per cent of the total number of adult males of Brazil are illiterate, clearly the lower classes were not present."[18] A further indication of the elitist nature of Brazilian university students is that—despite the fact that Brazil has few problems in race relations and no racial barriers per se—the observer in Brazil will notice very few, if any, *pretos* (literally, "blacks") or *mulatos escuros* (dark mulattos) in university classrooms.[19]

Since a great many of the students come from metropolitan areas, most of them live with their families while attending the university. Generalizations are difficult, however, for while in 1960, 70 per cent of the law students in São Paulo were from the metropolitan area, at the University of Minas Gerais law school in Belo Horizonte the majority of the students came from the interior. Students who do not live with their immediate families usually live together in inexpensive rooming houses (*repúblicas*), in special student houses (*casas dos estudantes*), or with relatives in the city.[20]

Although classes are not extremely formal, student-faculty contact remains rather perfunctory; as soon as they have finished a lecture, professors usually must rush off to a class in a different faculty or to another job. Some students simply do not attend classes, because they consider their professors incompetent.[21] Indications are "unmistakable that those students who do not attend class are more affluent than those who do"—probably in part because wealthier students feel that they are in the university only to fulfill their social obligation to obtain a degree.[22]

When university students are not in school or studying, they are most likely working. In 1960, 75 per cent of the law students held some type of employment. Similar data for all faculties taken in 1963 indicate that over two-thirds of the university students were employed in part- or full-time work. Fewer students were employed in the Northeast and in the Catholic faculties.[23]

Students who have free time can find practically no extracurricular activities in the university. There are no organized sports except for the annual intramural University Games and a few interfaculty competitions held once a year. These affairs are loosely organized by the students themselves. Almost all young men play soccer for recreation, but there are no regularly scheduled intercollegiate events in this popular national sport. Moreover, there are few other organizations, such as debate teams, auto clubs, outing groups, intellectual clubs, or the like. As in "Colombia and Mexico, where the extracurriculum is virtually nonexistent, at least in the public universities, satisfaction of . . . leadership ambition must focus on participation in university management and in the opportunity to stimulate, organize, and inspire student group action."[24] Politics in this context becomes an important and popular extracurricular activity.

Student social life offers a further explanation of the penchant for politics among Brazilian university students. Lipset points out that "where students are poor, and where socially desirable girls are often kept from intimate social contact with male students by strict norms and watchful relatives, as in much of Asia and parts of Latin America, the situation may generate a good deal of free-floating frustration that becomes available for political involvement."[25] Although social relations among Brazilian university students are becoming more liberal, young women are still quite protected. Female students date and mix freely with young men in the daytime, but they are often chaperoned on evening dates. Dating patterns vary in different parts of the nation, but such restrictions certainly tend to add to student interest in politics as a chance to mix socially and relieve frustrations.

Another important key to understanding Brazilian university students lies in their view of their own role in society. The students see themselves as an important, special, fortunately privileged group representing the people of the entire nation. They already consider themselves adult participants in the political system. Moreover, they regard themselves as the only truly concerned, impartial, and uncorrupted group in Brazilian politics. Consequently, they not only feel a sense of mission to change and improve the nation but also assume a role of defending the national interest against domestic and foreign exploiters. In this idealistic self-definition, the students may exaggerate their actual significance in the political system.

Other Brazilians see the students quite differently. In general, the public does not appear overly interested in or upset by student actions. When there is a student strike or other academic disturbance, a typical reaction of the people is likely to be: "It's just the students acting up again." They take student riots and demonstrations in stride, as if the students were acting out a role specially reserved for them. The general public attitude is that this is the students' way of "shooting off steam," that they have always acted this way and always will.

Politicians, intellectuals, and other Brazilian leaders view the university students in a still different light. Nostalgically recalling their own idealistic student days, when they were politically active in one way or another, they at least pay lip service to student demands. In certain circumstances, they may actually feel out student attitudes and seek student support for practical political reasons. This politically attentive segment of the population tends to eulogize the university students as "public loudspeakers who represent rebellion and reform," as "those who are preparing to assume the responsibility of the destiny of the nation," and as the "awakener[s] of the sense of responsibility in Brazil." Others, however, suggest that the students are just another "pressure group" or "were more important in the past than they are today."[26] In any event, Brazilian leaders in various fields are aware of the special role of university students in Brazilian society and do not take them completely for granted.

Although only a relatively small number take active part in student politics, almost all university students are politically alert. According to the 1963 INESE survey, 95 per cent of all students "were interested in political affairs," and the same percentage considered the standard of living of most Brazilians unsatisfactory.[27] This same study revealed that university students in general look extremely favorably on "democracy," very favorably on "socialism," quite favorably on "free enterprise," skeptically on "capitalism," and quite unfavorably on "Communism." About four-fifths of the university students advocated both land reform and tax reform, but two-thirds felt that "popular agitation" was *not* necessary for reforms to occur. In addition, about half the students considered foreign companies harmful to Brazil and favored their expropriation with partial or full compensation. Finally, although many did not fully approve of the Alliance for Progress, only 20 per cent totally opposed it.[28]

Most students are only passively interested in politics. Out of 822 students interviewed in the INESE study, 14 per cent said they were "very" interested in political affairs, 64 per cent were "moderately" interested, 16 per cent were "somewhat" interested, and 5 per cent were "not at all" interested.[29] Other data showed that only 40 per cent of Brazil's law students believed student organizations should play an active role in national politics "regularly," while 28 per cent chose "sometimes" and 26 per cent "not at all."[30] Even in one of the most highly politicized faculties in the country, the Faculty of Philosophy of the University of Brazil, only 59 per cent of those polled felt that student organizations should participate "in political questions."[31] Nevertheless, the leaders of the National Union of Students (UNE) were extremely active in national politics, for UNE tended to represent the truly interested and involved students.

Apparently, at least 20 to 30 per cent of the students are active in student politics. One observer estimated that 30 per cent of a select group of students he sampled were student activists.[32] In another survey, 36 per cent of the respondents said they participated in student politics and 22 per cent actually reported holding student government office.[33]

Most active are the student leaders, who more probably come from middle-class backgrounds than not. Among Brazilian law students, for example, those from middle-class backgrounds were reported to be slightly more active in student politics than their colleagues. In the Catholic law faculties, which tend to attract even more affluent students, there was a still higher degree of interest and participation in student politics.[34] Another researcher found "a tendency toward an association of class and political position; the traditional elite tends to conservative and reformist positions, the middle class clusters in the reformist position and the aspiring middle class tends to subscribe to reformist or revolutionary positions." But he also concluded "that the association of class and political position is far from absolute; reformists and revolutionaries may be drawn from any social class represented in the universities."[35]

According to one profile, the politically active student is likely to be an unmarried male day student from the interior who attends classes less regularly than his inactive colleagues.[36] Although politics is still not considered "proper" for young ladies, those who do become active often play key roles. In the office of any student organization, a girl student may be an important adviser to an executive officer, mustering votes for him among her female colleagues and keeping him well informed. Part of UNE's traveling *UNE Volante* (Flying UNE) team was made up of young women. Day students are more active because most student "politicking" takes place in the afternoon and evening, when night students may be working or attending classes. Understandably, single students can devote more time to politics than married students.

It is interesting to note that students from the rural interior appear more active than those from the large urban centers. These inland students often come from regions where politicians, particularly the local boss or *coronel,* are powerful and admired. Politics in rural Brazil has fewer competing diversions than it has in the metropolitan areas. Students from the interior can hope to make a name for themselves in urban university student politics and thereby to enjoy greater esteem when they return home. Finally, since they live away from home, their activities are less subject to familial constraints.

Politically active students tend to advocate extreme positions, particularly on the left.[37] In 1963, these students were much more in favor of government ownership of major industries than were their less active colleagues. They had a higher opinion of "socialism" and a lower opinion of "capitalism." Whereas they valued "democracy" slightly more than most students, they also had a much higher opinion of "Communism." Nevertheless, many student activists were critical of Communism and only half of them advocated "popular agitation" to bring reforms to Brazil.

The more active and politically interested students were also more critical of foreign companies in Brazil and favored their expropriation; yet, a clear majority favored working closely with the United States to promote Brazilian development. Finally, an overwhelming majority of students keenly interested in politics supported UNE and its leadership just prior to the military take-over in April 1964.[38] With the more active and politically interested students holding these viewpoints, it is easy to see how the student movement in Brazil had become "radicalized" prior to the coup.

Student leaders in Brazil are natural politicians. Since most of them are in the academic environment for only a short period of time, they must try to move quickly into the limelight. They usually have very strong personalities and are excellent orators and debaters. In a very few cases, however, they may quietly exercise political power from a minor position on a student directorate or from behind the scenes. Either type is usually well known and highly regarded among his peers and commands a strong allegiance from his friends and followers, for the personalist element, so evident in national politics, stands out in student politics as well. A popular student leader can easily gain strong support from within his faculty; if he is especially outstanding and from a reasonably large faculty, he may become influential in local or even state student politics. Before the 1964 revolution a top student leader could become president of the UNE. Most UNE presidents came from Minas Gerais, São Paulo, and metropolitan Rio de Janeiro, areas with large student populations and numerous faculties that controlled approximately one-half of the votes at the annual UNE Congress. On the whole, the presidents of student organizations on all levels have been dynamic, charismatic, and politically adroit. Several have gone on to make a name for themselves in national politics.

Lesser officials of student organizations have generally been much less powerful in student politics. Many were included on a slate of candidates solely to attract certain groups of voters. This was especially true on the local and state levels; but even nationally, lesser candidates were often selected to balance the slate geographically. In this manner, representatives from Pará, Maranhão, and other less important states gained posts on the UNE Directorate. A political balance was also sought: moderates, progressives, socialists, Communists, and radical Catholics could all be found on the same UNE Directorate.

Student leaders are normally genuine, enrolled students between twenty and twenty-five years of age. Some are academically outstanding, while others appear to use their educational status only for political ends. Among law students in Brazil in 1960, 26 per cent planned to participate in national politics in the future, but only 2 per cent said their reason for attending law school was "to enter politics."[39] They are generally most active during their third or fourth year; by the fifth year, their interest falls off as they begin to look to the future and adult job possibilities.

Although numerous tales exist that "professional" students or various political party "agents" control the Brazilian student movement, there is little evidence to support these allegations, particularly on the state and local levels. On the national level, such elements were present but not predominant. For example, the President of UNE in 1959–60 was unusually old at twenty-nine years of age; he had enrolled in the Faculty of Philosophy, Sciences, and Letters in São Paulo to keep his student status. Yet the 1962–63 UNE President, a fourth-year economics student from Minas Gerais, was only twenty-one when he took office. There are few indications that "professional" students have played any dominant role in the student movement.

UNE: A Political History

The birth of the National Union of Students in 1938, under the Vargas dictatorship, and the subsequent creation of the state student unions served to consolidate and institutionalize the student tradition in postwar Brazil. Through well-defined national, state, and local organizations, the students joined together to take increasingly progressive stands on the issues facing the nation in the postwar period. The student organizations, subsidized by the federal government, were financially independent from political parties and thus relatively free to pursue their political preferences and control their own affairs. The bipolarized Cold War world beyond their national frontiers stimulated the students to question Brazil's traditional alignments and speculate on the advantages of different economic and political models for national development. Bombarded by propaganda from all directions, the students sought new, radical, "Brazilian" solutions to national problems.

Economic nationalism, which had led to the creation of a national steel industry at Volta Redonda in the early 1940's, now focused on the exploitation of oil and mineral resources. The university students began the fight to establish a national monopoly for petroleum extraction, *Petrobrás*. UNE held study groups and meetings to examine the national oil question, and the creation of *Petrobrás* became one of its key goals. Together with nationalist intellectuals and military officers, the students grew increasingly enthusiastic in the campaign to defend Brazilian natural resources from foreign exploitation.

During this period there was a general government crackdown on Communist subversion in Brazil. The more radically nationalistic students, who had gained control of UNE in 1947, were accused of being Communists and pro-Soviet. Indeed there were a "handful" of young Communist students active in Rio de Janeiro, but they worked on the fringes of important student activity. UNE and the student government in general were in the hands of democratic, but strongly nationalistic, student elements.[40] As the UNE leadership began to advocate a more active role for university students in national politics, some student leaders began calling themselves "Marxist reformers." Under the stanchly anti-Communist policies of the Dutra administration (1946–51), clashes between students and police became more frequent. Several students were arrested, and the police closed down the impressive UNE building on the Praia de Flamengo in Rio for short intervals.[41]

By late 1950, less radical elements gained control of the UNE Directorate. But the Union continued to press for educational reforms, demanding more funds for higher education, backing scattered student strikes, and seeking more scholarships. It also fought for student privileges: inexpensive restaurants, lower transit fares, better health facilities, and the like. In the national arena, UNE issued a plan to combat illiteracy, and printed materials to get such a program under way.

Continuing its campaign for *Petrobrás*, UNE sent a letter to the presidents of the Brazilian Senate and Chamber of Deputies, urging that Brazil's mineral wealth be wrested from foreign control.[42] UNE headquarters served as a meeting place for a national congress for the "defense of petroleum." Amid shouts of *"O Petróleo é nosso!"* ("The oil is ours!"), the President of UNE cried out: "The Brazilian university class, the intransigent defender of the democratic principles that rule the destinies of a free people, will always fight, and each time more decidedly, for the national exploitation of our oil!" At the end of the session, the meeting degenerated into shooting and violence. The following day, UNE condemned certain "noxious elements . . . at the mercy of foreign and subservient interests" for having tried to "divert" the campaign.[43]

In the realm of foreign affairs, UNE "violently" opposed the sending of Brazilian troops to Korea, and dispatched a memorandum to the United Nations urging peaceful settlement of the conflict; it also condemned Perón in neighboring Argentina for closing the newspaper *La Prensa.*

Petrobrás was legally established in 1953. University students of all political leanings celebrated the event. Although the Brazilian Congress, the military, and President Vargas were ultimately responsible for the formation of *Petrobrás,* the students had been instrumental in making the oil monopoly a symbol of Brazilian nationalism. Later, the students were quick to "defend" the state enterprise from foreign and domestic "enemies." In return for this support, *Petrobrás* made substantial "contributions" to finance the activities of UNE and other student organizations.[44]

A brief interlude of relative tranquillity within the student movement, from 1952 to 1956, was shattered by the dramatic *bonde* (streetcar) strike in late May 1956. Protesting the 100 per cent increase in the trolley fare of the Canadian-owned transit company in Rio, UNE and the Metropolitan Union of Students in Rio de Janeiro (UME) joined the city's workers in a massive demonstration, blocking major intersections and overturning *bondes* to paralyze the traffic. When President Kubitschek called out the militia to halt the protest, several students and workers were wounded and 150 were arrested; tanks patrolled parts of Rio and the armed forces were kept on alert for two weeks.

The demonstrations quickly spread to other large cities. Students throughout the nation sent representatives or telegrams to Rio to express their solidarity with the action taken against the foreign-owned transit company. Several leftist federal deputies and liberal university officials also lent their support. Although President Kubitschek denounced the *bonde* strike as "Red-inspired," members of the Brazilian Congress decried the violence of the police in subduing the demonstrators. When the *carioca* (Rio) students called for a three-day nation-wide student strike against police brutality, they received overwhelming student support from all parts of the country. Finally, after the Presidents of UNE and UME met with President Kubitschek and other high officials, the new trolley fares were cut in half. The students had won.

The *bonde* strike marked a turning point in Brazil's student political tradition. From 1956 on, UNE was a center of increasingly leftist and radical politics. The national student organization never again returned to the control of the more moderate elements. Although anti-UNE and less radical student groups emerged in several localities at different periods after 1956, none of them was strong enough to take over the national student union.

Through congresses, meetings, and propaganda, UNE's leaders urged the youth of Brazil along radical paths. UNE became extremely important in "politicizing" the majority of the student population in Brazil, for it continuously emphasized the need for students to take action. In the minds of most students, the politicians and the "old guard" were not going to do anything for Brazil; only the student "class" could trigger or force reforms.

During the period of "nationalism and development" under the administration of President Kubitschek (1956–61), UNE and the state student unions received increased federal government subsidies through Minister of Education Clovis Salgado. Funds were released for numerous academic conferences convened to discuss the politics of educational reform, the creation of a university press, student professional interests, and regional social and economic problems. In addition, the Ministry of Education continued to help finance the annual national and state student congresses, where student leaders were elected and educational and political problems debated.

UNE maintained cordial relations with *Petrobrás,* defending it as the "untouchable" symbol of Brazilian nationalism. They also "guarded" the nation's atomic mineral deposits with the slogan "Brazil will not export the future!" The students were especially sensitive to United States investment in Brazil. To allow American investment to enter the nation and "suck out" profits, they argued, was to betray Brazil. When John Foster Dulles visited Rio in August 1958, strict security regulations went into effect. But the students draped the UNE building in black and displayed signs such as "Go Home, Dulles!," "*Petrobrás* Is Untouchable!," and "The U.S. Has No Friends, Only Interests!" Other students jeered the statesman from rooftops.

By 1958, UNE had declared itself "fundamentally an entity of political representation of the university class"[45] and called on students to clarify national problems for the workers and the people *(o povo).* The Union remained violently opposed to foreign investment for Brazilian development, labeling its advocates *entreguistas* ("sellouts").

UNE maintained ties with the Superior Institute of Brazilian Studies (ISEB), an independent, government-financed organization aimed at promoting national development through social science research.[46] But when ISEB published a controversial book arguing that foreign exploitation of Brazil's oil resources could assist Brazil's development,[47] UNE protested. Shortly thereafter, a split in ISEB caused some of its more moderate members to withdraw, charging that "emotionalism" had taken over the Institute.[48] UNE's mentor, the nationalist Álvaro Vieira Pinto, subsequently became Director of ISEB and UNE renewed its support.

In ensuing years, UNE intensified its work in the national political arena. Students campaigned for the nationalization of foreign-owned meat-packing plants, for restrictions on profit remittances by foreign investors, and—together with labor groups—against the inflation that continued to push up bus fares, food prices, and the cost of private education. UNE also criticized a U.S. advisory team's report on Brazilian oil reserves as written by "an agent of the North American trusts and monopolies" and condemned the United States—owned Hanna Mining Company's operations in Brazil.

UNE also sponsored numerous meetings to discuss national problems.[49] For example, in March 1961, UNE and the state student union of Pernambuco held a week-long Study Seminar on the Northeast to examine the problems of that underdeveloped region. Nine months earlier in Bahia, with the assistance of the Ministry of Education (at a cost of 3 million cruzeiros, or about $30,000), UNE hosted the First Latin American Congress on the Reform and Democratization of Higher Education. The final statement of the conference named the "common enemies" of Latin American students: "North American imperialism, the vestiges of colonialism, and the semifeudal oligarchy, which are responsible for the backwardness of our countries, the persistence of antidemocratic governments, and the backwardness and deformity of our universities."[50]

The Cuban revolution further radicalized Brazil's student movement. Students throughout the nation saw in Fidel Castro a fascinating new symbol of revolt. When President Eisenhower visited Brazil in early 1960, the UNE building displayed a "We Like Fidel Castro!" banner. UNE leaders wrote an open letter to the American President warning that "any intervention in Cuba will be an aggression against Latin America." When Jânio Quadros, then a federal deputy and a presidential candidate, headed a bipartisan committee to visit Castro's Cuba, the President of UNE was included in the delegation. Later, in response to the Bay of Pigs invasion in April 1961, UNE and other student organizations held rallies, sent telegrams, and vehemently denounced the "mercenary forces at the service of imperialism." Thus UNE "intransigently defended the democratic principles of the Cuban Revolution, its self-determination and its right to choose its destiny. . . ."[51]

Quadros, elected President of Brazil, advocated a more neutral stance in world affairs and sought closer relations with Cuba and other Communist countries. His resignation in August 1961 after only seven months in office sparked widespread student protests. UNE and other student organizations formed a "Front of Democratic Resistance" and declared a strike to forestall any attempt to prevent Vice President João Goulart from assuming office. Students of almost all political leanings, with the support of many professors and administrators, defended Goulart's constitutional right to the presidency. UNE leaders were jailed for their activities. After Goulart became President, under a special parliamentary arrangement that weakened his powers, many students still sought constitutional "legality" and the restoration of his full prerogatives. The President himself encouraged popular demonstrations, including student strikes and rallies, on his behalf.

In 1962, the radical leftist elements controlling UNE—still defending Cuba and calling for "revolution" throughout Latin America—tried to establish ties with labor and rural peasant workers by promoting a "Student-Worker-Peasant Alliance." The UNE leadership became preoccupied with the "politicization of the masses." With increased funds from the federal government, UNE expanded its Popular Culture Center and established its own University Press *(Editôra Universitária)* to spread the Union's views.

The idea of the Popular Culture Center quickly spread to the state student organizations. In these Centers students and young actors performed nationalistic and often anti-American plays and skits for the poor and illiterate, using language and themes the audiences could clearly understand. The Centers used heroes and villains from popular folklore to show the urban *favela* dwellers and rural peasants how miserable their living conditions were and how they should take action to improve them.[52]

The highlight of student politics in 1962 was a massive strike for university reform, in which university students throughout the nation demanded that one third of the members of the congregations (or governing councils) in the faculties be students. The strike lasted just over two months and triggered innumerable incidents between students, police, and the Ministry of Education. Although they gained limited participation in some faculty organs and on the university councils, the students failed to achieve one-third representation in the congregations. As the strike dragged on without further results, many students grew disappointed and returned to class. The strike hurt UNE's public image and weakened the Union in the eyes of many of the more moderate students who had previously supported the organization's general line.

UNE's image deteriorated further when violence broke out at its 1962 Congress, held at the lavish Brazilian mountain resort of Quintandinha during the latter days of the strike. Newspapers condemned the violence and the increasingly radical orientation of the student movement. Deputy Raimundo Padilha called for a Congressional investigation of UNE. The conservative newspaper *Estado de São Paulo,* which had earlier called UNE a "branch of the Soviet Union," noted the vast sums of money that the students had received for the UNE Congress from the federal budget, the Ministry of Education, *Petrobrás,* commercial firms in Rio, and the government of the state of Rio Grande do Sul under leftist Governor Leonel Brizola.[53] The Rector of the University of Paraná (and future Minister of Education under the Castelo Branco regime) called UNE a "Communist center." A Rio daily editorialized about the 1962 Quintandinha Congress: "There was everything of the pomp of the Habsburgs in the meeting of those professionalized Communist-nationalists."[54]

Despite the growing criticism, UNE maintained its militant posture and retained relatively strong support from students, leftist politicians, and reform-oriented Catholic priests. Still receiving substantial government funds, UNE and other student organizations continued their activities, denouncing the U.S. blockade of Cuba, demonstrating further solidarity with the Castro regime, and holding regional seminars on a host of national and regional problems.

In January 1963, UNE supported the national plebiscite that restored full presidential powers to João Goulart. By mid-1963, the Union had joined with several leftist federal deputies of the Nationalist Parliamentary Front (FPN) and the Communist-dominated General Workers' Command (CGT) to form the radically nationalist Popular Mobilization Front (FMP). The new Front advocated mobilizing the masses to press Goulart and the Congress to adopt a more radical position and to legislate far-reaching reforms. As a "superpressure group" of the left, the Front tried to coordinate the activities of the FPN, CGT, UNE, the Peasant Leagues, and other radical nationalist groups. An extremely loose-knit organization, the Front's internal solidarity rested largely on personal relationships and shared political sentiments. UNE leaders, through their ties with Front officials, tried to work within the Front's general line.

Political tensions mounted in late 1963. In October, Goulart lost a great deal of student support when he tried to obtain special powers by requesting that Congress declare a state of siege *(estado de sítio)* and when his Minister of Education and Culture, the ultra-nationalist Paulo de Tarso, who had funneled huge sums from the Ministry into the student movement, resigned. The students complained that Goulart was taking no steps toward urgently needed radical reforms.

Goulart finally decided to act in February 1964. He called for the expropriation of selected uncultivated areas and of the remaining private oil refineries. He also submitted a law giving illiterates the right to vote and decreed the lowering of rents in Rio and the immediate rental of all unoccupied apartments. When he appeared at a mass rally held on his behalf in Rio on March 13, 1964, Goulart thought he had regrouped and harnessed the forces of the radical left, including the students. In fact, he had merely incited the military to oust him from office the following month.

The "revolution" of April 1, 1964, revealed the weakness of the radical left, since it was incapable of generating any meaningful resistance to the coup. Student protest demonstrations were few in number and received little student support. In Rio, the UNE leadership from within their headquarters, and right-wing groups on the street outside, burned the UNE building on the Praia de Flamengo. One student tried to attack the troops in Rio and was killed. In Recife, a group of students marched on the governor's palace and left two of their colleagues dead, but not martyred, in an action regarded as more foolhardy than heroic. Throughout the nation leftist student leaders were arrested or went into hiding, and many student organizations were closed down by police. In Rio, three members of the UNE Directorate, including the UNE President, took refuge in the Bolivian Embassy.

The April coup threw the student movement into a state of confusion, but four alert and politically moderate state student union presidents quickly joined forces to form a student junta to run UNE until the regular UNE Congress scheduled for July. While the new regime of Castelo Branco threatened to legislate UNE out of existence, the student junta tried to muster support to preserve the organization. But the annual UNE Congress failed to meet in July for lack of student support and fear of reprisal from the government. The regime decided to abolish the Union, to replace it with a government-controlled National Student Directorate (DNE), and to prohibit student organizations from engaging in political activity. UNE ceased its legal existence under the Suplicy Law of November 9, 1964, named after Castelo Branco's first Minister of Education and Culture.

In late 1964 and early 1965 there were no student demonstrations against the military government, but students did keep UNE alive at the margin of the new law. The first public show of student discontent occurred in March 1965, when some four hundred students walked out on President Castelo Branco as he was about to speak at the University of Brazil in Rio. Police arrested several student leaders. They were quickly released on orders from the President, who declared he would not permit "a return to the climate of terrorism in the streets of Rio and the halls of the universities"; he promised to review student demands that tuition-free higher education be maintained, free student elections held, and political restrictions on student organizations removed.[55]

In July 1965, undisturbed by the government, the students held the UNE Congress in São Paulo. The Congress, condemned as "illegal" by Minister of Education Suplicy de Lacerda, gathered a relatively small and not strictly representative cross-section of students; only about one-third of the faculties were represented. But it did elect a full slate of officers, all from the leftist Popular Action (AP) faction within the student movement. The delegates pledged to repudiate the Suplicy Law and boycott the local student elections for the new DNE to be held the following month. Although not observed in all parts of the nation, the boycott was effective in the states of São Paulo, Minas Gerais, and Guanabara, and at the University of Brasília in the Federal District. In addition, anti-government candidates won many of the local student elections.[56]

In late 1965, serious disturbances broke out at the University of Brasília. Professors were dismissed and several students arrested. Police closed the University for serving as a "center of subversion." The incident reflected growing student discontent with Castelo Branco's educational policies and his restriction of student activities. In an attempt to establish better rapport with the students, the President replaced his strongly disliked Minister of Education with Pedro Aleixo, the majority leader in the Chamber of Deputies, who himself had been a student leader in Minas Gerais in the late 1920's. But government policy toward student political activity did not change.[57]

In 1966, despite government prohibition and suppression, student leaders kept UNE alive. When they tried to hold the annual UNE Congress in Belo Horizonte, in the state of Minas Gerais, Castelo Branco suspended the activities of the Minas Gerais student union. Students demonstrating on behalf of UNE were arrested, and the police occupied the university hall where the Congress was supposed to meet.

Approximately 150 students finally held the Congress informally in a nearby Franciscan monastery. There they drew up an eighteen-point proclamation. In the statement the students expressed their determination to struggle against the regime's policies and to seek the return of a freely elected, democratic government in Brazil.[58]

By September 1966, students were openly demonstrating against the imposition of nominal university tuition fees, student arrests, and the indirect election of state governors and of the President-elect, General Costa e Silva. In an attempt to mollify the students, President Castelo Branco announced reforms for the Federal University of Rio de Janeiro and attempted to open a dialogue with the students. But student opposition persisted. In the fall of 1966, "energetic police action" throughout the country served to halt, at least temporarily, student oppositionist activities, which the Castelo Branco regime claimed were coordinated by "Communist agitators directed from abroad." But the students remained an important, if silent, voice of discontent.[59] During 1967 and in early 1968, sporadic, but serious agitation emerged against the Costa e Silva government.

The Forms of Student Political Action

In articulating student demands, the student leadership in Brazil speaks and acts in the name of the entire "university class." In fact, however, the leadership most often enjoys the support of those students who are already strongly interested in political affairs. Their tactics of political action take a variety of forms.

Demonstrations. Student political demonstrations include public rallies, strikes, and the freshman initiation parades (*trotes*). These activities can either raise new issues or spotlight old ones. The history of one student political demonstration may serve to illustrate the general case.

In 1963, when President Goulart sought emergency powers from Congress, many students feared he might be maneuvering for a dictatorial take-over. In Rio, UNE publicly opposed Goulart's request that a state of siege be declared and cabled the state student unions urging them to mobilize immediately against emergency powers for the President. The President of the Pernambuco student union promptly convened an emergency session of state student representatives in the Recife law school. At that meeting, he presented to the delegates a prepared statement opposing any declaration of emergency powers. After an hour of heated discussion that produced minor changes in the text, the statement was approved and sent to the local newspapers for publication. Although many student leaders were politically moderate and did not completely endorse UNE's position, they worked closely with the more radical elements in Recife to oppose the projected state of siege. At the end of the meeting, several student leaders announced that a rally against Goulart's move would be held in front of the governor's palace at noon two days later.

On the morning of the rally, the students distributed mimeographed flyers and over a portable loudspeaker urged the public to join in the demonstration. After assembling at the law school to listen to a few speeches, the students paraded through the center of town to the governor's palace. There, the President of the state student union addressed a small but enthusiastic crowd of students, workers, and bystanders. This orderly demonstration continued for about an hour.

The same day, President Goulart withdrew his request for emergency powers. Student leaders in Pernambuco and elsewhere claimed a great victory. In fact, the demonstration in Recife and other similar student protests had little influence on Goulart's decision to retreat, a decision dictated largely by his inability to muster congressional or even military support. But the students' action did help bring the issue squarely before the public eye.

This case history reflects the efficacy of Brazilian student protest demonstrations in general. Most have had no significant direct impact on specific political decisions or on the formation of government policy, but they have helped move issues into the arena of public controversy. Other examples include student demonstrations against the outlawing of the Brazilian Communist Party in 1947, against the visits to Brazil of Eisenhower and Dulles, against the Alliance for Progress, against the International Monetary Fund, and to protest the resignation of pro-UNE Minister of Education Paulo de Tarso in October 1963.

Generally speaking, the more tangible the issue, the more effective the protest. Perennial student opposition to the rising transit fares is a case in point. Students protesting such increases usually sought to preserve the special low student rates as well. After picketing transit company offices, disrupting traffic, and perhaps damaging several buses or streetcars, the students could usually gain easy access to public officials to present their demands. The most dramatic example of this kind of protest was the successful 1956 streetcar strike in Rio, already discussed.

Students have also effectively prevented certain politicians hostile to their views from speaking. In January 1964, pro-Communist students at the National Faculty of Philosophy in Rio de Janeiro managed to keep the entrance to the faculty blocked, forcing Governor Carlos Lacerda to postpone a graduation speech. Similarly, politically moderate law students in São Paulo compelled Goulart's leftist Superintendent for Agrarian Reform, João Pinheiro Neto, to cancel a speech he was scheduled to give to the students of that faculty. Under the Castelo Branco and Costa e Silva regimes, however, the police did not permit such actions.

Acting alone, students are rarely able to mobilize nonstudents to demonstrate on any massive scale. They can and do, however, combine and coordinate with other groups to enhance the impact of a protest. In 1960, UNE sponsored a series of public demonstrations of solidarity with the Cuban regime, coordinating its efforts with leftist labor leaders. A number of student-politician, student-labor, and student-peasant rallies and strikes occurred in 1962 and 1963. In 1964, UNE and other student groups took part in the huge rally of March 13 that triggered the move to oust Goulart. On the whole, in the important mass demonstrations on nonacademic political issues, students have played only a secondary, supporting role.

One final type of student demonstration is the annual faculty *trote* (literally, "trot") , or parade of freshmen held as an initiation into the faculty. During the *trote,* incoming freshmen are dressed in gunnysacks, rags, or absurd costumes and marched through the streets of the city; they carry signs, make jokes, and disrupt traffic. In recent years, these festive occasions have often been used to attack certain politicians and policies or to call for drastic reforms. The *trote* has become just one more outlet for the students' political energies.

It is important to note that these public demonstrations have not prevented the students from gaining, with remarkable ease, direct access to high public officials such as state governors, the Minister of Education, and even, at times, the President. In the past, the students often used official contacts to obtain government subsidies not only for UNE but for the state and local organizations as well. More recently, Castelo Branco and his Ministers of Education occasionally met with discontented student leaders. Student demands were sometimes answered by the replacement of a government official or the granting of a token concession; far more often, public officials merely sought to pacify the students by assuring them their demands would receive "due consideration."

Conferences and Communications. The university students have also expressed their political demands in conferences and meetings. In the late 1940's and the 1950's, for example, UNE sponsored a number of seminars on the problems of the national petroleum industry and the creation of *Petrobrás.* But not until the 1960's did such meetings become an important method of student action.

In 1961, UNE and the state student organizations began organizing regional student seminars on the need for basic social and political reforms. These sessions were promoted "to awaken the Brazilian university student's conscience," to examine and "better understand Brazilian society," and to seek solutions to regional and national problems. Speakers at these meetings included prominent politicians and nationalist intellectuals.[60] Among the topics discussed were agrarian reform, the role of regional education, literacy programs, the "military-political crisis," the national power structure, "conditions of the existence of man in the Northeast," the self-determination of peoples, "colonialism and imperialism," the vote for illiterates, and the Student-Worker-Peasant Alliance. At the end of the seminars, the students approved resolutions calling for sweeping reforms but offering few, if any, practical suggestions for change. UNE also initiated a series of national conferences on university reform and encouraged state student meetings on the Popular Culture Centers, the establishment of a national drug industry *(Farmacobrás)*, and the consolidation of all national airlines into one government-owned unit *(Aerobrás)*.

Another important means of student political action is the printing press, such as the one UNE operated before the 1964 coup. Student journals and newspapers provide key channels of political communication among students at the faculty, university, and national levels. In addition, students and the reading public can follow student activities through the generally full accounts of student events to be found in the regular daily papers.

Almost every local student organization has its own newspaper, which appears from time to time depending on the availability of funds and talent. These "house organs" cover their organizations' latest social, political, cultural, and sports activities; many deal with national student and nonstudent politics as well. They reflect the political views of the students holding organizational power at the time, and their readership does not extend much beyond the university student community.

The state student unions, on the other hand, seldom publish their own journals, for they usually cannot cover the printing costs. An exception is the powerful Rio-based Metropolitan Union of Students. UME publishes a weekly, *O Metropolitano*, which covers national as well as local student news and enjoys a wide circulation among student leaders not only in Rio (the state of Guanabara), but throughout the nation. Prior to 1963, when for several years UME and UNE shared similar political viewpoints, the UME weekly also served as an unofficial national UNE weekly and expressed the strong leftist-nationalist position of UNE. At that time, *O Metropolitano* circulated on Saturdays as an insert in the independent Rio daily, *Diário de Notícias*, which could be purchased in all parts of the country. But when the opposition gained a victory in UME after the 1962 UNE Congress, the UME weekly adopted an independent-nationalist stance and circulated on its own. UNE reacted in mid-1963 by publishing its own weekly journal, *Movimento*, distributed nationally as an insert in the leftist-nationalist *Brasil, Urgente*. Both student newspapers carried a heavy concentration of articles on national political problems.

In addition, UNE published a monthly magazine, also called *Movimento*, dealing almost exclusively with national economic and political issues. Expressing UNE's radical leftist-nationalist viewpoint, it ran articles by or interviews with nationalist intellectuals, leftist politicians, and members of the Brazilian Communist Party. Among other student journals were the *Jornal Universitário* and the *Correio Acadêmico*. The former was the weekly of the anti-UNE Democratic Youth Front (FJD), while the latter was sponsored by a group of nationalist, anti-Communist students in Rio. Both had circulations largely limited to metropolitan Rio and São Paulo. They tended to carry fewer articles strictly related to politics and more social, cultural, and sports news.

A content analysis of ninety-nine articles from six randomly selected student newspapers and periodicals published in 1962 has shown just how highly politicized Brazil's student publications were at the time.[61] Sixty-two per cent of the articles were classified as "political," 38 per cent as "nonpolitical." Eighty-five per cent of the articles were concerned with national or local issues, while only 15 per cent dealt with foreign affairs. Of the latter, 60 per cent were anti-American. The study also confirmed this author's own observations that the publications of the larger, more important student organizations tend to be the most political.

The impact of these publications on Brazilian university students as a whole must be seriously questioned. The INESE survey showed that 87 per cent of Brazil's university students never read UME's weekly *O Metropolitano* and that 59 per cent never read the FJD's *Jornal Universitário*.[62] Nevertheless, the student press has certainly reached the politically attentive and active students and helped them keep up with student activities in other parts of the nation.

Even UNE, however, with all its resources prior to early 1964, did not reach an appreciable nonacademic audience with its publications.[63] A more effective channel for communicating student political demands to the general public has been the adult daily press. Hardly a day goes by without some mention of student activities in the regular newspapers.

Major student incidents—strikes, demonstrations, or violence—usually receive front-page coverage. For example, in 1962, during the protracted student strike for one-third representation on the faculty congregations, most of the major newspapers in Brazil carried an article daily for several months on the latest news of the strike. All UNE congresses and important local or regional student meetings enjoyed ample press coverage and often provoked editorial comments.

The student leaders realize the value of publicity and frequently issue statements in press-release form. These declarations are often quoted in part or in full by the newspapers. Such statements have included declarations of sympathy with striking workers, opposition to the Cuban "quarantine," sorrow at the death of President Kennedy, protests against French lobster fishermen off the Brazilian coast, opposition to a speech by the American ambassador, "defense" of *Petrobrás,* and reiteration of the UNE's eighteen-point proclamation against the Castelo Branco regime. In reporting student public statements and events, the daily newspapers thus play an important role in presenting student political demands to the general reading public and in emphasizing to the nonacademic community the political role of university students.

Elections, Political Parties, and Labor. University student electoral action in Brazil has been limited. Although almost all university students are qualified to vote, they total less than 1 per cent of the national electorate.[64] Individual students often work in electoral campaigns for reasons of personal ambition, friendship, or family ties. Student organizations, on the other hand, have been noticeably reluctant to throw their support behind one candidate or another. By not openly choosing sides in a political contest, they have remained independent and have avoided the risk of alienating a future mayor, governor, or President.

Nevertheless, in areas with a high concentration of university students, such as Rio de Janeiro and São Paulo, student organizations have occasionally come out strongly in support of particular candidates. For example, during the 1962 congressional elections, UNE leaders helped nationalist politician Leonel Brizola in his successful campaign for a seat as federal deputy from the state of Guanabara (the city of Rio). The victory of leftist-nationalist Paulo Alberto, who ran for state deputy on the Labor (PTB) ticket in Guanabara, has been attributed to the campaigning and votes of university students. A graduate of the Catholic University in Rio and a former editor of the UME weekly, *O Metropolitano,* he was said to have been the "students' representative" in the state assembly. But these instances are exceptions to the rule.

The students' nonpartisan stance has been reflected in their relations with political parties. Unlike many of their colleagues in other Latin American countries, young Brazilians have had only few and minor affiliations with the political parties. With the exception of the Brazilian Communist Party, party youth wings have been practically nonexistent.

There are several reasons for this. First, because they lack clearly defined ideologies, the parties have failed to offer the students a meaningful theoretical political position. For intellectual guidance, the students have turned instead to the writings of Brazilian nationalist intellectuals. Second, the students have seen no particular advantage in joining the parties. Receiving adequate funds from the federal government, and thus avoiding financial dependence on the parties, the student organizations have been relatively free to pursue their own interests and control their own affairs. Finally, and most important, the political parties themselves have failed to organize the university students. Because of the highly personalistic nature of party leadership and the relative insignificance of the party label, politicians have not been able to develop meaningful party structures to coordinate their own partisan activities, let alone plan for youth or student activities within the party framework.

Although the students have not had strong party ties, they have formed "alliances" with other groups from time to time. In general, these arrangements have been loose and informal, based on a broad common interest in reform.

The most explicit student "alliance" has been with labor. During the mid-1950's, student leaders in Rio and São Paulo began a series of loose alliances with labor groups to protest the rising costs of living. In these mainly symbolic associations, student leaders verbally supported labor's demands for higher wages and improved working conditions, while workers joined the students to protest rising transit fares and to advocate educational reforms. By the early 1960's, a few student leaders were attending trade union meetings and inviting labor representatives to participate in their conferences and demonstrations. In the Student-Worker-Peasant Alliance, UNE hoped for a united front of urban and rural labor and students to bring "revolutionary" change to Brazil. The "Alliance" existed more in theory than in practice; its major strength prior to April 1964 lay in São Paulo, where student members of Workers' Politics (POLOP) sought to join with urban and rural workers in a Marxist class struggle.

In the impoverished Northeast, a small group of students worked with the rural Peasant Leagues (*Ligas Camponesas*) to help them organize for higher wages and improved living conditions. However, these few students were looked upon as "fanatic reformers" by many of their colleagues, who preferred to remain in the city and support the peasants' cause verbally. The students were highly sympathetic to the plight of the agrarian workers, but very few actually went into the countryside to work with peasant groups. They were eager to point out the need for rural education and political organization, but their commitment usually stopped at that point. They did, however, help make the general public more aware of the plight of the agrarian worker.

As we have noted, the students did finally join in a formal alliance with pro-Communist labor leaders and leftist federal deputies in the Popular Mobilization Front in 1963; but even this was little more than a symbolic gesture. The Front was easily shattered by the 1964 military coup. Since then, the students have had no formal alliances with other groups in the political system.

Conclusion: Some Effects of Student Political Action

Through these several tactics, then, Brazilian university student leaders articulate their demands on the political system. As loudspeakers of opinion calling for major changes in the status quo, their ability to generate publicity and activate, if not influence, public opinion is far out of proportion to their numerical size. But their *direct* impact on national policy has been minimal. Except in those cases where their interests have coincided with or complemented the interests of other key groups, student demands on the political system have not been met. As Brazilian sociologist Marialice Foracchi writes, "Student action only acquires societal amplitude *under the condition that it is joined with the action of other forces of renovation manifest in Brazilian society.*"[65]

On the other hand, student political action may have important *indirect* effects on the Brazilian political system in the long run. This proposition is extremely difficult to prove, for one can only speculate about the intricate causal relationships that may link past student action with present political phenomena, but it does seem plausible in at least three senses.

First, by constantly pressing for revision of the existing order, the students have undoubtedly helped prepare the way for reforms. Over the years, cases in point have included student support for the abolition of slavery, the removal of the Vargas dictatorship, the establishment of a state petroleum monopoly, and the expansion of education. These causes were not, of course, successful simply because students espoused them, but student support did help create a national climate of opinion conducive to their success. In this sense, students have served as catalytic agents for change within the political system.

Second, and perhaps more significant, student politics are indirectly important for the Brazilian political system because they serve to induct young Brazilians into their political culture.[66] In their strikes, demonstrations, congresses, and publications, students find an opportunity to gain first-hand knowledge and experience of politics and political action, to experiment with new ideas, and to develop and reappraise their attitudes toward government and policy.

Finally, student politics fulfills an important recruitment function for the political system. In the universities, young Brazilian leaders-to-be can test their political talents and learn the political rules of the game. Reflecting on his own experience, one former student activist who went on to become a federal deputy and adviser to a recent President of Brazil has argued: "Student politics is more political than politics itself—much tougher. That's where politicians get their start, where leaders are made. Their importance for the politics of Brazil cannot be overemphasized."

NOTES

1. See, for example, Renato Bahia, *O estudante na história nacional* (Bahia: Livraria Progresso Editôra, 1954).

2. For a detailed description in English of the educational system, see August F. Faust, *Brazil, Education in an Expanding Economy,* U.S. Department of Health, Education and Welfare, Office of Education, Bulletin 1959, No. 13 (Washington, D.C.: U.S. Government Printing Office, 1959); Robert J. Havighurst and J. Roberto Moreira, *Society and Education in Brazil* (Pittsburgh: University of Pittsburgh Press, 1965); *U.S. Army Area Handbook for Brazil,* Department of the Army Pamphlet No. 550-20 (Washington, D.C.: U.S. Government Printing Office, 1964), pp. 153–86.

3. Brazil, *Lei de diretrizes e bases da educaçao nacional* (Rio de Janeiro, 1963), p. 110.

4. In May and June of 1964, following the military coup that ousted President João Goulart in April of that year, the prominent intellectual Gilberto Freyre was extremely influential in forcing the resignation of the Rector of the University of Recife. The two prominent men carried on an open debate concerning the administration of the University by the Rector in the *Jornal do Commércio,* an important daily newspaper in Recife. After a series of attacks and rebuttals in the press and other political pressure, the Rector resigned. See *Jornal do Commércio* (Recife), May 3–June 13, 1964.

5. In material kindly supplied to the writer, Dr. Aaron Feinsot found that among 743 university students in different disciplines throughout the nation, 68 per cent thought student-professor relations were "formal" rather than "informal." For an English and Portuguese version of his questionnaire, see Aaron Feinsot, "Brazilian Images of the United States: A Study of Brazilian University Students" (unpublished Ph.D. dissertation, New York University, 1965).

6. A survey taken by the *diretório acadêmico* of the school of engineering in Recife in 1963 showed that 56 per cent of the students in that large faculty cheated in their academic work. Students explained to the writer the elaborate methods used by their colleagues to smuggle information into written exams. Cheating was not respected, but certainly accepted.

7. In 1966, the Castelo Branco government announced it would begin to reform Brazil's system of higher education to make more efficient use of existing financial, physical, and personnel resources in an effort to modernize the university. *The New York Times,* September 30, 1966.

8. Personal communication from Dr. Bryant Wedge of the Institute for the Study of National Behavior, Princeton, New Jersey.

9. In late 1966, to provide students with an opportunity to work in domestic community development, President Castelo Branco presented a plan for a national volunteer service similar to the VISTA program in the United States.

10. The *União Brasileira dos Estudantes Secundários* (UBES) was the secondary student counterpart to UNE. The secondary students have numerous state and local student political groups.

11. (Antônio) de Almeida Junior, "Os estudantes também constroem," *Revista brasileira de estudos pedagógicos,* XXVIII, No. 67 (July-September, 1957), 229.

12. União Nacional dos Estudantes, *Luta atual pela reforma universitária,* Cadernos de coordenação universitária, No. 4 (Rio de Janeiro: União Nacional

dos Estudantes, 1963), pp. 30–32. For an example of a request by students for more funds for Brazilian higher education, see *The New York Times,* September 1, 1965, p. 12.

13. For general information on the university reform movement see Gabriel del Mazo (ed.), *La reforma universitaria* (2d ed.; La Plata: Centro Estudiantes de Ingenieria, 1941); and *University Reform in Latin America, Analyses and Documents* (Leiden, Netherlands: International Student Conference, n.d.).

14. Officially these faculties are "philosophy, sciences, and letters." Equivalent to the liberal arts colleges in the United States, they were instituted under the higher education law of 1931. Their popularity has increased greatly in the last twenty years.

15. See L. Ronald Scheman, "The Brazilian Law Student: Background, Habits, Attitudes," *Journal of Inter-American Studies,* V (July 1963), 335; and Instituto de Estudos Sociais e Econômicos (INESE), "Student Study" (mimeo.; São Paulo, 1963).

16. The median figure was supplied to the writer by Dr. Aaron Feinsot of New York University. The second 1963 survey referred to is INESE, *op. cit.* see also Scheman, *op. cit.,* pp. 334–35, and René Ribeiro, *Religião e Relações raciais* (Rio de Janeiro: Ministerio da Educação e Cultura, 1954), p. 158. Ribeiro found that among 249 students from various faculties at the University of Recife in 1952, student ages were between 18 and 33, with an average of 22.7 years.

17. Scheman, *op. cit.,* p. 341. Scheman found that 83 per cent of the law students classified themselves as middle-class. In information supplied to the writer, Feinsot noted that 87 per cent of his respondents considered themselves as middle- or upper-class. Also see Bertram Hutchinson, *Mobilidade e trabalho* (Rio de Janeiro: Centro Brasileiro de Pesquisas Educacionais, 1960), pp. 150–53. His figures show that 73 per cent of São Paulo students placed themselves in the middle class.

18. Scheman, *op. cit.,* pp. 346–47, 355.

19. See Era Bell Thompson, "Does Amalgamation Work in Brazil?," Parts I and II, *Ebony,* XX, Nos. 9 and 11 (July and September 1965), 27–41 and 33–42, respectively.

20. Scheman, *op. cit.,* p. 336. In a personal communication to the writer, Bryant Wedge indicated that at the University of São Paulo 60 per cent of the students lived with their families, 22 per cent lived in student houses and dormitories, 14 per cent in *repúblicas,* and 4 per cent had other arrangements. (The *república,* a private student house, is a carry-over from student living quarters of the nineteenth century; it is slowly dying away.)

21. Feinsot found that 24 per cent of the students believed the quality of higher education available to students in Brazil was "generally low throughout all faculties." Seventy-one per cent of the students considered it "excellent in some faculties, not good in others."

22. Scheman, *op. cit.,* p. 342.

23. *Ibid.,* p. 345. Feinsot supplied the 1963 figure. See also Marialice M. Foracchi, "O estudante universitário: resultados iniciais de uma investigação sociológica," *Anhembi,* XLV (February 1962), 422–45. Fifty-nine per cent of the students she interviewed were working.

24. E. Wight Bakke, "Students on the March: The Cases of Mexico and Colombia," *Sociology of Education,* XXXVII (1964), 203.

25. Seymour Martin Lipset, "The Political Behavior of University Students

in Developing Nations" (mimeo.; prepared for presentation at the UNESCO Conference on Students and University Education in Latin America, Bogotá, Colombia, July 13–19, 1964), p. 52.

26. Excerpts, respectively, from an interview with José Honório Rodrigues, Rio de Janeiro, August 20, 1964; a mimeographed letter from Hélio de Almeida (President of UNE, 1942–43) to the Brazilian Minister of Education, Suplicy de Lacerda, dated June 29, 1964, p. 3; Aben Athar Netto, *Psicologia do estudante brasileiro* (Rio de Janeiro: Gráfica Olímpica Editôra, 1959), p. 18; Themistocles Brandão Cavalcanti, "Grupos de pressão," *Revista de direito público e ciência política*, I (1958), 8; and an interview with Guide Holanda, Rio de Janeiro, July 6, 1964.

27. INESE, *op. cit.*

28. In another 1963 study, almost all the students sampled favored assistance programs for Brazil, but most thought the Alliance for Progress could "make some difference, but not enough in Brazil's social and economic development." Personal communication from Dr. Aaron Feinsot.

29. INESE, *op. cit.*

30. Scheman, *op. cit.*, p. 351.

31. See Leonard D. Therry, "Dominant Power Components in the Brazilian University Student Movement Prior to April, 1964," *Journal of Inter-American Studies*, VII, No. 1 (January 1965), 29.

32. Personal communication from Dr. Bryant Wedge.

33. Scheman, *op. cit.*, p. 349. The 22 per cent figure covers appointive as well as elective positions, graduation dance committee members along with student directory presidents. It seems nonetheless strikingly high when viewed from the perspective of a North American campus.

34. *Ibid.*, p. 350.

35. Personal communication from Dr. Bryant Wedge.

36. Scheman, *op. cit.*, p. 349.

37. Glaucio A. D. Soares has shown that there is a strong tendency for the most active participants in university student politics in different parts of the world, including Brazil, to be also the most radical:

> Not only is a radical ideology associated with broader interest and participation in political affairs in general, but radicalism is closely linked with party membership and active participation in meetings, demonstrations, rallies, etc. Therefore, if one tries to estimate the real extent of student radicalism by mass demonstrations, severe distortions are bound to appear as the radical leftist groups are likely to be greatly overrepresented among demonstrators.

Glaucio A. D. Soares, "The Active Few: Student Ideology and Participation in Developing Countries," *Comparative Education Review*, X, No. 2 (June 1966), 212.

38. INESE, *op. cit.*

39. Scheman, *op. cit.*, p. 350.

40. Conversation with Fernando Pedreira, New York City, October 1965.

41. Although the UNE building was not on any university grounds, it is worth noting that—in contrast to the Spanish American countries, where, until the recent events in Argentina and Venezuela, university premises have been "off-limits" to the police and "sacred ground" for student rioters—in Brazil the police may enter the universities, close down buildings, and arrest students. Students cannot seek asylum in university buildings.

42. União Nacional dos Estudantes (UNE), *Relatório, 1950–1951* (Rio de Janeiro: União Nacional dos Estudantes, 1951), p. 29.

43. *Ibid.,* pp. 33–34.

44. For example, in 1962 *Petrobrás* contributed Cr $802,500 (about $1,700) to UNE and other student groups. In 1963 it gave a total of Cr $2,206,869 (about $3,600) to student organs. See Brazil, *Diário do Congresso Nacional,* XIX, No. 74 (April 28, 1964), Section I, 2662.

45. Sônia Seganfreddo, *UNE, instrumento de subversão* (Rio de Janeiro: Edições GRD, 1963), pp. 49–50. Miss Seganfreddo's book is a highly biased diatribe against Communist subversion in UNE. It does, however, provide a useful historical view of UNE and several good illustrations of Brazilian student political activity.

46. See Frank Bonilla, "A National Ideology for Development: Brazil," in K. H. Silvert (ed.), *Expectant Peoples, Nationalism and Development* (New York: Random House, 1963), pp. 235–36.

47. Hélio Jaguaribe, *O Nacionalismo na Atualidade Brasileira* (Rio de Janeiro: ISEB, 1958).

48. Interview with José Honório Rodrigues, Rio de Janeiro, August 20, 1964.

49. UNE, *Relatório, 1960–61* (Rio de Janeiro: União Nacional dos Estudantes, 1961), pp. 11–15.

50. Luciano Martins, "UNE: quebrar bonde é reivindicar reformas para o ensino," *Jornal do Brasil* (Rio de Janeiro), July 3, 1960.

51. UNE, *Relatório, 1960–61*, pp. 21–22.

52. See Robert Myhr, "Cultural Nationalism in the Brazilian Student Movement," in David Spencer (ed.), *Student Politics in Latin America* (Philadelphia: U.S. National Student Association, 1965), pp. 250–52.

53. *Estado de São Paulo* (São Paulo), June 26, July 21, 1962.

54. *Jornal de Commércio,* July 26, 1962.

55. *News Features* (New York), VI, No. 3 (March 30, 1965), 4.

56. *Ibid.,* VI, No. 9 (August 25, 1965), 1–2; *Youth and Freedom* (New York), VII, Nos. 4–5 (1965), 24–25.

57. *Ibid.,* VIII, Nos. 1–2 (1966), 27–28; Brazilian Embassy in Washington, D.C., *Boletim Especial,* No. 10 (January 19, 1966).

58. *Correio da Manhã* (Rio de Janeiro), July 27–31, 1966.

59. *The New York Times,* September 15, 18, 25, 27, 30, 1966.

60. Among them were Leonel Brizola, Almino Afonso, Magalhães Pinto, Mauro Borges, Celso Peçanha, Darcy Ribeiro, Franklin de Oliveira, Seixas Doria, and Gabriel Passos.

61. Edward Chaszar, "Report on the Brazilian Student Movement" (manuscript prepared for the Kossuth Foundation, New York, 1963), pp. 21–33.

62. INESE, *op. cit.*

63. The idea of a student-run "university press" dates back to 1955–56, when UNE sponsored two national conferences on the subject. The students suggested that each university establish its own press, which they could help administer and use to publish materials they had selected. Finally, in 1961, UNE received an allocation of 10 million cruzeiros (about $30,000) from the federal budget to purchase printing equipment. UNE's University Press (*Editôra Universitária*) began operations the following year. (Allegations that UNE received money from Czechoslovakia for this equipment have not been proved.)

UNE used the Press to print the monthly *Movimento,* several pamphlets on university reform, and materials for the Popular Culture Centers. UNE also began publishing its own books. The first (in 1962) was Álvaro Vieira Pinto's Marxist-oriented *A questão da universidade (The Question of the University),* in which the author identified university reform as part of the greater struggle for the economic and social transformation of the nation. Next (also in 1962) came a collection of essays entitled *Cristianismo hoje (Christianity Today),* edited by Herbet José de Souza, stressing the need for Christian action for social change in Brazil to replace the "accommodationism and indifference to humanity" of traditionally "mystical and formal" Christianity. The book reflected both the influence of the Catholic left within the student movement and UNE's desire to reconcile its radical views with those of moderate-progressive elements in the Church.

Other University Press books (titles here translated into English) included a highly critical *Analysis of the Three-Year Plan,* also published in 1962. Co-authored by a Communist (Mário Alves) and a Socialist (Paul Singer), the book attacked Celso Furtado's economic development plan for 1963–65 as a "policy of conciliation with imperialism and landowners" against "the Brazilian people." Other UNE titles included: *How Brazil Helps the United States, Inflation: Arm of the Rich,* and *The Third War.* Although UNE's books and pamphlets could be purchased at some newsstands, they were normally sold at student congresses and at special student book sales, where they reached their primary audience: the university student community.

64. Brazilian voters must be literate and over eighteen years old. The 1963 INESE study showed that only 13 per cent of the university student population was under twenty; of these, most were probably between the ages of eighteen and twenty. In the 1962 Congressional elections, 14.7 million votes were cast, while the total university student population at the time was only 110,000.

65. Marialice M. Foracchi, *O estudante e a transformação da sociadade brasileira* (São Paulo: Companhia Editôra Nacional, 1965), p. 294. Emphasis in the original.

66. For a discussion of the process of induction into the political culture of a nation, see Gabriel A. Almond and G. Bingham Powell, *Comparative Politics: A Developmental Approach* (Boston: Little, Brown, 1966), pp. 42–72.

9. CHILE

MYRON GLAZER

How deeply involved are university youth in political activities? What political attitudes do they hold? What factors influence these activities and attitudes? These are only a few of the questions to which scholars concerned with students, politics, and modernization are currently seeking answers in a variety of national settings.

The research for this chapter was conducted at the University of Chile in Santiago in 1963–64.[1] The results suggest that political activism was not as widespread among Chilean students as some observers believed. Rather, the highly politicized university atmosphere was the result of intense activity by a small percentage of politically and ideologically committed students. Furthermore, it became quite clear that student political attitudes were not the consequence of intense intergenerational conflict. The views of the overwhelming majority of students questioned sharply reflected those of their fathers. The leftward thrust of the major political parties and the decline of conservative strength, moreover, created

I am pleased to acknowledge the generous assistance of various organizations that have supported this project. The Inter-University Study of Labor Problems in Economic Development and the Industrial Relations Section of Princeton University provided time and facilities during the planning stage, and Doris McBride and other members of the Section staff always responded to our many requests for help. The Henry L. and Grace Doherty Foundation financed the field work and the Center for International Studies of Princeton University supported the writing of the study materials. The work on this article has directly benefited from the generosity of the Comparative National Development Project of Harvard University and a grant from Smith College. I also extend my sincere appreciation to Marcia Alexander, Penina M. Glazer, Mohammed Guessous, Terry Lichtash, and Joel S. Migdal for their insightful criticisms of the manuscript. My many Chilean friends have earned my everlasting gratitude.

a climate in which the students' ideals were paralleled by those of national leaders.

To present the findings on which these, and other, conclusions are based, we shall introduce a small cast of composite characters. Although Luis, Jaime, Rosa, Hector, and Roberto cannot be found among the real-life students of the University, the attitudes and experiences they typify can.

Political Socialization in the University of Chile: Luis and His Friends[2]

The School of History. Luis, along with one hundred other students, enrolled in the School of History of the Pedagogical Institute (*Pedagogico*) in March 1964. Like the great majority of his peers, he had had little contact with political groups in secondary school, but he was, of course, aware of the struggles between the different national parties. He had even considered studying in the School of Law, the breeding ground of politicians. Although the law profession is more highly esteemed than secondary school teaching, Luis feared that the law school entrance requirements were more difficult and that competition within the school was keener. Even if he were to become a lawyer, he felt that his lower-middle class background would not afford him the contacts which were so useful in starting a professional practice. In the end, he decided he would have a more successful career in the teaching profession. He had always felt that his history courses in secondary school could have been far more interesting. His goals in entering the School of History were to become a good teacher, to attain a secure position in Santiago, and to interest his future students in the history and current problems of their country.

During his first days at the *Pedagogico* Luis was very much impressed by the pleasant campus. It is unlike those of other divisions of the University, which consist of old buildings and new annexes, spread out all over the city of Santiago.[3] Luis observed a spirited atmosphere when advanced students gathered in front of the school to have long discussions. These were often continued at the cafeteria, located alongside the history building. He sensed that many of these conversations derived from the political agreements or differences among the students. Luis was also almost immediately beset by partisans of various political groups who handed out literature presenting their point of view or calling attention to articles in the national press. It was obvious to him that the divergent ideas were taken very seriously by the student groups in his school.

These groups, student miniatures of the national parties, were highly competitive and hostile to one another. Their representatives tried to contact each incoming student personally. Luis and all other first-year students were approached by the Christian Democrats. Their organization impressed him, as did their efforts to help orient him to the routine of the school and assist him with any registration problems. Students of the University Leftist Movement (*Movimiento Universitario Izquierdista,* or MUI), who described their group as a leftist coalition including Communists, Socialists, and independents, seemed to be less efficient in contacting the incoming students. Luis, however, was told that they had a file on every history student and his political preference.

At the time Luis entered the University, in March 1964, the national presidential campaign had just officially begun. With the withdrawal of the candidate of the incumbent conservative coalition, the Democratic Front (*Frente Democrático*), in the aftermath of a defeat in a local election, the center-left Christian Democrats and the far left, largely Socialist-Communist Front of Popular Action (*Frente de Acción Popular,* or FRAP) alone remained as potential victors. The two competing forces differed less in policy than in style and reputation. Their programs were strikingly similar, especially in their general emphasis on the need for sweeping social change. Both, as opposition parties, could freely attack the incumbent regime.

The basic program of the Christian Democratic party had been spelled out by its President, Renan Fuentealba, the previous year. Attacking the FRAP and charging it with proposing "revolution with dictatorship," he characterized the Christian Democratic program as a "revolution in liberty." The party's platform, as he presented it, stressed the need to democratize and modernize state and nation through extensive reform in all areas: economic, legislative, administrative, judicial, agrarian, educational, urban, and diplomatic. Under economic reform, for example, the Christian Democrats proposed participation by workers in industrial ownership and management, the fullest use and control of Chile's natural resources for the sole benefit of her people, and "an end to the power and privileges of accumulated money."[4] Christian Democratic leaders declared, in a manner characteristic of their whole campaign, that theirs would not be a government of a single man or party, but a collectivity, responsible in its action to all the people, who would themselves lead in the struggle for their own liberation and betterment. Their program, however, did not advocate the nationalization of American-owned copper mines.

The program of the FRAP was set forth almost a full year before the election;[5] it too focused on the need for agrarian reform, economic controls, industrialization, democratization, and an independent foreign policy. The major divergence between the FRAP and the Christian Democrats lay in the former's stated intention to nationalize Chile's major extractive industries.[6] The FRAP urged this as a vital step to prevent the exodus of millions of dollars in foreign profits and to permit their reinvestment in the national economy. The FRAP claimed that Chile had too long been bled by North American copper companies, whose operations were blatantly imperialistic. Chileans, warned the FRAP, could no longer ignore the fact that parent companies in the United States set the prices for the raw copper mined by their Chilean subsidiaries or that the highly profitable refining process still took place thousands of miles from Chile. So long as foreign capitalists controlled her most vital resource, the leftist coalition bitterly predicted that Chile was doomed to remain a servant nation.

As the campaign progressed Luis realized how difficult it was to remain neutral or aloof. The great contest stepped up the tempo of student political life and stimulated the recruitment and propaganda activities of opposing student partisans, who worked to organize support not only in the University, but also in metropolitan Santiago.

Luis' friend Jaime was one of these ardent campaign workers. Jaime had been active in a political group in high school, and had decided, even before entering the School of History, to join the University affiliate of the same group. To Jaime, the highly politicized atmosphere of the school was a great attraction. An admirer of the FRAP candidate, Senator Salvador Allende, and strongly influenced by Fidel Castro and the Cuban Revolution, Jaime believed that student radicals had an important part to play in the modernization of their country. He reminded Luis that the Student Federation (*Federación de Estudiantes de Chile,* or FECH) had been very active in politics for over fifty years, struggling to overcome the inequalities and injustices of Chilean society. This heritage continues to inspire contemporary students. In the words of one observer:

> Over and above nationalistic feeling and the commitments to party, there exists a set of canons governing and inspiring student action. . . .

They include the courage to hold and defend a point of view on fundamental issues, a readiness for self-sacrifice, loyalty in friendship, love of
country, hatred of dictators and distrust of the military, a sentimental
identification with the working classes, and solidarity with youth of
other Latin American countries. Students have been a force for progress
within the university; their dedication to democratic ideals, their readiness to protest injustice, and their resistance to political repression have
helped keep Chile politically moderate.[7]

This was Jaime's image of what a student should be.[8] In discussions with Luis, he argued that the student's privileged position
in Chile, a country with so many pressing problems, *obliged* him
to engage in social and political action; the alternative, to concentrate on his studies and professional training, could only be a
betrayal of the suffering masses. Jaime rejected the view that student
organizations should be concerned only with "student" issues, such
as financial aid and housing, and denied the charge that student
political groups were merely party tools. He also disagreed with
those who believed that students could never be politically relevant.
To illustrate his case, he reminded Luis of the front-page newspaper
coverage recently given a meeting held between a high government
official and the leaders of FECH to discuss the nation's border dispute with Argentina.

Jaime also maintained that student political work in the *callampas*
(urban slums) and rural areas could help awaken the people to
their needs and rights. Urging Luis to accompany him on such a
mission the following Saturday, Jaime said: "See the waste of our
precious resources and tell me that Chile does not need a social
revolution. Look at the poverty and try to side with those who
speak of 'democracy' and moderation. Talk to our Chilean *rotos*
(broken ones) and tell me you cannot fight our exploiting aristocracy. Don't discuss the rights of the 500,000 who live in the
gracious Chile known by tourists and visitors.[9] Speak instead of the
millions who go hungry in spite of rich soil, who drown in squalor
while we attend our lovely schools."

Rosa, another good friend of Luis, responded to the campus
political environment quite differently. Unlike Jaime, she came
from a secondary school in the northern province of Coquimbo.
The world of politics was strange to her. Luis saw her struggling to
"define" herself. She realized it was difficult not to identify with a
political group. Yet her inherent dislike for political activity was
so strong that she was alienated by all the attempts to recruit her
and by the political machinations she saw going on in the school.

She was aware of the many problems facing the teaching profession, the lack of good jobs in the cities, the poor pay, and the low prestige. Yet she rejected political agitation as the answer. A conscientious student, she was disturbed by the chronic strikes that plagued the *Pedagogico*. Good training, she felt, was most essential if she were ever to help her future students. Luis understood the two opposing views of his friends and felt himself caught in the middle.[10]

After his initial exposure to the political currents of his school, Luis could now better understand the great rivalry between the two major groups. They seemed to have almost the same number of members and were continually battling for the sympathies and votes of the uncommitted (Table 1).

Through his many conversations with other students, Luis became aware that although few actually joined the groups, many (49 per cent) were strong sympathizers.[11] As he began to spend more and more time in political conversations in front of the history building and in the *casino* (student union), he saw that the MUI appeared slightly stronger than the Christian Democrats. This was somewhat unusual, for both in the *Pedagogico* and in the University-wide offices the Christian Democrats retained most of the major positions. The strength of the MUI in his school, in fact, had led a few of his classmates to identify more closely with the Christian Democrats than they ordinarily would have; some had even become members primarily for this reason. One of his friends explained, "The Marxists are very strong in this school, and since I am in sympathy with the Christian Democrats, I feel I should actively support them." The high degree of politicization of the school was markedly increased by the competition between the two major groups. Since each feared the other would gain an undue advantage, both tended to define all issues on the campus in highly political terms.

This situation was intensified as the presidential campaign became a widening spiral of claim and counter-claim, charge and counter-charge. Under the pressure of such exchanges and because of the similarity of the two programs, partisan allegiances were personalized. Both candidates—Eduardo Frei of the Christian Democrats, Salvador Allende of the FRAP—had developed substantial personal followings over the years. Increasingly, FRAP supporters defined themselves as Allendistas, and many Freistas also appeared.

Although there were some instances of personal attacks on the candidates themselves, much more energy was devoted to vilifying the supposed "real powers behind the thrones." There was a power-

TABLE 1

UNIVERSITY POLITICAL GROUP MEMBERSHIP BY SCHOOL AND YEAR

(In Per Cent)

	SCHOOL					YEAR		
	History	Engineering	Medicine	Physics	Total	I	II-III	IV-VI
Nonmembers	67 (63)	93 (87)	82 (81)	97 (29)	82 (260)	85 (88)	81 (86)	80 (86)
MUI coalition[a]	16 (15)	4 (4)	5 (5)	—	8 (24)	7 (7)	8 (9)	7 (8)
Christian Democrats	13 (12)	2 (2)	6 (6)	3 (1)	7 (21)	5 (5)	9 (10)	6 (6)
Other groups[b]	1 (1)	1 (1)	—	—	1 (2)	—	1 (1)	1 (1)
Rejected[c]	3 (3)	—	7 (7)	—	3 (10)	3 (3)	—	6 (7)
Total	100 (94)	100 (94)	100 (99)	100 (30)	101 (317)	100 (103)	99 (106)	100 (108)

Note: Because of rounding, percentages do not always total 100. Absolute figures are in parentheses.

[a] Includes seven students who specifically identified themselves as Socialists and two who identified themselves as Communists, the latter both in the School of History.

[b] The Radicals and Liberals, with one member each.

[c] Responses unclear or missing.

ful attempt to associate the FRAP coalition with Communist domination and to depict the Socialist Allende as a pawn whom the Communists would soon dispose of, were he elected, in order to set up their own dictatorship.[12]

Guilt by association also became a major FRAP weapon, particularly after the right-wing parties gave their support to Frei. A flood of headlines in the Communist press linked various *latifundistas* (large landowners) and "exploiters" with Frei and his party.[13] Attempts were even made to associate the Christian Democratic candidate with fascism and with a small Nazi group that supported him as the lesser of two evils.[14]

In addition to making drastic attempts to discredit the opposition, each group also worked to widen the base of its own support. Ideological consistency became far less important than victory. After the demise of the right-wing coalition in the provincial election in Curico, the Christian Democrats were greatly strengthened by an infusion of conservative support. The party accepted this backing, notwithstanding its vehement attacks on these same groups only a short time before. After March 1964, Frei stated his readiness to accept the endorsement of any group willing to support his program, but said he would not be compromised in any manner. Sarcastically attacking this position, Allende derided those who believed that support would be given "with no strings attached." Yet it was Allende himself who made an impassioned, but unsuccessful, plea to the middle-of-the-road Radical Party immediately after the breakup of the conservative coalition.[15] Each national coalition, then, attempted to build its own positive image, with which a vast cross section of the population could identify, and to portray its opposition as representing only narrow and alien interests. The opposition, in turn, was at once engaged in projecting its own image, creating a negative image of its political competitors, and rejecting the negative image of itself.

As he followed the course of the campaign, Luis, like many of his peers, became increasingly aware of Chile's social and economic problems and the programs proposed to remedy them. Yet none of the current student groups attracted him. He would have much preferred a group with an independent approach and without commitments to any national political leader. He believed Chile needed students who were dedicated to solving national problems but who were not overly committed to any particular party.

In the relatively partisan atmosphere of the School of History, Luis' views were in the minority. In many other schools, however, a majority of the students believed that all the existing groups were too involved in *politiquería* (dirty politics) to merit the students' support. They felt they should try to make their contribution as intelligent, unaffiliated critics of society.[16] Many were simply uninterested in politics. Others were politically concerned but critical of the politicians' behavior and unconvinced by the campaign rhetoric. They saw little to be gained through partisan action on behalf of an existing political alternative.

The School of Engineering. Several times a month, Luis and a good friend studying in the School of Engineering met downtown. Their conversations often turned to a comparison of their experiences. Hector reported that in the School of Engineering very few students had actually joined a political group and that the proportion who were avowed sympathizers also seemed relatively small. In the School of Engineering, unlike the School of History, the Christian Democrats controlled the elective student offices and enjoyed much more sympathy than the MUI.[17] The School of Engineering seemed to lack the "leftist" flavor of the School of History. While history students usually identified themselves as "leftists," those in the Engineering School were much more likely to describe themselves as being of the "center" (Table 2). In both schools, a few

TABLE 2

STUDENTS' POLITICAL SELF-DEFINITION BY SCHOOL

(In Per Cent)

	History	Engineering	Medicine	Physics	Total
Left	51	28	39	40	39
	(48)	(26)	(39)	(12)	(125)
Center	17	41	29	23	29
	(16)	(39)	(29)	(7)	(91)
Right	3	6	2	3	4
	(3)	(6)	(2)	(1)	(12)
Uninterested[a]	23	18	23	23	22
	(22)	(17)	(23)	(7)	(69)
Others[b]	5	6	6	10	6
	(5)	(6)	(6)	(3)	(20)
Total	99	99	99	99	100
	(94)	(94)	(99)	(30)	(317)

[a] Apolitical.

[b] Six "leaders," six "independents," four "center-leftists," two "humanists," and two who did not answer.

ideologically committed activists set the tone for a large majority of sympathizers and uninvolved students. This led many to complain about the over-politicization of the schools. Even many of the sympathizers believed that the political activity had deteriorated into machinations, factionalism, and manipulations, instead of leading to serious efforts to solve societal problems.

Over 40 per cent of the history students complained that their school was too politicized and that many of their peers were too interested in political maneuvering. An additional 12 per cent specifically mentioned *politiqueria,* the "dirty" aspects of politics, as one of the school's major problems.

A comparable reaction to political participation and activity was found among the engineering students; 50 per cent of those in their first year cited excessive politicization as a major problem. Several of them reported that they had been advised to avoid entanglement in political activity in order to prevent the loss of valuable study time. They were aware of the great work demands made on engineering students and of the very high repeat and failure rate among their more advanced peers. They also knew that the attainment of an engineering degree would assure them a secure and highly prestigious social position.

In the entire sample, many of the unaffiliated students (51 per cent) considered over-politicization of the University a problem, while far fewer of the FRAP supporters (29 per cent) did. The latter seem to adapt better in a politically charged environment. Christian Democratic students, as well as conservatives, tended to see the University in less militant political terms.

These tendencies are not confined to Chilean students. They reflect a most important distinction in many other Latin American countries.

> Radical and Conservative students have different role images. A radical orientation seems to be connected with an *integrated* role image, in the sense that the student role is not separated from the citizen role. Student life is seen as *part* of national political life.
>
> Conservative students, on the contrary, tend to see themselves as full-time students preparing for a career. They are more concerned with technical problems rather than with national issues. They feel unhappy when university life is interwoven with national politics. A conservative orientation seems to be closely associated with a *compartmentalized* and more professionalized student role image.[18]

The School of Medicine. As Luis' experiences in the School of History differed from those of his friends in the Engineering School, so did they diverge from those of young Chileans entering the School of Medicine. Roberto, a first-year medical student, was well aware of the social problems of his country. In fact, this was one of the reasons he had decided upon a career in medicine. Yet, it was also obvious to him that his major challenge in the next few years would be to learn the basic materials in the biological sciences. Together with the majority of his classmates, he realized that in the Medical School a student was in training. To become a good doctor had to be his major concern. He was proud of his acceptance to the school and knew of the high reputation that Chilean doctors had secured for themselves.

He knew from what other students had told him that in his school professional commitment and political interest were kept quite separate. The classroom was a place where medical knowledge was imparted and learned. Politics had to be put aside at the door. While other schools might be affected by strikes, the medical students, engaged in study, research, or clinical training, had to remember that their major responsibility was to their work. The school was obviously intent on training highly skilled physicians, through an intensive exposure to the most modern and specialized forms of medical treatment.

Roberto was not, however, oblivious to the political activity going on around him. He listened to many discussions in the cafeteria and read the propaganda posted in the halls. As in all other schools, when the FECH elections approached heated arguments broke out between those who supported MUI and those who supported the Christian Democrats. Roberto learned that in recent student elections the majority of his school had voted for the Christian Democrats, but that more than one class delegate and sometimes even the school's student president had come from the opposing group.

Roberto also noticed an important change in the attitudes of many medical students as they advanced through the school. They tended to become more confident of their ability to complete the required work and surer that some day they would be doctors. He saw that they grew more concerned with the broader problem of effecting change in the society. They had begun to believe, or so it seemed, that they could make only a limited contribution through technical competence alone. They were critical of the emphasis on specialization. Were they in fact being prepared to practice the kind of basic medicine that Chileans most required? As students went through the medical training program their interest in politics sharpened and they moved to the left. Increasingly, they believed that government policy strongly affected medical progress throughout Chile and thus found it difficult to separate the professional from the political.

Indeed, when confronted with a direct question asking whether gaining technical competence or participating in change-directed activities was more important, a high percentage of student doctors chose the latter (Table 3) .[19] Students in the upper years of both medicine and engineering seemed least convinced of the primary importance of their studies. Chilean students, generally, saw the intake of technical knowledge as the primary rationale of university study.[20] Yet as they drew closer to accepting full professional responsibilities, many became less convinced that this was the best way to contribute to social progress. Perhaps because they had completed most of their training, had gained practical experience in applying their professional skills, and had seen the extent of Chile's problems, they now more seriously questioned the central significance of professional concerns.[21]

Student Political Partisanship: Origins and Content

Early membership in political groups appeared to affect subsequent university activity. Just over one-half of the forty-three students who joined while in secondary school went on to play an active political role in the University. While these early joiners represented only 14 per cent of the total sample, they comprised 25 per cent of the activists.

Religious definition strongly influenced early joiners' adherence to parties. Of all the Catholics who joined the Christian Democrats in the *liceo* (secondary school) , 77 per cent later identified with that party in the University. Several students indicated that their early membership had resulted from involvement in the social action programs sponsored by the Catholic secondary schools. They had had an early and obviously meaningful exposure to national social problems and to the Christian Democratic youth groups in the parochial schools. Not one of the Catholic early joiners indicated a preference for the FRAP when he entered the University. In contrast, of the early joiners who indicated no religious affiliation, 70 per cent supported the FRAP.[22]

At all levels of family socio-economic status,[23] the Christian Democrats had more supporters than the FRAP (Table 4) . Interestingly, proportionately more of them (41 per cent) came from lower-middle- and lower-class families than did the FRAP supporters (22 per cent). In general, it can be said that support for the two groups

TABLE 3

PREFERENCE FOR STUDENT ROLES: TRAINEE VERSUS ACTIVIST BY SCHOOL AND YEAR

(In Per Cent)

	SCHOOL				Total	YEAR		
	History	Engineering	Medicine	Physics		I	II–III	IV–VI
Trainee[a]	65	72	65	67	67	82	66	55
	(61)	(68)	(64)	(20)	(213)	(84)	(70)	(59)
Activist[a]	27	24	29	17	26	15	27	35
	(25)	(23)	(29)	(5)	(82)	(15)	(29)	(38)
Others[b]	9	3	6	17	7	4	7	10
	(8)	(3)	(6)	(5)	(22)	(4)	(7)	(11)
Totals	101	99	100	101	100	101	100	100
	(94)	(94)	(99)	(30)	(317)	(103)	(106)	(108)

[a] For an explanation of these terms, see Note 19.

[b] Includes those who did not answer and those who rejected both roles.

TABLE 4

STUDENTS' POLITICAL PREFERENCES BY SOCIO-ECONOMIC STATUS OF FAMILY[a]

(In Per Cent)

	Upper	Upper-Middle	Middle-Middle	Lower-Middle	Lower	Unknown	Total
Christian Democrats	28 (5)	35 (25)	30 (35)	40 (34)	44 (11)	—	35 (110)
FRAP	11 (2)	24 (17)	20 (23)	23 (19)	24 (6)	50 (2)	22 (69)
None or other	61 (11)	41 (29)	50 (57)	37 (31)	32 (8)	50 (2)	44 (138)
Total	100 (18)	100 (71)	100 (115)	100 (84)	100 (25)	100 (4)	101 (317)

[a] Political preference as used here means preference for a university political group. For an explanation of how status was defined and scaled, see Note 23.

tended to diminish with higher status. Upwardly mobile students seemed more likely than their upper-class colleagues to identify with political positions that were reformist and aimed at broadening economic and social opportunities.

These findings lend further weight to the hypothesis that recruitment of children from lower-middle- and working-class families to the university tends to increase the number for whom university politics is an important concern.[24] But this does not necessarily result from their lesser ability to accommodate themselves to university life. More likely, politics is seen as an important means of changing an iniquitous social order and, simultaneously, as a way of gaining a place in it. In countries like Chile, student politics is an excellent way to *belong* to society and yet be, or believe oneself to be, engaged in its transformation.

These effects of social class were reinforced by the choice of school. History, the most politicized school, was the only one of the four sampled with a majority of its students located beneath the middle-middle-class level.[25] Of the history students from lower-middle-class backgrounds, 36 per cent preferred the FRAP, while only 13 per cent in medicine, 9 per cent in engineering, and none in physics did so. In the schools preparing future doctors and engineers, on the other hand, the Christian Democrats received especially strong support from lower-middle-class students. It would appear that those students from more modest backgrounds who had gained admission to the schools of higher social prestige were less likely to favor the Marxist parties. Apparently this was because their future professional positions held out the promise of substantial economic comfort and social recognition.

Of further interest is the consistency between the fathers' political views and those of their children. Of the students who said their fathers supported right-wing parties, 71 per cent were neither for the Christian Democrats nor the FRAP (Table 5). Many said they favored no political group in the forthcoming national election, but in subsequent questions, indicated positive support for the incumbent conservative government of Jorge Alessandri. Sons of right-wing fathers were the single largest group implicitly or explicitly supporting the Alessandri regime.

Striking generational continuity can also be seen in the case of FRAP and Christian Democratic supporters. Sixty-one per cent of the students whose fathers favored the FRAP had the same preference. Even more revealing is the fact that among those whose fathers identified with the Christian Democrats, only 4 per cent hoped for a

TABLE 5

STUDENTS' POLITICAL PREFERENCES BY FATHERS' POLITICAL PREFERENCES[a]

(*In Per Cent*)

	Christian Democrats	Center	Right	Radical	FRAP	Independent	Unknown or Unavailable	Total
Christian Democrats	57 (41)	33 (1)	21 (9)	21 (12)	20 (10)	10 (1)	32 (27)	32 (101)
FRAP	4 (3)	—	7 (3)	35 (20)	61 (30)	40 (4)	13 (11)	22 (71)
None or other	39 (28)	67 (2)	71 (30)	44 (25)	18 (9)	50 (5)	55 (46)	46 (145)
Total	100 (72)	100 (3)	99 (42)	100 (57)	99 (49)	100 (10)	100 (84)	100 (317)

[a] Students' political preference here and in Table 7 means preference for a national political group.

FRAP victory; the majority (57 per cent) duplicated their fathers' political position.

The children of supporters of the Radical Party represent a special case. During the previous decade, the Radical Party had lost almost all its influence among university students and grown increasingly inept on the national scene, although it continued to maintain a tight grip over the large government bureaucracy through extensive patronage. Frequently, however, the children of Radical fathers did not basically disagree with the fathers' political ideology but rather rejected the Radical Party as simply too ineffective to warrant support. It was not inconsistent with their fathers' reformist ideology that many of these students now embraced the programs of the left-wing parties. This was no doubt a major factor among many of the 35 per cent who supported the FRAP. Given the strong secular tradition among the Radicals, allegiance to the Christian Democrats was predictably less (21 per cent).

Our findings fully support a conclusion of Frank Bonilla's study of FECH leaders during the mid-1950's. He noted a strong coincidence between the political affiliations of Chilean student leaders and those of their fathers. This, he wrote,

> help[s] to explain the generally moderate tone of University politics and FECH action in this final period. The powerful psychic charge of intergenerational or parental conflict does not seem to be an important motivating factor behind the political activities of most of today's student leaders. Insofar as this works in favor of a more rational and unemotional attack on political problems, it favors the development of the technical, managerial approach associated with the "bargaining interest group" or the reformer rather than the intransigence of the agitator or revolutionary.[26]

These findings seem relevant to other Latin American countries as well. Kalman Silvert has pointedly observed that

> the Latin American university student is the child of his parents. To assume that the student is but a hot-eyed revolutionary is to presume that somehow registering in a university is sufficient to cut family ties, break class and other group identifications, and produce a special kind of creature divorced from his society. The intellectual community can be "ahead" of society as a whole, but it must have identifications with some sectors of the community, and can pull along only those people susceptible to its particular suggestions or prodding.[27]

Students reflect in their political attitudes both the current center-left trend in Chilean politics and the relatively substantial influence of their fathers. Contemporary student politics, strongly reformist in tone, enjoy considerable support in Chilean national life. The integration of student with national politics in Chile both mirrors and serves to reinforce political stability while simultaneously inhibiting independent student action.

Student Political Attitudes: A Profile

Chile is one of the most highly developed of the Latin American countries. Yet it suffers from severe agricultural problems, growing urban slums, and serious health and educational deficiencies. The difficulties of economic development are aggravated by its precarious position in the international market. Most students were deeply aware of this situation but differed in their selection of the most important factor inhibiting national development.

Respondents were asked to list the problems that they saw as the most formidable barriers to national progress.[28] Their selections can be loosely divided into four groups: deficiencies inherent in the character of the Chilean people; the significance of personal contacts rather than competence; foreign imperialism; and an internal monopoly by an elite, which could be overcome only through basic structural changes amounting to a social revolution.

The student responses were highly consistent in their emphasis on the last or structural impediment to Chile's development: 44 per cent of the students identified this as the most important factor. There were no striking differences in this result by school, but when broken down by year, the data showed that entering students placed less emphasis on this problem than did their peers in later years. Only 19 per cent of the total sample blamed the actual character of the Chilean people. A larger number, 25 per cent, pointed to a still potent remnant of traditional Chilean society: the ascriptive, highly personal character of national life. These students urged a shift toward achievement as the sole criterion of personal advancement. In response to another question the overwhelming majority of all students felt that performance and competence should be the prime criteria in attaining professional success. Many were aware that Chilean realities diverged greatly from this ideal.[29]

Finally, only 8 per cent named imperialism as the major obstacle to Chile's progress.[30] The much-publicized controversy over the United States–owned copper mines would have led one to predict far greater emphasis on this factor. Bonilla reported that "anti-imperialism became a permanent and unifying formula of student protest in Chile beginning about 1930."[31] This orientation is not peculiar to Chileans or to students.

> The elites of the emerging nations see themselves and their countries as part of the suppressed strata of the world though they themselves may be among the well-to-do not only within their own country but even by a world standard. Awareness or concern with the inferior position of the nation is most acute among those who have received or are receiving a university education, since the culture and the university community has such close ties with the international community of scholars and universities.[32]

In any case, in the context of the electoral campaign in Chile in 1964, attacks on imperialism were associated with the extreme partisan left, and especially the Communists. This may explain why so many students did not identify imperialism as a major problem.

The largest segment, then, fell into a center-left category. They emphasized basic structural factors as the greatest obstacle to Chilean progress but did not exclude other, less radical causes. These responses reveal a void between the students' beliefs and their degree of political involvement. While many students were quite aware of the severity of national social problems, they strongly resisted the call to political action. Some students were cynical about the possibility of implementing proposed solutions. Others were suspicious of the motivations of the activists. Nonetheless, the widespread belief in the necessity of social change certainly strengthened the position of those students who saw no alternative but direct political action. Their control of major student organizations and their ideological fervor were reinforced by the political tendencies of the large majority of their fellow students. Even though this majority may have been uninvolved and many were highly critical of the character of certain aspects of student politics, they still provided the proper climate for the activists' dominance and influence during a time of national political crisis. In their over-all goals the student activists represented most of their peers.[33]

The Christian Democrats most frequently cited (37 per cent) the structural problem of "upper-class monopolies" blocking progressive change. One-fifth mentioned "inequality of opportunity" as the nation's foremost problem. While "imperialism" was the problem least often chosen by the Christian Democrats (2 per cent), it proved to be the one most frequently selected by FRAP students (28 per cent). FRAP supporters also focused on "upper-class monopolies" (23 per cent), "inequality of opportunity" (20 per cent), and the "need for social revolution" (16 per cent).

Further evidence of the center-left tendencies of the student body came in response to a question asked of those with a stated national party preference: "What should be the general policy of the government of your choice should it come to power?" The students were divided almost evenly between those who preferred a policy of "substantial" reforms (45 per cent) and those who desired a more radical alternative of "structural" changes (43 per cent). Only 12 per cent believed "moderate" reforms would suffice.[34] By political preference, the FRAP students (65 per cent) most often proposed "structural" changes. Among the Christian Democrats, on the other hand, "substantial" reforms (52 per cent) were more frequently supported than "structural" changes (34 per cent).

In general, then, the students viewed Chile's problems as largely structural and called for substantial to sweeping changes in the social order. How does the pressure of such beliefs affect their commitment to the democratic process? Students with a stated preference for a national political group were asked to recommend a course of action for their party should it fail to win power through the ballot box in the foreseeable future. Only 7 per cent of these students advocated the use of extra-electoral means. Almost all of these were FRAP supporters who were primarily history students. Ninety-nine of the 101 Christian Democrats, whose party went on to win the presidential election in 1964, preferred to remain in the legal opposition in the event of failure at the polls.

A second question testing commitment to the democratic process divided the students far more sharply. They were asked: "Do you think that any group, no matter how detrimental you believe its policies to be, should be allowed to assume office if it wins the next presidential election?" Again, a majority chose to respect the electoral outcome, but 38 per cent answered negatively or were undecided (Table 6). Although the students were not formally asked to specify which groups they would deprive of electoral victory, informal conversations showed the objectionable groups to be the Nazis and the Communists. For some, particularly in the School of Physics, the prospect of any Nazi in power was complete anathema. Some of these students were sons of Jewish refugees who had fled from Hitler. Although Nazism was not an issue in the 1964 presidential election, Jorge Prat, an extreme right-winger associated with fascist ideas, was a candidate for a short time. This threat, perhaps heightened by the history of an active Nazi movement in Chile in the 1930's, did generate some fear on the part of those already sensitive to this issue.

TABLE 6

Should Any Group That Wins Be Allowed To Take Office? By School and Year

(In Per Cent)

	SCHOOL					YEAR		
	History	Engineering	Medicine	Physics	Total	I	II-III	IV-VI
Yes	61 (57)	56 (53)	69 (68)	57 (17)	62 (195)	57 (59)	61 (65)	66 (71)
No	22 (21)	25 (23)	18 (18)	33 (10)	23 (72)	26 (27)	22 (23)	20 (22)
Undecided	15 (14)	19 (18)	13 (13)	10 (3)	15 (48)	16 (16)	16 (17)	14 (15)
Other	2 (2)	—	—	—	0 (2)	1 (1)	1 (1)	—
Total	100 (94)	100 (94)	100 (99)	100 (30)	100 (317)	100 (103)	100 (106)	100 (108)

There is little doubt, however, that the major group at issue was the Communist Party. For some students, the victory of a Communist-supported coalition (FRAP) in the presidential election was a real and frightening possibility. Many of those who felt that Chile could never recover from a "Communist-type" government were willing to exclude the Communists from their definition of democracy.

A breakdown by degree of political activity is particularly revealing (Table 7). The activists (69 per cent) are the most democratic, while the politically uninvolved students are both the most uncertain (28 per cent) and the least affirmative (51 per cent) in upholding the electorate's right to decide. This pattern undoubtedly reflects strong anti-Communist feelings among the politically inactive students.

There were significant differences between the FRAP students and the Christian Democrats. We had predicted that the former would most strongly defend the democratic process since they stood to lose the most by the hardening of a "military coup" mentality. The FRAP supporters on a national level attempted to expose such thinking in its every form. Yet, paradoxically, 11 per cent of the FRAP students stated that they were "undecided," and 24 per cent were against letting any elected group assume office. The intense struggle for political power seems to have had a detrimental effect on Chilean democratic thought. The FRAP supporters apparently feared that a "reactionary" government could destroy the power that they had struggled so hard to attain. The nonaligned students would have presumably preferred a temporary limitation on democratic action rather than risk the dangers of an "extremist" government. Only the Christian Democrats, whose ideology precluded the use of force, resisted the expedient of denying to political opponents one's own cherished prerogatives. The students' responses to the two questions on political methods accurately reflected Chile's democratic political system and its history of occasional military intervention and repressive government action.

Summary and Conclusions

Although the intensity and extent of student involvement vary considerably by school, we can identify three basic groups in the University as a whole: a minority of leaders and activists; a much larger group of sympathizers; and a third group, roughly equal in size to the activists, with little interest in politics. Not only the third group, but a considerable number in all three groups, are

TABLE 7

SHOULD ANY GROUP THAT WINS BE ALLOWED TO TAKE OFFICE?
BY POSITION ON POLITICAL ACTIVITY-ATTITUDE SCALE AND POLITICAL PREFERENCE

	Active Partisans[a]	Critical Sympathizers[b]	Noninvolved[c]	Total	Christian Democrats	FRAP	None or Other
Yes	69 (61)	62 (94)	51 (40)	62 (195)	73 (74)	63 (45)	52 (76)
No	19 (17)	26 (40)	19 (15)	23 (72)	15 (15)	24 (17)	28 (40)
Undecided	10 (9)	11 (17)	28 (22)	15 (48)	12 (12)	11 (8)	19 (28)
Other	1 (1)	—	1 (1)	0 (2)	—	1 (1)	1 (1)
Total	99 (88)	99 (151)	99 (78)	100 (317)	100 (101)	99 (71)	100 (145)

[a] Students who stated they were leaders in, members of, or sympathizers wholly in accord with a particular university political group.

[b] Those who (a) sympathized with one group but expressed strong reservations either about it or about the usefulness of any kind of political involvement, or (b) did not sympathize with any university group but voiced a distinct preference for one of the national parties and voted for its campus affiliate in the student elections.

[c] Those who claimed no political affiliation, defined themselves as having no interest in politics, and showed no consistent voting pattern.

concerned with the over-politicization of the University.

The effectiveness of student political groups in asserting their power is very much affected by the nature of the learning experience in each school. Thus, in the School of Medicine, political activity is limited by the difficulty of course demands, the obligations of hospital work, and the insistence by many professors that politics be kept out of the classroom. In the School of History, on the contrary, the free time resulting from limited academic requirements; the disadvantageous position of the students' future career (teaching) in the larger society; and the nature of the courses, which are focused on historical and contemporary problems, reinforce the attractions of politics. Our findings support the hypothesis that the greater the curricular challenge, the lower the probability of student political activity. Thus, less demanding programs may result in increased political activity.[35] This is especially true when political action can effect social change that will directly benefit relatively underprivileged professional groups.

Our data also lend weight to the view that the student political role is strongly influenced by the characteristics of transitional societies and their political institutions. The quality and amount of student political involvement seem to reflect the responsiveness of political institutions and the strength of various groups representing major interests. The more rigid the institutions and the weaker the established interest groups, the greater the students' political involvement. Students as a political force can be most effective in crisis situations. When political institutions fail or a vacuum in public leadership occurs, student leaders may suddenly find themselves enjoying national prominence and a real opportunity to influence the course of events.[36]

In 1964, a wide variety of Chilean political parties were permitted to vie for political power without fear of repression. There was no dictatorship and no need to "mount the barricades." Major sectors of the population, including the most underprivileged, had important spokesmen at the national level. These leaders articulated the policies to which student activists responded. Disruptive action was not encouraged.[37]

Many students were active in the presidential campaign. The more astute among them were alert to the realities of political life in Chile and the shortcomings of its leaders. Should reforms—demanded by the students, promised by the politicians, and desperately needed by the people—fail to materialize, these active, dedicated students and their presently nonaligned peers may well serve as the fulcrum of future political change.

NOTES

1. Data were gathered in several ways. Contemporary Chilean newspaper and journal articles, as well as scholarly and government sources, were used to secure a picture of official and popular thinking on educational problems in general and the student's role in particular. Persons well acquainted with Chilean education, including social scientists, university professors, professional practitioners, and university students, were also relied on as informants. Finally, a lengthy interview schedule, drawn up during the first few months after our arrival in Chile in September 1963, was utilized to probe the attitudes of a representative sample of university students.

The interview schedule covered family and educational background, professional training experiences and attitudes, political background and experiences, and political attitudes. The political questions were developed almost entirely from observation of Chilean life and politics in 1963–64. The schedule was pretested and discussed at great length with Chileans of all political persuasions to ensure that queries focused on those matters considered most relevant by local observers.

The actual interviews were conducted—over half by the author and his wife, the remainder by Chilean assistants—with students in four schools of the University of Chile, the largest and most important university in the country. These schools train students in fields that are essential for national development: medicine, engineering, secondary school (history) teaching, and physics.

Seventy-five per cent of the School of Physics' 40 students were interviewed. History had approximately 250 students; the number interviewed there was somewhat less than 40 per cent. The sample in Medicine represented about 8 per cent of 1,225 students. In Engineering, with almost 1,500, the sample represented around 6 per cent. All samples were stratified by year and randomly drawn. The interview schedule appears in Myron Glazer, "The Professional and Political Attitudes of Chilean University Students" (unpublished Ph.D. thesis, Princeton University, 1965), Appendix II.

Chile has seven state-recognized universities with a total enrollment of more than 25,000 students. The University of Chile accounts for almost half that number. The bulk of the universities are concentrated in the major cities of Santiago and Valparaíso, although the University of Concepción is located well to the south. The Roman Catholic Church supports two universities whose combined enrollment represents one-fourth of the higher education enrollment.

In the past, the most important student political activity has been in Santiago. Yet, left-wing influence has been quite strong in Concepción. A comparable study there might well find a high degree of student political involvement. An investigation at the Catholic universities, however, would probably yield findings indicative of the higher social class background of the students and of their more conservative political views. For an overview of Chilean higher education, see Clark C. Gill, *Education and Social Change in Chile* (Washington, D.C.: Government Printing Office, 1966).

An abbreviated version of the present chapter appears in *Daedalus*, XCVII (Winter 1968).

2. My analysis will focus on students in the Schools of History, Engineering, and Medicine. For further discussion of the School of Physics, see my "Field

Work in a Hostile Environment: A Chapter in the Sociology of Social Research in Chile," *Comparative Education Review*, X (June 1966), 367–76. Professional socialization in these schools is discussed at length in the author's "El proceso de socialización profesional en cuatro carreras chilenas," *Revista Latinoamericana de Sociología*, II (November 1966), 333–67.

3. Lipset's observations are pertinent here. "The ecological concentration of universities within a limited area, bringing together many young men and women in a similar situation in life, and isolating them for the most part from the motley routine of adult life contributes to the perpetuation of student restlessness." ("University Students and Politics in Underdeveloped Countries," *Minerva*, III [Autumn 1964], 35.)

4. *El Mercurio* (Santiago), October 20, 1963. All translations are the author's. For a discussion of Chilean politics during the election, see Ernest Halperin, *Nationalism and Communism in Chile* (Cambridge, Mass.: M.I.T. Press, 1965).

5. See *El Siglo* (Santiago), October 27, 1963. The election took place in September 1964.

6. See, for example, Nilo Rosenberg, "Nacionalización de cobre es un imperativo," *El Siglo*, June 28, 1964.

7. Frank Bonilla, "The Student Federation of Chile: 50 Years of Political Action," *Journal of Inter-American Studies*, II (July 1960), 326–27. Bonilla discusses in detail the levels of student political organization at the University.

8. E. W. Bakke writes that one of the stimulants for student involvement in public demonstrations is the "public expectancy that students form one group that can, and probably will, do something about obstacles to justice and human welfare." ("Students on the March: The Cases of Mexico and Colombia," *Sociology of Education*, XXXVII [Spring 1964], 214.)

9. The tourist's image of Chile has been reinforced by such laudatory books as *Chile Through Embassy Windows, 1939–1953* (New York: Simon and Schuster, 1958), by Claude G. Bowers, a former U.S. Ambassador to Chile. Frederick B. Pike, *Chile and the United States, 1880–1962* (Notre Dame: University of Notre Dame Press, 1963), presents a far more realistic picture. See especially chap. x.

10. Most of his professors tried not to get involved in political discussions in class. Because of the nature of the material, however, it was often difficult not to digress onto subjects of contemporary significance. Whether or not this occurred, the professors' political inclinations were usually known to the students and seemed to have a subtle influence upon them.

The majority of students (78 per cent) interviewed in all four schools reported that their professors neither encouraged nor discouraged political activity. The students' perceptions of their professors' attitudes were often influenced, however, by the extent of their own activity. Of the most politically involved, 30 per cent saw their professors taking a stand in favor of, and only 3 per cent as opposing, political activity. We were informed, moreover, that in some cases, especially in the School of History, students tended to seek out as teachers those with whom they agreed politically.

11. One hundred and thirty-four of the 276 students who answered this question reported sympathizing with either the Christian Democrats (89) or the MUI coalition (45, including Socialists and Communists). The leftist coalition's showing was strongest in the School of History, where they tied the Christian Democrats with 18 sympathizers apiece, and weakest in Engi-

neering, where Christian Democratic sympathizers outnumbered theirs almost four to one.

12. The conservative *El Mercurio*, in particular, played up the fear of Communist domination. In addition to frequent lead editorials on the subject, the newspaper carried full-page pictures and articles on the "atrocities" of life under Communism. See, for example, the issue of June 26, 1964, p. 5.

13. The Communist daily *El Siglo*, for example, ran a series of articles in June 1964 entitled "Explotación en Libertad" ("Exploitation in Liberty"), deriding the Christian Democrats' slogan, "Revolution in Liberty," and identifying members of the landed aristocracy who supported Frei.

14. In the press and at mass rallies, Frei was often portrayed as a cross between Uncle Sam and Hitler.

15. The election in the province of Curico in March 1964 resulted in the collapse of the conservative incumbent *Frente Democrático*. Its candidate, Julio Duran, had gambled heavily on the victory of the right-wing candidate for deputy from Curico, promising to withdraw if he were defeated. Duran's withdrawal gave the Conservative and Liberal parties the freedom to realign themselves. Within the month, they announced their support for Frei, while Duran was subsequently renominated by his own Radical Party and ran as a third candidate.

16. In Physics, when asked to choose between this independent viewpoint (paraphrased in the text) and the view that "a student who is interested in the future of Chile should assume the responsibility of working with a political group with whose ideals he is basically in accord in order to help it realize its program," 60 per cent of the students adopted the former stance. In Engineering, 55 per cent did so; in Medicine, 50 per cent. But in the School of History, only 38 per cent preferred the "independent-critical" view.

It is interesting to note the equal-peaked U-shaped distribution of the respondents' preferences. Ninety-six students (30 per cent of the total) *strongly* endorsed the "affiliated-partisan" position; an equal number *strongly* supported the "independent-critical" alternative. The latter view gained slightly more adherents at the level of mild agreement, to win the argument over all, 49 to 45 per cent. (The residual 6 per cent declined to choose.)

17. Of those in the four schools answering the question on political sympathies, Engineering had the lowest proportion of avowed sympathizers (32 per cent). On Christian Democratic strength there, see n. 11 above.

18. Glaucio A. D. Soares, "The Active Few: Student Ideology and Participation in Developing Countries," *Comparative Education Review*, X (June 1966), 206.

19. The following choice was posed:

"A" says that the most important factor for the development of Chile is to have well trained and prepared people. Therefore, the major responsibility of the student is to devote the majority of his time to learning the materials in his field and only a minimum of time to other activities.

"B" says that Chile needs basic social changes before it can bring about any other changes effectively. He believes that the student has a responsibility to devote a good part of his time to political activities, even if this reduces somewhat the amount of time he can spend on his studies.

With whom do you agree?

20. In fact, when scaled by their intensity, the responses drop off sharply toward the extreme pro-activist end. Specifically, of all 317 students, 32 per

cent strongly agreed with proposition "A" (above) that students should limit themselves to the trainee role and 35 per cent expressed mild agreement, while only 18 per cent mildly agreed with and a scant 7 per cent strongly endorsed proposition "B." (Seven per cent rejected both alternatives or declined to answer.)

21. In the study of comparative student activity there is a dearth of material collected over time. Since the dropout rate is usually quite high, statements about the differences among students at different points of their training must be made with great caution. Panel studies would also be extremely useful in shedding light on the factors separating the successful from the unsuccessful degree seekers.

22. None of the fifteen Protestants and only one of the eighteen Jews had joined a political group while in secondary school.

23. The socio-economic index used in Table 4 was based on student responses to questions on the fathers' education and salary. Those who stated earnings of E° 1,000 (*escudos*) or more per month were assigned ten points; E° 500–999, seven points; E° 200–499, four points; one point was assigned to those who indicated an income of less than E° 200. Father's education was scored as follows: three points for a complete or incomplete university education, two points for a complete or incomplete secondary education, and one point for elementary school attendance. Mother's education and salary were given minor weight, except where there was no father in the household, on the assumption that class is largely determined by the position of the father. If the mother worked, half a point was added. If she had a job of high prestige or salary that could significantly change the family's status, one point was added. (All figures refer to 1963–64 prices).

Students' families were then divided into five categories. Thirteen points was the minimum for the upper class (high income plus high education), ten points for the upper-middle group (high income plus middle education or middle income plus high education), and six points for the lower-middle class (low income plus middle education or middle income plus low education). Anyone with five points or less was classified as lower class. These results were roughly verified, and complemented when necessary, with information on parental occupation, a further indicator of social class position.

24. Lipset, *op. cit.*, p. 47.

25. The percentages of lower-lower-class students per school sample were History, 57; Engineering, 32; Physics, 23; and Medicine, 18.

26. Frank Bonilla, "Students in Politics: Three Generations of Political Action in a Latin American University" (unpublished Ph.D. thesis, Harvard University, 1959), p. 257. Major sections of this will appear in Frank Bonilla and Myron Glazer, *Student Politics in Chile* (New York: Basic Books, 1969).

27. Kalman H. Silvert, "The University Student," in John J. Johnson (ed.), *Continuity and Change in Latin America* (Stanford: Stanford University Press, 1964), p. 225. It is, of course, possible that students may have influenced their parent's response. Our data do not permit drawing any inference in this regard, but it raises a fascinating area for future research. For another incisive discussion supporting this point, see Arthur Liebman, "Children of their Fathers: The Politics of Puerto Rican University Students" (unpublished Ph.D. thesis, University of California, 1967).

28. For a full listing of the choices presented to the respondents, see Myron Glazer, "The Professional and Political Attitudes of Chilean University Stu-

dents" (unpublished Ph.D. thesis, Princeton University, 1965), Appendix II.

29. For further discussion of this point, see Myron Glazer, "The Professional and Political Attitudes of Chilean University Students," *Comparative Education Review*, X (June 1966), 283–85.

30. The nature of the question may partially explain this result. While three of the twelve problems suggested fell into the "structural" category, only one cited imperialism. Of those students who did cite imperialism, 64 per cent were in the School of History.

Many contemporary students, social scientists, and politicians are obviously concerned with the extent of U.S. influence in Chile. The type of suspicion that many students expressed about our project was one clear indicator. See Glazer, "Field Work in a Hostile Environment." For an elaboration of this theme that focuses on the problems resulting from the demise of Project Camelot and the military sponsorship of overseas research, see M. Glazer and P. M. Glazer, "Los Chilenos y Los Gringos: Social Science Research and the Real World," *Revista Latinoamericana de Sociología* (forthcoming).

31. Bonilla, "The Student Federation of Chile," p. 315.

32. Lipset, *op. cit.*, pp. 28–29.

33. For an elaboration of this and other pertinent issues, see Seymour Martin Lipset, "Students and Politics in Comparative Perspective," *Daedalus*, XCVII (Winter 1968).

34. The students were asked to choose one of three alternative answers: "make mild reforms"; "make major reforms, but preserve the general structural framework of Chilean society"; and "make major structural changes in the society."

35. Lipset, "University Students and Politics in Underdeveloped Countries," p. 35.

36. Bonilla, "The Student Federation of Chile," p. 313. Lipset, in "Students and Politics in Comparative Perspective," cites a variety of other case studies supporting this observation.

37. This was most readily evident during the general strike in March 1964 and the rupture of diplomatic relations with Cuba in August. Both the Christian Democrats and the FRAP were intent on maintaining order to preclude any excuse for military intervention.

10. CUBA

JAIME SUCHLICKI

Among Latin American nations, Cuba has had a prominent tradition of student political involvement. In the last decades of the nineteenth century, the University of Havana became the nation's hotbed of anti-Spanish sentiment. In the early 1930's, students at the University fought hard to bring down the dictator Gerardo Machado, in power since 1924. In 1933, they succeeded; a University of Havana physiology professor was named Cuba's provisional President. Under the dictatorship of Fulgencio Batista (1952–58), students first demonstrated and rioted against Batista, then joined the insurrection that overthrew his regime; a number sacrificed their lives in the struggle. Fidel Castro's revolutionary victory in 1959 was a turning point in the history of Cuba's student movement: his conquest of the University marked the nadir of student political opposition.[1]

Several factors enhanced the political importance of University of Havana students during the 1950's. First, the more than 17,000 students attending the University were represented by only one organization, the Federation of University Students (*Federación Estudiantil Universitaria,* or FEU), giving that body concentration and strength.[2] Second, the location of the University in the heart of the capital city exposed the students to the shock waves of Cuba's

This chapter is based on research conducted in 1965 for an M.A. thesis at the University of Miami and in 1966–67 for a Ph.D. dissertation at Texas Christian University. The author is presently completing a comprehensive study of university students and politics in Cuba as part of a Ford Foundation-supported research program on Cuba and the Caribbean area undertaken by the University of Miami's Center for Advanced International Studies. The author is indebted to many Cuban informants for their help and to Professor Donald E. Worcester of TCU for reviewing the manuscript.

political turmoil and placed them in an ideal situation for making their political views known. The inadequate student recreational and library facilities and a staff of part-time teachers who lacked a sense of pedagogic responsibility diminished still further the campus' educational atmosphere. Finally, the University's autonomy—originally a sheltering device against government encroachment—converted it into a sanctuary for political agitators. Because police were not allowed to enter the campus, the students had a safe emplacement from which to carry on activities against the government.[3]

Students Against Batista: 1952–55

When, on March 10, 1952, General Fulgencio Batista and a group of army conspirators overthrew President Carlos Prío Socarrás' constitutional government, University of Havana students were the first to oppose the new regime. During the first three years of Batista's rule, student opposition was limited to sporadic riots, demonstrations, and protests. Although at the time these unorganized acts may have seemed unimportant, they did help awaken the Cubans to the oppressive nature of Batista's rule, and thus paved the way for the insurrection that followed.

Batista was neither personally popular nor accepted as the island's legitimate ruler. Nonstudent opposition soon developed. The two major political parties, *Ortodoxo* and *Auténtico,* and most of Cuba's politicians opposed Batista through peaceful means, hoping for an honest election. A faction of the *Auténticos,* however—followers of the deposed President Prío—went underground and began planning insurrectionary activities.

During the first few years of Batista's regime, political parties exerted considerable influence upon the students in Havana. The *Ortodoxos* were particularly popular and influential among students because of the party's uncompromising attitude toward Batista, the mystique of its martyred leader, Eduardo Chibás, and the fact that its more prominent members included several professors at the University of Havana. The National Revolutionary Movement, an offshoot of the *Ortodoxo* party, also commanded strong student support. Led by a professor at the University, Rafael García Bárcena, this group recruited a number of students for an attack on the military camp that had given Batista the command of the army. Batista's intelligence police averted the plot and arrested Bárcena and several fellow conspirators in April 1953. After being brutally beaten by the police, they were tried and sentenced to prison.[4]

The government also attempted to influence the students. Batista appreciated the "trouble-making" capabilities of the students and tried by two methods to reduce their power. First, he publicly criticized the University's autonomy. In October 1952, the Federation of University Students (FEU) accused the government of planning to intervene in the University and destroy its autonomy. The University Council, composed of professors and administrative officials, strongly supported the students' accusations.[5]

Realizing the futility of any frontal assault, Batista tried a second tactic. He attempted to form parallel student organizations to challenge the predominance of FEU. The first attempt occurred on the occasion of the Eighth Mexican Congress of Architecture, scheduled for August 1952 in Mexico City, to which FEU sent a delegation. The government recruited a group of students and provided a military plane for their flight to the Congress. While in Mexico, these students voiced support for Batista. As soon as they returned to Havana, FEU called an assembly to judge their actions. Amid flying chairs and fists, the Federation condemned their behavior. All but three of the twenty-one members of the pro-Batista delegation made public statements supporting FEU and explaining they had no intention whatsoever of backing the regime.[6]

The government then organized within the University the "First Student Committee for Batista for President." Its purpose was to support Batista's presidential ticket in the approaching national elections, and to run its own candidates in student elections. FEU opposed this new maneuver and issued a declaration aimed at ending all further government penetration of the University. The statement reminded the students that they were not to engage in any political activity that would contradict FEU's position against the regime. "Our action is justified," said the Federation, "by the support we have received from the student body."[7] FEU President Alvaro Barba later reaffirmed this stand and added that the mission of the Federation was to coordinate the opposition forces and unite the nation against Batista's usurpation of power.[8]

The relations between Batista and FEU, which had never been cordial, deteriorated rapidly. Early in 1953, police shot and killed a University of Havana student during a demonstration in front of the school. A national student strike followed. Disorder spread throughout the island; demonstrations against the government occurred almost daily. When the regime announced that the 1953 national elections would be postponed for a year, FEU quickly accused Batista of perpetuating himself in power. The Federation demanded general elections as soon as possible and a neutral government that could give all parties ample guarantees.[9]

The mock elections of November 1954, from which Batista emerged victorious, placed Cuba at a dangerous crossroads. The opposition wanted new elections, while Batista insisted on remaining in power until his new term expired in 1958. Throughout 1955, numerous meetings were held in an attempt to find a compromise. The failure to reach an agreement forced the Cuban people reluctantly onto a road leading to civil war, chaos, and revolution.

At the end of 1955, a series of student riots shocked the country. On November 27, FEU organized a ceremony to honor the memory of eight students shot by Spanish authorities in 1871. When the meeting turned into an anti-Batista rally, police arrested several student leaders, while others had to be hospitalized as a consequence of brutal police methods. Similar events occurred in Santiago, capital of Oriente province, where police ruthlessly beat students who tried to observe the November 27 commemoration. In protest, FEU called a student strike, which quickly spread throughout the island. All universities, colleges, and secondary schools closed down. For three weeks daily sorties were made against the police all over the country.

On December 2, 1955, students on a march from the University of Havana were stopped and beaten by the police. The new FEU President, José Antonio Echeverría, and Vice President, Fructuoso Rodríguez, were hospitalized. On December 4, during a baseball game, a group of fifteen students carrying banners condemning the regime ran onto the field. Several dozen policemen, who had been waiting for the demonstrators, surrounded them and beat them brutally, in front of thousands of astonished spectators and television viewers. In clashes during the following months, more than thirty persons were wounded, many by gunfire. Finally, on the pretext of searching for hidden arms, government forces entered the University, demolished the rector's office, and destroyed documents, scientific equipment, and furnishings. The action was decried as a violation of university autonomy, and Rector Clemente Inclán suspended classes indefinitely.[10]

While these riots and demonstrations were going on, other Cubans not connected with student activities were plotting to unseat Batista. Fidel Castro was an early advocate of armed action against the government. After several years in jail following his unsuccessful July 26, 1953, attack on the Moncada barracks, he traveled to the United States and Mexico, seeking followers and funds for the revolutionary cause. In 1956, he vowed to overthrow Batista or to die fighting in the attempt. Another group, known as *Montecristi,* plotted with army officers to overthrow the regime; Batista uncovered the conspiracy and arrested its principal instigators in April 1956. That same month another group, belonging to former President Prío's *Organización Auténtica,* unsuccessfully attacked the Goicuría army barracks in Matanzas province.[11]

The Directorio Revolucionario: 1955–57

Instead of seeking to discourage rebellion by moderation, the regime encouraged it by meeting terrorism with a murderous counter-terrorism that defeated its own ends. By the end of 1955, the leaders of FEU realized that the efforts of nonpartisan organizations to reconcile government and opposition were futile. They proposed the creation of an insurrectionary movement to lead the struggle for freedom. As the FEU proposal found little response among the electorally oriented politicians, the students formed their own clandestine organization—the Revolutionary Directorate *(Directorio Revolucionario)* —in December 1955. In a secret meeting at the University of Havana on February 24, 1956, Echeverría, as head of the *Directorio,* announced its creation.[12]

The reasons for organizing the *Directorio* were varied. One of its founders, Félix Armando Murias, told the author that the students had maintained close contact with labor leaders willing to participate in coordinated actions against the regime. An organization was needed to lead such actions. "Furthermore," said Murias, "members of FEU who advocated an insurrection against Batista met with opposition within the Federation, adding a note of urgency to the need for a separate organization."[13] In another interview, Armando Fleites, also an active member of the *Directorio* since its inception and later a commander of the guerrilla forces that fought Batista, explained that during 1955 many labor and professional leaders, disappointed with the electoral negotiations and having no underground movement to which to turn, approached Echeverría to coordinate armed resistance against Batista. Since the Federation operated under the aegis of the University and therefore could not incorporate these nonstudent elements, it was necessary to create an organization outside FEU that could lead the resistance against Batista.[14]

Out of interviews with former *Directorio* activists, the following portrait emerges. The student leaders were admirers of Eduardo Chibás and José Martí, sharing the latter's vision of an idealized *patria*: a socially united, racially harmonious, and economically independent nation. They were democrats, strongly nationalistic, and anti-Communist. "We opposed agreements with Cuban Communists," said Murias, "whom we considered opportunists and collaborators with Batista since the 1930's."

The students advocated economic reforms: agricultural diversification, industrialization, and agrarian reform. They opposed administrative corruption and other evils of Cuba's public life, and wanted to see the 1940 Constitution fully re-established and free elections held. Most of them did not aspire to political office, limiting their involvement in politics to the immediate objective of Batista's overthrow, but a few were interested in using student politics as a steppingstone to national prominence. (After Batista's fall, several *Directorio* leaders showed their eagerness for positions in the Castro government.) In general, they were well-intentioned, idealistic, politically immature young people who desired the best for their country. It is significant to note that several of the FEU and *Directorio* leaders were from areas other than Havana and many came from poorer or lower-middle-class homes. Living away from their families and exposed to the loneliness of a new urban environment, these students were apparently more prone to political involvement than the average city student.

The *Directorio* differed from other anti-Batista insurrectionary organizations in several ways. First, the *Directorio* was predominantly a student organization. Not until 1957, after the death of its principal leaders, did nonstudent elements enjoy a degree of importance in the organization and share in making its decisions. Second, its leaders believed in assassination as the means of overthrowing the dictatorship. They were, however, strongly opposed to indiscriminate terrorism that might kill innocent people.

The *Directorio*'s plans called for establishing contact with other leaders advocating armed opposition to Batista. One of these was Fidel Castro, who had been training an expeditionary force in Mexico and planned to land in Cuba at the end of 1956. Early that year, Echeverría led a student delegation to Mexico, where he signed an agreement with Castro known as *La Carta de México* ("The Mexican Letter"). The students pledged a series of diversionary riots in Havana to coincide with Castro's landing on the island.[15] "Since the landing date had not yet been set," Murias explained, "Castro promised to advise the students as to his exact plans."

A few days after the students returned to Cuba, the *Directorio* undertook one of its first operations: an attempt on the life of

Colonel Antonio Blanco Rico, head of Batista's Military Intelligence Service. On October 28, 1956, two members of the *Directorio,* Rolando Cubela and Juan Pedro Carbó Serviá, fired at Blanco Rico and a group of his friends in a Havana nightclub, killing him and wounding several of his companions. In the ensuing chaos, the attackers escaped.[16]

The assassination brought censure from several sectors of society. Sensing this indignation, Castro told a reporter in Mexico in November: "There was no need to kill Blanco Rico; others deserved to die much more than he did."[17] On the eve of his landing in Cuba, Castro attempted to appear before the Cuban people as an advocate of mass struggle against Batista, and as opposed to actions of the type perpetrated by the *Directorio.* He also wanted to discredit the student leaders, whom he considered rivals in the quest for power.

In Oriente province, a small but well-organized underground led by Frank País prepared for Castro's arrival, set for November 30. On that day commando groups attacked several military installations, touching off a wave of sabotage throughout the province. The terrorists exploded bombs, derailed trains, and sabotaged power lines, blacking out entire towns.

In Havana, the leaders of the *Directorio* watched the Oriente developments anxiously, awaiting word from Castro to go into action in the capital. "Fidel's notification," said Murias, "did not come until December 2—the day he was landing in Oriente."[18] By that time, the uprising had already been crushed and most of the leaders of Castro's July 26th Movement were either dead or in jail. Batista suspended constitutional guarantees and imposed total censorship of news. The dreaded military police patrolled the streets of Havana day and night, rounding up suspected revolutionary elements.

Castro's action was supported neither by the general public nor by the regular opposition parties. The army remained loyal to Batista. Castro found refuge in the Sierra Maestra mountains and from there began waging guerrilla warfare against the regime. Lacking word from Castro, afraid the regime might have infiltrated the revolt, and appalled at the speed with which Batista's forces repressed the uprising, the *Directorio* leaders in Havana failed to support the Oriente insurgents.[19]

The events in Oriente prompted the University of Havana Council to suspend classes temporarily on November 30, 1956. But as terrorism and violence continued, the Council indefinitely postponed the reopening of the University, which remained closed until early in 1959.[20]

Batista and his clique welcomed the closing of the University. For more than four years, the students had been a thorn in their side. Now the government expected to neutralize student opposition. But the closing of the University instead threw almost 18,000 students into the vortex of national politics. As time went on, and the University remained closed, the impatience of the students grew and many began joining insurrectionary organizations. The students narrowed their focus, as their predecessors had in the successful struggle against Machado in the 1930's, to a single, immediate goal: to end the dictatorship.

The fall of Machado had ushered in almost two decades of political freedom and constitutional government. The students, and the Cuban people in general, saw Batista's regime as only a temporary interruption of Cuba's democratic political development, as the consequence of Batista's own ambitions for power and Prío's corrupt rule rather than a symptom of more profound national problems. The reduced importance of political institutions at the local level, the reliance on *personalismo,* the economy's continuing dependence on a single crop, widespread administrative corruption—these conditions were not given the recognition they deserved. The elimination of Batista's dictatorship became the panacea to cure all of Cuba's ills. This simplistic thinking served Fidel Castro's purposes well during his stay in the Sierra Maestra, where he proclaimed the overthrow of the regime as the nation's sole, overriding task, avoiding ideological questions as much as possible and advocating only the most obviously popular reforms.

The *Directorio* planned to overthrow the government by assassinating Batista. The students leaders reasoned that such a fast and decisive action would cause the regime to crumble and would prevent unnecessary loss of life in a possible civil war. Castro blamed Echeverría for the *Directorio*'s inaction at the time of the abortive Oriente uprising. Echeverría apparently felt it was a question of honor to prove both his own courage and the *Directorio*'s determination to fight.[21]

A two-pronged plan to overthrow Batista got under way. On March 13, 1957, a combined force of *Directorio* members and followers of former President Prío stormed the presidential palace and succeeded in penetrating to the second floor of the building. But despite the audacity of the assault, the strong palace defense held out. The poor quality of the attackers' weapons and the failure of reinforcements to arrive turned possible victory into costly defeat. According to the official government report, twenty were killed, including five members of the palace guard. That figure, however, did not include the many conspirators who were hunted down and killed by the police after the event.

At the same time, another group, led by Echeverría, stormed a Havana radio station. Unaware of the failure at the palace, the students broadcast an announcement that Batista had been killed and his regime brought down. The students' joy was short-lived. In an encounter between students and government forces minutes later, the police shot and killed Echeverría and wounded several other students.[22]

Students, Communists, and Castro: 1957–58

Fidel Castro, from his hide-out in the mountains, criticized the students' attack. In a televised interview, Castro called it "a useless waste of blood. The life of the Dictator is of no importance. . . . Here in the Sierra Maestra is where to fight."[23] Throughout his stay in the mountains, Castro opposed a military coup, the assassination of Batista, or any other violent act by any group not directly under the control of his July 26th Movement.

Another group that spoke against the attack on the presidential palace, and against Castro's landing in Oriente as well, was the *Partido Socialista Popular* (PSP), Cuba's Communist Party. The head of the PSP, Juan Marinello, wrote to Herbert L. Matthews on March 17, 1957, explaining the official Party line: "In these days and with reference to the assaults on barracks and expeditions from abroad—taking place without relying on popular support—our position is very clear: we are against these methods." The Communists advocated, as the correct strategy against Batista, a mass struggle based primarily on the mobilization of the proletariat and leading toward national elections. They called for the creation of a Democratic Front of National Liberation to form a government representing the workers, peasants, urban petty bourgeoisie, and national bourgeoisie, all under the leadership of the proletariat.[24]

But the PSP leaders were following a dual strategy. While publicly advocating peaceful opposition to Batista, they were secretly making overtures to the insurrectionary groups for closer collaboration. As early as December 1955, Raúl Valdés Vivó, Secretary General of the *Juventud Socialista,* the youth branch of the PSP, held meetings with *Directorio* leaders Echeverría and Fructuoso Rodríguez pressing for closer relations with their organization. Vivó also advocated a "united front" of all students, including the *Directorio,* but under the leadership of the FEU.[25] The Communists, encouraged by their success in electing Amparo Chaple, a member of the *Juventud,* to the presidency of the School of Philosophy at the University of Havana in November 1955, apparently believed they could eventually dominate FEU and neutralize the *Directorio* by placing the latter under the Federation's control. But no union emerged from these early Communist contacts with the students. Echeverría and other student leaders were not ready for an alliance with the Communists and went ahead with their own plans for the *Directorio.*[26]

Throughout most of Batista's rule, the Communists had enjoyed virtually complete liberty, and several of them had even held posts in the government. Batista took certain measures against the PSP, principally to appease the United States government. These were minor, however, compared to the persecution suffered by the non-Communist opposition. The PSP, directly and through its University Bureau at the University of Havana, consistently sought to undermine, infiltrate, and control the groups combating Batista. The importance of the *Directorio* as a dangerous rival for power and the militant anti-Communism of several of its leaders were constantly present in the minds of the top members of the PSP.

The defeat suffered at the palace was further aggravated by the assassination a month later of four of the *Directorio*'s remaining top leaders. On April 20, 1957, police surrounded an apartment building on Humboldt Street in Havana and massacred acting FEU President Fructuoso Rodríguez, along with Joe Westbrook, Juan Pedro Carbó Serviá, and José Machado.[27] That the police could have located the students' hide-out without inside help seemed almost impossible to the friends and families of the murdered youths. Every indication pointed toward a police informer among the students. An investigation, however, would have to await Batista's downfall.

The "Humboldt event," as this episode was later known, the failure of the attack on the presidential palace, and the death of Echeverría, at the time perhaps the most popular figure opposing Batista, left the *Directorio* leaderless and disorganized. Almost a year went by before the organization recovered from the blow, and even then it never regained the prestige and importance it had enjoyed prior to the palace assault. While the *Directorio* declined, Castro, unchallenged in the mountains, grew in prestige, strength, and following. He gained adherents in the cities and won over many discontented elements that, whatever differences with his July 26th Movement they might have had, found no other insurrectionary organization to join.

The remaining *Directorio* leaders went into exile and began reorganizing under the direction of Faure Chomón. In a speech in Miami on October 20, 1957, Chomón advocated unity among the revolutionary groups, called for "a nationalistic united party of the Revolution," and condemned the United States for selling arms to Batista.[28] Chomón also supported the unity efforts of representatives from seven anti-Batista organizations, including the *Directorio* and the July 26th Movement, who had gathered in Miami following Castro's July 1957 "Manifesto of the Sierra Maestra," which called for a united front to overthrow Batista.[29] Out of that meeting, a unity pact was signed on November 1, 1957, a Cuban Liberation Council (*Junta de Liberación Cubana*) organized, and Felipe Pazos, a distinguished economist, appointed provisional President of Cuba to take over in the interim after Batista's overthrow.

The *Junta*, however, was short-lived. In a letter sent to members of the Council on December 14, 1957, Castro explained that he opposed the Miami unity pact because it failed "to reject foreign [U.S.] intervention in Cuba's internal affairs and to repudiate a military junta after Batista's downfall." Castro wrote further that the *Junta's* pretensions "to approve or disapprove of the provisional President's appointment of cabinet members and to incorporate all revolutionary forces into the armed forces after victory" were unacceptable. "The July 26th Movement," asserted Fidel, "claims for itself the functions of directing the revolutionary struggle and of reorganizing the armed forces of the nation."[30] After Batista's overthrow, Castro disclosed that he had withdrawn from the *Junta* because he realized he was not strong enough to dominate the other groups in a single front.[31]

Following the murder of the July 26th Movement's underground leader, Frank País, by Batista's police on July 30, 1957, a spontaneous strike broke out in the three easternmost provinces of Cuba. This strengthened Castro's conviction that a general strike could topple the regime. The July 26th Movement did finally organize a general strike on April 9, 1958, but it failed, setting off an ideological struggle within the Movement. The main subject of controversy was apparently the problem of relations with the Communists. Although the PSP had sent representatives to the Sierra Maestra prior to the April strike, apparently no formal agreement had been reached with Fidel. The Communists failed to support the strike, blaming its failure on the July 26th Movement's "unilateral call, without counting on the rest of the opposition or on the workers themselves."[32]

Meanwhile, the *Directorio* leaders prepared to resume their struggle against Batista. Early in 1958, they sailed from Miami to start guerrilla activities in the mountains of central Cuba. But differences soon arose within the *Directorio*. One group, commanded by Faure Chomón, claimed that the correct strategy was to *golpear arriba* (strike at the top); it advocated moving back to Havana to reorganize the *Directorio* underground and assassinate Batista. Another group, led by Eloy Gutiérrez Menoyo and Armando Fleites, urged a continuation of guerrilla warfare. Menoyo and Chomón also clashed over who should direct the military operations and over Chomón's decision to send a supply of badly needed weapons to Havana.

In mid-1958, the two factions finally split. Fleites told the writer that his group, later known as the "Second Front of the Escambray," continued to fight Batista as an independent organization opposing alliances with the July 26th Movement or any other group. Toward the end of 1958, he said, his force numbered about 1,000 men, mostly farmers and residents of the area.[33] Of the remaining members of the *Directorio*, some, led by Chomón, returned to Havana and began rebuilding the underground, while others, commanded by Rolando Cubela, carried on small guerrilla operations in the mountains. Finally, faced with mounting repression in the capital, Chomón went back to the mountains. There the *Directorio* joined the July 26th Movement forces under Che Guevara, three months before Batista fell.[34]

Castro Takes Over: 1959–60

The crumbling of Batista's regime on January 1, 1959, marked a turning point in the history of Cuba's student movement. Advocating unity among the revolutionary forces that had fought Batista, and claiming that State and University were now identical, Castro proceeded to sieze control of the student movement and the University of Havana, expelling dissident students and professors.

How was this accomplished? Of the several groups that had fought Batista, the July 26th Movement had an almost undisputed claim to fill the vacuum left by the dictator. Castro's charisma and his revolutionary prestige made him in the eyes of the Cuban people the logical occupant of Batista's vacant chair; he was the man of the hour, the new messiah. The other insurrectionary organizations lacked the mystique, the widespread support, and the organized cadres of Castro's movement. The Second Front of the Escambray was a localized guerrilla group without much following in the cities. The Civic Resistance Movement, formed by prominent professionals and university professors, was an amorphous group that followed Castro's leadership. The PSP had accepted Castro's leadership and seemed willing to cooperate with the "petty bourgeois" revolutionary. Most politicians had lost prestige by participating in Batista's rigged elections of November 1958. Furthermore, the regular army, which might otherwise have been able to take over, was leaderless and demoralized. Castro's bid for power seemed unchallenged.

The *Directorio Revolucionario*, however, had a chance to confront the national hero from a position of strength. Prior to Castro's triumphant arrival in Havana, the *Directorio* underground, led by Faure Chomón, occupied key positions in the city, including the presidential palace and the University of Havana. The students also took large quantities of weapons from a military base near the capital and moved them to the University. "Some *Directorio* leaders, and especially Chomón," *Directorio* activist Jorge Nóbrega said later, "wanted an active role in the new government."[35] Angered because a provisional government had already been formed in Santiago de Cuba without its participation, the *Directorio* demanded that the other insurrectionary organizations be allowed to share power. "The victory belongs to all," emphasized Chomón at the time, "and none should try to impose his will."[36]

As soon as he arrived in Havana, Castro demonstrated his tactical ability by outmaneuvering his young rivals. In his first victory speech, he pleaded with the students' mothers to take their weapons away. "Arms for what?" asked Castro. "The time to fight is over. What we now need is unity."[37] In a televised appearance the next day, he criticized the *Directorio* leaders, particularly Chomón.[38] Portraying the students as ambitious divisionists, he was able to turn public opinion against them. Faced with mounting pressure, the *Directorio* had no choice but to end its defiance and turn over its strongholds to the July 26th Movement.

Castro immediately rewarded those willing to support him. Former *Directorio* leader Major Rolando Cubela was appointed military attaché to the Cuban Embassy in Spain and later Under Secretary of the Interior. José Naranjo, who had worked closely with the July 26th Movement while he was *Directorio* coordinator in the United States in 1958, was appointed Minister of the Interior. Although remaining outside the government in 1959, Chomón decided to support Castro's move to the left and endorsed the ensuing purge of anti-Communist elements within the revolution.[39] Castro rewarded Chomón with an ambassadorship to the Soviet Union in 1960 and later with a cabinet post. A host of minor governmental positions went to less prominent *Directorio* members. Some students, however, were alienated by Castro's accelerating shift leftward throughout 1959; others quietly resumed their studies.

The University of Havana reopened its doors early in 1959. Old student leaders and new ones, emerging out of the insurrectionary struggle, took provisional charge of FEU. They saw as their first task the transformation of an archaic university into an academically modern, politically progressive institution. To that end, students and faculty formed a University Reform Commission. The Commission immediately organized revolutionary tribunals to purge professors, students, and employees who had collaborated with Batista. Once the Alma Mater had been "purified," the Commission drew plans to reform the University's structure and curriculum, and called for student elections in October 1959 to renew FEU's leadership.[40]

The approaching elections prompted the government to intervene. To mobilize and indoctrinate the students, control of FEU was essential. Castro advocated unity among the various student factions and urged the "election" of one candidate by acclamation. In a meeting held with Rolando Cubela and Pedro L. Boitel—the two candidates for President of FEU—and with other students, Castro's brother Raúl backed Cubela.[41]

There were several reasons for this choice. Cubela worked with the government and supported the Castro brothers. Although he was not directly involved in student affairs, he enjoyed great popularity at the University. The Castros may also have seen in Cubela personality weaknesses to be exploited to their own advantage.[42] Finally, the alternative to Cubela, Pedro Boitel, opposed and was opposed by the Communists.[43] To ensure complete control, Raúl placed three unconditional Castro supporters as Cubela's running mates: Major Angel Quevedo, Ricardo Alarcón, and José Rebellón.

As the election approached, government pressure increased. The day before the voting, Fidel asked Boitel to resign his candidacy.[44] The next morning, October 17, 1959, the official government newspaper *Revolución* carried on its front page Castro's exhortation to the students to unite and name the FEU President by acclamation rather than by election. "All students," the paper quoted Fidel, "should proclaim one President unanimously. That will really be a victory for all and not the Pyrrhic triumph of one group." Then Raúl Castro, to leave no doubt where the government's support lay, accompanied Cubela to the University and spoke to the students on Cubela's behalf. In addition, Minister of Education Armando Hart met with the two candidates and asked Boitel to withdraw from the race.[45]

Under these pressures, Boitel called a student assembly and offered not to run. But the students demanded an election. Their insistence should not be interpreted as a rebuke of Fidel, but rather as part of the student political tradition at the University of Havana, where elections had been held every year prior to 1956.

The revolutionary regime enjoyed the support of a great majority of the students and, for that matter, of the Cuban people. The students were largely unaware of the pressures and maneuvers going on behind the scenes. Many, reading Castro's appeal in the newspapers on the morning of the election and hearing rumors that Boitel had withdrawn his candidacy, expected no elections and stayed away from the polls. With approximately half of the student body voting, Cubela won the election. He received 52 per cent of the votes to Boitel's 48 per cent.[46] There were no other elections until 1962, when José Rebellón was "elected" President of the FEU. He was the sole candidate.[47] Pedro L. Boitel had been sentenced to forty-two years in prison in 1960 for "counterrevolutionary activities."

Cubela's election gave Fidel Castro only partial control of the University. Its autonomy still sheltered the campus from further interference; the University Council could still decide internal matters. Castro's desire to direct the university reform movement became the issue over which State and University clashed. Autonomy was the obstacle, and control the prize.

An early attempt to subvert the University's autonomy occurred simultaneously with the FEU election campaign in 1959. On October 7, Professor Raúl Roa, Minister of Foreign Relations, proposed that the University Council ask the government to appoint several cabinet members to form a joint committee with the deans of the faculties to plan university reform. The Council, pretending that this proposal was not contrary to university autonomy, adopted Roa's proposal and petitioned the government accordingly.[48] The uproar this request produced among teachers and students and the regime's stake in the approaching student elections, however, convinced the government that the time was not yet ripe for such a move. Castro shelved the Council's petition.

A second assault on the University's autonomy occurred in 1960. At a time when the government's power was expanding into every sector of Cuban society, the University still enjoyed relative independence. Arguing that autonomy had special significance when State and University clashed, but was anachronistic when they coincided, Castro's cabinet proposed to participate in planning university reform and sent representatives to explain this view to the student-faculty University Reform Commission established early in 1959. The government demanded a role for the Ministries of Education and Finance and the National Institute of Agrarian Reform in shaping university policy.[49] But this threatened intervention again met with the professors' stern opposition.

The government then made a final attempt, this time through the Student Federation. In a joint declaration issued in April 1960, FEU in Havana and its counterparts at the Universities of Las Villas and Oriente requested the creation of a "Higher Council" composed of government representatives and faculty members and students from the three state colleges to coordinate Cuba's university education. Although opposing this new attempt, the University Council did agree that two students and two faculty members from each university should form a committee—without government representation—to coordinate reform plans.[50]

Despite this concession, the University Council remained in control. But the government-controlled FEU refused to cooperate and the new committee soon died out. Meanwhile, the 1959 University Reform Commission had lapsed into inactivity. The Federation needed an incident to justify the government's complete intervention in university life. This occurred in mid-1960. The crisis was provoked after the University Council refused to approve the actions of several engineering students, led by José Rebellón, who had accused two professors of being "counterrevolutionary"; the students had ejected the professors from the University of Havana, barred them from their classrooms, and—without any legal authority—advertised in the press for replacements.[51] The Council sided with the two professors while FEU, although it apparently had not been formally involved in the "expulsion," supported Rebellón's action.

Verbal attacks and counterattacks followed. Castro's official press began a defamatory campaign against the Council. Charging that "reactionary" professors were attempting to provoke a crisis to damage the revolution, FEU demanded that Council members resign. Several professors resigned. Pro-Castro students occupied university buildings. Finally, on July 15, a group of about fifty professors and the leadership of FEU organized a new revolutionary council. The professors who refused to accept the new junta were expelled, forced to resign, or pensioned off. The government soon sanctioned this university coup and at the request of the new Council passed legislation legalizing its functions. Nearly 80 per cent of the old faculty members were replaced with professors favorable to the revolution.[52] The regime dealt a final blow to university autonomy on December 31, 1960, when it created a Higher Council of Universities, patterned after the Higher Council proposed by the students in April and headed by the Minister of Education, to rule the three state universities.[53]

The students' coup converted the autonomous University of Havana into an extension of the state. Credit for this transformation must also be given to Carlos Rafael Rodríguez, one of the PSP's top theoreticians. In March 1960, Rodríguez became Professor of Political Economy at the University. Working together with Hector Garcini—a law professor and legal adviser to Cuba's President, Osvaldo Dorticós—and with FEU leaders, Rodríguez helped plan the take-over. Minister of Education Armando Hart and two student leaders, Ricardo Alarcón and Isidoro Malmierca, also played key roles in the July crisis.[54]

Rodríguez remained in the background, allowing others to occupy important positions. By the end of 1961, however, he became the University's representative on the Higher Council of Universities and the guiding force behind plans for reform.[55] At the time of the July events, Rodríguez explained to a reporter, the Communists' tactic had been "thorough cooperation with Castro"; the government and the PSP had agreed that non-Communists as well as Communists could teach at the University, but that the institution would have to be dedicated "to the complete service of the revolution."[56] Having fulfilled his mission at the University of Havana, Rodríguez moved in February 1962 to the presidency of the National Institute of Agrarian Reform. In January of that same year the President of the PSP, Juan Marinello, became Rector of the University.[57]

Students Against Castro: The Opposition Fails

Although it is difficult to specify student attitudes under Castro with any precision, at least three general orientations can be distinguished during the first year and a half of Castro's rule.

One group of students supported both the revolution and its shift to the left. Some of these students backed Fidel faithfully, but—in keeping with the Latin American tradition of *personalismo*—followed the man rather than his ideas. Others in this group supported Castro's policies: his stand against the United States, his implementation of economic and social reforms, and his insistence on ending administrative corruption. Many of these pro-Castro students were caught up in the mystique of revolution, eager to do whatever was necessary to help the government. The regime, furthermore, fostered the students' feeling of participation by increasing their opportunities to join in the revolutionary process. Still others, coming from lower-income families, found that by aligning themselves with the revolution they could better their social status and strike back at more privileged students. A common characteristic of all the students in this first group was their identification with the "fatherland" rather than with any specific ideology, such as Marxism. The group included, however, a small but militant and disciplined Marxist-Leninist element, which usually followed PSP directives and which strongly influenced other pro-Castro students.

A second group, quite small, opposed the revolution. Its ranks were filled mostly with students whose families had been adversely affected by Castro's reforms.

A third group of students favored the revolution but opposed Communist influence in the government. Their opposition had varied origins. Some of those who had participated actively in the anti-Batista struggle abhorred Castro's purges of revolutionary figures.[58] Others resented the rapid and often chaotic changes brought on by Castro's reforms. Many feared the regime's absolutist tendencies and its intervention in university affairs. But overriding these views was a fourth orientation, shared by virtually all students during this early period: a willingness to justify government excesses as the natural result of transitional times.

Student opposition to the Castro regime was at first amorphous, but as the tempo of the revolution increased and the Communists gained in strength, it took on definite form. Late in 1959 and throughout 1960, anti-Castro organizations established branches within the University of Havana.[59] One group, known as *Trinchera* (the Trench), soon acquired some prestige and importance. Its leaders were former members of the Catholic University Association (*Agrupación Católica*). The Church provided the framework for these students' anti-Communist activities, offering them a doctrinal alternative to Communism. Through their newspaper, *Trinchera*, they were among the first to denounce Communist gains within the revolution. One of the leaders of the group, Juan Manuel Salvat, told the author that throughout 1959 *Trinchera* supported the revolution but—aware of the struggle between Communists and non-Communists within the government—was committed to fight to prevent the Communists from taking control.[60]

The *Trinchera* group sought to alert the Cuban people to the Communist challenge mainly through protests, riots, and propaganda. In February 1960, they demonstrated against Soviet Vice Premier Anastas Mikoyan's visit to Havana. Minutes after Mikoyan had placed a wreath on the statue of José Martí in the city's Central Park, the students attempted a similar ceremony to show their discontent. Police fired shots into the air and arrested twenty students. The following month, while *Trinchera* students marched from the University in support of Luis Conte Agüero, a popular radio and television commentator then waging an anti-Communist campaign, FEU leaders and student militias recently organized by FEU gave them a brutal beating.[61]

Soon after these events, seeking to organize and lead an active struggle against the regime, the *Trinchera* group joined the Revolutionary Recovery Movement (MRR). The MRR's origins dated back to the insurrectionary era, when it was called the Legion of Revolutionary Action. One of its military leaders, Manuel Artime, had fought briefly against Batista in the mountains and had later worked with the revolutionary government. After breaking with Castro, he and other rebel army officers organized the MRR. Several student leaders had belonged to and kept in close contact with Artime's organization; after the anti-Mikoyan demonstration, they formed the Revolutionary Student Directorate (*Directorio Revolucionario Estudiantil,* or DRE) of the MRR within the University of Havana and tried to build a student underground.[62]

The activities of the DRE and other anti-Castro groups interfered with the government's attempts to control the University. Castro and the controlling group within the FEU recognized the danger and acted accordingly. The Federation set up disciplinary tribunals to judge and expel "counterrevolutionary" students and suspended some of its own officials who had been involved in the anti-Mikoyan demonstration. FEU President Cubela called for the expulsion of "the traitors who conspired against the University."[63] Students burned bundles of *Trinchera* and other anti-Communist propaganda. Dissenters, including DRE leaders Alberto Müller and Juan Manuel Salvat, were beaten, threatened, and bodily forced off the campus. At the same time, Raúl Castro inaugurated a new scholarship plan through his Ministry of Defense to expand opportunities in higher education for the children of workers and peasants.[64] In the process, support for the regime from these less privileged social sectors naturally increased. By implementing this plan, the government was able to swell university enrollments with loyal followers and effectively stifle student opposition.

Denied the shelter of the University, the DRE leaders had to choose between the underground, imprisonment, and exile. In mid-1960, after several months in the underground, Müller and Salvat escaped to the United States. In Miami, the DRE broke with the MRR and joined the Democratic Revolutionary Front, a loosely coordinated body of anti-Castro organizations. Shortly thereafter, the two students, together with several others, returned clandestinely to Cuba to organize resistance in schools and universities.[65]

As a group, the DRE students were an interesting lot. Most came from middle- and upper-class families, usually professionals and businessmen. Some were active in Catholic youth organizations. The Church's influence on them was strong, although decreasingly so over time. A few came from areas outside Havana, but most were from the capital. They were young, usually in their early twenties. Some belonged to the old anti-Batista generation; others had entered the university after Castro came to power. Like their predecessors in the *Directorio,* these students were well intentioned and courageous, but lacked political maturity. Beyond the overthrow of Castro, they had no clear goals. Recognizing the U.S. government as the world's most powerful anti-Communist force, they sought and welcomed its help. "We expect aid and weapons from our neighbors to the North and will always be grateful [to them]," wrote Müller in January 1961, "but we will never be servants or vassals."[66]

The ideas of the DRE leaders were within the mainstream of Cuban political thought. The students shared Martí's vision of an ideal *patria,* friendly to but not dependent upon the United States. They had supported the program of nationalism, social justice, and political democracy expounded by Castro in the early days of his regime. When it became evident, however, that the revolution was moving toward Communism, they joined the anti-Castro ranks.

The DRE leaders adhered to Christian ideals. They felt their task was to warn the Cuban people of the materialistic, atheistic nature of Communism. In an editorial in *Trinchera,* they claimed the Communists denied "human freedom, property rights, freedom of thought, and family, love, and religion," and accused the PSP of "treachery to the spiritual values of Martí's fatherland." "While the Communists are materialists," they wrote, "the Cuban people and students are humanists." After the hoped-for overthrow of the

Castro regime, the DRE advocated a "national Christian order based on freedom and justice and a youth movement based on Christian principles and ideals."[67]

The DRE never attained the prominence of the anti-Batista *Directorio*. There are several reasons for this. While the *Directorio* was organized after nearly four years of Batista's rule, when opposition was widespread, the DRE was formed when Castro still enjoyed a great deal of support. Furthermore, the DRE had a more limited base of support; unlike the *Directorio*, it worked exclusively among students. Finally, the DRE lacked a leader comparable in popularity to José Antonio Echeverría. Even had they had such a figure, it is doubtful that the anti-Castro Cubans would have been ready to place their complete faith in one man, disillusioned as they were with the *personalista* tradition Castro had so effectively appropriated. The unwillingness of many anti-Castro Cubans to accept any strong, charismatic leader is perhaps an important reason why they remain disunited to this day.

By the summer of 1960, Porfirio Remberto Ramírez—a student leader closely connected with the DRE, who had fought against Batista and after Castro's victory been elected President of the FEU at the "Marta Abreu" University in Las Villas province—was completely disenchanted with Castro and with the mounting Communist influence in his government. Ramírez took up arms again, hoping to open a guerrilla front in the mountains of central Cuba. A Castro firing squad ended his brave gesture on October 13, 1960.[68]

In the months that followed Ramírez' execution, the activities of the DRE and the anti-Castro underground reached their high-water mark. When Fidel spoke at the University of Havana on November 30, several bomb explosions reaffirmed the DRE's determination to end his regime. In January 1961, the DRE sabotaged Havana's electric power plant and in February, on the first anniversary of the anti-Mikoyan demonstration, it organized a partially successful national student strike. In April 1961, a small group led by Alberto Müller began guerrilla activities in Oriente province.

Also in April, the DRE was to participate in a coordinated plan to assassinate Castro and capture Havana. Men and weapons had been requested from exile organizations for this so-called April 9th Plan. Its leaders had no program other than the establishment of a provisional government. Manolo Ray's Revolutionary Movement of the People (MRP) had been given the task of assassinating Castro. The DRE shared the MRP's view that the underground forces were indispensable to success in overthrowing Castro's government. The two groups saw the landing of the United States–sponsored Cuban invasion force, then being trained by the CIA in Guatemala, as the culminating event to follow a series of uprisings and acts of sabotage they hoped would split Castro's army throughout the island and weaken the regime's hold over the people.[69]

The plan was doomed to fail. The forces in exile disregarded the underground forces in Cuba and placed an unjustified faith in the invasion's success. The DRE inside Cuba watched the Bay of Pigs disaster in confusion and frustration.[70]

The failure of the invasion and the brutal repression that followed smashed the entire Cuban underground. On the first day of the invasion, the regime arrested thousands of real and suspected oppositionists. The resistance never recovered from the blow. Müller was captured by Castro's army, tried, and sentenced to twenty years in prison. Of the other DRE leaders, many were apprehended—a few were executed—and many went into exile.[71]

After a short stay in Miami, a small DRE force led by Fernández Rocha was smuggled into Havana to begin rebuilding the underground. But early in 1962, the DRE was infiltrated by Jorge Medina Bringuier, a captain in Castro's intelligence service. Taking advantage of his friendship with several students, Medina posed as an anti-Castroite and attained an important position within the remnants of the DRE's Havana underground.[72] The final blow fell in mid-1962, in an operation planned and directed by Raúl Castro. Most of the remaining DRE members were arrested. A few were purposely not captured in hopes they would in turn reorganize and expose others.[73]

Castro in Control: Mobilization and Purification

Castro had promoted loyal *Fidelistas* as FEU Presidents, ended university autonomy, purged dissenting students and professors, and destroyed the DRE. But he still needed a centralized body that could control Cuba's youth and ensure their loyalty to his regime. Early in 1960, Castro established the Association of Young Rebels (AJR). In October 1960, the youth branches of the July 26th Movement, the PSP, and the *Directorio* (the latter still under Chomón's leadership) merged into the new association.[74] Over the next two years, the AJR expanded until it controlled every youth group in Cuba. In the case of the FEU of the Unversity of Havana, however, a special arrangement was made. While it too merged with the AJR, FEU maintained its existing structure and leadership. In 1962, the Association of Young Rebels changed its name to the Union of Young

Communists (UJC) and organized a University Bureau in charge of political indoctrination within the University of Havana.[75]

Two reasons can be advanced for the special treatment given FEU. First, the Federation's prestige abroad enabled Castro to influence international student movements and congresses, and provided an ideal vehicle for the penetration of Latin American universities. Second, the dissolution of FEU would have alienated many students who still revered the organization's traditional and past importance.

By 1967, the government felt it unnecessary to preserve the University Bureau of the UJC and the FEU as two distinct organizations within the university. On November 21, 1967, claiming that university students now shared the same ideology, the FEU President explained that there was no need for two parallel organizations and announced the fusion of the FEU and the UJC in a new body, to be called the University Bureau UJC-FEU. This process was repeated at the universities of Las Villas and Oriente.[76]

The joining together of all youth groups was only one phase of a larger fusion of Communists and *Fidelistas,* and seems to indicate that as early as 1960 Castro was considering merging his July 26th Movement with the PSP. In August 1960, PSP Secretary General Blas Roca had advocated the union of all revolutionary forces in a single movement. It was not until 1962, however, that *Fidelistas,* Communists, and *Directorio* members formally merged into the Integrated Revolutionary Organizations (ORI), a preparatory step toward the creation of the United Party of the Socialist Revolution (PURS), later transformed into the Communist Party of Cuba (PCC) —the island's present ruling party.

This apparent harmony concealed an internal struggle for power. Although Castro had eliminated opposition outside the revolution, he still had to contend with inside factions that challenged his desire for absolute hegemony. Of these, the PSP was clearly the most dangerous. Throughout 1961 and part of 1962, Castro accepted the principle of "collective leadership," allowing old-guard Communists widespread control. By 1962, however, feeling his position threatened, Castro purged the old-time Communist leader Aníbal Escalante and moved toward direct personal control. In November 1963, at a time when he leaned toward Communist China, Fidel appointed Juan Mier, Vice Minister of Higher Education and a lesser PSP member, to replace the more important old-guard Communist leader Juan Marinello as Rector of the University of Havana.[77]

One episode in this power struggle brought into the open Communist maneuvers in the University of Havana student body. This was the trial of Marco ("Marquito") Armando Rodríguez. As a Communist informer, Marquito had exposed the hide-out of the four *Directorio* leaders assassinated by Batista's police on Humboldt Street on April 20, 1957. After fleeing to Mexico, he had received aid and protection from Joaquín Ordoqui and his wife, two leading PSP members. Ordoqui had obtained a scholarship for Marquito to study in Czechoslovakia and had helped him to become an official member of the *Juventud Socialista*, the youth wing of the PSP. In 1961, at the insistence of the *Directorio*, which had discovered Marquito's guilt, Castro requested his arrest and extradition from Prague to Havana. Deported shortly thereafter, Marquito remained in jail in Cuba until his trial in March 1964.

The trial—especially the testimony of Marquito—shed light on an important and previously unclear matter: the tactics of the PSP in dealing with the student movement during the 1955–57 period. At first, the Communists had tried to infiltrate the *Directorio*. Marquito explained that the youth branch of the PSP had ordered him to concentrate on intelligence work within the *Directorio*. "All information," said the accused, "was transmitted to the University Bureau [the PSP group that worked within the University of Havana] to be sent on to its final destination . . . the Party."[78]

Later, in 1956, the Communists, realizing they could not gain control of the *Directorio*, had attempted to influence the creation of a "United Student Front" composed of delegates from the *Directorio*, the July 26th Movement, and the PSP. The Communists had reasoned that any such front would reduce the *Directorio*'s power and eventually fall under their own control. Marquito recounted the failure of that attempt and the differences that had arisen between three factions. Finally, he explained the refusal of the *Directorio* to allow his participation in the plans for the presidential palace attack in 1957 and admitted having revealed the students' hide-out to Batista's police.[79]

Castro used the trial to reassert his own power. He tried Marquito and took advantage of the opportunity to put the Communist PSP on the bench with the accused. All the top leaders of the PSP testified; they took pains to deny that the accused had been a member of the *Juventud Socialista* or had been connected with their party. Toward the end of the trial—perhaps thinking of his economic dependence on the Soviet Union and fearful of provoking Moscow's wrath—Fidel exonerated the PSP from guilt in the "Humboldt event" and ordered Marquito's execution. Whether Marquito had acted on his own initiative or followed the directives of the Party when he betrayed the four students is still not known. The trial did, however, reveal that the Communists had used Marquito in their efforts to undermine the non-Communist revolutionary forces, especially the *Directorio*.[80]

Another challenge to Castro's authority arose early in 1966. This time it involved a full-fledged conspiracy within the armed forces led by the former President of FEU, Major Rolando Cubela, and involving the exiled MRR leader Manuel Artime. The plotters planned to assassinate Castro, land an expedition under Artime's leadership, and establish a provisional regime with Cubela and Artime sharing top posts. Castro uncovered the conspiracy in March 1966, arrested Cubela and six others, and sentenced them to long prison terms.[81]

The Cubela affair is significant for the disillusionment it revealed in a generation of students hitherto loyal to Castro. Cubela was well known at the University of Havana and had been extremely popular there. During the trial, while the prosecution was requesting the death penalty for Cubela, students at the University demonstrated against the regime and distributed leaflets warning Castro that he would also die if Cubela were executed. The protests reached such a high pitch that Castro had to order the army to occupy the University. Many students were arrested; others were silenced by the threat of imprisonment. Perhaps aware that killing Cubela would only cause more resentment, Castro sent a letter to the prosecutor asking him not to insist on the death penalty. The tribunal obediently sentenced Cubela to twenty-five years in prison.[82]

In June 1965, Castro's party (PURS) had established its first full-fledged cell at the University of Havana to ensure what Castro called the "second revolution" in Cuban education. The first one had involved the quantitative spread of educational facilities, and the second would focus on qualitative aspects, namely Marxist indoctrination.[83] But, as the events surrounding Cubela's trial showed, neither "revolution"—nor even Raúl Castro's scholarship program to create a new, more loyal student generation—had suceeded in quelling student opposition completely.

Conclusion: The Social Context of Revolution

In the late 1940's and early 1950's, the University of Havana was a microcosm of Cuba's public life. Unscrupulous individuals used the prestige associated with being a student leader to further their political ambitions and obtain governmental positions for friends and relatives. The presidency of FEU degenerated into a stepping-stone to national politics. Violence became a common means of settling student disputes. University politics required not only public speaking abilities but also survival skills: toughness and shrewdness. The activities of the *bonches* (student gangs) became so conspicuous that Havana's daily *El Mundo* lamented, "Professors and students are nothing but the prisoners of a few groups of desperados who impose their will and pass their examinations at pistol point."[84]

Despite this breakdown in discipline and morals, many students shared a redemptionist fanaticism, a readiness to sacrifice everything for Cuba's political salvation. In the University, more than anywhere else, the nation's problems were evoked and debated. Theories of all sorts vigorously flourished. The authoritarian ideas of fascism and Communism, offering ready formulas to bring order out of Cuba's chaos, were widely discussed. But above all, the nationalistic program of the *Ortodoxo* party—economic independence, political liberty, social justice, and an end to corruption—captured the imagination of Cuban youth. *Ortodoxo* leader Eduardo Chibás, the most revolutionary exponent of an idealistic generation seeking to bring justice and honesty to Cuba's public life through democratic means, became the idol of university students.[85]

It was in this environment that Fidel Castro and other revolutionary leaders received their first schooling in politics. Fidel, while studying law at the University of Havana in the late 1940's, had not been a prominent student leader. Yet he participated in the activities of student gangs, enrolled in an aborted expedition against the Trujillo dictatorship in 1947, attended an anti-imperialist student meeting timed to coincide with the Ninth Inter-American Conference gathered in Bogotá in 1948, and joined the *Ortodoxo* party soon after. His university years exposed him to the realism of power politics, the idealism of Chibás program, and the authoritarianism of fascism and Communism.

Batista's coup d'état in 1952 further stimulated student political involvement. Students laid their rivalries aside, directing all efforts against the new regime. Militantly anti-Batista student leaders emerged with effective political power not only in the student community but nationally as well.

Today, with the Communist Party of Cuba directing student activities and the universities shorn of their autonomy and geared to socio-economic development, student involvement in politics has reached a low ebb. Fidel unquestionably enjoys student support, but its intensity and extent cannot be accurately determined. Student opposition has been contained primarily by the coercive strength of the Castro regime. Dissident students are periodically purged, strict discipline is imposed by student militias and other repressive forces, and "counterrevolutionaries" are prevented from enrolling in the universities.[86]

Other factors can also be adduced to explain the present lack of student political opposition. First, the regime maintains the students, and for that matter the entire Cuban population, in a state of emergency and mobilization. Castro's propaganda incessantly warns that Cuba is surrounded by powerful enemies, that the future of the revolution is at stake. Students share in the continuous mass mobilizations and spend many weekends cutting sugar cane in the fields. These and other extracurricular activities required by the government exhaust the students' energy and leave little time for politics.[87]

Castro's constant exhortations to the students to participate in these chores, and his criticism of "pampered youths who lack a revolutionary conscience and willingness to work for society" may indicate a decrease in nation-building enthusiasm.[88] Apparently, university students still retain their elitist, middle-class attitude toward manual labor. More than the abstract goal of "working for society," what probably motivates them is ambition and a mixture of fear and hope for the future. Furthermore, the charismatic appeal exerted by Castro has probably eroded over time; today many students may have grown apathetic and immune to the regime's constant revolutionary exhortations.

A second factor is the new orientation of university education in Cuba. In the past, liberal arts studies were emphasized and the universities produced a crop of underemployed intellectuals every year. Today the emphasis is on technical and scientific studies, and the government absorbs almost all university graduates. An assured salaried job and a guaranteed social position after graduation are undoubtedly important disincentives to opposition activity. Since "good behavior" is one of the requisites for government aid, the regime's scholarships have also contributed to political conformism.[89]

This government control over scholarships and future jobs is, however, a double-edged sword. Since the regime makes a considerable investment in educating a student, it will hesitate before stopping his career, especially in its later stages. Students realize and take advantage of their privileged position. In a December 1966 speech at the University of Havana, Castro lashed at government-supported technical students "who think they are doing society a favor." "They know," said Fidel, "that technicians are needed, and that bourgeois technicians are leaving; therefore, they think they are important."[90]

Third, the class composition of the university student body has changed. Although statistics are not available, sons of workers and farmers probably constitute a much larger proportion of the student body today than in the past. The regime has started special preparatory course programs to qualify industrial workers for university study. Also, students from poor families receive priority attention from the government in the granting of scholarships. This assistance naturally tends to build loyalty to the regime among recipient students.

A fourth factor is the establishment of the UJC at the University of Havana. Besides its coercive influence, the UJC offers the students a legitimate channel, in addition to FEU, through which they can operate and voice their discontent directly to the Party.

These factors indicate that anti-Castro student activity of any significance in the future is extremely unlikely. If criticism of the regime develops, it will probably come not from students of middle-class origin, but from those of worker or peasant origin. Whereas the latter might feel a little freer to voice their opinions, the former, in order to avoid calling attention to their social background, will probably remain politically inarticulate. Yet a small potential for opposition remains. Whether or not it will be ignited —and, if so, whether by the students themselves or only in the context of some larger national crisis—is difficult to say.

NOTES

1. See Jaime Suchlicki, "University of Havana Students and Politics, 1920–1966" (unpublished Ph.D. dissertation, Texas Christian University, 1967). Some information on the anti-Machado struggle can be found in Rubén de León, *El origen del mal* (Coral Gables: Service Offset Printers, 1964); Eduardo Suárez Rivas, *Un pueblo crucificado* (Coral Gables: Service Offset Printers, 1964); and Raúl Roa, *En Pie* (Santa Clara: Universidad Central de Las Villas, 1959). These books were written by participating student leaders. On the anti-Batista insurrection, see J. Suchlicki, "The Role of the University of Havana Students in Cuban Politics 1952–1957" (unpublished M.A. thesis, University of Miami, 1965). Luis Boza, *La situación universitaria en Cuba* (Santiago de Chile: Editorial del Pacífico, 1962) is valuable for the Castro era.

2. The presidents of the University's thirteen student associations (one for each faculty) formed the Federation and selected its President. Elections were

held annually. For the structure of FEU, see José Ramón Rolando Puig y Pupo, *Apuntes sobre la escuela de Derecho y la Universidad de la Habana* (Havana: Imprenta de la Universidad, 1959). University of Havana students were chosen for this study because they played a historically more important role in Cuban politics, had a greater impact on the Cuban revolution, and are far greater in number than students in the other universities, although the latter have also been politically active. Prior to Castro's revolution, there were in Cuba three state-controlled universities, one private university, and several private colleges, with a total enrollment of approximately 21,000. More than 17,000 of these students attended the University of Havana. After the revolution, private institutions were abolished or nationalized; the Catholic University "Santo Tomás de Villanueva" in Havana was transformed into the Makarenko Institute for adult teachers. University instruction is now offered at the universities of Havana, Oriente, and "Marta Abreu" of Las Villas. Enrollment at the University of Havana had decreased to 13,430 students by 1962. See Dudley Seers (ed.), *Cuba: The Economic and Social Revolution* (Durham: Seeman Printing, 1964), p. 256. By 1967 there were 20,029, students enrolled at the University. See *Cuba 1967, The Educational Movement* (Havana: Ministry of Education, 1967).

3. Until 1933, the University was under government jurisdiction. Decree No. 2059 of October 6, 1933, established the University's autonomy and provided for a governing University Council of professors and administrative officials. The 1940 Constitution later guaranteed this grant of autonomy. The University, however, continued to depend financially on the government. For a brief history of the University, see Luis Felipe Le-Roy y Gálvez, *La Universidad de la Habana: síntesis histórica* (Havana: Imprenta de la Universidad, 1960). In 1952–53, the state universities received 2.6 per cent, or $2.2 million, of the educational budget, while in 1967 they secured 8.9 per cent, or $37 million. *Cuba 1967, op. cit.*, p. 84. There has been a substantial increase in governmental expenditures for higher education under Castro. The 1967 figures, it should be noted, were supplied by the Cuban government.

4. "Resolverá el Tribunal de Urgencia situación de los detenidos," *Diario de la Marina* (Havana), April 7, 1953, p. 1. See also "En Cuba," *Bohemia* (Havana), No. 16 (April 19, 1953), p. 77, and No. 22 (May 31, 1953), pp. 68–69. Bárcena had no program beyond a return to the 1940 Constitution and the holding of free elections.

5. See "En Cuba," *Bohemia*, No. 41 (October 12, 1952), p. 90; No. 50 (December 14, 1952), p. 73; No. 7 (February 15, 1953), p. 68. See also *Del Consejo Universitario a la opinión pública* (Havana: Imprenta de la Universidad, 1953).

6. *Bohemia*, No. 47 (November 23, 1952), p. 72.

7. *Ibid.*

8. "Interview with Alvaro Barba," *Bohemia*, No. 1 (January 4, 1953), pp. 36–37.

9. For a description and photographs of the murdered student's funeral, see *Vida Universitaria*, No. 32 (March 1953), pp. 13–14. Also see "Interview with José Joaquín Peláez," *Bohemia*, No. 10 (March 8, 1953), pp. 70–71.

10. On these events, see Suchlicki, "The Role of the University Students in Cuban Politics, 1952–1957," pp. 84–89.

11. On these events, see "Carta a varios líderes políticos de Cuba," *La*

Sierra y el llano (Havana: Casa de las Américas, 1961); "La conspiración del 3 de Abril," *Bohemia*, No. 16 (April 15, 1956), pp. 63–77; "Cuartel Goicuría, 29 de Abril," *Bohemia*, No. 24 (June 10, 1956), pp. 60–65. The *Organización Auténtica* was an insurrectionary offshoot of the *Auténtico* party.

12. See Suchlicki, *op. cit.*, pp. 97, 178–80.

13. Interview with Félix Armando Murias, Miami, Florida, July 19, 1965. Murias and all other persons interviewed participated actively or were closely connected with the events described in this chapter. Although these interviews constituted the main source of data, they were supplemented whenever possible with documentary evidence: newspapers, magazines, pamphlets, personal letters, tape-recorded speeches, and manifestos. Obviously, the interviews varied in value because of the intense involvement of some individuals and the faulty memories of others. All interviews have, therefore, been used with caution.

Of the eight original founders of the *Directorio*, José A. Echeverría, Fructuoso Rodríguez, Joe Westbrook, and Tirso Urdanivia died in the struggle against Batista, Faure Chomón and René Anillo are in Cuba supporting the revolutionary regime, René Valls is in jail in Cuba, and Murias is in exile.

14. Interview with Armando Fleites, Miami, July 12, 1965.

15. On the students' dealings with Castro, see Suchlicki, *op. cit.*, pp. 100–104. For the text of the "Mexican Letter," see *ibid.*, pp. 181–84.

16. "La muerte del Coronel Blanco Rico," *Diario de la Marina*, October 27, 1956, p. 1. Also see "La trágica muerte del Coronel Blanco Rico," *Bohemia*, No. 45 (November 4, 1956), pp. 60–66. Carbó Serviá sought refuge in a Latin American embassy and Cubela escaped to Miami.

17. "Interview with Fidel Castro in Mexico," *Bohemia*, No. 11 (January 6, 1957), p. 6.

18. Similar statements, claiming that Fidel failed to notify the *Directorio* in advance of his landing, were made in other interviews, by Juan A. Rodríguez, Miami, May 7, 1965; Annaelis Esteva, Miami, May 11, 1965; and Armando Fleites, Miami, July 12, 1965.

19. Several years later, *Directorio* leader Faure Chomón, justifying the students' inaction, said that at the time the students lacked "the necessary means" (i.e., weapons) to stage a revolt in Havana. Testimony of Faure Chomón at the trial of Marco Armando Rodríguez, *Hoy* (Havana), March 24, 1964, p. 8.

20. "Suspenden clases en la Universidad," *Diario de la Marina*, December 1, 1956, p. 1; December 3, 1956, p. 1. Also see "Calmada la capital de Oriente después de dos jornadas de sucesos," *ibid.*, December 2, 1956, p. 1.

21. Interview with former FEU leader Juan A. Rodríguez, Miami, May 7, 1965.

22. On these events, see Suchlicki, *op. cit.*, pp. 116–31.

23. "En Cuba," *Bohemia*, No. 20 (May 28, 1957), p. 97.

24. The text of Marinello's letter can be found in Herbert L. Matthews, *The Cuban Story* (New York: George Braziller, 1961), pp. 51–52. See also Theodore Draper, *Castroism, Theory and Practice* (New York: Frederick A. Praeger, 1965), pp. 30–31.

25. Testimony of Raúl Valdés Vivó at the trial of Marco Armando Rodríguez, *Hoy*, March 25, 1964, p. 4.

26. Later, in February 1957, in a letter to the July 26th Movement, the PSP leaders also called on Castro for "closer understanding" based on a "coincidence" of strategy. They insisted that armed action was the wrong tactic and

repeated their disagreement with Fidel's "methods and tactics." They noted, however, that among the different groups in Cuba the July 26th Movement "came closest" to the Communists' "strategic conception." "Carta del Comité Nacional del Partido Socialista Popular al Movimiento 26 de Julio," February 28, 1957, quoted in Draper, *op. cit.,* pp. 29–30.

27. Interview with Dora Rosales, Miami, June 14, 1965. Mrs. Rosales, Joe Westbrook's mother, took up the fight against Batista after her son's death. She went into exile and traveled throughout Latin America denouncing Batista. After Castro came to power, she returned to Cuba and supported the revolutionary regime. When it became clear to her that Communism had gained control in Cuba, she again went into exile and denounced the Castro regime.

28. A tape recording of Chomón's original speech was supplied to the author by Ada Azcarreta in Miami, May 7, 1965.

29. For the text of the manifesto, see Gregorio Selser (ed.), *La Revolución Cubana* (Buenos Aires: Editorial Palestra, 1960), pp. 119–26.

30. For the full text of the letter, see *ibid.,* pp. 127–40.

31. *Revolución* (Havana), December 1, 1961. Responding to Castro's invitation to new unity talks, the *Directorio* sent delegates to the Sierra Maestra in mid-1958. (Testimony of PSP leader Carlos Rafael Rodríguez at the trial of Marco Armando Rodríguez, *Hoy,* March 26, 1964. Carlos Rafael Rodríguez also went to the Sierra Maestra at the same time.) In July, representatives from several anti-Batista organizations, including the *Directorio* and the July 26th Movement but excluding the PSP, met in Venezuela and signed a new unity pact known as the "Caracas Letter." The meeting accepted, as head of the provisional government to be established after Batista's overthrow, Dr. Manuel Urrutia, a distinguished judge.

> The "Caracas Letter" of July 28, 1958, called for a common strategy of armed insurrection, a brief provisional government that would guide the country back to normality through constitutional and democratic means, and a minimum government program guaranteeing the punishment of the guilty, workers' rights, order, peace, freedom, the fulfillment of international agreements, and the economic, social, and institutional progress of the Cuban people.

For the full text, see Selser (ed.), *op. cit.,* pp. 152–55.

The Communists were excluded from the Caracas meeting because of the opposition of several groups represented there. Castro, however, was holding parallel talks with PSP leaders at the time. Draper claims (*op. cit.,* pp. 32–34) that Castro surreptitiously negotiated a separate unity pact with the Communists in 1958.

32. See "Declaraciones del PSP: Las mentiras del Gobierno sobre la huelga y la situación," PSP leaflet of April 12, 1958, quoted in Draper, *op. cit.,* p. 32.

33. Fleites interview. Fleites reported that when a PSP representative, Ovidio Díaz, visited his headquarters in the mountains in August 1958 to propose unity, "he [Díaz] met with our stern opposition to any pacts with the Communists."

34. Interview with Lázaro Fariñas, Miami, July 2, 1965. Fariñas, a *Directorio* member, fought under Cubela in the Escambray Mountains.

35. Interview with Jorge Nóbrega, Miami, September 12, 1966.

36. "Hará el gobierno justicia serena pero muy enérgica," *Revolución,* January 7, 1959, p. 5.

37. "Armas para qué?," *ibid.*, January 9, 1959, p. 1.

38. "Resolverá el gobierno," *ibid.*, January 10, 1959, p. 1.

39. Chomón described his role in these terms: "When in 1959 the July 26th Movement, the PSP, and the *Directorio* worked jointly to decide the true course of the Revolution . . . we organized the so-called left among the insurrectionary groups to defeat the right." Testimony of Faure Chomón at the trial of Marco Armando Rodríguez, *Hoy*, March 21, 1964, p. 5.

40. "Comisión Mixta para la depuración universitaria," *Revolución*, March 25, 1959, p. 1. For the Commission's reform plans, see *Acuerdos de la Comisión Mixta de Reforma Universitaria* (Havana: Imprenta de la Universidad, 1959).

41. Interview with Jorge Nóbrega, Miami, September 12, 1966. Also see Boza, *op. cit.*, p. 24. For the government's version of events surrounding the 1959 election, see *La Universidad de la Habana al Consejo Ejecutivo y a la Asamblea General de la Unión de Universidades de América Latina* (Havana: Universidad de la Habana, 1964), pp. 44–50.

42. As has already been noted, the assassination of Blanco Rico in 1956—in which Cubela took part—met with considerable indignation in Cuba and was criticized by Castro in Mexico. According to the *Directorio's* representative in Miami at the time, this censure disturbed Cubela so deeply that, after escaping to the United States, he underwent psychiatric treatment. (Interview with Ada Azcarreta, Miami, May 7, 1965.) In interviews with the author, Jorge Nóbrega, Juan A. Rodríguez, and several other student activists who knew Cubela well portrayed him as unstable and easily influenced.

43. Boitel belonged to the July 26th underground in Havana. Prior to Castro's December 1956 landing in Cuba, sporadic cells had been organized throughout the island, one of them among University of Havana students. This underground, a part of the July 26th Movement, grew in size and importance after the ill-fated attack on the presidential palace in March 1957. Although students joined both the underground and the guerrilla forces, the July 26th Movement never included a substantial student participation. During the insurrection, the Communists were never able to infiltrate the underground to the degree they did the guerrilla forces.

44. Juan Miguel Portuondo de Castro, *Como se apoderaron los comunistas de la Universidad de la Habana* (Florida: Directorio Magisterial Cubano, 1962), p. 21. Dr. Portuondo, a distinguished Cuban physician, was then Professor of Physiology at the University of Havana. See also *La destrucción de la enseñanza universitaria* (Florida: Directorio Magisterial Cubano, n.d.), p. 13.

45. Boza, *op. cit.*, pp. 29–30.

46. *Ibid.*, p. 31. When the University reopened in 1959, the old system of indirect election for FEU President (see note 2) had been changed and students were allowed to vote directly for candidates.

47. "Elections" were held again in February 1965. Jaime Crombet became the new FEU President, the students having cast their votes for a single preselected list of candidates presented at a general assembly of the entire student body. In January 1966, the regime reshuffled the leadership of the Federation, replacing Crombet with Francisco Dorticós as President. This *fait accompli* was later "publicly approved" by an assembly of the student body. See "Directed Democracy for FEU," *Youth and Freedom*, VII, No. 2 (1965), 16, and "Reestructuran las dirigencias de la FEU y la UJC," *Vida Universitaria*, April-May 1966, pp. 6–8. Crombet became Secretary General of the Union of Young Communists (UJC).

In an attempt to raise the Federation's prestige, the regime did allow elections in December 1966. Former FEU Vice President Enrique Velazco, with 7,771 votes to medical student Juan Vela's 7,544, became President of FEU. Both candidates were members of the UJC. "Daily News from the Cuban Radio" (USIA, Miami), December 7, 1966, p. 6. See also "New Officers for FEU and UJC," *Youth and Freedom*, IX, Nos. 1–2 (1967), 30.

48. "Pide el Consejo Universitario al Gobierno actue en su crisis," *Revolución*, October 8, 1959, p. 1.

49. "Una sola reforma para las 3 universidades oficiales," *ibid.*, April 6, 1960, pp. 1, 6. Also see "Universidades," *ibid.*, April 11, 1960, p. 18.

50. "Piden un consejo de Enseñanza Superior," *ibid.*, April 21, 1960, p. 2; "Comisión coordinadora para las Universidades," *ibid.*, May 5, 1960, p. 7.

51. See *ibid.*, June 17, 1960, p. 7. Also "Expulsará la Universidad a Aureliano Sánchez Arango," *ibid.*, June 20, 1960, p. 1.

52. See Portuondo de Castro, *op. cit.*, pp. 48–49. On the events described, see *ibid.*, p. 43; "Rechaza la FEU la actitud del Consejo Universitario," *Revolución*, June 29, 1960, p. 2; "Acusa la FEU al consejo," *ibid.*, July 2, 1960, p. 1; "Constituída la Junta Superior de Gobierno de la Universidad," *ibid.*, July 16, 1960, p. 1. Also see Pedro Vicente Aja, "La crisis de la Universidad de la Habana," *Ensayos* (Quito), August 1962, pp. 39–46.

53. *La Reforma de la Enseñanza Superior en Cuba* (Cuba: Consejo Superior de Universidades, 1962), p. 14. This monograph describes the new structure of Cuba's three state universities. For other educational changes, see U.S. Office of Education, Division of International Studies, *Educational Data: Cuba* (Washington, D.C.: Government Printing Office, November 1962); Richard R. Fagen, *Cuba: The Political Content of Adult Education* (Stanford: Stanford University, The Hoover Institution on War, Revolution, and Peace, 1964); and Joseph S. Roucek, "Pro-Communist Revolution in Cuban Education," *Journal of Inter-American Studies*, VI, No. 3 (July 1964), 325–35.

54. Interview with Luis Fernández Rocha, a prominent student leader in Havana at the time and later coordinator of the anti-Castro Revolutionary Student Directorate (DRE) in exile, Miami, September 18, 1966.

55. Boza, *op. cit.*, pp. 180–5. Also see *La Reforma de la Enseñanza Superior en Cuba*.

56. For Max Frankel's interview with Carlos Rafael Rodríguez, see *The New York Times*, November 27, 1960, p. 1.

57. *Ibid.*, January 11, 1962, p. 1.

58. The most important cases were the dismissal of the first President, Manuel Urrutia, in July 1959; the arrest of Major Huber Matos, commander of the rebel army in Camagüey Province, in October; and the removal of two ministers, Faustino Pérez and Manolo Ray, in November.

59. Some of the more important were *Rescate*, the Triple A, the Revolutionary Recovery Movement (MRR), and the Christian Democratic Party.

60. Interview with Juan Manuel Salvat, Miami, September 14, 1966. The *Trinchera* group drew its name from one of José Martí's maxims: "Trenches of ideas are stronger than trenches of stone."

61. Salvat interview; interview with Juan A. Rodríguez, Miami, September 17, 1966; "Saludo a Anastas Mikoyan," *Revolución*, February 6, 1960, pp. 1, 16; "Chiflaron a Conte Agüero," *ibid.*, March 26, 1960, p. 1. Early in 1960, the FEU organized student militias within the University of Havana. Only FEU leaders and students of "revolutionary militancy" were allowed to join.

62. Salvat interview. Artime was later closely involved in the ill-fated invasion attempt at the Bay of Pigs.

63. "Respaldo a la FEU," *Revolución*, March 28, 1960, p. 1. See also "Instauran tribunal para universitarios," *ibid.*, February 6, 1960, p. 4.

64. "Plan," *ibid.*, March 31, 1960, p. 1.

65. "In its beginning," said Salvat, "the DRE had only 100 student members. But by 1961 it had grown into a clandestine army of 1,800 in Havana alone." (Salvat interview.) These figures cannot, of course, be verified.

66. *La cruz sigue en pie* (Caracas: Directorio Revolucionario Estudiantil, n.d.), p. 35. This pamphlet contains a short biography of Müller and a collection of his writings.

67. *Ibid.*, pp. 21, 28–29.

68. "Cumplidas las sentencias a alzados del Escambray," *Revolución*, October 13, 1960, p. 1.

69. Rocha and Salvat interviews.

70. Arms that were to be shipped to DRE forces in the mountains never arrived and communications between the exile and underground forces were sporadic and confused. "The lack of support from the groups in exile," DRE leader Fernández Rocha later complained bitterly, "and their failure to supply badly needed war matériel, frustrated the 'April 9 Plan' in its early stages." Rocha claimed further that "the underground was not advised at all of the invasion plans. Not until April 17, the very day of the landing, did we receive word that the invasion had been launched." (Rocha interview.)

71. Virgilio Campanería, law student, and Alberto Tapia Ruano, architecture student, for example, were executed on April 18, 1961. A list of students executed or jailed can be found in Boza, *op. cit.*, pp. 189–99.

72. Later, while on a trip to East Germany, Medina defected from the Castro regime.

73. According to Salvat, there are a few DRE activists still in Cuba, but "their activities are very limited. They don't know whom they can trust." (Salvat interview.)

74. "Crearán una organización de toda la juventud cubana," *Revolución*, October 24, 1960, p. 1.

75. "Tomó la AJR el nombre de Unión de Jóvenes Comunistas," *Hoy*, April 1, 1962, p. 1. Also see Jaime Crombet, "La UJC en la Universidad de la Habana," *Vida Universitaria*, March 1964, pp. 10–12. By December 1966, the UJC University Bureau had a membership of 1,902 students. "UJC—Comite Universitario," *ibid.* (December 1966), p. 39.

76. "Daily News from the Cuban Radio" (USIA, Miami), November 21, 1967, p. 2.

77. In June 1965, Salvador Vilaseca, President of Cuba's National Bank, became the new Rector. See "Nuevo Rector Universitario," *ibid.*, August 1965, pp. 4–6.

78. "La Revolución no ha de ser ni tolerante ni implacable," *Hoy*, March 27, 1964, p. 6. The full text of the trial was published, among other places, in *Hoy*, March 24–27, 1964. *Hoy* was the official PSP newspaper. It merged with *Revolución* in 1966 to form *Granma*, the present official newspaper of Cuba's Communist Party.

79. On the Marquito affair, see Suchlicki, *op. cit.*, pp. 152–63. Also see *Humboldt 7 y el Comunismo Cubano* (Panamá: Directorio Revolucionario Estudiantil, n.d.) and Janette Habel, "Le procès de Marcos Rodriguez et les

problèmes de l'unité du Mouvement Révolutionnaire à Cuba," *Les Temps Modernes*, No. 219–20 (September 1964), pp. 491–531.

80. Only a few months after the trial, Joaquín Ordoqui was arrested and accused of "political crimes." His wife, Edith García Buchaca, was relieved of her post at the National Council of Culture. On February 15, 1965, Fidel purged Carlos Rafael Rodríguez as Director of the National Institute of Agrarian Reform and appointed himself to that position. Other old PSP leaders were scorned and attacked by Castro's press.

81. "Ordenó Castro que no se aplique la pena de muerte a Cubela," *Diario Las Américas* (Miami), March 10, 1966, p. 1. See also the "Proceedings of the Trial of CIA agents which took place at La Cabaña Fortress in Havana and started on 7 March, 1966," *Cuban Embassy Information Bulletin* (London), No. 8 (1966). In interviews with the author, Edgar Sopo, one of Artime's top lieutenants and a prominent MRR member, reported that Cubela had been conspiring within Cuba's armed forces since 1961. According to Sopo, while attending a student congress in Europe early in 1965, Cubela met with Artime in Spain, where they drew up plans to kill Castro. Artime left immediately for Central America and Cubela returned to Cuba to prepare the assassination attempt. The MRR supplied Cubela with the murder weapon, a high-powered telescopic rifle. (Interviews with Edgar Sopo, Miami, September 21 and 23, 1966.)

82. "Ordenó Castro que no se aplique la pena de muerte a Cubela." Also see "Fue Tomada militarmente la Universidad de la Habana," *ibid.*, March 18, 1966, p. 9.

83. See *The New York Times*, June 15, 1965, p. 12, and "Nuevo núcleo del PCC en la universidad," *Vida Universitaria*, March 1966, pp. 16–17.

84. *El Mundo* (Havana), September 5, 1949, p. 3.

85. Chibás, an elected Senator, shot and killed himself during one of his weekly radio programs in August 1951. He felt his suicide would awaken the Cuban people to the corrupt nature of the *Auténtico* administration, creating the necessary conditions for the emergence of an honest, reformist government. Instead, his death created a political vacuum, left the masses leaderless, produced a rift in the *Ortodoxo* party, and thus prepared the way for Batista's coup d'état in 1952.

86. See Lee Lockwood's candid interview with Castro in *Playboy*, January 1967, pp. 59–84.

87. Mobilization for productive labor has also been a factor in reducing the time available for study. Recently, FEU leaders have been emphasizing academic excellence as the students' most important goal.

88. See, for example, Castro's December 1966 speech at the University of Havana, published among other places in *Vida Universitaria*, January 1967, pp. 3–16.

89. During 1966, the government gave financial aid to 103,386 university, secondary, and other students. Of these, almost 8,000 were University of Havana students. See "De la ignorancia a altos niveles de estudio," *Vida Universitaria*, June 1967, p. 45.

90. *Vida Universitaria*, January 1967, p. 10.

11. VENEZUELA

WILLIAM L. HAMILTON

In February 1928, Venezuelan students took to the streets in a spontaneous antigovernment protest that marked the beginning of the modern Venezuelan student movement. Those members of the "generation of '28" are now at the peak of what have in many cases been illustrious careers. Meanwhile, the Venezuelan student movement has been variously united and disorganized, peaceful and violent. The students have fought against dictatorships, for and against democratic systems, for and against socialist revolution. They have been concerned with university reform, labor organization, the composition of the cabinet, economic policy, and international affairs. They have worn the colors of every conceivable political position. They have acted in five different political systems: two dictatorships, a limited-base democracy, and two democratic systems based on universal suffrage.

Thus Venezuela presents in the span of a single generation an immensely diverse panorama of student political activity. A few relatively spectacular incidents in recent years have tended to draw attention away from this diversity; the result has been a quantity of generalizations about Venezuelan students based on their response to one very specific situation. The real value of the Venezuelan case, however, is that it brings quickly and clearly to view nearly all of the characteristics of student movements in Latin America.

This chapter is based on research conducted in 1965–66 in Venezuela and the United States for a Ph.D. dissertation at the Fletcher School of Law and Diplomacy. The author wishes to acknowledge the assistance of Professor William S. Barnes of the Fletcher School, and to thank Dr. José A. Silva Michelena and the staff of the *Centro de Estudios del Desarrollo* of the Central University of Venezuela for assistance in the use of data from their study "Conflict and Consensus in Venezuela."

This chapter will first consider the political student and then his role in national politics. It will identify the various participants in student politics and briefly characterize the student leader. The student's political roles under dictatorships and in periods of political transition will be considered as an introduction to an analysis of his place in today's political system. The chapter will conclude with a speculative look at the possibilities open to student politics in Venezuela's future.

The Political Student

Identifying the Political Student. Like so much convenient terminology, "student politics" is a loosely used expression that can easily convey erroneous ideas. Not all students participate in student politics; nor are all the participants in student politics university students. This discussion will therefore begin by identifying the components of the student political sector in Venezuela.

The most significant component is the university student. In 1963–64 there were 35,259 students enrolled at seven universities in Venezuela.[1] Of these, nearly 50 per cent were at the Central University (UCV) in Caracas. Approximately 35 per cent attended the other national universities: the University of the Andes (ULA) in Mérida, the University of Zulia (LUZ) in Maracaibo, the University of Carabobo (UC) in Valencia, and the University of the East (UDO) with faculties in several cities. The remaining 15 per cent of the students were enrolled in the two private universities in Caracas, Andrés Bello University (UCAB) and Santa María University (USM).

As might be expected from this distribution of students, the Central University is by far the most important center of student political activity. Factors other than mere numbers contribute to this importance. The UCV is the oldest and most prestigious of the Venezuelan universities; its prestige persists despite the fact that in some faculties its academic reputation is equaled and even surpassed by the University of the Andes, the University of Zulia, and Andrés Bello University. The age of the universities is particularly relevant to student politics since in 1928 and 1936, the two dates generally regarded as periods of exemplary student activity in Venezuela, only the UCV and the ULA were functioning and the latter was so small as to be of negligible significance.[2] Furthermore, the Central University was the only university located in Caracas, the power center of the nation, until the University Law of 1953 permitted the establishment of private universities.[3] Even today, however, the private universities do not compare with the UCV in importance, because of their relatively small enrollments and the fact that their organization deliberately hinders significant political activity on the part of the students.

Still another factor contributing to the dominance of the Central University students is the structure of student organization in Venezuela. No single organization represents all the university students in the country. Each university has a Federation of University Centers (*Federación de Centros Universitarios,* or FCU) but the various federations are not officially related. There was an unsuccessful attempt to establish a national confederation after the fall of President Pérez Jiménez in 1958; the same partisan political motives that caused its failure preclude any such organization today. With the student organizations thus atomized, the federations at the University of the Andes and the University of Zulia are the only ones that can begin to rival that of the UCV in any contest for attention.

In none of the universities do all students participate in political activities. With regard to such participation, three broad categories of students can be defined: the militants, the sympathizers, and the nonparticipants. The militants, constituting perhaps 10 per cent of the student body,[4] are active members of a political party. Some hold office in student organizations, some have official positions within their parties; all are employed in the organizational and propaganda efforts of the party on campus, sometimes to the partial or complete exclusion of their studies. The sympathizers, amounting to about 40 per cent of the student body, agree with and generally support the position of one of the parties active on campus, although they are not active members of the party. These are the students who attend the meetings, support the strikes, and always vote in the student elections. The remaining half of the students are nonparticipants, which is not to say that they are politically inert. They may indeed be uninterested in politics. More often, they oppose student political activity on principles or disagree with the positions of all the active parties; in particular, they may find themselves to the right of the active parties (an unpopular position to articulate).

The line between the sympathizer and the nonparticipant is often so thin that the two proportions change radically depending on the issue; there is also considerable variation among universities. In general, the Central University, the University of the Andes, and the University of Zulia are considered the most active politically. Such activity is less significant elsewhere, particularly in the private universities, Andrés Bello and Santa María, where less activity is permitted and a smaller range of political opinion is represented. Furthermore, some faculties are traditionally more active than others; at the Central University, for example, the law and economics faculties are considered to be the most active and medicine the least.[5] Thus those who do participate in student politics do not form a representative microcosm of the national student body.

The microcosm is further distorted by the fact that many participants in student politics are not university students. The most significant extra-university participants in Venezuela have been secondary school students. Three decades ago, in fact, there was no definitional or organizational difference between the student movements on the university and secondary school levels. Today, the two levels are separated primarily by the national political parties, almost all of which have coexisting university and secondary school sections in the youth faction of the party. Some connection outside the parties is provided by the fact that many university students teach part-time in the secondary schools and can acquire personal followings among the younger students, but in general cooperative action is taken only at the direction, or within the framework, of the party.

The political activities of secondary school students are generally of limited significance. In terms of national politics, their influence is greatest on issues concerning secondary school education, but only rarely do such issues become nationally important. On issues involving education in general or noneducational politics, it is the voice of the university student that is more clearly heard and carefully attended. Furthermore, the secondary student is organizationally even more fragmented than his university counterpart. Attempts to establish a truly national secondary student organization have foundered on the problem of partisanship—domination by one party leading to the withdrawal of others. Such organization is made even more difficult by the great difference in the amount of political activity permitted in the public *liceos* and the private *colegios*, the latter including nearly 30 per cent of the secondary student population.

This is not to say that secondary student politics is not intensive or even occasionally significant. In the *liceos*—though not in the much more restrictive *colegios*—it is not uncommon to hear of demonstrations, strikes, and even armed violence,[6] and their annual elections call forth nearly as much sound and fury as those of the universities. The secondary school is a recruitment center not only for sympathizers but for future leaders, and "not a few *liceo* students come out transformed into magnificent youth leaders and very bad students."[7] Participation by secondary school students can add emphasis to a general student action, particularly by bringing the issue to areas outside the eight cities containing university centers. Finally, the secondary school organizations can be an alternate means of expressing student political opinion when the universities are unable to do so because of unusually thorough government control or closure.

Although the most important and the most consistent nonuniversity participants in Venezuelan student political activities have been the secondary students, other elements have at times been visible. This is especially true of the years from 1928 to 1937, when the students were the only organized political force outside the government and their actions attracted a wide variety of adherents. In 1928, the first arrests of students after the "Week of the Student" in February brought into the streets groups of students, workers, women, young middle class employees, and other varieties of protestor. The military rebellion of April 7, 1928, was a cooperative effort of university students, young officers, members of the military college, and a few of the "bank clerk" class.[8] With the death of the dictator Juan Vicente Gómez in 1936, student activities regularly included workers, as well as anyone who wanted to express a political opinion other than that of the government. By 1937, however, there were labor organizations, women's associations, and above all political parties; since then, despite student efforts to involve other groups, especially the urban proletariat, the mass of participants in student political activity has been composed almost exclusively of students.

The extra-university actors in student politics thus far mentioned have all been followers; with the occasional exception of the secondary students, they have done no more than follow the university students' lead, adding numbers and perhaps broadening the political impact of a given action. There have, in addition, been instances when the actual leadership, or at least a contribution to the leadership, of the university student movement has come from outside elements. The two such influences worthy of note are the university professors and the professional politicians.

The university professor is naturally in a position to exert much influence on students. The extent to which Venezuelan professors have fostered particular political sympathies and even action on specific issues, though impossible to measure, must be great. To some extent the influence is circular, since the student voice can be important in the selection or retention of professors. A political leader may become a professor as frequently as a professor becomes a political leader. Nonetheless, not a single professor has achieved prominence as a leader of the Venezuelan student movement.[9]

The influence of the professional politicians is also difficult to measure, although for somewhat different reasons. Nearly all of the major student leaders, whether full-time, part-time, or only nominal students, are in fact professional politicians. This has been true since the founding of political parties in Venezuela. The professional status of these individuals does not, in general, mean that they are less respected or regarded as less legitimate student leaders. The extensive involvement of the student movement with partisan politics in Venezuela makes it exceedingly difficult to draw a boundary line between indigenous and outside elements in the movement, or between "trained Communist agitators" and ordinary student leaders. Most students would not object strongly even to the presence on campus of a politician with no pretensions to student status, for the simple reason that student leaders are expected to be in contact with the machinery and authorities of the party they represent.

The variety of other persons who may participate in student political activity, either in the leadership or in the rank and file, does not in the end alter the fact that it is the university students who are the key to an understanding of that activity. The focus of this chapter, therefore, will be on the university students; when "student politics" is meant to include other elements, they will be specified.

Characterizing the Political Student. At the center of student political activity is the student leader. In identifying some of the important characteristics of the political student, we shall be concerned principally with this figure. The student leader will be defined as anyone holding a major elective position in a Venezuelan university. There are four such positions: member of the faculty center (the organization representing the students in a given faculty—elected by the students of that faculty); member of the federation of centers (the university-wide student organization—elected at large in the university); member of the faculty council (the administrative organ of the faculty—student representatives elected by the students of that faculty); and member of the university council (the university-wide administrative body—student representatives elected at large).

This definition was used in a study—"Conflict and Consensus in Venezuela" (ConVen)—carried out jointly by the Center for Development Studies at the Central University and the Massachusetts Institute of Technology.[10] Extensive interviews were held with respondents in thirty-four sample groups in six major categories: government, economy, rural sector, cultural sector, special groups (including student leaders), and Guayana (an eastern region of Venezuela). A universe of 387 student leaders[11] was identified, of which 197 (or 51 per cent) were interviewed. The percentage interviewed was approximately equal in all universities but Andrés Bello, where it was slightly higher.

In general, this sample can be regarded as being qualitatively as well as quantitatively representative of the student leadership. The one bias that may have occurred concerns leaders affiliated with parties that have little student support. Since the offices in question are normally divided among the two or three parties receiving the bulk of the vote, leaders of the smaller parties might not be represented. The sample might not include, for instance, any members of the *Acción Democrática* (government party) at the Central University.

To what extent is the student leader a reflection of the student body as a whole? A number of comments on "professional students,"[12] have implied that student leaders are a subculture unto themselves, "representative" of their fellows only in the political sense of the word. It is, fortunately, possible to contrast on four basic variables—age, sex, marital status, and father's occupation—the ConVen student leadership sample and the student body of the Central University (UCV). The comparison is obviously incomplete, but since only the Central University has published this type of information, it is all that is feasible.

The statistics show, in general, a high correlation between the characteristics of the student leader sample (SLS) and those of the UCV student body. The age distribution of the two groups is given in Table 1.[13] The most significant divergence between the two distributions shows a bunching of student leaders in ages twenty-two and twenty-three. This reflects two facts. First, a student is not normally a candidate for a university post until he has had a year, and more likely two or three, of party militancy within the university. Second, after one or two years in an elected position the student normally either graduates and leaves the university or curtails his militancy to concentrate on completing his course work.

The proximity of the percentages beyond age twenty-five sheds

TABLE 1

AGE DISTRIBUTIONS OF CENTRAL UNIVERSITY STUDENT BODY (UCV) AND OF
CONVEN STUDENT LEADERSHIP SAMPLE (SLS)

(In Per Cent)

	UCV	SLS
Under 19	12	1
19	10.5	4
20	12.5	7.5
21	13	15
22	11	21
23	10	19
24	7	10.5
25	5	7.5
26	3	4.5
27	3	2
28	2	2.5
29–32	5	4
Over 32	6	1.5
Total	100 (N=17,507)	100 (N=197)

some light on the issue of the professional student. A few student
leaders do prolong their stay at the Central University in order to
carry on political activity; their advancing age is not a liability on
a campus where 11 per cent of the student body is age twenty-nine
or over. In the spring of 1966, for example, the outgoing president
of the Federation of University Centers (FCU) of the Central University was twenty-nine years old, having been a student in four
different faculties for a decade; his successor was twenty-eight years
old and had also been a university student for ten years (counting
two years at the University of Mexico), in two faculties.[14] The
prominence of such individuals, however, should not obscure the
fact that the student leaders' over-all age distribution is far from
unrepresentative of that of the student body.

The relatively low rate of active participation in organized politics by Venezuelan women is reflected in the sex distribution statistics. While 33 per cent of the Central University student body was female—and there is no reason to suspect much difference in the case of the other universities—women comprised only 7 per cent of the student leader sample.

The data on marriage are interesting in view of the common hypothesis that political activity is limited by the student's other time-consuming commitments. Sports and rigorous academic requirements are often cited in this regard, and marriage would seem to be as time-consuming as either of these. Yet there is virtually no difference in the distribution on marital status in the two groups, 89 per cent of the student leaders and 87 per cent of the student body being single.

The student leader sample and the UCV students are also similar when their fathers' occupations are compared. The one significant divergence, shown in Table 2, is in the category of children of public employees, which covers 21 per cent of the student body but only 3 per cent of the student leaders. Part of the explanation for this contrast lies in the probability that the proportion of children of public servants is much higher in the Central University than on the other campuses. Furthermore, children of government employees probably either support the government party or remain quiet to avoid embarrassing their fathers; the possibility of a sampling bias against the small parties (which the government parties are on most campuses) has already been mentioned, and politically inactive students are, of course, not represented.

It should be noted that there is no obvious difference in class origin between the two groups. Proportionally more student leaders than students classify their fathers as workers, but the difference is small. Table 2 does not support the idea that lower-class backgrounds lead to increased political action.[15]

Given the limitations of the data, it would be rash to conclude that there are no important differences between the student leaders and Venezuelan students as a whole. However, the marked similarities shown do cast doubt on the idea that student leaders are an atypical phenomenon.

The Political Student and His Image. Since the impact of student activity depends greatly on what people think of students, it is important to know what perception of the student obtains in Venezuela and how it relates to present reality. The Uruguayan writer José Enrique Rodó drew a picture of the ideal student that is still relevant today, not only in Venezuela but throughout Latin America:

Ariel [the Latin American student] is reason and higher feeling. Ariel is the sublime idea of perfectibility. . . . Ariel is to Nature the supreme crowning of her work. Ariel triumphant means ideals and order in life, noble inspiration in thought, disinterest in morality, good taste in art, heroism in action, delicacy in manners.[16]

In Venezuela, this golden image of the student is based on four main assumptions: (1) that the student is pure, idealistic, and free of the corrupting interests and influences of adult life; (2) that the student will and should take an active interest in the nation's political and social life; (3) that the student has a direct contact with and understanding of both the national values and the *pueblo* ("the people" in a general sense) ; and (4) that the student will and should be radical and perhaps even revolutionary.

The concept of the student as a purer being than others who may participate in politics is based more on a generational than a functional separation: youth is distinguished from age, rather than those who study from those who do not. This derives from the fact that youth is a period, as S. N. Eisenstadt puts it, of "role moratorium, . . . a period in which one may play with various roles without definitely choosing any. It does not yet require the various compromises inherent in daily participation in adult life."[17] In

TABLE 2

FATHER'S OCCUPATION: UCV STUDENT BODY AND STUDENT LEADERSHIP
SAMPLE (SLS) COMPARED[a]
(*In Per Cent*)

	UCV	SLS
Independent farmer	7	6
Professional or independent technical worker	19	22
Independent businessman or industrial employer	30	36
Rural worker	1	3
Urban worker	10	14
Public employee	21	3
Private employee	12	16

[a] Subtracted before calculation of the percentages shown were all cases where the respondent did not answer or where his answer did not fit any of the occupational categories used. Such cases totaled nearly 30 per cent of the UCV sample and 15 per cent of the student leader sample (SLS).

Venezuela, this "unattached" condition is said to allow youth to act without regard for material concerns or the interests of any group representing an entity smaller than the nation. In the case of the students, it is further assumed that the uncompromised purity of their position in life will render their actions in politics selfless and idealistic.

In the history of the Venezuelan student movement, the one period that seems to justify the "pure and idealistic" facet of the student image is the year 1928. The students went into the streets in a spontaneous protest against the dictator, with no plan, organization, or special interests in mind. The fact that the students were unsure of what ideals they were defending—were not even sure what they meant by their key word, "liberty"[18]—by no means detracts from the idealism of their gesture. Never since 1928, however, have the students acted with such complete lack of outside interests or such thorough commitment to a single ideal. In 1936, political parties were established and the student movement split on ideological grounds into two organizations. A strong commitment to party interests and bitter hostility between opposing student organizations have marked Venezuelan student politics ever since.

Today, it is taken for granted that the student leader will represent the interests of a political party. The number of independents in the leadership ranks is small and almost none achieve positions of university-wide importance. (The exception is Andrés Bello University, where a well-organized nonparty group regularly wins elections.) The party tie is reflected in a ConVen question that asks whether the informant has participated in any of three partisan activities (political meetings, active work for a party or candidate, strikes). Of the thirty-four samples included in the study, the affirmative response of the student leader sample was among the highest for all three activities.[19]

The involvement in party politics obviously encourages the representation of a specific interest and may lead to corruption as well.[20] It has not, however, eliminated the tendency of the students to act in response to ideals, provided the definition of "ideals" includes "ideology." To some extent, action in response to an ideological program is inherent in partisan activity, especially in Venezuela, where ideology is more important in the formation of party policy than in the United States, but the students sometimes carry the ideological response further than do other elements in the party.

A recent example was the case of Abdón Vivas Terán, Christian Socialist Party (COPEI) candidate for the Presidency of the FCU at the Central University, who was dramatically removed from his post as head of the youth wing of the party just before the university elections. It was widely assumed that the conflict was based on competing ideologies, that Vivas and his supporters occupied a position to the left of the party hierarchy. In fact, the difference lay more in style than in content; one reason given for Vivas' dismissal was that he had argued at an international conference that one of the causes of economic underdevelopment was "foreign capitalism," while the official COPEI thesis was that "national and foreign capital have some part" in underdevelopment.[21] The two statements represent not differing ideological beliefs but differing degrees of respect for the political necessities of a large party.

Vivas' statement is the more uncompromising, and "compromise" is the operational word. *Acción Democrática,* which as the dominant party in Venezuela since 1958 has had to make many compromises, has very little support in the universities; its student representatives are somewhat contemptuously regarded as unprincipled. Idealism remains not only a characteristic of student action but a requirement of the students themselves.

The second facet of the student image—that he must take an active interest in the political and social life of the nation—is a part of the general perception of the intellectual's role in society. The university-trained elite is expected to be capable of leadership in both politics and culture. A political leader without a book to his name, be it poetry or economic analysis, is a rare creature in Venezuela. This dependence on the university man naturally includes the student. As Kalman Silvert has noted, "The word *universitario* denotes anyone connected with the university, whether student, teaching assistant, professor, or graduate."[22]

Even within the general reliance on the *universitario,* the student is singled out for special emphasis. "That the students worry about problems of the State and of the world is not only inevitable but indispensable,"[23] for otherwise, as adult leaders, they will lack a sense of "historical responsibility." The norm applies even at the secondary level: "Be it in the *liceo* or in the university, our South American students must necessarily feel political and social unrest."[24] This theme is so prevalent in Venezuelan writing that even those most opposed to university political activity admit the need for students to understand and respond to political and social factors.

The student leaders are intensely interested in politics. Proportionately more than any of the thirty-three other ConVen samples, they reported being "very interested" in political matters. Theirs was the highest affirmative response (98 per cent) when asked whether they discussed politics with friends. They were also among the best informed politically, as measured both by their use of communications media and by their knowledge of specific events. On these criteria, they easily meet the requirements of the student image.

Much more difficult to pin down is the direct and almost mystical contact that students are supposed to have with the *pueblo*. That the period of university study, culminating a long effort to inculcate societal values and norms, may be regarded as "the only [time] in which full identification with the ultimate values and symbols of the society is attained" is not surprising.[25] Less easy to understand, but equally prevalent, is the further assumption that the possession of these values renders the student uniquely qualified to comprehend and interpret the *pueblo,* a term used to mean something similar to Rousseau's "general will," but also connoting the masses, lower classes, or proletariat.

Again, the best examples of the students' living up to their image come from the early years, especially 1928 and 1936. Student political actions on those occasions elicited such broad—and disorganized—popular support that no name save the *pueblo* would fit. Since those years, the student movement has, in general, tried hard to identify with the *pueblo* (usually as represented by the labor movement) and has assiduously promoted this part of its image. But there are many difficulties inherent in such a role.

One obvious problem in any linkage between students and *pueblo* is the fact that the students are overwhelmingly of middle-class origin. The very image of the student is based on eminently middle-class values.[26] A most vivid expression of the resulting difficulty can be found in a novel by Uslar Pietri, set in the heady atmosphere of 1936. The student protagonist, marching in a large, motley street demonstration, exulting in his new-found love for the *pueblo,* makes a remark to which a worker responds:

> "That's very good, *bachiller.* That's true now."
> That title [designating a graduate of a *liceo*] marked a distance, and Alvaro regretted it—the distance that separated the manual worker from the son of the well-to-do family studying in the university.
> "Here there is no *bachiller.* Call me *compañero.* We are fighting companions."
> "That's the way it is, *bachiller.*"[27]

Because the *pueblo* cannot be a clearly defined group, communion with it is hard to organize. When the ULA student federation attempts to illustrate its contact with the *pueblo* by citing petitions for the release of political prisoners, protests against the high cost of living, and participation in a transport union strike,[28] one is left with the feeling of a point unproven. Nonetheless, the student leaders seem to feel that they have close ties with, and represent the interests of, the *pueblo*. Asked about their communication with other groups, 94 per cent of the ConVen sample claimed they had some contact with workers at least once a month and 64 per cent claimed the same frequency for contact with peasants. But an average of 63 per cent in the lower-class urban and 86 per cent in the rural samples responded that they had never, or only "a few times in my life," had any contact with student leaders. In other words, although most student leaders are in frequent touch with the lower classes, this contact is with only a small portion of the members of those classes, most of whom practically never see a student leader.[29] It is hard to conclude that the student today has the direct contact with the *pueblo* prescribed by his image.

The final component of the student image is the idea that his approach to life, and especially to politics, must be radical or revolutionary. What is remarkable is not that radicalism should be expected—it is probably the most universally noted characteristic of student political behavior around the world—but that it should be considered desirable even by members of the ruling elite, that leading intellectuals can say, "Unhappy is the people or nation whose students are not excited by revolutionary sentiments,"[30] and "The excesses of the fight do not discredit the fight itself."[31]

In radicalism, unlike other aspects of the image, Venezuelan students have done more to justify their reputation in recent than in earlier years. In 1928, the students had heard of the Russian Revolution but knew almost nothing of its content. What few programmatic notions they had were derived from nineteenth century liberalism; the most contemporary influence on their thinking was Woodrow Wilson. Even in 1936, although they were labeled as Communists by the government,[32] the students were engaged in little more than a flirtation with Communism, later to be ridiculed by their more ideologically sophisticated successors.[33] The street protests and stone-throwing, regarded as radical in the earlier epoch, have been surpassed by more "revolutionary" methods of action. A claim to the title of "revolutionary" is now a prerequisite to respectability in the student movement. The ConVen data indicate that this is not mere semantics: asked to name solutions to Venezuela's most pressing problems (as identified by the respondent), 23 per cent of the student sample responses fell in the "revolutionary" category, while in no other sample did they exceed 8 per cent; responses on other items revealed the same tendency.[34]

There is reason to suspect that the student's radicalism is limited to those areas of life that could be described as political, and that on other subjects he holds the traditional values of his class. The response patterns of the student sample on such questions as divorce, birth control, the qualities necessary to success in work, and sanctions of antisocial behavior did not differ significantly from the over-all pattern of responses. This limitation of radicalism to the field of politics, combined with the generally held assumption that political radicalism fades after the student leaves the university, may explain why the incumbent elites can afford to tolerate and even encourage this characteristic of student behavior.

It has been seen that the characteristics of the student image diverge from reality on a number of points. To what extent are such deviations perceived and how do they alter, if at all, the popular image of the student? Measurement of belief in the image, difficult in any case, is made even more so by the fact that the principal propagators of the image are the intellectuals (who are often former student politicians) and the students themselves. Since these two groups produce virtually all of the literature on the subject, it is almost impossible to find an unbiased view of the situation.

Such evidence as is available, however, suggests a confrontation between fact and image. Events of the last few years, especially student involvement in terrorist activities, appear to have lowered the general positive appreciation of student politics. The ConVen data, representing only a single point in time, are of little value in identifying any trend. The one significant indicator, a question asking for an evaluation of the contribution of various groups to the nation, shows the students' prestige in a lower position than one would expect if the best of the image were universally believed but still higher than one would expect, for instance, in the United States.[35] Significantly, the most common criticism of student politics, as heard in conversation and reflected in newspaper editorials, is that of excessive partisan activity, and the most frequent recommendation is for continued student political concern and activity divested of compromising party allegiances.[36] In other words, the image is still held, at least one deviation from it is perceived, and the reaction is to demand that the students shape themselves back into the image.

The Political Student and National Politics

Venezuela today has a constitutional, democratic, party system of government, but this has been true for a relatively short period of time. An understanding of the place of students in present-day national politics requires consideration first of the roles students have played under dictatorial regimes and during the transition to democracy.

The Political Student Under Dictatorships. Recent Venezuelan history offers examples of both primitive and relatively modern versions of military dictatorship. The first was that of Juan Vicente Gómez, a military leader of peasant origins who ruled the country from 1908 until his death in late December 1935.[37] Gómez' government was small and tightly centralized; its high offices were filled largely by his relatives, and its power base was the army with which he had acquired the presidency. Political parties were only names remembered from the previous century, and labor organizations were virtually nonexistent.[38] Opposition to the government was sporadic, undertaken largely on behalf of other military *caudillos* (strongmen) and always quickly suppressed.

The one outstanding instance of opposition to Gómez occurred in 1928. In February of that year, members of the recently organized Federation of Venezuelan Students (*Federación de Estudiantes Venezolanos,* or FEV) planned a series of social, cultural, and fund-raising events to occur during a "Week of the Student." The opening speech was a thinly veiled cry against the dictator; it set the tone for the week. Several students were arrested, another large group delivered themselves into voluntary arrest as a gesture of solidarity, and there followed an unprecedented series of public protests and demonstrations. Most of the students were released shortly thereafter, and on April 7 they and a group of young officers tried to overthrow Gómez in a military rebellion. The attempted coup failed. Many students were imprisoned or put to work on road-building projects; others went into exile. Gómez tightened control over the UCV and, aside from a few exiles who took part in an abortive invasion attempt, the students remained quiet until after the dictator's death.

In this period, the students played three roles. They voiced a political viewpoint opposed to the government, they acted directly in an attempt to overthrow that government, and they served as a focal point for other opposition groups. None of these roles is extraordinary, and the first two were not even new to the Venezuelan scene. Students had previously spoken out against Gómez and had even participated in direct action against him, without receiving more than passing attention.[39] There was nothing new in the program of the students in February—if in fact it could be called a program rather than simply a vague cry for liberty—and nothing new about the April rebellion except that it came closer to success than had some earlier coup attempts.

What was new was the fact that students served as a catalyst for urban opposition to the government. They were incorporating into the political process "sectors of the population that were there on the national scene, innocent of all political work but charged with potential."[40] At the same time, they began a transfer of the center of resistance from the countryside to the city, from the *caudillo* to the masses. Venezuelan commentators tend to emphasize the new participation of the masses, but it is important to note that this transfer of power benefited the students' own class, the urban elite. The government would now have to pay less attention to rural *caudillos* and more to organized urban interest groups, and it would be above all members of the upper middle class—in many cases, those very students of 1928—who would first organize and lead the lower classes.

The modernization of the political process signaled by the events of 1928 had wrought important changes on Venezuela by the time of the dictatorship of Marcos Pérez Jiménez (1948–58).[41] Pérez Jiménez has sometimes been described as another Gómez, and many aspects of his regime were similar. Power was again centralized around the military, several political parties were outlawed, and labor organizations were controlled. But the Venezuelan government had grown much larger and more complex in the interim. In a sense, the previous political institutions did not disappear; they simply went underground. Popular expectations of what a government should be and do were so strong that Pérez Jiménez felt constrained to justify his rule with elections and public works. The days of unadorned centralism under Gómez were over.

One political group the Pérez Jiménez government tried to suppress was the students. Their reaction was as hostile as it had been to Gómez. Throughout the life of the regime they engaged in minor harassing actions and antigovernment propaganda. There was one major strike, "the glorious strike of 1951 and 1952,"[42] but it did little more than inspire the regime to close the Central University for a year and reopen it under much tighter control. The next major incident occurred late in 1957, when a student strike marked the beginning of a general uprising that culminated in the fall of Pérez Jiménez in January 1958.[43]

The functions of student political activity in the Pérez Jiménez period were essentially the same as those of the Gómez period. In their propaganda and harassment activities, they presented the opposition point of view and kept a certain amount of attention focused on it. In 1957, they helped plan and participated in direct action against the government, and in this period, especially during the turbulent weeks of January, they again served as a catalyst for the opposition.

However, the political development that distinguished the Pérez Jiménez period from the Gómez era caused a basic change in the students' role. Although they were performing the same functions as before, they now generally did so not as free agents but as the representatives of political parties. The clandestine documents they distributed were printed almost entirely at the direction of the parties. The strike of 1951 was first planned not by the central student organization but by a strike committee composed of five students who were direct emissaries of their party leaders.[44] The students' strike of 1957 and their participation in subsequent activities were part of a plan developed by the *Junta Patriótica,* an underground resistance group of which the students were a minor, and party representatives the major, component.

This suggests that the primary role of the students in the Pérez Jiménez period was to help keep alive the most important political structures functioning before the dictatorship, namely, the parties. When the known party leaders were exiled, unknown students were there to take their places. When the normal expression of party opinion was blocked, the students provided alternative outlets. Significantly, the student strike of 1951, which failed to gain large popular support, took place while some parties were still legally functioning and before their chances of gaining representation in the government had been eliminated by the electoral fraud of 1952. In such a context, the strike failed to attract broad popular support. But in 1957 the government proposed a plebiscite to replace the constitutionally prescribed elections, thereby underscoring how far the emasculation of normal political processes had progressed; support for that year's student strike approached unanimity.

The Political Student in Times of Transition. At the end of the two periods of dictatorship, in 1936 and again in 1958, Venezuela faced the task of establishing a democratic system in a situation where, in the one case, democratic political institutions had never existed and, in the second, they had suffered a decade of energetic repression. At both times, the students played a critical role in the transition.

The beginning of 1936[45] saw General Eleazar López Contreras, the successor to Gómez, surrounded in government by numerous infighting court factions, and in the country by a nervously milling populace anxious for a taste of freedom but ignorant of how to get it or of exactly what it was. The Student Federation (FEV), outlawed after 1928 but reorganized clandestinely in 1934–35, sprang back into life and took the lead in building up pressure against the government. The FEV's biggest moment came on February 14, 1936, when it led a massive demonstration against a new suspension of constitutional guarantees. The demonstration turned into a riot, and the homes of some of the old Gómez officials still in power were looted. As a result, several of these officials were immediately dismissed; a week later, López Contreras announced a conciliatory "February Program."[46] For several months, the FEV was the principal nongovernmental political force in the nation.[47]

Events following the fall of Pérez Jiménez[48] recreated many of the uncertain and fluid aspects of the situation in 1936, and again the students' political power was magnified. In the chaotic days of Pérez Jiménez' ouster, student-led demonstrations forced the exclusion of two military men from the new governing junta. The student organizations maintained close contact with the new government in 1958, and on two occasions when the possibility of a rightist coup appeared, the students mobilized and armed themselves to fight against any such occurrence.[49]

The amount of political power achieved by the students on these two occasions surpasses by far that of any other period of the student movement. A large part of the explanation lies in the chaotic political situation, in which the majority of the possible sources of influence were "in such disarray as to elevate the relative power of any organized group."[50] This holds particularly for the 1936 period, when for a few months the FEV was virtually the only organized political association and as such attracted the support and active participation of most nonstudent elements of similar viewpoint. The causes of the "disarray" of other power centers, especially the repressive tactics of the dictatorship, have less effect on students. The latter form a relatively small, homogeneous group with excellent internal communications and good organizing abilities,[51] and their youth, even under dictatorships, generally warrants them a degree of immunity unavailable to others.[52] In fact, the dictator, by providing a concrete goal upon which all students can agree (his removal), has in Venezuela inspired a degree of unity in the student movement not seen in freer times. So the students tend to be organizationally at their best when all other groups are at their worst.

The fall of a dictator marks the point of highest prestige for the student, the time when his image is most completely accepted. He is uncorrupted, having made no compromises with the former government. Actions that might be regarded as excessive at other times are forgiven and even overcredited: "Although dissident army officers actually sparked the revolt that overthrew the dictator in January 1958, and although his departure . . . was brought about by a general strike and an uprising on the part of the entire population of the nation, the public looked upon the students as having been the earliest and the hardest workers toward the desired goal."[53] The student is portrayed and portrays himself as the nation's fiercest lover of democracy, an aspect of the image that is much more difficult to attain when he is disagreeing with a freely elected government.[54] And if the government he would really like to see established is considerably to the left of the one actually forming, this is not a problem in the first months, during which he tends to concentrate on the prevention of backsliding rather than the accomplishment of any specific program.

The students' antidictatorial power in moments of transition is not, however, their only contribution to the establishment of a democratic system in Venezuela. Very important has been their influence in the development of a national political infrastructure. The two largest political parties in Venezuela today are descendants of student organizations. The exiled students of 1928 returned in 1936 to become the leaders of the Venezuelan Organization (ORVE). ORVE was outlawed in 1937; its successor was the clandestine National Democratic Party (PDN), which consisted primarily of the ORVE leaders and "an enthusiastic group of workers and students."[55] The PDN was legalized in 1941 under the name *Acción Democrática* and is today Venezuela's governing party. Another group of student leaders split from the FEV in May 1936 to form the National Student Union (UNE). Of Roman Catholic orientation, the UNE eventually led to the formation of the Christian Socialist Party (COPEI).[56]

The students were also active in the founding of labor organizations, and the FEV in 1936 and 1937 organized and operated a number of "popular universities" to provide workers with basic primary-level education and instruction in political action.[57] The students have thus been important contributors of personnel, ideas, and institutions to the present political system of Venezuela.

Student Political Roles in a Party System. Since 1958—specifically, since the elections in December of that year—Venezuela has enjoyed a representative democracy based on political parties. As the parties have become the primary paths of political action, the character of student politics has changed accordingly. The parties now express political points of view that only the students voiced under the dictatorships, and the parties' full-time organizations nullify the students' former advantages in this regard.

The Role of Future Leader. The parties see the universities above all as centers for the recruitment of future party leaders. The ascent from student politics to the top rung of party politics has been well traveled: virtually all of the highest party officials in Venezuela today were once student leaders. Many student leaders have held important appointive and even elective party positions while still enrolled in the university.

The party sections on campus lead very smoothly into the national organizations. *Acción Democrática* (AD) is a typical example.[58] At the bottom rung within the university are the militants, the rank-and-file party activists. These are generally younger students with little or no experience in the party, although some have participated in secondary school activities. Their numbers fluctuate, rising in national election years and around university election times. The first official position a militant can achieve is that of class representative (*responsable del curso*). Several such representatives will be assigned to each class (e.g., first-year law students, third-year students in the Faculty of Sciences), the number depending on the size of the class. At the next level is the three-man committee in each faculty—generally third- or fourth-year students who have had two or more years in the party. The top rung within the university is the University Bureau, consisting of five members and normally including any party members who hold high elective posts on campus.

Above the University Bureau comes the regional section of the AD youth wing, concerned with university and secondary school activities in the area; at the top of the ladder within the youth wing is the Youth Committee. The Youth Secretary is a member of the National Executive Committee, the highest continuously functioning organ of the party.

A party militant within the university may be paid by the party, although this is rare even for a member of the University Bureau. More often, if he needs money, the party will find him a part-time job or see that he gets a scholarship so that he can devote more time to party work. A member of the party organization graduating from the university may stay in the youth wing of the party until he reaches age thirty, although he often leaves earlier; he can then move into one of the other sections of the party (e.g., syndical wing, international affairs bureau). He may, of course, decide not to continue his party work; this decision is particularly common among those who have reached only the lower and middle ranks during their university careers. But if he continues—and a majority of the top student leaders do—then the party has a man with at least four or five years of active experience and often (though not so often in AD as in the parties with greater campus support) a ready-made personal following.

The Role of Voter. In addition to recruiting leaders, the parties are naturally concerned with the basic political problem of gathering votes. In a country with an electorate of about 3 million, the 50,000 votes contributed by the universities are not to be disdained. It is uncertain, however, to what extent university students' political allegiances are subject to change, for many already have firm preferences when they enter the university. A study conducted at the Central University suggests that (1) younger students tend to prefer the parties at the ends of the political spectrum, (2) preferences tend to move left with time spent in the university, and (3) older students tend to have less interest in politics of any kind, but (4) none of these tendencies shows any relation to party efforts at proselytizing.[59] Nonetheless, all the parties seem to feel the need to keep active members on campus, if only to present the party's position to the students.

More important to the parties are the votes cast in the annual university elections. The elections in the Central University are front-page news in newspapers throughout the country, and even the returns from Mérida and Maracaibo receive considerable coverage in the Caracas-based national dailies. There is thus much value in prestige and propaganda to be gained by the parties that make an impressive showing. Furthermore, national elections in Venezuela are held only once every five years; the university elections provide one of the few interim tests of electoral strength, and the returns are anxiously awaited as indications of party growth or decline.[60]

The general election returns from the Central University in the years 1961–66 are shown in Table 3. As the figures indicate, COPEI has been the strongest single party in the University for the past several years, although it has been beaten by the Marxist parties, which despite some conflicts have consistently managed to mount an electoral coalition. That COPEI's strength is inflated by an independent anti-leftist vote that simply does not like *Acción Democrática* is suggested by COPEI's loss of votes in 1964 to the FND,[61] a party founded in that year around the person of Arturo Uslar Pietri. Significant is the shift within the leftist bloc in favor of the Communist Party, which has lately followed a "soft line" while the MIR has given "hard-line" support to the guerrilla movement of the Armed Forces of National Liberation (FALN).[62]

The extent to which the tempo of national politics influences political activity on campus is reflected in the numbers of votes cast in various years. The highest rate of voting came in 1962, when over 80 per cent of the total student enrollment cast valid ballots. That was the year in which the Communist Party and the MIR were outlawed—in fact, the initial decree was issued in May, very close to the time of student elections—and openly called for revolution. Many students saw themselves renewing the gallant opposition of the Pérez Jiménez period; others saw themselves resisting a violent, foreign (Castro-oriented) Communism; many were confused. But nearly all were excited by the discussion of the "big questions" and the feeling that they were at a critical point in history.

By the following year, this intellectual turbulence had waned. Even though 1963 was the year of the national elections the leftists had promised to prevent, most students had made their decisions and acted on them long enough before for the election to have lost some of its glamour. In the UCV elections of that year, slightly over 65 per cent of the students voted. By 1964, the big questions had been answered, for the time being at least, and the percentage of voters dropped to nearly 60 per cent. In the following years, as new issues arose, the turnout increased, but even when the number of voters reached their highest total, in 1966, the percentage of students voting was less than 70 per cent.

One important trend is only slightly visible because of the lack of figures for the years prior to 1961: the decline of AD from the major power in 1958—a result of party splits that created the MIR and the PRN—and its partial resurgence to a plateau of about 9 per cent. AD officials predict a further recovery as the secondary school students, among whom the party is very strong, move on to the University, but they also admit that university students tend not to support the government, and it is possible that AD will not gain significantly while it continues to hold power.[63]

Among the other universities, the major divergence from the UCV pattern is at Zulia. There COPEI is the dominant force, receiving about 43 per cent of the votes in 1966; AD has gained strength, running a close third to the leftist coalition, with 25 per cent in 1966. At the University of the Andes, the order is the same as at the Central University, although COPEI comes closer to beating the leftist coalition and AD has proportionally more support than at UCV. The other national universities, with fewer students voting, receive little attention despite generally close contests. The Andrés Bello elections interest only those who enjoy the irony of a Social-Christian party (COPEI) regularly being defeated by independents in a Catholic university.[64]

University elections have a special importance for the MIR and the Communist Party (PCV). Since these groups were outlawed in 1962, the university has been the only place where they can compete with the other political parties. Their consistently strong showings on the campus are not only a source of prestige but a means of demonstrating to the Venezuelan public that they are still a live and active force. Furthermore, their well-publicized participation in university elections tends to improve their image, since acts of violence are the only other actions of these parties that normally become public knowledge.

The Role of Spokesman. Students serve all of the political parties as an instrument for publicizing the party's viewpoint on any given problem. Their image is still so well accepted, particularly in contrast to that of the politician,[65] that a student's word on some occasions may be worth more to the party than a senator's. Not surprisingly, the student is conceded more attention on educational issues—especially questions involving the university—but his utility as a party spokesman is by no means limited to this area. In election years, touring campaign parties invariably include one or two student leaders, and any political rally numbers at least one student among its speakers.

In addition, students are useful in many of the lower-level organizational and propaganda activities in which a party is continually engaged. They distribute leaflets, affix posters (or, as is common in Venezuela, paint the party name or the name of the leader on walls), and carry word of political meetings to stimulate interest

TABLE 3

VOTING PATTERNS IN UCV ELECTIONS, 1961–66[a]

(In Per Cent)

	1961[b]	1962	1963	1964	1965[b]	1966[b]
Communist Party (PCV)[c]	24.0 (2,619)	50.6 (7,376)	52.7 (6,628)	51.8 (6,033)	22.7 (3,098)	30.0 (4,559)
Movement of the Revolutionary Left (MIR)[c]	24.9 (2,721)				28.7 (3,928)	23.8 (3,592)
Social Christian Party (COPEI)	38.2 (4,169)	42.3 (6,159)	38.2 (4,797)	31.5 (3,666)	36.9 (5,052)	36.9 (5,592)
Democratic Action (AD)	9.9 (1,078)	2.7 (391)	5.1 (641)	9.4 (1,094)	9.0 (1,169)	9.3 (1,412)
Others	3.0[d] (328)	4.4[e] (641)	4.0[e] (501)	7.3[f] (851)	2.7[f] (368)	— —
Total	(10,915)	(14,567)	(12,567)	(11,644)	(13,615)	(15,155)

ª Sources were newspaper accounts (*El Nacional, El Universal, La Esfera*), which were not always in agreement. In case of conflict, the more detailed account was used.

ᵇ There are two stages to the UCV elections. In the first, the students elect representatives to the larger, usually less political, administrative bodies. In the second, they elect the members of the faculty centers and the federation of centers (FCU). In 1961, 1965, and 1966, the first election was used to show the PCV-MIR proportions; in all other years, the FCU votes are shown. Probably because of the competition between the PCV and MIR in the first election, there is a tendency for the leftist vote to be slightly higher then than in the second. In 1966, the leftist coalition in the second election obtained 50.4, the COPEI party 39.1, and AD 10.5 per cent.

ᶜ The PCV and MIR ran in coalition in all elections in 1962, 1963, and 1964. In 1965 and 1966, they used the first election as a test of their relative strengths, the winner between the two naming the coalition candidate for President of the FCU.

ᵈ In 1961, this was the Republican Democratic Union (URD), which in later years ran in coalition with the PCV-MIR. In 1964, the left wing of the URD was expelled and became the Popular National Vanguard (VPN), which continued in the coalition. URD moderates did not run a separate slate in 1964–66 and probably voted with AD in those years.

ᵉ In 1962 and 1963, this was a group that broke from AD, calling themselves "AD-opposition" and later the Revolutionary National Party (PRN). In 1964, they did not name a slate of candidates. In 1965 and 1966, they ran in coalition with the MIR-PCV.

ᶠ In 1964 and 1965, this was principally the National Democratic Front (FND).

and attendance. Often they are active in helping to establish, and occasionally even to lead, ward- or precinct-level organizations; they may also conduct small classes for prospective members. Although this type of activity takes place principally in the cities, *Acción Democrática* and COPEI make special efforts to get the students to the countryside, where both parties find a disproportionately large amount of their support. In 1941–45, the major organizing years for AD, students were especially important in this regard.

The student role as party spokesman and "ward heeler" is much more important to the outlawed PCV and MIR than to the legal parties. Even the small legal parties, more often than not, have at least one personality of national prominence whose statements are given extensive coverage. But were the high officials and recognized personalities of the illegal parties to speak publicly, they would deliver themselves over for arrest. Only the university, with its traditional autonomy, offers immunity to those who speak for an outlawed party. The only other political group in which the Communist Party has enough strength to make itself heard is the labor movement, where Communists dominate the antigovernment workers' organization (CUTV). But labor leaders do not enjoy as much freedom as do the students, either in the sense of freedom from punishment or in the range of subjects on which they are considered competent to speak. And the MIR, now composed predominantly of students, has no voice in any nonstudent organization. Thus the students have become the one institutional outlet the illegal parties can use to publicize their views.

Another important service, provided only to the illegal parties, is the recruitment of participants in terrorist and guerrilla activities.[66] Here, students have been crucial, not only in adding numbers to the extralegal opposition but, by virtue of their image (especially the belief that students should be revolutionary), tinging the movement with a romantic and even respectable aura it could never attain were it composed only of "hardened" politicians.

Insofar as they are keeping alive a suppressed political viewpoint, the students' service to the illegal parties is much the same as their role under the Pérez Jiménez dictatorship. This situation is reflected in the students' frequent complaint that the revolution of 1958 was "betrayed" or, more specifically, that today's system is not the complete democracy for which they hoped in that year.

The Role of Critic. Another function sometimes attributed to students in the Venezuelan party system is that they constitute a point of entry into the parties for new ideas and philosophical directions. In the furor surrounding the removal by COPEI leaders of Abdón Vivas Terán from his post as head of the party's youth wing, for making statements deemed inconsistent with party policy, it was sometimes argued that he had been exercising this innovative function and therefore should not have been dismissed. Not uncommon in the press were statements such as the following: "The National Command of the Revolutionary Youth of COPEI will press the Central Committee of COPEI to adopt a more revolutionary position toward the government . . . in order that it may express completely the position of the Venezuelan people."[67]

The role of critic is of course quite consistent with the image of the political student, but there is reason to doubt that students have much real influence in the processes of program formation in the parties. In the first place, all the major parties, including COPEI, have elaborate and well-established ideological programs. Changes in these programs are made through a very formal procedure in which the relative influence of the youth wing is small. In the case of the parties actually responsible for governing, their primary concern must be with the necessities of day-to-day policy decisions; this concern is reflected in the fact that AD student leaders claim little or no programmatic influence for themselves.

Even the dispute within COPEI sheds less light than it might on the problem. The importance of the conflict was magnified because it occurred just before the UCV elections, in which Vivas ran for FCU President, and because it reflected in part a long-standing internal division between the older generation, whose political careers date from the 1936–45 era, and the younger, post-1945 generation of COPEI leaders. Furthermore, many of the specific points of difference turned out to be more stylistic than substantive. In any event, the relative ease with which the party replaced the dissidents suggests that the students' direct influence on general policy is small.

Student Political Influence. There is one factor, however, that could radically alter student influence not only on the parties but on the whole pattern of national political development. This is the delayed effect of participation in student politics, the effect that makes itself felt long after the individual has left the university. The classic assumption is that student politicians will "grow up," will accept the values of their society and behave no differently from persons who had no political experience as students. It seems most unlikely that this could be completely true, that the patterns of thinking and action engendered by an intensive experience lasting four or five years could simply disappear without a trace. On the contrary, it seems probable that student political activity has an important influence on the degree and on the style of future political activity.

The political student has, or develops, a greater interest in national politics than his fellow students. He also acquires a wealth of knowledge of the operation of the political process and a confidence in his own ability to act in that process. The ConVen data, although providing no comparison with the nonpolitical student, clearly illustrate the general idea. On three measures of political efficacy—how important the respondent thought the political opinions of people like himself, whether he could do anything about a national government plan or policy he disliked, and whether he could do anything about a local government plan or policy he disliked—the students ranked second, first, and first among the thirty-four samples. Significantly, trade union leaders were the only other group consistently scoring at this high level. In this light, it seems likely that the ex-student politicians would tend to use political institutions more—and more effectively—than persons without their special experience.

At the same time, however, student politicians develop a very special approach to the political process. One of the most important characteristics of student politics is irresponsibility, or non-accountability. The students are never given real decision-making power; they never have to put their pronouncements into practice and answer for the results. This condition may be reflected in the ConVen data: when reacting to political statements, the student leaders tended to cluster at the extreme ends of the response range, and especially in the "firmly disagree" category.[68] They led all samples in identifying national problems, but tended to offer fewer solutions.[69]

Unfortunately, the available data do not permit measurement of the extent to which the students' degree and style of political activity change in later years. If the degree of participation is greatly lowered, then the question of style may be purely academic. But if participation remains high and the students' estimate of their ability in the political process is accurate, then whether their political style changes or continues to have the characteristics of political irresponsibility may be a critical factor in national development. The difference between constructive and negative, or flexible and extreme, styles of action could mean the difference between the development of stable and effective political institutions and the collapse of an overly brittle political structure.

On a more immediate level, the students can to some degree influence national politics by acting as an independent political interest group. In general, there are two basic strategies open to them: they may try to apply pressure directly on the policy-makers or indirectly through some other group. Direct pressure is usually used on issues directly affecting the university, and more often than not is exercised informally, for instance, in private talks with officials of the university or the Ministry of Education.[70] The normal indirect approach is through the political parties, which must represent the students before the government in return for student support. A less common approach is to attempt to force some other group to react in such a way as to bring about the desired pressure; an example is the terrorist campaign in 1962–63, one of whose aims was to prevent the 1963 elections by provoking the military into a coup. In any of these approaches, the effectiveness of student action is limited by the condition of the student movement, the issue at stake, and the general political situation at the time.

To be effective as an independent pressure group, the students must be—or at least appear to be—united. In Venezuela, this has seldom happened, except under dictatorships. Juan Vicente Gómez had been dead less than six months when the student movement split into the FEV and the UNE; never again, not even under Pérez Jiménez, were the students completely united organizationally. There have nevertheless been occasions when all groups could agree on a single goal, such as repelling the rumored coups of 1958 or supporting university autonomy, and these have been the students' moments of greatest effectiveness. Also important is the state of the student image, which has tended to be most favorably and most widely accepted immediately after the unifying experience of a dictatorship.

Equally important is the particular issue involved, for it affects both student actions and their public reception. In general, the issues on which the students can act most effectively are those dealing with education, and especially with the university. These are the issues on which the students are most likely to agree and least likely to be divided by general party policies. At the same time, because they are the areas in which the individual most directly affected is the student himself, his word is accorded more weight than that of persons less directly concerned. Finally, these are the areas in which the students can most precisely apply pressure on the relevant decision-makers (for example, by preventing the university from functioning) with the least outside support.

In policy areas outside education, it is likely that the student's position will be governed by that of his party (e.g., in supporting a candidate for national office). Other interest groups (e.g., the chamber of commerce on questions of economic policy) will receive prior hearing. In some areas (e.g., foreign policy) there may be no means by which the student can apply direct and discriminating pressure on the decision-maker. Only in the field of educational policy do all three factors—unity, recognized interest, and the availability of effective means—operate in the student's favor.

Another condition of student effectiveness is the configuration of national politics. The political "disarray" of other sectors during periods of dictatorship has already been mentioned, but even in more settled times it can happen that organizations of political expression and influence decline, or do not exist for all sectors. The students may then move into the vacuum, as they did in 1936, when they took the place of political parties and labor unions. "Periods of uncertainty and excitement,"[71] marked by rumors of coups and revolutionary unrest, tend to increase the effectiveness of student action. Conversely, in periods of calm, when the political system is functioning adequately and all major interests are represented, the students' sphere of effective influence is extremely limited.

In addition to contributing to the political process, the university can itself become an issue in national politics. "University reform" covers many aspects of the university and its relations with society.[72] In Venezuela, the debate has almost always centered around the problem of university autonomy.

The issue of university reform or autonomy was not, as it was in some other countries,[73] the starting point of the modern Venezuelan student movement. But as soon as the students gained the freedom to organize and to influence the government, university reform became a rallying cry. Since 1936, there has been no student disagreement on the necessity of autonomy; first granted under the *Acción Democrática* regime in 1946, autonomy has been considered a basic principle of democratic government. As conceived by the law of 1946 and continued by a decree of the governing junta shortly after the fall of Pérez Jiménez, autonomy includes administrative independence from the national government (students having a voice in the administration) and financial independence by means of a guaranteed annual allotment of a specified percentage of the national budget.[74]

As the commitment to university autonomy has grown, however, so has the importance of the university to the government. As it has grown in size and complexity, the government has come increasingly to rely on the university for trained personnel. The commitment to national planning held by all major parties encourages an active interest in how many students will be graduated in which specialties at what time. Increasingly, too, the government has become dependent on the research skills and specialized expertise of the university staff. Yet while the government cannot control the administrative decisions relevant to its needs because of the rules of autonomy, these same rules give administrative influence to the student leaders. The government's appreciation of the latter is not enhanced by their marked tendency to prefer opposition, and especially illegal, parties.

In the future, the government would like to gain some influence on the development of the university and would like to see a general rise in academic standards. *Acción Democrática,* in particular, considers a reduction in the level of political activity a prerequisite of almost any sort of progress in higher education. This idea has inspired a quantity of literature that tends to justify a limitation of autonomy with the argument that some elements of the present system are anachronistic—antidictatorial devices when there are no more dictators—and lead to "excesses" instead of a harmonious resolution of national problems.[75]

The aims of the universities—as generally expressed by the student leaders—are to acquire sorely needed additional funds while maintaining the administrative and political status quo. The student leaders tend to interpret the government's statements as purely an attack on themselves because of their political position, and they enjoy citing the formerly fervent support of autonomy by current government figures as proof of duplicity.

Overt conflict on this general issue has been rare. In one open test in 1964–65, the students of the University of the Andes defeated a proposal for competitive entrance examinations to limit admission to the Faculty of Medicine. A more important case was the three-year fight conducted by Central University student leaders against the implementation of a "repeaters rule." Designed to prevent students from repeating a year more than once,[76] the rule could be a serious blow to student politicians. The government quietly but strongly supported the measure; representatives of the legal opposition parties tended to be neutral or mildly opposed; and the extremist parties, so heavily dependent on student politicians, were in vociferous and bitter opposition. Largely because a significant segment of the student body believed the rule a necessary step in the improvement of the University, it appears finally to have been successfully implemented.

The repeaters rule controversy may indicate the direction the final solution of the conflict over autonomy will take; if so, it also indicates that a complete solution—especially a completely acceptable solution—will be a long time in coming.

Conclusion: Venezuelan Prospects

Any attempt to predict the future direction of Venezuelan student politics must take into account two almost inevitable trends: more students and more government. The university population has been growing rapidly in the years since Pérez Jiménez and there is no reason to think this expansion will cease. Many of the additional students will go to the Central University, but it is likely that the increase at the provincial and private universities will be disproportionately higher. The counterbalancing effect of the creation of strong centers of student opinion in competition with UCV will be further enhanced by improving national communications. At a larger Central University, more political viewpoints will be represented organizationally as today's minor groups (such as the VPN and PRN, which presently are forced to act in coalition with larger parties) attain the minimum absolute size needed to make independent organization practical. Although these factors will not necessarily change the students' role in the political parties, they will tend to fragment student politics and make it harder to achieve the unity necessary for effective independent action.

Likewise the government, which under any party and probably even in a nondemocratic system will increase in size and complexity, will continue to grow more dependent on the products of the university system. Almost surely, it will find a way to exert increased influence, if not direct control, over some university operations. Students will be channeled away from the traditional disciplines and into the newer technical fields with their more stringent academic requirements, and the academic quality of the university as a whole will be upgraded. Although there may be no direct control of student politics, rising academic pressures will tend to diminish the intensity of such activities.

The most important determinant of the role of student politics, however, will be the political system, which might take one of three main shapes: a dictatorship, a socialist revolution, or a democracy.

A new dictatorship in Venezuela would probably have most of the characteristics of the Pérez Jiménez years, in particular the immediate or delayed suppression of all institutions that tend to act as vehicles for the expression of political viewpoints opposed to the government. Because of technical advances in police methods, the suppression of free student political activity would undoubtedly be at least as thorough as under Pérez Jiménez. The students would nonetheless continue clandestine efforts on behalf of the other suppressed institutions, and on occasion would take their opposition dramatically (if unsuccessfully) into the streets. Unless the dictator fell quietly because of inter-clique maneuvers, the students would be in the vanguard of the forces participating in his eventual overthrow. Again a large portion of the students would aim for a complete social revolution, and this time, with more sophisticated clandestine training and the lessons of the past to guide them, they might succeed.

In a socialist revolution—whether it originates in a coup d'état, an agrarian guerrilla movement, or an urban proletarian uprising—students would certainly be among both its most vigorous supporters and its most vigorous opponents. Since almost all students desire a social revolution, and since the line between a social and a socialist revolution is far from distinct, it seems likely that in the beginning those in favor would far outnumber those opposed. Judging from the examples available,[77] students would not be allowed an independent role within a socialist regime. They would serve the Party in much the same ways they now serve the parties. Such influence as they might have would probably be directed toward liberalizing some of the totalitarian aspects of the regime.

The possibility of a counterrevolution raises fascinating questions. It is an axiom of student politics that students are radical and leftist. What happens, then, when to be radical is not to be leftist? When the established order is socialist, would students support a revolution moving to the right because they are radical, or would they support the established order because they are leftist? From the present vantage point, the best guess seems to be that students would be among the most determined and energetic supporters of both sides.

The final possibility in Venezuela's future is the continuation of the present system with only minor alterations. In this case, the most significant trend would be the continued institutionalization of the political process. The greater the acceptance and common utilization of standard organizations and procedures in the expression of political desires, the more limited will be the area of effective student action. When all political viewpoints have access to such institutions—including the viewpoints now represented by the illegal parties—then student power will be restricted almost entirely to the educational sphere, and perhaps to the representation of newly developing points of view that have not attained institutional acceptance.

But however limited the power of student political action, and however great the restrictions imposed by the government or by academic requirements, student politics seems unlikely to cease in Venezuela. In the Venezuelan political system, students have for a generation and more played roles, often crucial, for which they were uniquely fitted. The need for such roles may diminish in the future, but the students will certainly remember and may be prepared to repeat or surpass their past service to the nation.

NOTES

1. Venezuela, Ministerio de Educación, *Educación para todos* (Caracas, 1965), p. 47. The academic year 1963–64 is the latest year for which adequate data are available. Total university enrollment in 1966–67 was probably slightly over 50,000.

2. In 1935 it had only 153 students, while the UCV had 1,259. Ministerio de Educación, *Memoria y cuenta, 1935* (Caracas, 1935).

3. Miguel Angel Mudarra, *Historia de la legislación escolar contemporanea en Venezuela* (Caracas: Tipográfica Vargas, 1962).

4. This figure is a personal guess, but it was upheld in conversation with many persons connected with the Venezuelan universities. A discussion of the proportion of students who participate in political activity in several Latin American countries can be found in Orlando Albornoz, "Student Opposition in Latin America," *Government and Opposition*, October 1966-January 1967.

5. This phenomenon is discussed in S. Walter Washington, "Student Politics in Latin America: The Venezuelan Example," *Foreign Affairs*, April 1959.

6. An example was a four-month series of disturbances in the spring of 1965, triggered by the expulsion of a student from the Technical and Industrial School in Caracas and eventually involving action by secondary and university students throughout the nation. See *La Esfera, El Nacional*, March 11, 1965, and subsequent issues.

7. Editorial in *El Nacional*, August 9, 1966.

8. Information on the "Week of the Student" and the April rebellion can be found in Thomas Rourke, *Gómez, Tyrant of the Andes* (New York: William Morrow, 1936); John D. Martz, "Venezuela's 'Generation of '28': The Genesis

of Political Democracy," *Journal of Inter-American Studies*, January 1964; John D. Martz, *Acción Democrática* (Princeton: Princeton University Press, 1966); Joaquín Gabaldón Márquez, *Memoria ye cuento de la generación del 28* (Buenos Aires: Imprenta Lopez, 1958); Rodolfo Luzardo, *Notas histórico-económicas, 1928–1963* (Caracas: Editorial Sucre, 1963); Rómulo Betancourt, *Política y petroleo* (Mexico: Fondo de Cultura Económica, 1956); Pedro N. Pereira, h., *En la prisión: los estudiantes de 1928* (Caracas: Editorial Avila Gráfica, 1952); Francisco Betancourt Sosa, *Pueblo en rebeldía* (Caracas: Ediciones Garrido, 1959); and Raúl Agudo Freytes, *Vida de un adelantado* (Caracas: Universidad Central de Venezuela, 1948).

9. This has not always been true elsewhere in Latin America. For example, Alfredo Palacios, as politician and professor, but especially as the latter, was a widely recognized leader of the Argentine university reform movement. Rómulo Gallegos, Venezuela's most famous author and the nation's President in 1948, was regarded as the mentor of the generation of 1928. However, in 1928 he was a secondary school teacher and did not have a direct and active role in the student movement. See Juan Liscano, *Rómulo Gallegos y su tiempo* (Caracas: Universidad Central de Venezuela, 1961).

10. Most of the interviews in this study were carried out in 1963–64. Analysis of the data is still in progress, but some preliminary analyses and general descriptions are available in Frank Bonilla and José A. Silva Michelena (eds.), *Studying the Venezuelan Polity* (Cambridge, Mass.: Massachusetts Institute of Technology, 1966).

11. At UCAB and UDO, university and faculty council members could not be counted because such positions do not exist there. In addition, no faculty council members from ULA and no students at all from USM were included.

12. An example is Robert D. Barton, "The Militant Latin Campus," *The Nation*, August 12, 1961, pp. 75–78. He cites Venezuela as "the country most plagued with this type of student agitator."

13. The figures on the UCV student body were taken from Universidad Central de Venezuela, Oficina de Estadistica, *Información estadistica*, No. 3 (1964).

14. *Vértice*, April 1966, pp. 27–29. *Vértice* is a student publication at the Central University.

15. The relation of class origin to political activity is discussed in Seymour Martin Lipset, "University Students and Politics in Underdeveloped Countries," *Minerva*, III (Autumn 1964), 47, and in Albornoz, *op. cit.*

16. José Enrique Rodó, *Ariel* (Mexico: Imprenta Universitaria, 1947), p. 126.

17. S. N. Eisenstadt, "Archetypal Patterns of Youth," in Erik H. Erikson (ed.), *Youth: Change and Challenge* (New York: Basic Books, 1963), p. 27.

18. In fact, their rallying cry was not even "liberty," though the word appeared frequently enough, but a meaningless mouthful of syllables variously reported as *"sigala y balaja"* and *"sacalapatalajá."* The utility to the movement of this meaningless shout and other romantic symbols is discussed in Domingo Alberto Rangel, *Los andinos al poder* (Mérida: Talleres Gráficos Universitarios, 1965), pp. 236 ff.

19. Students had the second-highest affirmative response rate on the question of political meetings, the second in work for a party or candidate, and the highest on the question of strikes. Labor union leaders ranked first, first, and second, respectively.

20. Orlando Albornoz cites examples, among them a case where student-

controlled professorial appointments were made contingent on political contributions, in his *Libertad académica y educación superior en América Latina* (Caracas: Dipuven, 1966), pp. 46–47.

21. *El Nacional,* June 17, 1966.

22. Kalman H. Silvert, "The University Student," in John J. Johnson (ed.), *Continuity and Change in Latin America* (Stanford: Stanford University Press, 1964), p. 219.

23. Rafael Caldera, "Universidad y política," *El Nacional,* June 16, 1966.

24. *El Nacional,* August 9, 1966. An example of the opposing point of view can be found in Arturo Uslar Pietri, *La universidad y el país* (Caracas: Universidad Central de Venezuela, 1962). Uslar Pietri is the only leading intellectual—he is also a leading politician—who has consistently spoken against the political activism of the Venezuelan university.

25. Eisenstadt, *loc. cit.*

26. An identification of some of these values can be found in Orlando Albornoz, *Valores sociales en la educación venezolana* (Caracas: Facultad de Economía, Universidad Central de Venezuela, 1962). The middle-class origins of student leaders have been noted in many general and specific works, for example, Silvert, *op. cit.,* and Frank Bonilla, "The Student Federation of Chile: 50 Years of Political Action in a Latin American University" (unpublished Ph.D. dissertation, Harvard University, 1959).

27. Arturo Uslar Pietri, *Un retrato en la geografía* (Buenos Aires: Editorial Losada, 1962), p. 134.

28. Federación de Centros Universitarios, *Prospecto estudiantil de la Universidad de los Andes* (Mérida: Talleres Gráficos Universitarios, 1960), p. 53.

29. It must be remembered that there is a considerable difference in the total numbers of the two groups. The universe of student leaders was only 387, while that represented by the urban and rural proletariat samples was over 235,000.

30. Francisco Betancourt Sosa, *op. cit.,* p. 11.

31. Angel Oscar Matheus B., *Valor de una generación* (Mérida: Federación de Centros Universitarios, Universidad de los Andes, 1964), p. 9.

32. See, for example, Eleazar López Contreras, *Proceso político y social, 1928–1936* (Caracas: Editorial Ancora, 1955).

33. Such as Domingo Alberto Rangel, *op. cit.*

34. The question was open-ended and the answers categorized into ten groups, such as economic measures, institutional political measures, "change the government," revolutionary measures, cooperative measures, and so on. It must be remembered that these data were collected in the academic year 1963–64 at the peak of terrorist and guerrilla activity, a time when the students were more than usually caught up in the idea of revolution.

35. Among the twelve groups evaluated, the students ranked fifth. The order was teachers, peasants, priests, businessmen, students, journalists, military, judges, union leaders, police, government officials, and politicians. (This ranking was based on responses by only twenty-three of the thirty-four samples.)

36. See, for example, Foción Febres Cordero, *Reforma universitaria* (Caracas: Universidad Central de Venezuela, 1960), and Albornoz, *Libertad académica y educación superior en América Latina.*

37. For general accounts of the Gómez period, see Rourke, *op. cit.;* John Lavin, *A Halo for Gómez* (New York: Pageant Press, 1954); and José Rafael Pocaterra, *Gómez* (Paris: André Delpeuch, 1929).

38. On political parties, see Manuel Vicente Magallanes, *Partidos políticos venezolanos* (Caracas: Tipográfica Vargas, 1959). On labor, see Rodolfo Quintero, *Sindicalismo y cambio social en Venezuela* (Caracas: Universidad Central de Venezuela, 1966).

39. Some of the earlier movements are described in Pocaterra, *op. cit.;* Luzardo, *op. cit.;* and Humberto Cuenca, *La universidad revolucionaria* (Caracas: Editorial Cultura Contemporanea, 1964).

40. Rangel, *op. cit.,* p. 238. Rómulo Betancourt saw this moment as the first confrontation between "two complementary energies . . . : the masses without intellectual leaders and the intellectual leader without the masses," in Luis Enrique Osorio, *Democracia en Venezuela* (Bogotá: Editorial Litografía Colombia, 1943), p. 156.

41. General works on the Pérez Jiménez regime include Tad Szulc, *Twilight of the Tyrants* (New York: Henry Holt, 1959); Robert J. Alexander, *The Venezuelan Democratic Revolution* (New Brunswick: Rutgers University Press, 1964); José Rivas Rivas (ed.), *El mundo y la época de Pérez Jiménez* (Caracas: Pensamiento Vivo, 1961).

42. Manuel Alfredo Rodríguez, José Francisco Peñaloza, and Régulo Briceño, *Autonomía y reforma universitaria* (Caracas: Ediciones del Comité Estudiantil Nacional Revolucionario, 1961), p. 17. Rodríguez goes on to call the strike "really extraordinary, because for the first time professors, authorities, and students united to defend the autonomy of the University." Other observers saw the activity as excessive and the resultant closure in a different light: "Public opinion received [the closure] with some pleasure, since it saw in the intervention nothing more than measures tending to 'normalize' and 'pacify' the University." Foción Febres Cordero, *Autonomía universitaria* (Caracas: Universidad Central de Venezuela, 1959), p. 44.

43. The best account of the fall of Pérez Jiménez is José Umaña Bernal, *Testimonio de la revolución en Venezuela* (Caracas: Tipográfica Vargas, 1958). Material can also be found in Rivas Rivas, *op. cit.;* José Rivas Rivas, *Los manifiestos de la liberación* (Caracas: Pensamiento Vivo, 1958); and Alexander, *op. cit.*

44. This is not apparent from the literature but was reported to the author by a member of the strike committee.

45. The most important general sources on this period are José Rivas Rivas, *De Gómez a Gallegos* (Caracas: Pensamiento Vivo, 1963); Rodolfo Luzardo, *op. cit.;* López Contreras, *op. cit.;* and Martz, *Acción Democrática.*

46. Venezuela, Presidencia de la República, *Documentos que hicieron historia* (Caracas: Editorial Arte, 1962), p. 187.

47. A popular joke had it that the government was located not at Miraflores (the presidential palace) but at Miracielos (the location of FEV headquarters). Juan Blanco Peñalver, *Historia de un naufragio* (Maracay: Editorial Nuestra América, 1962), p. 158. See also *Fantoches,* a satirical weekly of this period.

48. The best general sources are Umaña Bernal, *op. cit.;* José Rivas Rivas, *Un año con Wolfgang Larrazabal* (Caracas: Pensamiento Vivo, 1964); and Alexander, *op. cit.*

49. Discussed in S. Walter Washington, "The Political Activity of Latin American Students," in Robert D. Tomasek (ed.), *Latin American Politics* (New York: Doubleday, 1966). See also Umaña Bernal, *op. cit.*

50. Silvert, *op. cit.,* p. 217.

51. See Philip G. Altbach, "Students and Politics," *Comparative Education Review,* June 1966, p. 178.

52. Lipset, *op. cit.,* p. 18.

53. Washington, "The Political Activity of Latin American Students," p. 124.

54. The students' own devotion to democratic systems seems to be more intense in such periods. In 1958 they could say, "Democracy is the only system that satisfies the Venezuelans' traditional and genuine aspirations to liberty and equality." (*Declaración de principios de los gremios universitarios* [Caracas: Universidad Central de Venezuela, 1958].) But in the ConVen data, on two questions in which respondents were asked to give an order of priority to various possible objectives of the government, the student gave lower rankings to the two objectives most specifically related to the democratic system ("stabilize the electoral system" and "maintain democracy") than did any other sample group except the priests.

55. *Acción Democrática: doctrina y programa* (Caracas: Secretaría Nacional de Propaganda. Accion Democrática, 1962), p. 6. See also Martz, *Acción Democrática.*

56. See Magallanes, *op. cit.,* pp. 95 ff.

57. *F.E.V.* [a review published by the FEV], December 1936.

58. The information in this section comes from an interview held in Caracas with several members of the AD youth wing, on January 18, 1966.

59. José M. Salazar Jiménez, *Determinantes y dinámica de las actitudes políticas de estudiantes universitarios* (Caracas: Universidad Central de Venezuela, 1961). Although Salazar's interpretations are interesting, his data are weak. The first section of the study, from which he draws conclusions (1) and (3), was based on a sample of 343 students from four faculties (out of a UCV total of 11 faculties and over 10,000 students for that year); the sample base for conclusion (2) was 41 students in two faculties.

60. As an indication of how seriously the elections are taken, estimates of the amount of money spent on posters and other propaganda on the UCV campus—and the bulk of such funds comes directly from the parties—exceed a half-million bolivars (over $100,000) per year. *Vértice,* April 1966, p. 29.

61. Given the long COPEI rivalry with AD and the basic anti-Communist plank in the COPEI platform, it seems unlikely that a person who had supported COPEI would turn to either AD or the PCV-MIR coalition. The FND, on the other hand, occupied an ideological position near that of COPEI, though without the religious connection, and would be a logical choice for such a voter. Adjusting for the general decline in voting, we find that the absolute number of votes lost by COPEI was just about 100 less than the FND's total vote.

62. The breakdown of the MIR-PCV vote for 1965 was available from only one source and may overemphasize the suddenness of the shift in 1966. The author's impression is that the shift took place over the previous two or three years.

63. See Sección Juvenil, *La juventud de Acción Democrática y las pasadas elecciones universitarias* (Barcelona: Acción Democrática, 1961).

64. The independents who win are generally considered to occupy a position to the ideological right of COPEI, reflecting the upper-income orientation of the university.

65. Note the difference in ranking of students and politicians given in n. 35 above.

66. Accounts of this recruitment are included in James D. Cockroft, "Venezuela's Fidelistas—Two Generations" (unpublished paper, Stanford University, 1963) and in John L. Sorenson, *Unconventional Warfare and the Venezuelan Society* (China Lake, Calif.: U.S. Department of the Navy, 1964).

67. *El Nacional,* June 30, 1966.

68. Respondents were asked to place themselves on a scale of agreement-indifference-disagreement in relation to ten statements about the proper role of the state in the economy. Five of the statements were in favor of direct state influence, five were against. In eight of the ten cases, proportionally more of the student leaders' responses fell into the "firmly disagree" category than did those of any other sample, and their relative concentration at this end of the spectrum on the other two statements was almost as great.

69. The two questions used—"What worries you most about Venezuela's present situation?" and "What can be done to improve this situation?"—were both open-ended, allowing the respondent to name several answers if he desired to do so. The response rate (total answers per number of respondents) of the student sample was the highest of all groups on the first question but just slightly above average on the second.

70. According to one ex-student leader, most of these issues are settled by such informal means. Overt, formal actions such as strikes are used only after informal means have failed.

71. John J. Johnson, "Whither the Latin American Middle Sectors?," *Virginia Quarterly Review,* August 1957, p. 516.

72. For a general discussion of the content of university reform, see John P. Harrison, "The Confrontation with the Political University," *Annals of the American Academy of Political and Social Science,* March 1961. For a general account of the history of university reform in Venezuela, see Febres Cordero, *Autonomía universitaria.*

73. Notably Argentina. See Gabriel Mazo, *La reforma universitaria* (La Plata: Centro de Estudiantes de Ingeniera, 1941) and, by the same author, *La reforma universitaria* (Buenos Aires: Compañía Editora y Distribuidora de la Plata, 1957).

74. Venezuela, Ministerio de Educación, "Estatuto Organico de las Universidades Nacionales—Decreto 408 de la Junta Revolucionaria de Gobierno," October 1, 1946, Articles V and VI.

75. For example, *AD y el problema universitario* (Caracas: Secretaría Nacional de Propaganda, Acción Democrática, 1964).

76. Universidad Central de Venezuela, "Resolución reglamentaria sobre los requisitos de admisión para alumnos repitientes," undated flyer put out by the UCV. According to the rule, a student may not register for the same year in the same faculty (e.g., second-year law) more than twice. He may register again for that year after four years have passed, or he may sign up in another faculty.

77. See Lipset, *op. cit.,* pp. 21–27.

12. CONCLUSION

DONALD K. EMMERSON

A major danger in writing about student political activity in developing nations is that its ubiquity, intensity, and striking triumphs may blind us to its absences, fragility, and no less striking failures. The roster of governments whose downfall followed major student protests in the last ten years is long: Venezuela in 1958 (Marcos Pérez Jiménez), Japan in 1960 (Nobusuke Kishi), South Korea in 1960 (Syngman Rhee), Turkey in 1960 (Adnan Menderes), South Viet-Nam in 1963 (Ngo Dinh Diem), Bolivia in 1964 (Víctor Paz Estenssoro), the Sudan in 1964 (Ibrahim Abboud), and Indonesia in 1966 (Sukarno). But the list of governments that have successfully resisted student opposition in the same period is far longer, ranging from the constitutional democracy of Venezuela and the monarchies of Morocco and Iran to military regimes of the right and left in Algeria, Burma, South Viet-Nam, Argentina, Brazil, the Dominican Republic, Nicaragua, and Paraguay, to cite only a few examples. In the toppling of governments, including many of those that have fallen in the wake of student action, the central figure has been the army officer, not the student.

If the significance of student political activity should not be exaggerated, neither should its extent. Students in developing nations, at least in those where survey data have been gathered, tend to be politically aware, interested, and active in sharply decreasing degrees. On the average, a third of the students in each of nine

The Social Science Research Council and the American Council of Learned Societies were kind enough to support me financially as a Foreign Area Fellow during the preparation of this final chapter, whose contents and conclusions Professors Robert Axelrod and Herbert Feith, as well as a number of the co-authors of this volume, were kind enough to criticize. To all the above, whose help does not of course entail responsibility, I should like to express my warm appreciation.

countries (Nigeria, India, Iran, Pakistan, Turkey, Argentina, Brazil, Colombia, and Panama) who answered comparable survey questions reported that they were very interested in politics.[1] In one case, Iran, the proportion exceeded 50 per cent, but only 15 per cent of the respondents could be classified as "highly politicized"[2] in their actual behavior. Other studies comparing student interest and activity show a similar narrowing. In surveys conducted recently in Latin America, respondents who were very interested in student politics compared to those reporting active participation in four or more strikes or demonstrations declined from 41 to 12 per cent in Paraguay, from 20 to 8 per cent in Colombia, from 17 to 4 per cent in Mexico, and from 21 to 3 per cent in Puerto Rico.[3] At the University of Puerto Rico, the activist core of the militant Pro-Independence University Federation (FUPI) numbers only 60 to 100 students, or about 0.3 per cent of the student body.[4] Even at the time of the student demonstrations against the United States–Japan Security Treaty in Tokyo in 1960—one of the most massive and sustained student protests of the past decade—only about 5 per cent of the students at Tokyo University, the center of the movement, could be classified as *"Zengakuren* activists."[5]

A second danger lies in the deceptive radicalism of the most intense—and most widely reported—forms of student activism. As Glaucio Soares has shown,[6] radicals are only a small minority of the student population in most developing countries, and are greatly overrepresented among those who believe students should play an active role in politics and who act on that belief in demonstrations and strikes. Such activities tend therefore to involve the tail ends of any given distribution of student opinion and not its central modes.

A third, subtler danger is the temptation to view students as isolates, as part of an international stratum of intellectuals rather than in the unique contexts of their national societies. Studenthood is everywhere a phase of academic learning, career preparation, and personal discovery in the transition from adolescence to adulthood. The university is everywhere a place where knowledge is imparted, skills are exercised, and values are transmitted wholly or partly in a tradition of institutionalized scholarship extending unbroken from medieval Europe to the modern world. A critical dynamic of the process of modernization itself, it has been argued, is the expansion of an emergent "world culture" (Lucian Pye)[7] or "modern intellectual culture" (Edward Shils)[8] whose natural and often sole novitiates and carriers are the university-educated.

Such generalizations are useful, but they must be qualified. The personal experience and social meaning of studenthood are not cross-culturally invariant. The genus *Universitas* covers a great diversity of organizational forms, political functions, and curricular contents.[9] We need not adopt a posture of extreme cultural relativism to recognize the vital influence of diverse national conditions on the political attitudes, roles, and significance of university students.[10]

This needs to be said with force because our present task is comparative, a search for the general rather than the limiting case. In the pages that follow, we shall examine the influence on student politics of a number of "independent variables": at the biographic level of the individual student, at the level of his university environment, and in the context of broader social and political change. These are not rigid distinctions—a student's academic specialization, for example, could be viewed as his major (biographic variable), his faculty (university variable), or his occupational training (societal variable)—but they will serve to structure our discussion.

Student Politics: Biographic Variables

Under this heading, we shall examine the relationships between sex, age, religion, family, and personality factors on the one hand,[11] and student political attitudes and behavior on the other.

Sex, Age, and Religion. One of the most consistent findings of contemporary political science is that men are on the whole more politicized than women. Students are no exception. In general, female students are politically less informed, less interested, and less active, and those who are politicized are less leftist, than their male counterparts.[12] The explanation lies in the sheltered, passive, family-centered roles reserved for women in most developing nations.

The influence of age is less clear-cut. Seymour Martin Lipset has suggested that "the greater the number of years the student spends at the university, the greater the likelihood of student political activity," and has noted the presence of "professional" student politicians at universities where it is possible to retain one's student status without advancing academically.[13] In parts of Latin America and Asia, prolonged student status is not uncommon and the "professional" student activist is definitely not a mythical figure. Among the students who graduated from the University of Buenos Aires in 1956 was one who had been registered in the Faculty of Law for forty-one years.[14] In 1963, Efren Capiz Villegas led a student revolt at the University of Morelia in Mexico; he had been a student for seventeen of his forty-five years.[15] In 1960, Juan Campos Lama led a massive strike at the University of San Marcos in Peru; "in his balding mid-thirties,"[16] he had been a student for fourteen years.[17] Joseph DiBona has noted the power wielded by ten- and nine-year veterans of student politics at the University of Allahabad in India.[18] "Older, tougher, more ingenious, often seductively attractive," Shils has written from his Indian experience, "these 'professional' students are often catalysts who agitate lambs into lions."[19]

However, as William Hamilton shows in the chapter on Venezuela, such individual cases do not characterize the broader community of student leaders, whose age distribution is not that strikingly out of line with the age curve of the student body as a whole. A study of University of San Carlos students in Guatemala found that leaders were in fact on the average younger than nonleaders.[20] At the same time, advanced age alone does not disqualify a student leader from enjoying popularity on the campus, particularly in Latin American and Asian countries where the matriculation-graduation ratios of a number of universities are so high that there is little or no peer disapproval of students who fail to graduate in the formally allotted time[21] and where student and politician roles are not clearly differentiated.

The relationship of age (and class year) to student politicization is apparently mixed. On the one hand, older students with years of university experience behind them are more likely to hold positions of leadership in political groups; on the other hand, as students advance toward the prospect of employment, political interest and activity may give way to more career-centered concerns.[22] Data from Argentina and Colombia suggest that political activity and leftist radicalism increase through roughly the first three years in the university and then decline as the majority of students in terminal classes turn away from politics toward occupational concerns, leaving a few who remain active, maintain their radical views, and perhaps become "professional" student politicians.[23]

Whether an individual student's experience conforms to this or some other curve of politicization as he moves through the university will depend on many factors. One of them is religious belief. The available survey data indicate that the more religious the student the less likely he is to be interested, active, or leftist in politics.[24] In several of the countries studied, this negative relationship is statistically significant even when social background variables are controlled for.

Given the historically conservative role of the Catholic Church and the anticlerical connotations of a leftist stance in politics in Latin America, the negative association between religiosity and leftist radicalism on that continent is not surprising. Neither the Church nor the left in Latin America is monolithic, however. Somewhat different patterns may prevail among student leaders in countries such as Chile and Venezuela, where center-left social Christian parties enjoy considerable campus support, or in Brazil, where the Catholic left has contributed a number of radical activists to student politics.

Given the close integration of Islam historically with nationalism and doctrinally with the realm of politics, one might expect religion to play a wholly different role in student politicization in the Muslim world. Indeed, the role of the General Union of Algerian Muslim Students (UGEMA) in the Algerian revolution and that of the Islamic Student Association (HMI), the leading member of the Indonesian Students' Action Command (KAMI), in the recent upheaval in Indonesia (see Chapters 1 and 6) suggests a positive correlation between religiosity and politicization. But the "Muslim" in UGEMA's name and the street prayers of KAMI in Djakarta in 1966 were not expressions of religious belief so much as political tactics based on a recognition of the ideological uses of religious identification, and were directed in both cases against leftist opponents.[25]

On campuses in other countries, politico-religious student organizations take still different forms. Yet the Catholic and Buddhist student leaders in South Viet-Nam, the Calvinist Afrikaners of the *Afrikaanse Studentebond* (ASB) in South Africa, and the Catholic Pax Romana circles from which Lovanium student leaders in the Congo (Kinshasha) apparently tend to be recruited—merely to cite examples from the preceding chapters—all have one thing in common: a predominance of political or communitarian values over strictly religious faith and practice. In almost any African, Asian, or Latin American nation, university students as a group are more secularly inclined than the adult community, and student political leaders, although they may employ religious symbols for political ends, are less devout than the student body as a whole.

The Family. In 1922, the famed Peruvian student leader Víctor Raúl Haya de la Torre cited the words of a Chilean student as the cry of Latin American youth: "Let us be different from our fathers!"[26] In subsequent years, generational revolt has become a common theme in the literature on student politics.[27] Now, accumulated empirical evidence allows us to chart more precisely the influence of the family on student politicization. We shall examine this evidence under three headings: the student's residence at or away from home, his parents' social status, and his parents' political interest and participation.

In general, and particularly in Asia, students residing in university housing, student hostels, or rented rooms are politically more active and more radical than those who live at home.[28] This finding can be attributed to a sense of release from family constraints, to the disorienting effects of an urban environment, or to the increased opportunity for interaction with their peers that students away from home experience. If the student's home is in a rural area, the transition may be particularly stressful. When the university functions effectively *in loco parentis*, however, the mere fact of residence away from home is unlikely to play a significant role in politicization. Nor is political activity the necessary result of such dislocation; apathetic withdrawal, involvement in nonpolitical campus cliques, or compulsive immersion in study are also possible outcomes.

The effect of family social status on student politicization is not entirely clear. Several studies have shown that upwardly mobile students tend to be more politicized than those from higher-status backgrounds.[29] Evidence also exists for several countries suggesting that lower-status backgrounds are conducive to radical leftist views.[30] But other investigations indicate the opposite: that upwardly mobile students are likely to be *less* politicized[31] and *less* radical.[32] Finally, there is also evidence for the hypothesis that social status is not related, or at least not unambiguously related, to politicization[33] or radicalism.[34]

The diversity of these findings is in part a result of diversity in research designs. In these studies, social status is variously specified according to father's occupation, income, or education. Sometimes these or other attributes are blended to form an index. Occasionally, the respondent's self-assigned position in a status hierarchy or along a "status satisfaction" scale is used.

It should also be kept in mind that the distribution of parental status in virtually any representative sample of university students in a developing nation is skewed toward the middle or the upper end in comparison with the distribution of status in the adult population. "Lower status" in such samples thus tends to identify "lower-middle class" students rather than the children of poor peasants or unskilled workers. To the extent that educational opportunities expand, class structures differentiate, and "middle sectors" develop and widen, the skewness will decrease, as it already has in many countries. But broadening the social base of recruitment to higher education need not mean that the student body will become markedly less homogeneous in *self-assigned* status, or that the impact of social background variables on student politicization will necessarily be heightened. For the upwardly mobile student, the relatively high status he acquires merely by successfully competing for entrance into a university is likely to blur the influence of his social origin on his political attitudes and activity. This is one reason why the power of strictly class-based analysis to explain student political behavior is so low.

The "contradictory" hypotheses are still there to be tested: that lower social origin leads to leftward politicization because the student is poor, disoriented, frustrated, and identifies more easily with the deprived strata in society, or, on the contrary, that lower social origin leads to conservative or apolitical careerism because the student identifies with higher social strata, whose ranks he has a longed-for chance to enter, because he lacks the economic margin to allow for "time wasted" in politics, and because radical political activity might endanger his career security and the enjoyment of material advantages hitherto denied him. Similarly, higher social origins can be linked to conservative or apolitical views or to a leftist, activist posture. The point is that whatever status-derived "explanation" is found to fit a given case, it will probably apply not because one or another of these interpretations is cross-culturally valid but because other variables interact to create the particular conditions in which parental social status can operate in a given direction. For, finally, the diversity of empirical findings on the matter shows that parental status alone is a weak and unstable cross-national predictor of student political attitudes and behavior.

Turning to the influence of parental political interest and opinion, we find no evidence of "generational revolt." On the contrary, in several studies patterns of generational continuity in political orientations emerge,[35] while others suggest that parental and student participation in politics are not related.[36] The student who adopts a given political position solely or even largely because it is contrary to his father's views seems to be a rare creature indeed.

In sum, family influences on student politics vary widely. The leaders of the Chilean Student Federation (FECH) whom Frank

Bonilla interviewed in 1957 enjoyed warm, permissive, and democratic family relationships; political involvement for these students was not a means of escape from family conflicts. Arthur Liebman, on the other hand, observed that the most militant leaders of FUPI in Puerto Rico tended to come from broken homes and to have been brought up by their mothers. Bonilla concludes that the FECH has been a democratizing force for moderation, tolerance, and reform in Chile. FUPI, on the other hand, is "anti-American" in the most bitterly alienated sense of the term and its leaders' vehement attacks against U.S. influence in Puerto Rico may, as Liebman suggests, be in part a projection of their own personal search for identity.[37] Whatever the role of the family in manifest political socialization—i.e., in the explicit transmission of specifically political information, values, and feelings[38]—the student does acquire basic personal values within the family unit, values that will help to shape the future direction and content of his overtly political orientations.

This brings us to our final biographic variable: personality.

Personality. Little is known about the role of personality in student movements. The portrait of the young radical as someone driven by his crisis of identity and sense of alienation to seek a new self-image in ego-asserting, tension-relieving, morally purifying action has great intuitive appeal, but relatively little empirical validation. The survey data we have cited, almost without exception, reflect surface attitudes, not core motivations.

The portrait itself is richly suggestive. "Is it not probable and in fact demonstrable," Erik Erikson has suggested, "that among the most passionate ideologists there are unreconstructed adolescents, transmitting to their ideas the proud moment of their transient ego recovery, of their temporary victory over the forces of existence and history, but also the pathology of their deepest isolation, the defensiveness of their forever adolescing egos—and their fear of the calm of adulthood?"[39] Shils, writing of Indian students, refers to "the need of Indian youth for a unitary, immediately present, integral, and morally pure authority."[40] Robert Scalapino asks why Chinese students in Japan in the early twentieth century were so preoccupied with the idea of radical change, and concludes that their radicalism was

almost a psychological necessity . . . a dramatic, simple act relieving personal tensions, reducing the possibility of being "corrupted," and liberating some of the pure, action-oriented desires among a deeply frustrated group. Blood had to flow. Traditional elites and institutions had to be uprooted. The old had to be levelled before the new could be established. In much of this, one sees romanticism and myth, a defiance of reason, and the espousal of a type of anti-intellectualism that refused to acknowledge complexity, catered only to the simple.[41]

This line of argument should not lead us to treat politics as pathology. Scalapino notes that the Chinese students in Japan in the years 1900–1910 had become politically conscious at a time when their homeland was undergoing profound external humiliation (the Sino-Japanese War, expanding foreign spheres of influence) and internal upheaval (the Hundred Days' Reform, the Boxer Rebellion). In this light, the students' radical nationalism was eminently rational. Similarly, to cite a current example, psychologically based interpretations of radical nationalism among Vietnamese students should not be allowed to obscure the empirical circumstances that make such a response rational: the humiliating weight of the American presence in South Viet-Nam and the systematic dismemberment of Vietnamese society.

But personality—loosely conceived as an image of the self—does exert an important influence on student political style. In 1918, the student authors of the famous manifesto that launched the university reform movement in Latin America wrote: "Youth always lives in a heroic moment. It is disinterested, pure. It hasn't yet had time to corrupt itself." Theirs, they announced, was a "holy revolution," a "revolution of conscience."[42] "The most important class is the student class because we are clean," the radical president of Latin America's largest national student union declared nearly half a century later. "Other groups have interests that are dirty."[43] This emphasis on purity and righteousness is widely characteristic of radical student movements.[44] Perhaps its most critical psychological function is that it permits simultaneously an assertion of self and a denial of selfishness. We shall return briefly to its political implications after the university, society, and polity have been explored as contexts for student politics.

University Variables

Under this heading, we shall examine the influence on student politicization of the university's location, auspices, quality, and faculties.[45]

Location, Auspices, and Quality. Understandably, the political potential of the student body at a large university in a capital city exceeds that of students enrolled in colleges in comparatively isolated rural areas. In the capital, the students' proximity to government and opposition, their easy access to political information and commentary, and the ready availability of a national audience via the capital-centered communications media all tend to facilitate the task of the activist. These conditions hold with particular force where the capital city is unquestionably the center of political gravity in the nation; the University of San Marcos in Peru, the Central University of Venezuela, and Seoul National University in Korea are among the many institutions that fit this pattern. Even in countries with large, dispersed systems of higher education such as China, Indonesia, and Japan, the epicenters of student upheaval are found in universities in capital cities. Exceptions to the latter rule are India and Pakistan, where student unrest is concentrated not in the national capitals but in the northeastern and eastern regions, respectively.[46]

Elsewhere, notably in Africa, the nation's major university may be located near the capital in a self-enclosed "university city." In Sierra Leone, Ghana, Uganda, and Tanzania, and perhaps in Algeria and the Congo (Kinshasha) as well, this spatial insulation seems to have facilitated a certain apolitical elitism among many students.

At least three aspects of university administration are relevant to student politicization: public vs. private auspices, secular vs. religious orientations, and the degree of student involvement in university decision-making. In general, one might expect the highest incidence of student activism in secular state institutions where students have an important voice in university affairs. Most of the major universities in Latin America fit this pattern. But state financial support does not necessarily entail political control; in Latin America, traditions of university autonomy are strong and jealously guarded by students and teachers alike, and the University of Havana model has yet to be duplicated.[47] Furthermore, the fact of public auspices alone cannot account for the wide variations in levels of student political activity among state institutions.

In Asia, there are several striking exceptions to the general tendency for public institutions to outweigh private schools in political influence. For example, Waseda University in Japan and the Lyceum of the Philippines, both private institutions, are important centers of student opposition. In each instance, the explanation stems in part from a distinctive tradition of student involvement in public affairs. Waseda, founded in 1882 by a leading opponent of the government, "was intended as the breeding ground of future opposition politicians. Its core departments were those of politics and economics, and of law, and the character of the new school was sufficiently clear for the government to take the precaution of enlisting spies among its students."[48] Although the public universities in Japan have generally been more prominent than private institutions as centers of student activism in recent years, Waseda's tradition of public concern has not dimmed. Similarly, the Lyceum in Manila was established in 1952 by José Laurel, President of the Philippines during the Japanese occupation, expressly to promote nationalism and a spirit of national service among Filipino youth. Today, the largest chapter of the radical leftist *Kabataang Makabayan* (Nationalist Youth) is at the Lyceum.[49]

Religion, whose importance as a biographic variable we have already noted, allows for a somewhat better discrimination between politically active and politically passive campuses, particularly where Catholic colleges are involved. Shils notes that "Jesuit institutions in India are notoriously strictly governed, and they practically never have troubles with discipline."[50] Newton observes that the Catholic-sponsored universities in Buenos Aires have acquired "a reputation for internal orderliness."[51] Similar observations could be cited for other countries.[52]

Why should this be so? There are probably several reasons. Catholic institutions generally impose stricter discipline on their students. A shared religious commitment in a highly structured campus environment allows the Catholic university to function more effectively *in loco parentis*. To the extent that Catholic universities draw their students from a more conservative clientele that can afford to pay the relatively high fees required, the attractions of radicalism may be further diminished (although, as we have noted, high social status need not necessarily discourage student activism or leftism). The tendency for many of these institutions to maintain small enrollments and high academic standards is probably also involved.

In Muslim countries as well students at religiously oriented universities have not been notably more active than their colleagues in secular institutions. In the past—at the traditional Al Qarawiyin University in Morocco, for instance—students at Islamic universities who have felt occupationally restricted and disadvantaged by their predominantly religious education have occasionally expressed their anxieties in various forms of unrest. But the steps taken to modernize Islamic higher education—at Al Azhar University in Cairo, for example—have considerably reduced these fears. By and large throughout the Muslim world, the large secular universities—of Rabat, Karachi, Dacca, and Djakarta, among others—have played more important roles in student politics than Islamic colleges.

A consideration of student participation in university policy-making brings us back to Latin America, where student representation in university organs (*cogobierno,* or co-government) has been widely institutionalized.[53] Although this unique tradition is an important referent for student politics, the consultative process of *cogobierno* should not be confused with direct action in demonstrations, rallies, and so on. Nor should we assume that a student role in decision-making automatically politicizes the campus. Above all, *cogobierno* should not be seen simply as a means whereby irresponsible student leaders are able to distract the university from its main pedagogic task. Evidence from Argentina and Central America, for example, points in a contrary direction, namely that student participation can be on the whole a positive force for academic reform and improvement.[54] By providing a forum for student grievances, *cogobierno* also encourages action within rather than against the university; as a former rector of the University of Buenos Aires put it, "I would rather have the students across the table from me than across the street."[55]

Far more important than the university's location and auspices in accounting for student *inquietudes* (unrest) and "indiscipline" is the quality of university life. The relative absence of activism in sub-Saharan Africa, for example, is in part a reflection of this region's markedly lower student-population ratios when compared to those of North Africa, Asia, and Latin America. University students in black Africa are also absolutely less numerous, constitute a lower proportion of total enrollment, and enjoy lower student-staff ratios than their counterparts in the other three areas.[56] As the authors of the chapter on Ghana have argued, student political activity tends to be disvalued in numerically restricted, proportionally elitist systems of higher education in which the university graduate is virtually assured future employment.[57]

In contrast, in the university where underpaid, part-time professors lecture to anonymous crowds, where "education" means passing examinations and "learning" means cramming for them, where the student is unsupervised, unstimulated and, finally, unrewarded—under these conditions, student unrest is almost inevitable. This picture is exaggerated, but one or more of its elements can be found in many of the overexpanded, underdeveloped mass systems of higher education in Asia and Latin America today.

The underpaid "taxi professor," for example, so named because he must commute between jobs, is a ubiquitous figure in Latin America.[58] In India and Pakistan, inadequate classroom facilities, insufficient student housing, and an almost obsessive reliance on formalistic, externally administered examinations as indicators of student performance combine to create a thoroughly unacademic atmosphere at many colleges.[59] A student welfare official who visited the University of Calcutta in 1951 reported that more than 5,000 students had no accommodations at all. These students—many of whom slept on train station platforms and studied by the light of street lamps—were probably among those he saw making up half the length of a Communist protest march four miles long.[60] If, as a Pakistani professor wrote in 1963, "complete passivity in the classroom is considered a virtue,"[61] it is not surprising that intense activity outside the classroom, misnamed student "indiscipline," has become an almost endemic feature of university life on the subcontinent.

Exacerbating these conditions are the low output-input ratios found in many universities. Where students enter in waves and graduate in a trickle, education is not a process but a log jam. Once having acquired the coveted student status, often after several unsuccessful attempts to matriculate, students are naturally unwilling to be "selected out" on any grounds, including academic failure. Whether because of pressure from student representatives on university bodies, threatened demonstrations, or both, plans to sacrifice quantity for quality are often exceedingly difficult to implement. As the dean of an Indian law faculty put it, "I would not dare to limit admissions; it would mean endangering my life."[62] Or in the blunt language of a Peruvian professor: "I am now correcting exam papers, and at least half of these poor bastards deserve to fail. They don't know anything and they don't come to class. But if I failed them they would fire me. Believe me, I take a great risk in flunking 10 per cent of my students, which few other professors would dare to do."[63]

Whatever the accuracy of these complaints, the problem they evoke is critical not only to the quality of higher education in these countries, but to the extent of student opposition as well. The strict implementation of measures such as the "three F rule" in Burma[64] or the "repeater's rule" in Venezuela,[65] aimed at preventing the perpetual re-enrollment of academic laggards, may be one effective means of dampening activism, particularly if undertaken in conjunction with other steps to upgrade the quality of the university.

In the first application of the "repeater's rule" at the Central University of Venezuela (UCV), the Dean of Engineering dropped some 260 students from his register,[66] but it is too early to tell what effect such actions will have on UCV student insurgents. If the Burmese experience is any indication, it will be considerable. Since 1964, the military government in Burma has carried out a complete reorganization of higher education to depoliticize the university, raise its standards to benefit serious students and eliminate "hangers-on," and to harness its curriculum to the priorities of economic development (by emphasizing the sciences over law and letters). As a result, the Burmese university, once among the most turbulent in Asia, has begun to approximate the apolitical, elitist African model.[67]

Faculties

"What is your major?" the fat student asked Gopi.

"Natural Science," said Gopi.

"Lucky chap," said Rajan.

"Why don't you like your major?" Gopi asked.

"You can't even get a clerk's job after studying History, Economics and Logic. H.E.L. Add one more 'L' and it is hell," Rajan said.

"You could have taken up science," said Gopi.

"No. I'm not that intelligent. I think I'll study law and get into politics."

This conversation between two characters in K. Bhaskara Rao's novel of Indian student politics, *Candle Against the Wind*,[68] is fictional, but the relationship it suggests between faculty and politicization is not. Indeed, evidence from nineteen countries shows that, on the whole, students in the social sciences, law, and the humanities are more likely to be politicized[69] and leftist[70] than their colleagues in the natural and applied sciences. Before asking why this should be so, we will use a single case, the University of Buenos Aires (UBA) in Argentina, to qualify the conclusion in three important ways.

First, faculties of philosophy, letters, and other liberal arts subjects that have a high proportion of female students often do not follow the general trend toward greater politicization and leftism in the humanities, law, and social sciences. The effect of sex as an intervening variable is clearly shown in the UBA Faculty of Philosophy and Letters, whose student body is predominantly female. In a study by David Nasatir of the University's ten faculties, only engineering and dentistry ranked lower than philosophy and letters in the proportion of students reporting that they frequently got as excited about political events as about events in their personal lives.[71]

Second, the political *reputation* of a faculty is more likely to rest on the reported views and actions of an activist minority than on the actual distribution of opinion in the student body. Thus, for example, the leftist reputation of the UBA Faculty of Engineering[72] is in large part a reflection of the fact that student leaders in engineering are decidedly more politicized and leftist than nonleaders. In a 1964 study of the faculty, 90 per cent of the leaders felt that the university should be directly involved in the solution of social problems, and 40 per cent believed that student politics should be a form of apprenticeship for party political activity; the figures for the nonleaders were 15 per cent and none, respectively. Similarly, the distribution of the leadership sample along a leftist-centrist-rightist scale was skewed sharply to the left compared with that of the nonleaders.[73]

Third, in comparing faculties cross-culturally, we must make allowance for differing meanings behind the same academic label. Silvert and Bonilla, using a set of questions tapping levels of political activity, found that students in the Faculty of Economics at UBA were slightly *less* politicized than their colleagues in medicine and exact sciences.[74] But, as Lipset points out, the Faculty of Economics is in fact more of a business school than a place where economics is taught as a social science discipline. Lipset goes on to underline the need for greater conceptual clarity in these matters and to suggest a refining distinction between faculties that prepare students for specific occupational roles and those that do not.[75]

One possible explanation for the finding that humanities, law, and social science faculties tend to have more politicized and leftist student bodies than the exact and applied sciences focuses on the content and structure of the two curricular types. In the first set of faculties, political, social, and economic problems are actual subjects of study; in the latter, the student's contact with public affairs takes place only outside the classroom. In the first set, the student is concerned with man, the mind, and social interaction; in the second, with matter, the body, and physical laws. In the exact science faculties, the student is also likely to be under a somewhat more rigorous and demanding academic regimen.

But it is not enough to distinguish curricular types. This line of reasoning may account for variations in levels of political information, but it does not necessarily follow that the study of public affairs leads the student toward political action. More important than the formal content of an academic subject is how that subject is conceived and taught and how the student incorporates what he learns into his changing image of himself and his society. In this context, Lipset's distinction between "role-specific" and "role-diffuse" faculties may prove particularly fruitful.

The degree to which the faculties of a given university have distinctive value climates and traditions will also affect the utility of interdepartmental comparisons. In Latin America, for example, many universities are little more than administrative superimpositions on historically independent faculties. In the newer, more integrated residential universities of tropical Africa, on the other hand, the faculty tends to be more of a subsystem of the university than a system in its own right.

Finally, we should not discount the likelihood that secondary school students who are already inclined toward political activity may in part base their choice of a faculty on its curricular type, its extracurricular value climate, or its reputation for involvement in public affairs. This kind of "self-selection" may be an important mechanism in the relation between faculty and activism.

Before proceeding to the broader levels of social and political change, it will be useful briefly to illustrate the preceding discussion with a specific instance of interuniversity contrast. In a 1963 study of four major state universities in Pakistan (Dacca, Karachi, Lahore, and Peshawar), respondents at the University of Dacca in East Pakistan were most interested in politics and most frequently held leftist views, while those at Peshawar University were the least politicized and least leftist. Of the four samples, Dacca students also had the least respect for the political opinions of relatives, religious leaders, and government officials (on world affairs), valued service to others the least and personal ambition the most (as "guides to life"), were most pessimistic about the prospects for reducing inequalities in living standards within Pakistan, were most attracted to the use of force in effecting socio-economic change, and most frequently criticized student organizations as "politically influenced"; the Peshawar sample ranked at the extreme opposite end on each of these dimensions.[76] Peshawar has no university-wide students' union, while at the University of Dacca there is not only a Central Students' Union but also a separate union in each hall of residence.[77] The University of Dacca also has a much longer and stronger tradition of student activism than Peshawar.

Differences in location, religiosity, and the quality of student life all contribute to these polarities. Peshawar is a geographically isolated institution with an attractive residential campus; the University of Dacca is located in a densely populated city, and the conditions under which many of its students live are unsatisfactory.[78] According to one study, only slightly more than half the students at Dacca are attracted to Islam;[79] the corresponding figure for Peshawar is almost certainly much higher. Staff-student relations at Peshawar, although not unmarred by incidents, have been considerably better than those at Dacca, where a survey by Professor Ghulam Jilani revealed that roughly three-fourths of the students questioned felt frustrated by what they considered a stultifying university atmosphere and by poverty and inadequate facilities. Seventy-five per cent of Jilani's respondents reported that they had lost their traditional respect for teachers, while 77 per cent "were quite decided in their views that the students were being exploited by the politicians to serve their own selfish interests."[80] Students frequently referred to the "hidden hand" of politics at the university.[81] Finally, of course, the demographic density of the East, its Bengali language and comparatively Hinduized culture, and its economically disadvantaged position in relation to Pakistan's western section also help to shape this striking interuniversity contrast.

Student Politics and Social Change

Even if one could rank nations along some index of student activism—a delicate task indeed, given the formidable methodological problems involved[82]—it is unlikely that any strong correlations between quantitative levels of modernization (per capita income, for example) and student activism would emerge. The *quality* of a nation's modernizing experience, however, is a critical factor in student politics.

In Algeria and Viet-Nam, where independence came only after long and violent struggle, national liberation was an intensely politicizing experience, personally for the students who fought under its banner and vicariously for those who looked on from abroad. In the tropical African countries that acquired their independence through a gradual transfer of power from the metropole, university students were comparatively much less politicized as a group. Similarly, the recentness of student activism in the Philippines can in part be attributed to the relatively enlightened U.S. colonial administration of the islands, which effectively denied Filipino nationalism an anticolonial rationale by accommodating its basic demands. In Latin America, the drive for independence occurred so long ago that its effects on present-day student politics are purely symbolic. In Thailand, Ethiopia, and Liberia, countries that have had no colonial experience to speak of, student activism has been almost nonexistent. In general, the more tenacious the colonial regime, the greater its politicizing and radicalizing effects.

Independence brings with it new frameworks for student politics. As the student community within the nation expands (overshadowing the overseas student sector so prominently involved in the early phase of nationalism) and begins to conform more closely in social origins to the larger population, as attempts are made to reorient higher education toward new national priorities, and as the old anticolonial consensus is fragmented by re-emerging ethnic and regional cleavages, and emerging or re-emerging ideological ones, the university tends to lose its former position of "splendid isolation" and to open its gates to a variety of pressures from the host society.

Just as these pressures, as we have seen from the preceding chapters, form a unique setting for student politics in each country, the student's position in relation to these larger forces of change also varies. Table 1 illustrates the point.

TABLE 1

STUDENTS IN FOUR NATIONS COMPARED REGARDING "MODERNISM"
(In Per Cent)

Question: *"All things considered, are you more in favor of [respondent's country] retaining traditional customs or adopting more modern ways?"*

	Iran	Malaya	Pakistan	Thailand	Totals
"Traditionalists"	14	26	43	71	45
	(42)	(117)	(505)	(533)	(1,197)
"Modernists"	76	66	49	24	48
	(228)	(298)	(576)	(180)	(1,282)
No answer	10	8	8	5	7
	(30)	(36)	(94)	(37)	(197)
Total	100	100	100	100	100
	(300)	(451)	(1,175)	(750)	(2,676)

SOURCES: "Attitudes and Values of Iranian University Students" (mimeo.; United States Information Agency, Research and Reference Service, Washington, D.C., December 1964), p. 18; "Aspirations and Attitudes of University Students in Pakistan" (mimeo.; United States Information Agency, Research and Reference Service, Washington, D.C., December 1963), p. 23; "Student Views: Thailand and Malaysia" (mimeo.; United States Information Agency, Research and Reference Service, Washington, D.C., March 1965), p. 1. Absolute numbers are in parentheses.

A recent study of students in six African countries (the Congo [Kinshasha], Ethiopia, Ghana, Nigeria, Senegal, and Uganda) also shows interesting differences in "modernism." Proportionally more of the Ghanaian students defined themselves as "traditionalists" and believed that traditional authority should be given a place in the structure of government than any other sample, and Ghana ranked second-highest among the proportions who wanted to preserve traditional culture because it was "very valuable." The Congolese students, on the other hand, clustered at the "modernist" extreme; of the six samples, they proportionally most often defined themselves as "innovators" and most often held the view that traditional culture was "no longer valuable" and should be replaced.[83]

These variations should not be exaggerated. Table 1 shows that only in Thailand did a majority actually choose the "traditionalist" response. In none of the six African samples was the "traditionalist" self-image preferred; on the contrary, more than twice as many students in each country, on the average, chose the "innovator" role. The variations do, however, suggest important differences in receptivity to innovative change, differences that may be related to variations in political behavior. Iranian and Congolese students, for example, have been much more active politically than students in Thailand or Ghana.

If such crude comparisons are to be refined, however, a simple dichotomy of "traditionals" and "moderns" will not suffice. In each of the six African samples, an average of two-thirds of the students chose neither the "traditionalist" nor the "innovator" role but fell somewhere in between. Likewise, if the question in Table 1 had allowed respondents to favor a mix of "traditional customs" and "modern ways," the compromise alternative would no doubt have been selected by many, perhaps a majority, of the respondents.

An illustration from India may help to suggest some of the tensions and conflicts that modernization creates among these "transitional" students. B. V. Shah, using a male Gujarati sample, found that deviation from traditional norms had occurred at different rates in different spheres. In matters such as the selection of one's friends and occupation independently of family and caste considerations, deviation from traditional norms had advanced quite far. But in other areas—notably marrying within one's caste, living with one's joint family (parents, married brothers, and sisters-in-law) after marriage, and permitting one's wife to work outside the home —the students still largely accepted the dictates of Gujarati custom. The students were, on the whole, willing to take a "modernist"

view of the outward aspects of life, such as one's career and interaction with others in public, and to criticize traditional institutions
in principle, but were reluctant to forsake traditional sanctions in
practice in the concrete, personal spheres of family and marriage.
For example, 87 per cent of the students said they would dine with
members of castes lower than theirs (although only a little more
than one-fourth of these students had no reservations about doing
so), but 65 per cent of the sample flatly refused to consider marriage outside their own caste.[84] Similarly, 60 per cent criticized the
joint family system as an institution, but 90 per cent said they themselves planned to live with their joint families after marriage even
if separate residence were economically feasible.[85]

The tensions and frustrations reflected in these attitudes may
find expression in acts of student "indiscipline." Such students
may, in fact, be more change-resistant than change-prone, particularly in areas where their high status might be threatened if the
"modernist" principles they verbally espouse were actually put into
practice. One widely noted dimension of modernization, for example, is a shift from ascriptive to achievement-based status criteria.
The Gujarati students, Shah writes, "may wish others to compete
for higher positions openly and fairly on the bases of individual
interest, ability and achievement in the field and yet may exploit
ascriptive kinship and caste loyalties to further their own ends,"
for instance, in maneuvering to obtain or retain power in the students' union. Shah draws a similar contrast between these students'
demands for egalitarian, democratic relations with their superiors
and the unequal, authoritarian manner in which they may treat
those with less status than they.[86] If such students can be called
"modernizers," they are insecurely and defensively so.[87]

One of the sources of this insecurity is the contrast between what
the student wants out of life and what he expects to get, for it is
here that he feels most deeply the dislocative effects of socio-economic change. The notion that student protest activity is an outlet for frustration over "vocational prospectlessness," to use Shils'
phrase, has been widely discussed,[88] and perhaps some preliminary
conclusions are now possible.

Student occupational frustrations and anxieties have been particularly high in several Asian and Latin American nations and
strikingly low in sub-Saharan Africa, thus crudely reflecting the
relative levels of activism in these areas. Employment prospects
also tend to be particularly poor in oversupplied fields such as law
and the humanities and relatively bright, given the typical priori-

ties of economic development, in the applied sciences, thus reinforcing to some extent the differential effect of academic specialization on student activism.

Bleak employment prospects can work in various ways to enhance the attractions of protest activity. The student may feel "cheated" by his environment: both by the university that has raised his expectations and by the society that cannot accommodate them. He may be able to identify more fully with calls for sweeping, radical change because he feels he has nothing to lose and everything to gain by shaking up the status quo. He may seek in zealous partisanship a way of circumventing obstacles to his upward mobility, hoping to substitute political contacts for professional skills. But none of these reactions to "vocational prospectlessness" can be assumed; rather, an excess of aspirations over opportunities seems to contribute to student unrest only when other variables point in the same direction.

Finally, if the necessary steps are taken to redress the imbalance between the university's supply of graduates and the economy's manpower needs, student politics will be deeply affected. Generally speaking, as merit-based barriers to university entrance and to prolonged student status are raised, as scholarship and occupational incentives swing more students into "role-specific" disciplines, and as the academic quality of university life is upgraded, student activism is likely to decline.

Student Politics and National Politics

If patterns of occupational recruitment influence student politics, political recruitment does so far more directly. Party activities in universities in developing nations are so widespread that campus activism may indeed seem to many observers a kind of "proxy politics" in which students are used and manipulated by outside forces. The figure of the "professional" student, as we have seen, lends some weight to these views, but they must be placed in perspective.

In most countries, only a minority of students actually belong to political parties. In a recent Latin American survey, on the average one-fifth of the students sampled in each of six countries reported membership in a national political organization.[89] In sub-Saharan Africa, excluding such "no-party" states as Ethiopia and (at the time of writing) Ghana, the average is probably roughly the same or slightly lower.[90] In North Africa, the Middle East, and

Asia, student political party membership probably seldom exceeds these levels.

Parties are, of course, active in universities in all these areas. But the image of the party organizer as an omnipotent student puppeteer is at best simplistic and at worst incorrect. There are at least two reasons why this is so.

First, students everywhere are most concerned about the things that directly affect their lives. In the absence of an overriding national crisis, their concerns are likely to center in their immediate environment. Academic regulations, conditions of board and lodging, university autonomy, resented disciplinary measures, and the cost of intracity transport are the kinds of issues that can spark large-scale demonstrations and strikes. In the six-nation Latin American survey previously cited, for example, respondents in each country who approved of student strikes on university issues outnumbered on the average two to one those who felt students were justified in striking over national or international issues.[91]

The task of the party organizer in these circumstances has not changed since Lenin urged a group of young Social Democrats in St. Petersburg to support a proposed student strike against conditions in the universities of Russia. Such support, wrote Lenin,

> must consist chiefly and primarily in ideologically and organizationally influencing the broader strata which have been aroused by the conflict and for which this form of conflict is in many cases their *first* political conflict. . . . It is our duty to explain to the mass of "academic" protesters the objective significance of this conflict, to try to make it a *conscious* political one.[92]

It is sometimes fairly easy to politicize an academic protest, particularly if blame for university conditions can be laid at the government's doorstep. Repressive police action can quickly expand the activists' base of support. But the leaders cannot stray too far into obviously partisan political organizing without running a risk of factionalism and isolation from the student body. The rhythm of many student protests follows this general pattern: initial incident—initial protest—"repressive" counteraction—massive protest—attempts to organize for sustained activity—further and more explicitly political demonstrations—increasing partisanship and factionalism—a loss of enthusiasm—isolation—eventual decline. The "professional" student politician, if he is to be effective, must have a good sense of timing and a knowledge of the limits of his own power.

A second important limitation on the party organizer is the sensitivity of many students to the unsavory aspects of partisan politicking, their dissatisfaction with existing parties, and their belief that students should act autonomously. In Nigeria, student images of parties, politicians, and politics in general are overwhelmingly negative; in one survey, asked to rank twenty-four professions in descending order of prestige, the respondents gave "political party worker" the honor of twenty-fourth place.[93] Parallel attitudes were common in Ghana under Nkrumah (see Chapter 3) and are probably widespread elsewhere in English-speaking Africa, where student unions are independent of political parties.

In Asia, such attitudes also exist. We have already mentioned student aversion to the "hidden hand" of politics at the University of Dacca. Similar antipathies can be seen in India. In Korea, organizational student-party ties are illegal and professional student organizers comparatively rare.[94] In Japan, party discipline has proved extremely difficult to impose on the fractured student left. Even in China's regimented party-state, as Bruce Larkin has argued (Chapter 5), students have acted autonomously, whether by taking at face value an invitation to dissent (1957) or by moving in the interstices of larger factional conflict (1966). In the cross-national Latin American study cited earlier, substantial majorities said that student leaders should have nothing to do with political party interests and ideologies.[95] In Peru, one observer has written, "Within the university, party leaders attempt to minimize their connections with the national headquarters . . . in deference to the strong sentiment for student autonomy."[96]

This is not to underestimate the involvement of political parties in student affairs. In Asia, the Middle East, North and South Africa, and Latin America, parties play important and occasionally determining roles in student politics. But students in general make unreliable and unwilling tools. Where the party succeeds in galvanizing student support, its student spokesmen are more often than not popular campus figures in their own right.

Parties are not, of course, the only agencies of political change. Governments, labor unions, religious movements, and a host of other formal and informal groups are involved in the process of political development, in the creation and solution of political crises, and in the search for an appropriate balance between stability and change. The nature of the balance, or imbalance, is a critical variable influencing student activism.

Kalman Silvert has used such criteria to develop a highly suggestive "scale" of student political action in Latin America. His analysis bears quoting at length:

Situations of Stable Traditional Societies. In very rudimentary, almost bi-class social structures, necessarily governed under crude dictatorial forms, students normally play a very limited role in innovation and political activity. This was the situation in the colonial era, and present-day Nicaragua, Haiti, and Paraguay fall into this category.

Situations of Beginning Modernization and Disarray. As the city begins to grow, as an industrially oriented middle class emerges, and as the politics of change begin to operate, students assume a most important role in the importation and adaptation of ideology, in the organization of power as well as of ideas, and in government itself. Factionalism is one of the earliest signs of modern pluralism. El Salvador, Guatemala, Ecuador, Peru, the Dominican Republic, and Panama are currently in this stage. In a world of political factionalism, more than in any other social milieu, the student, as one of the aspirant elites, finds a situation sufficiently simple so that he can exercise relatively great power over political events.

More Mature Situations of Temporary Resolution. When the social structure is relatively complex, politics turbulent, and at least interim political decisions are made with the immediate future in mind, student groups are usually very active but limited in their role by other established interests. In such situations student activity can still be of great importance in defining issues and precipitating incidents or even full-scale revolts. But usually the university as an institution begins to turn inward, preparing to meet the demand for professionalism that always arises in times of rapid economic and political development. Colombia, Venezuela, and Bolivia, for varying historical reasons, all fall into this category.

Situations of Institutional Complexity and Relative Strength. Where the student finds himself in a plural-interest structure and complex class system, his relative power becomes even more limited. The Mexican experience is a useful case in point. . . . The strength of the Mexican government, the ideological weight of the Revolution and the institutional expression of this ideology by the state, the single governing party, and the intellectual community all combine to strip from the students much of their political reason for being. To take another example, active as the Cuban students were against the Batista regime, they are now contained by the ideological as well as military strength of Castro's modern dictatorship. In Argentina, even though the country exhibits institutional disarray, effective student action in public affairs is impeded by the massiveness of Buenos Aires, the strength of the competing interest structure, and the complication of motivations and values. In these situations the students may and usually do have much influence over university policy and affairs, but in national politics their role must of necessity depend on other, more primary definitions of interest. Brazil, Mexico, Argentina, Uruguay, Costa Rica, Chile, and Cuba are all within this category.[97]

Such criteria are applicable elsewhere. Malaysia, the Philippines, and Taiwan combine a degree of institutional complexity with relative economic strength and political stability; Thailand's less complex infrastructure has also been comparatively stable. In these countries, students have on the whole been politically quiescent. In parts of India and Pakistan, socio-economic crises of major proportions and long duration frame a general sense of resentment and frustration among students, which seeks release not so much in consciously or specifically political action as in the less focused, more anomic expression of "indiscipline." The Chinese case is in some ways similar: although the Great Proletarian Cultural Revolution was more political than economic, more engineered than endemic, the crisis setting was also unfocused (or at least, to the outside observer, not clearly focused) and the Red Guards also showed generalized frustration and a kind of "indiscipline." In contrast, the political crisis in Indonesia in 1965–66 was highly focused, and KAMI could gear its movement to a few explicit demands (see Chapter 6). But if crises create opportunities for student action, they can also destroy its potential effectiveness. In South Viet-Nam, students will remain politically active as long as the war lasts, but because they are split along the same religious, regional, and ideological lines that fracture the broader polity, they may remain impotent as well, unable to recapture the unity and purity they found in the struggle against Diem.

The civil war in Nigeria has had a similar impact. Ethnic solidarities have shattered the capacity of the student community to act as a unified, transregional "conscience" of the nation. Elsewhere in tropical Africa, the Congo (Kinshasha) excepted, the centrifugal forces of tribal affiliation have been more successfully incorporated within a developing sense of national citizenship, and major political crises have been comparatively few and brief. In part as a consequence, levels of student activism throughout this region, as we have observed, are low. But, over the years, as urbanization and social differentiation continue, as the presently elitist systems of higher education expand, and as post-graduate employment opportunities narrow, African students may turn increasingly to political action.

North and South Africa present additional contrasts. In multiparty Morocco, students have found an important source of support and guidance in the adult opposition to the monarchy and have been more active than their counterparts in Tunisia, where a single-party system has so far served to contain and channel student demands. In less stable Algeria, in the disillusioning aftermath of anticolonial struggle, the student community has turned away from partisan involvement, leaving a small minority of activists to pursue their various "revolutionary" paths under the vigilant eye of the party (Chapter 1). South Africa, on the other hand, displays "institutional complexity and relative strength," to use Silvert's terms; Legassick and Shingler (Chapter 4) have shown how totalitarian surveillance and control, a meliorist "white liberal" political culture, and the numerical restriction and spatial isolation of nonwhite students combine to limit student opposition to apartheid.

Summary and Conclusion

As the preceding chapters demonstrate, and as we have tried to show in this concluding essay, the student is not an isolate. His ties to family and community are not somehow magically severed by matriculation. Nor is he automatically an enthusiast in the vanguard of change. In part a product of modernization, he is psychologically exposed to its dislocations; often its prime beneficiary, he can number among its casualties as well. His age, religion, and personality, the proximity, social origins, and political attitudes of his family, the location, auspices, and quality of his university, his career preparations and perceived life chances, the politicians who proselytize him, the balance of stability and change in his nation—all these factors define the terms of the student's entrance into, or avoidance of, the political realm.

Student political activity has no single cause and no single predictable effect. It occurs most often on the margins of the polity, only occasionally dramatically touching the center of national concerns. For many of the peripherally participant, their experience in student politics will be remembered as a mere passing excitement at childhood's end. For some among the most actively involved, it will have been a rehearsal for adult political roles.

Righteous in tone, symbolic in content, student politics tends to differ from "adult" politics in the sense that it is more often the art of the *im*possible. This emphasis on style over program and commitment over compromise is at once the weakness of student movements and their strength. Student political leaders cannot always escape criticism for the irrelevance of their conceits, for dissipating their energies in proclaiming and protecting ideal images of self and society while ignoring the complex, mundane, "low-payoff" tasks of incremental reform. Yet in those very images—in the credibility of the myth of the students' innocence, in the purity of their rage against evil—lies the fragile chance to effect basic change, albeit not singly or directly but by triggering or accompanying larger forces into action.

It is in this sense that students gain potential strength from actual frailty and noninvolvement, for it is only as political virgins that they are truly virile, only as the powerless that they acquire real influence. It is in this sense too that, caught in the contradiction between purity and power, they are rarely able to consolidate their gains.

But whatever their success in opposing the injustice and oppression they so keenly feel, students can at least serve to break the silence, to indicate fresh directions for the polity. That, in itself, is no mean achievement.

NOTES

1. The figure of one-third is meant to be suggestive only. Each sample was asked the same question and was offered the same "very interested" response alternative. The other response categories (e.g., "moderately" and "not" interested in politics) were generally, but not always, identical in phrasing and number. The samples themselves and the sampling methods used varied widely. Percentages selecting the "very interested" alternative were: Iran (59), Panama (48), Pakistan (38), Colombia (33), India (32), Nigeria (24), Argentina (21), Turkey (20), and Brazil (14). The survey in Panama sampled only students in the University of Panama Law School, whereas the Argentine sample was limited to the Faculty of Engineering of the University of Buenos Aires. As we shall see in our discussion of university faculties, this may in part explain the high ranking of Panama and the low ranking of Argentina. In another, broader survey ($N = 630$) of University of Buenos Aires students, 38 per cent reported they "frequently" became as excited about political events as about events in their personal lives.

The references are: *Nigeria:* Charles S. Rooks, "University Students and Politics in Nigeria" (paper delivered to the Conference on Students and Politics [henceforth cited as CSP] sponsored by the Harvard University Center for International Affairs and the University of Puerto Rico, San Juan, Puerto Rico, March 27–April 1, 1967), p. 46. [Several of the CSP papers cited in this chapter have been edited and published in *Daedalus*, XCVII (Winter 1968).] Universe, sample, and sample as proportion of universe (if given): Universities of Ibadan (West), Nigeria (East), and Ahmadu Bello (North), N=642, or 10–20 per cent at each institution. *India:* Margaret Cormack, *She Who Rides a Peacock: Indian Students and Social Change* (New York: Frederick A. Praeger, 1961),

p. 139. Universities and colleges in eleven cities and towns, N=approximately 425. *Iran:* "Attitudes and Values of Iranian University Students" (mimeo.; United States Information Agency [USIA], Research and Reference Service, Washington, D.C., December 1964), p. 23. Teheran University, N=300. *Pakistan:* "Aspirations and Attitudes of University Students in Pakistan" (mimeo.; USIA, Research and Reference Service, Washington, D.C., December 1963), p. 11. Universities of Dacca, Karachi, Peshawar, and Punjab, N=1,175. *Turkey:* Leslie L. Roos, Jr., Noralou P. Roos, and Gary Field, "Students and Politics in Turkey," CSP paper, p. 34. University of Ankara Faculty of Political Science, School of Social Welfare (Ankara), and Economics and Business Sciences Academy (Eskisehir), N=667. *Argentina:* Juan Osvaldo Inglese, "Comportamiento de estudiantes y dirigentes," in Inglese, Carlos L. Yegros Doria, and Leon Berdichevsky, *Universidad y estudiantes/Universidad y Peronismo* (Buenos Aires: Editorial Libera, 1965), p. 21. University of Buenos Aires Faculty of Engineering, N=1 of every 60 students. *Brazil:* 1963 INESE study, cited by Robert Myhr, Chapter 8, n. 29, above. Universities in four states, N=822. *Colombia:* "En minoría absoluta los universitarios que tienen interés por la política," *El Tiempo* (Bogotá), June 7, 1964 (Sunday supplement), p. 7. Thirteen universities and institutions of higher education in Bogotá, N=611, or 3 per cent. *Panama:* Daniel Goldrich, *Radical Nationalism: The Political Orientations of Panamanian Law Students* (East Lansing: Michigan State University, Bureau of Social and Political Research, 1962), p. 33. University of Panama Law School, N=83, or 59 per cent.

For the larger Buenos Aires sample mentioned above, see David Nasatir, "University Experience and Political Unrest of Students in Buenos Aires," in Seymour Martin Lipset (ed.), *Student Politics* (New York: Basic Books, 1967), pp. 320 and 331, n. 8.

2. Defined as members of political organizations who were primarily interested in political activity. "Attitudes and Values of Iranian University Students," p. 29.

3. *Colombia:* Universities of Javeriana, Libre, Los Andes, Nacional, and Popayan (Gauca), N=1,594. *Mexico:* Autonomous University of Mexico and University of Guanajuato, N=830. *Paraguay:* University of Asunción, N=474. *Puerto Rico:* University of Puerto Rico, N=575. These surveys were conducted in 1965–66 by the Comparative National Development Project under the direction of Professor Seymour Martin Lipset. I would like to thank Professor Lipset for his kindness in letting me use these data.

4. For the estimate of FUPI strength, see Arthur Liebman, "Children of Their Fathers: The Politics of Puerto Rican University Students" (unpublished Ph.D. dissertation, University of California, 1967), p. 142. The student enrollment figure used in calculating the percentage is from *The World of Learning, 1966–67* (London: Europa Publications, 1967), p. 949.

5. George R. Packard III, *Protest in Tokyo: The Security Treaty Crisis of 1960* (Princeton: Princeton University Press, 1966), p. 265. Packard defines this activist group as those who "seldom attended classes and devoted almost full time" to the struggle against the treaty. The *Zengakuren* (All-Japan Federation of College Student Governments) led the protest.

6. See Glaucio A. D. Soares, "The Active Few: Student Ideology and Participation in Developing Countries," in Lipset (ed.), *Student Politics*, pp. 124–47.

7. See these works by Lucian Pye: *Politics, Personality, and Nation Build-*

ing: Burma's Search for Identity (New Haven: Yale University Press, 1962), pp. 10–14; "Introduction," in Pye (ed.), *Communications and Political Development* (Princeton: Princeton University Press, 1963), p. 19; *Aspects of Political Development* (Boston: Little, Brown, 1966), pp. 9–11, 198–200.

8. See Edward Shils, "The Intellectuals in the Political Development of the New States," in John H. Kautsky (ed.), *Political Change in Underdeveloped Countries: Nationalism and Communism* (New York: John Wiley, 1965), p. 199.

9. For example, in China (where an institution of higher education existed nearly 3,500 years before the influential twelfth-century universities of Paris and Bologna had been organized [see Ping Wen Kuo, *The Chinese System of Public Education* (New York: Columbia University Teachers College, 1915), pp. 7–13]), the Communist *kangta*-style university is the product of forces and models vastly different from those that shaped, say, the "tribal colleges" in South Africa. Sharp contrasts also exist between geographically proximate institutions: the traditional, Islamic Al Qarawiyin University (founded in the ninth century) and the modern, secular Mohammed V University in Morocco; the respectively British-, American-, and French-modeled Universities of Sierra Leone, Liberia, and the Ivory Coast; the Universities of Puerto Rico and Havana, Saigon and Hanoi; and so on.

10. For further discussion along these lines, see James S. Coleman, "Introduction" and "Introduction to Part III," in Coleman (ed.), *Education and Political Development* (Princeton: Princeton University Press, 1965), pp. 19–20 and 356, respectively.

11. This list is restricted by limitations of space and the availability of data. Secondary school experience may be a particularly notable omission. Goldrich, for example, found that in the University of Panama Law School, students who had been strongly attracted to politics in secondary school were significantly more likely to have adopted a radically nationalist stance (i.e., to strongly favor nationalization of the Panama Canal) in the University than were their colleagues. See Goldrich, *loc. cit.*

12. For survey data confirming these points, see: *Nigeria:* William John Hanna and Judith Lynne Hanna, "Notes on Political Practices and Perspectives of University of Ibadan and Makerere University College Students," CSP paper, p. 51. University of Ibadan, N=96. *Uganda: Ibid.* Makerere University College, N=135 [weighted]. *China:* Olga Lang, *Chinese Family and Society* (New Haven: Yale University Press, 1946), pp. 319–20. Twenty-two universities and colleges in various cities, N=1,164, or approximately 2.5 per cent of all students in higher education in China in 1936. *India:* Cormack, *op. cit.*, chap. X, especially pp. 139, 156. *Turkey:* Gary R. Field, "Political Involvement and Political Orientations of Turkish Law Students" (unpublished Ph.D. dissertation, University of Oregon, 1964), p. 103. University of Ankara Law Faculty, N=1,034, or 12 per cent. *Brazil:* L. Ronald Scheman, "The Brazilian Law Student: Background, Habits, Attitudes," *Journal of Inter-American Studies,* V (July 1963), 349. Fifteen law schools in various cities, N=1,250. *Chile:* The portrait of "Rosa" in Myron Glazer, Chapter 9 above. *Colombia:* Robert C. Williamson, "University Students in a World of Change: A Colombian Sample," *Sociology and Social Research,* XLVIII (July 1964), 406. National University of Colombia, N=610, or 10 per cent. *Puerto Rico:* Liebman, *op. cit.*, p. 91. *Venezuela:* William L. Hamilton, Chapter 11 above.

13. Seymour Martin Lipset, "University Students and Politics in Underdeveloped Countries," in Lipset (ed.), *Student Politics,* p. 24.

14. Another had been enrolled for thirty-five years, another for twenty-three, two more for twenty-one, and another for nineteen years. Kalman H. Silvert, "Other People's Classrooms," American Universities Field Staff (AUFS) Report, East Coast South America Series, V, No. 2 (January 1958), 12. Silvert does not say whether or not these students were politically active.

15. Francis Donahue, "Students in Latin American Politics," *Antioch Review*, XXVI (Spring 1966), 94.

16. Richard W. Patch, "Fidelismo in Peruvian Universities," Part II, AUFS Report, West Coast South America Series, VII, No. 3 (February 1961), 6.

17. Donahue, *op. cit.*, p. 102.

18. Joseph DiBona, "Indiscipline and Student Leadership in an Indian University," in Lipset (ed.), *Student Politics*, pp. 381, 386–87.

19. Edward Shils, "Indian Students: Rather Sadhus than Philistines," *Encounter*, XVII (September 1961), 17.

20. Artemio Rivera-Arroyo, "Characteristics of Student Leaders and Nonleaders in the University of San Carlos of Guatemala" (unpublished Ph.D. dissertation, Michigan State University, 1965), pp. 4.8, 6.7. N=5,704, or 100 per cent.

21. In many Latin American universities, less than 5 per cent of the student body graduates in any given year. In 1956, for example, in the largest university in Latin America, the University of Buenos Aires, only 4 per cent of the students graduated, while a third as many as were enrolled registered for entrance. (Silvert, *loc. cit.*) For comparable Central American output figures, see Barbara Waggoner, George R. Waggoner, and Gregory B. Wolfe, "Higher Education in Contemporary Central America," *Journal of Inter-American Studies*, VI (October 1964), 452; Harold R. W. Benjamin, *Higher Education in the American Republics* (New York: McGraw-Hill, 1965), p. 124. Brazilian higher education, in contrast, has had much higher output-input ratios. See *ibid.*, p. 151.

22. See: *Morocco:* Clement H. Moore and Arlie R. Hochschild, "Student Movements in North African Politics," CSP paper, p. 47, n. 1. Mohammed V University and Mohammedia Engineering School in Rabat, N=125, or 4 per cent. (Moore and Hochschild warn that their Moroccan sample is not strictly representative and that generalizing from it is therefore hazardous.) *South Korea:* Byung Hun Oh, "University Students and Politics in Korea," CSP paper, p. 34. *Turkey:* Roos, Roos, and Field, *op. cit.*, pp. 27, 30–31. *Chile:* Glazer, Chapter 9, Tables 1 and 2, above.

23. *Argentina:* Ronald C. Newton, "Students and the Political System of Buenos Aires," *Journal of Inter-American Studies*, VIII (October 1966), 644. Nasatir, *op. cit.*, p. 328. *Colombia:* Kenneth N. Walker, "Determinants of Castro Support Among Latin American University Students," *Social and Economic Studies*, XIV (March 1965), 100, 101, 104. Newton and Nasatir use political activity as the dependent variable; Walker uses leftist radicalism (i.e., support for Fidel Castro's programs). For Walker's universe and sample, see n. 12 above.

24. See: *Morocco:* Moore and Hochschild, *op. cit.*, pp. 37, 41a. *Tunisia: Ibid.*, p. 66. University of Tunis, N=500, or approximately 12 per cent. *Turkey:* Roos, Roos, and Field, *op. cit.*, p. 34. *Colombia:* Walker, *op. cit.*, pp. 98–99, 102. *Panama:* Goldrich, *op. cit.*, p. 31. *Puerto Rico:* Liebman, *op. cit.*, pp. 91–92, 155–56.

25. These comments could be extended to include other religiously defined student groups in Indonesia. Harsja Bachtiar notes, for example, that Catholics

comprise only a third of the membership of the Union of Roman Catholic Students of the Republic of Indonesia (PMKRI). See Chapter 6 above.

26. "Cronica del viaje de Haya de la Torre por Uruguay, Argentina y Chile," in Gabriel del Mazo (ed.), *La reforma universitaria*, VI (Buenos Aires: Centro Estudiantes de Medicina, 1927), 148.

27. Lewis Feuer, for example, has argued that student movements provide a stage for the prolonged reenactment of the rebellion of youth against their fathers. See his "Rebellion at Berkeley," *The New Leader*, XLVIII (December 21, 1964), 5.

28. For supporting evidence, see Lipset, "University Students and Politics in Underdeveloped Countries," pp. 25–26, and: *India*: "Political Attitudes of Indian Students" (mimeo.; American University, Bureau of Social Science Research, Washington, D.C., December 1955), p. 46. *South Korea*: Byung Hun Oh, *op. cit.*, pp. 36–37. *South Viet-Nam*: David Marr, Chapter 7 above. *Colombia*: Walker, *op. cit.*, p. 100. Notable examples of student dormitories that have served as centers of radical action are Komaba at the University of Tokyo and "Stalingrad" at the Central University of Venezuela.

29. See: *Morocco and Tunisia*: Moore and Hochschild, *op. cit.*, pp. 38–39 and 65–66, respectively. *India*: Soares, *op. cit.*, p. 131 (Table 3, recomputed), using data from the "Political Attitudes of Indian Students" study. Shils, "Indian Students," p. 16. *Japan*: Michiya Shimbori, "Zengakuren: A Japanese Case Study of a Student Political Movement," *Sociology of Education*, XXXVII (Spring 1964), 232–33. Jean Stoetzel, *Without the Chrysanthemum and the Sword: A Study of the Attitudes of Youth in Post-War Japan* (New York: Columbia University Press, 1955), pp. 147–48. *Chile*: Glazer, Chapter 9, Table 4, above. Frank Bonilla, "Students in Politics: Three Generations of Political Action in a Latin American University" (unpublished Ph.D. dissertation, Harvard University, 1959), p. 253. Major sections of this work appear in Frank Bonilla and Myron Glazer, *Student Politics in Chile* (New York: Basic Books, 1968).

30. See: *Algeria*: David Ottaway's discussion of the "social promotion" as a source of leftism in student politics, Chapter 1 above. *Morocco*: Moore and Hochschild, *op. cit.*, pp. 44, 46, 48a. *China*: Lang, *op. cit.*, pp. 317–18. *South Korea*: Byung Hun Oh, *op. cit.*, p. 37. *Argentina*: Soares, *op. cit.*, p. 130 (Table 2, recomputed), using data collected by David Nasatir. *Panama*: Goldrich, *op. cit.*, pp. 31–32.

31. See: *Nigeria*: Pamela Day, "An Opinion Survey of the Students in the University of Ife: 1962–1963," *Nigerian Journal of Economic and Social Studies*, VII (November 1965), 334–35. University of Ife, N=84, or slightly over one-third. *Turkey*: Roos, Roos, and Field, *op. cit.*, p. 46. *Argentina*: Kalman H. Silvert and Frank Bonilla, "Education and the Social Meaning of Development: A Preliminary Statement" (mimeo.; AUFS, New York, 1961), pp. 238, 257, 277. University of Buenos Aires Faculties of Economics, Medicine, and Exact Sciences, N=719. Nasatir, *op. cit.*, pp. 322, 324. *Brazil*: Soares, *op. cit.*, p. 132 (Table 4, recomputed), using data on applicants to the Air Force Technological Institute. Glaucio A. D. Soares and Loreto Hoecker, "The World of Ideology: The Role of Ideas and the Legitimacy of Student Politics," CSP paper, p. 18. University of Brazil Faculty of Philosophy. N=272.

32. See: *Brazil*: Soares and Hoecker, "The World of Ideology," p. 18. *Chile*: Glazer, Chapter 9, Table 4 and accompanying text, above.

33. See: *Nigeria*: William John Hanna, "Students," in James S. Coleman

and Carl G. Rosberg, Jr. (eds.) *Political Parties and National Integration in Tropical Africa* (Berkeley: University of California Press, 1964), p. 419 (Table 1, recomputed). University College of Ibadan, N=210, or 21 per cent. Hanna and Hanna, *op. cit.,* pp. 49, 52–53. *Uganda: Ibid. India:* Philip G. Altbach, "Students, Politics, and Higher Education in a Developing Area: The Case of Bombay, India" (unpublished Ph.D. dissertation, University of Chicago, 1966), p. 48. *Philippines:* John A. Lepper, "Student Politics in the Philippines," CSP paper, p. 39. *Argentina:* Soares, "The Active Few," p. 130 (Table 2, recomputed). *Brazil:* Scheman, *op. cit.,* pp. 350, 352. *Puerto Rico:* Liebman, *op. cit.,* p. 91. *Venezuela:* Hamilton, Chapter 11, Table 2 and accompanying text, above.

34. See: *Philippines:* Lepper, *op. cit.,* pp. 22–23. *Brazil:* Soares, "The Active Few," p. 132 (Table 4, recomputed). *Colombia:* Walker, *op. cit.,* p. 98. *Puerto Rico:* Liebman, *op. cit.,* pp. 163, 168.

35. See: *Ghana:* David Finlay, *et al.,* Chapter 3, n. 36, above. *Chile:* Glazer, Chapter 9, Table 5 and accompanying text, above. *Puerto Rico:* Liebman, *op. cit.,* pp. 91–92, 168.

36. See: *India:* Cormack, *op. cit.,* pp. 139–40. *Japan:* Yasumasa Kuroda, "Agencies of Political Socialization and Political Change: Political Orientation of Japanese Law Students," *Human Organization,* XXIV (Winter 1965), 329–30. Law students at the Universities of Tokyo and Kyoto and the Judicial Research and Training Institute, N=663. *Panama:* Goldrich, *op. cit.,* p. 30.

37. Bonilla, "Students in Politics," pp. 278, 293, 295; Liebman, *op. cit.,* pp. 155, 165.

38. This definition of manifest political socialization follows Gabriel Almond. See his "Introduction," in Gabriel A. Almond and James S. Coleman (eds.), *The Politics of the Developing Areas* (Princeton: Princeton University Press, 1960), p. 28. For evidence showing high respect for parental authority and low respect for parental political opinions (on world affairs), see: *Iran:* "Attitudes and Values of Iranian University Students," pp. 19–24. *Pakistan:* "Aspirations and Attitudes of University Students in Pakistan," pp. 7–8. *Thailand:* "Student Views: Thailand and Malaysia," (mimeo.; USIA, Research and Reference Service, Washington, D.C., March 1965), p. 3. "A Study of University Student Attitudes in Thailand" (mimeo.; United States Information Service, Bangkok, September–October 1957), p. 16.

39. Erik H. Erikson, "Youth: Fidelity and Diversity," in Erikson (ed.), *The Challenge of Youth* (Garden City: Doubleday Anchor Books, 1965), p. 25.

40. Shils, "Indian Students," p. 19.

41. Robert A. Scalapino, "Prelude to Marxism: The Chinese Student Movement in Japan, 1900–1910," in Albert Feuerwerker, Rhoads Murphey, and Mary C. Wright (eds.), *Approaches to Modern Chinese History* (Berkeley: University of California Press, 1967), p. 214.

42. "La Juventud Argentina de Cordoba a los hombres libres de Sud America," in Gabriel del Mazo (ed.), *La reforma universitaria* (2nd ed.; La Plata: Centro Estudiantes de Ingenieria, 1951), pp. 3, 5.

43. Gerald Clark, *The Coming Explosion in Latin America* (New York: David McKay, 1963), p. 54, citing Aldo Arantes, then President of the National Union of Students (UNE) of Brazil.

44. For examples outside Latin America, see: *Nigeria:* Rooks, *op. cit.,* p. 31. *Soviet Union:* Thomas J. Hegarty, "Student Movements at Russian Universities,

1855–1917: A Preliminary Survey," CSP paper, p. 61. *China:* Bruce Larkin, Chapter 5 above. *India:* DiBona, *op. cit.,* p. 389. *Japan:* Robert Jay Lifton, "Youth and History: Individual Change in Postwar Japan," in Erikson (ed.), *op. cit.,* p. 279. Michiya Shimbori, "The Sociology of a Student Movement: A Japanese Case Study," CSP paper, p. 46.

45. The usefulness of the university as a unit for comparative analysis has been noted by several scholars. For a theoretical scheme, see Bart Carter Pate, "Colleges as Environmental Systems: Toward the Codification of Social Theory" (unpublished Ph.D. dissertation, Boston University, 1964). For a discussion of the university as a focus for comparative social science, see Joseph Fischer, *Universities in Southeast Asia* (Columbus: Ohio State University for Kappa Delta Pi, 1964), pp. 1–42.

46. For a discussion of the Indian case, see Cormack, *op. cit.,* pp. 181, 190; Shils, "Indian Students," pp. 13, 15, 17, 19; DiBona, *op. cit.,* p. 376. For the Pakistani case, see below.

47. On the Cuban case, see Jaime Suchlicki, Chapter 10 above. The Cuban government does not deny the actual principle of university autonomy. For the government's socialist interpretation of autonomy, see *La Universidad de la Habana al Consejo Executivo y a la Asamblea General de la Unión de Universidades de America Latina* (Havana: University of Havana [1964]), pp. 29–35. A tradition of university autonomy is not, of course, sufficient guarantee against government incursion. The violation of autonomy by the Ongania government in Argentina in 1966 is a case in point. See Kalman H. Silvert, *et al., A Report to the American Academic Community on the Present Argentine University Situation* (Austin: Latin American Studies Association, 1967).

48. R. P. Dore, "Education," in Robert E. Ward and Dankwart A. Rustow (eds.), *Political Modernization in Japan and Turkey* (Princeton: Princeton University Press, 1964), p. 182.

49. For a fuller discussion, see Lepper, *op. cit.,* pp. 31–33.

50. Shils, "Indian Students," p. 20.

51. Newton, *op. cit.,* p. 638.

52. See, for example, the discussion of the Andrés Bello and Santa Maria universities in Hamilton, chapter 11 above.

53. For data on the various forms of *cogobierno* in South America, see Benjamin, *op. cit.,* pp. 54–55.

54. See Newton, *op. cit.,* pp. 650–51; Waggoner, Waggoner, and Wolfe, *op. cit.,* p. 457.

55. Riseri Frondisi, cited in Newton, *loc. cit.*

56. These statements are based on data to be found in the *World Survey of Education,* IV (Paris: UNESCO, 1966), 16, 18, 67–68, and *passim,* and in *The Development of Higher Education in Africa* (Paris: UNESCO, 1963), pp. 147–48, 226–27, 241.

57. For illustrations of the elitist model in Africa, see J. E. Goldthorpe, *An African Elite: Makerere College Students, 1922–1960* (Nairobi: Oxford University Press, for the East African Institute of Social Research, 1965); Dwaine Marvick, "African University Students: A Presumptive Elite," in Coleman (ed.), *Education and Political Development,* pp. 463–97; Manfred Stanley, "The New Elect: A Study of an Emerging East African Intelligentsia" (unpublished Ph.D. dissertation, New York University, 1965).

58. Ubiquitous, but not universal. In Uruguay, for example, full-time teaching is enforced by law. For statistics on full- and part-time professors in indi-

Conclusion 423

vidual countries, see Benjamin, *op. cit.,* pp. 63, 94, 121–22. Benjamin writes that university staff salaries in South America are "generally low" and "must be considered in most cases as being merely supplemental to the professor's usual professional income." *Ibid.,* p. 63.

59. See, for example, the severe criticism of Indian higher education in the *Report of the Education Commission, 1964–66: Education and National Development* (New Delhi: Ministry of Education, 1966), pp. 278–79.

60. "Student Conditions in S.E. Asia: Need for Relief," *The Times Educational Supplement* (London), August 3, 1951, p. 617.

61. M. Rashid, "Absorption of the Educated," in E. A. G. Robinson and J. E. Vaizey (eds.), *The Economics of Education* (New York: St. Martin's Press, 1966), p. 400.

62. Cited in DiBona, *op. cit.,* p. 380.

63. Cited in "With Mao on the Mountains," *The Economist,* January 29, 1966, p. 405.

64. Under the "three F rule," University of Rangoon students who failed their examinations three times could be dropped from the rolls. On the strong student opposition to the rule, see "Students in Revolt," *The Times Educational Supplement,* October 7, 1955, p. 1021. On another occasion, University of Rangoon students opposed a regulation assigning one-fourth of each final course mark to classroom work and successfully demanded a return to the former system of all-or-nothing examinations. See George Mannello, Jr., "Student Strike at an Asian University: A Case History," *American Association of University Professors Bulletin,* XLIII (June 1967), 251.

65. See Hamilton, Chapter 11 above.

66. Donahue, *op. cit.,* p. 103.

67. For a fuller discussion, see Josef Silverstein's "University Students and Politics in Burma," *Pacific Affairs,* XXXVII (Spring 1964), 50–65, and his "Burmese Student Politics in a Changing Society," CSP paper.

68. K. Bhaskara Rao, *Candle Against the Wind* (Bangalore: Samyutka Karnatak Press, 1963), p. 121. Nonfiction on student "indiscipline" in India abounds, but this little novel is possibly the best and certainly the most compelling single introduction to the subject.

69. See: *Ghana:* Finlay *et al.,* Chapter 3, n. 53, above. *Congo* (Kinshasha): Jean-Claude Willame, Chapter 2 above. *Sierra Leone:* Marvick, *op. cit.,* pp. 490–92. Fourah Bay College, N = roughly 100. *Tunisia:* Moore and Hochschild, *op. cit.,* pp. 64–65, 67a. *Burma:* Silverstein, "Burmese Student Politics in a Changing Society," p. 31. *India:* Metta Spencer, "Professional, Scientific, and Intellectual Students in India," in Lipset (ed.), *Student Politics,* p. 358, using data from the "Political Attitudes of Indian Students" study. Cormack, *op. cit.,* p. 187. *Philippines:* Lepper, *op. cit.,* pp. 6–7. *South Korea:* Princeton M. Lyman, "Students and Politics in Indonesia and Korea," *Pacific Affairs,* XXXVIII (Fall–Winter 1965–66), 290. Byung Hun Oh, *op. cit.,* pp. 32–33. *Turkey:* Roos, Roos, and Field, *op. cit.,* p. 24. *Chile:* Glazer, Chapter 9, Table 1, above. *Colombia:* Williamson, *op. cit.,* p. 408. Also see "En minoría absoluta. . . ," p. 7. *Venezuela:* Orlando Albornoz, "Student Political Activism in Venezuela," CSP paper, pp. 18–19.

70. See: *Yugoslavia:* Stanislaw Skrzypek, "The Political, Cultural, and Social Views of Yugoslav Youth," *Public Opinion Quarterly,* XXIX (1965), 94. Five major universities, N=3,889. *India:* Spencer, *loc. cit. Iran:* Spencer, *op. cit.,* p. 358, using data from the "Attitudes and Values of Iranian Univer-

sity Students" study. *Pakistan: Ibid.*, using data from the "Aspirations and Attitudes of University Students in Pakistan" study. *Turkey:* Roos, Roos, and Field, *loc. cit. Chile:* Glazer, Chapter 9, Table 2, above. *Colombia:* "Los estudiantes hablan del Canal del Atrato y de otras cosas," *El Tiempo,* May 24, 1964 (Sunday supplement), p. 5. For sample details, see n. 1 above. *Guatemala:* Solomon Lipp, "Attitudes and Opinions of Guatemalan University Students," *Sociology and Social Research,* XLIV (May–June 1960), 342. University of San Carlos and Guatemalan-American Institute, N=348, or 5–38 per cent in each university faculty and 10 per cent at the Institute. *Honduras:* Donahue, *op. cit.*, p. 104. *Mexico: A Study of Opinions of University Students in Mexico* (Mexico City: International Research Associates, 1964), pp. 16–19, 40–43, 123–32, cited in Lipset, "University Students and Politics in Underdeveloped Countries," p. 46, n. 52. *Puerto Rico:* Liebman, *op. cit.*, p. 154.

71. Nasatir, *op. cit.*, p. 325. As might be expected, Law and Economics held the top two ranks. (In 1957–58, Philosophy and Letters was 73 per cent female; Economics was 77 per cent male. Of those graduating from Philosophy and Letters in 1963, 83 per cent were females. See Silvert, "Other People's Classrooms," p. 5; Newton, *op. cit.*, p. 642, n. 31.) For a parallel illustration of the intervening effect of sex on faculty in a Colombian sample, using leftist radicalism as the dependent variable, see Williamson, *op. cit.*, p. 408.

72. See Silvert, "Other People's Classrooms," p. 5.

73. See Inglese, *op. cit.*, pp. 20, 26–27, 31, 35–37.

74. Silvert and Bonilla, "Education and the Social Meaning of Development," pp. 237, 256, 276.

75. Seymour Martin Lipset, "Research on Students and Politics," CSP Paper, pp. 37–39.

76. "Aspirations and Attitudes of University Students in Pakistan," *passim.*

77. *Report of the Commission on Student Problems and Welfare* (Karachi: Ministry of Education, 1966), p. 181. On the politicizing effects of the Dacca University hall unions, see *ibid.*, pp. 183–84. For a fuller discussion of Pakistani student politics, see *ibid.*, pp. 177–91. Also see Karl von Vorys, *Political Development in Pakistan* (Princeton: Princeton University Press, 1965), pp. 132–36 and *passim.*

78. See Louis Dupree, "Peshawar University," AUFS Report, South Asia Series, VII, No. 6 (April 1963). The *Report of the Commission on Student Problems and Welfare,* however, noted some improvement in student housing at Dacca.

79. Md. Afsar Uddin, "Notes on Researches about Student Problems at the University of Dacca," in Pierre Bessaignet (ed.), *Social Research in East Pakistan* (Dacca: Asiatic Society of Pakistan, 1960), p. 57. Also see Khalid B. Sayeed, *The Political System of Pakistan* (Boston: Houghton Mifflin, 1967), pp. 183–84.

80. Afsar Uddin, *op. cit.*, pp. 56–57. Also see Ghulam Jilani, *An Inquiry into the Factors Influencing the Academic Atmosphere of the Dacca University* (Dacca: Pakistan Institute of Human Relations, 1956).

81. Ghulam Jilani, *Teacher-Student Relationships at the Dacca University* (Dacca: University of Dacca, 1961), pp. 176–77.

82. Student political activity is not easily quantified across nations. Merely to identify the numbers of student demonstrations occurring in different countries over the same time period would be no easy task, given the selectivity

of international press coverage. But size, intensity, and purpose would also have to be taken into account—characteristics that are extremely difficult to determine with any precision from secondary sources. This is not to mention the distortion involved in limiting the dependent variable to demonstrations alone.

83. This study was conducted by Miss Marisa Zavelloni under UNESCO auspices in October-December 1965. Her sample N's were 291 in Ghana, 233 in Nigeria, 195 in the Congo (Kinshasha), 179 in Ethiopia, 97 in Senegal, and 64 in Uganda, all drawn from the major universities of these countries. The Ghana-Congo difference cited above is not a function of academic specialty, for both samples consisted wholly of social science majors. I should like to express my thanks to Miss Zavelloni for her kindness in letting me see her preliminary results.

84. B. V. Shah, *Social Change and College Students of Gujarat* (Baroda: Maharaja Sayajirao University of Baroda, 1964), pp. 168, 178. N=200, or 20 per cent of all male Gujarati students at the University of Baroda. Eighty-eight per cent of Shah's respondents came from the upper castes.

85. *Ibid.*, pp. 38, 46. For nationwide survey results that parallel these findings, see "Political Attitudes of Indian Students," pp. 66, 69.

86. Shah, *op. cit.*, pp. 201–2.

87. Among student leaders at Allahabad University in Uttar Pradesh, Di-Bona found a pattern of actual reversion to traditional norms:

> When the object of higher education was an administrative job with the British bureaucracy, it was natural to share the Englishman's love of Shakespeare, his faith in progress, and belief in the parliamentary forms of justice. Today one is more likely to hear a [Students'] Union speaker extoll Tulsi Das, the author of the local Ramayana, as the "greatest poet that ever lived." The important festivals for the students tend increasingly to be the Hindu festivals of *Shiv Ratri* or *Holi* and all political harangues allude to the importance of duty, piety, and respect for elders. Of the thirty-odd [student] leaders arrested and held five months in jail for the 1963 riots [at Allahabad], none of them objected to their parents' choosing their spouse. At home in the village, although it is otherwise on the campus, they observe all the caste ceremony and ritual attached to food and bathing. . . . In many ways, the new student strength is conservative: cow worship, vegetarianism, respect for parents, and caste are important. (Di-Bona, *op. cit.*, pp. 388, 390.)

88. Shils, "The Intellectuals in the Political Development of the New States," p. 204. For analyses and illustrations, see: *Egypt:* Walter Z. Laqueur, *Communism and Nationalism in the Middle East* (New York: Frederick A. Praeger, 1956), pp. 14 and 311, n. 17. *Nigeria:* Rooks, *op. cit.*, pp. 3, 60. *Soviet Union:* Hegarty, *op. cit.*, p. 58. *China:* "Unemployed 'White Collar' Workers and the North China Student Demonstrations," *China Weekly Review*, LXXV (January 18, 1936), 224–27. *India:* Shils, "Indian Students," p. 18. DiBona, *op. cit.*, p. 373. *Indonesia:* Lyman, *op. cit.*, p. 284. *Japan:* Lawrence H. Battistini, *The Postwar Student Struggle in Japan* (Tokyo: Charles E. Tuttle, 1956), pp. 141–42. Michiya Shimbori, "Zengakuren," pp. 238–39. *South Korea:* William A. Douglas, "Korean Students and Politics," *Asian Survey*, III (December 1963), 584. Byung Hun Oh, *op. cit.*, p. 31. Lyman, *op. cit.*, pp. 289–90. *Turkey:* Roos, Roos, and Field, *op. cit.*, p. 50. *Colombia:* E. Wight Bakke, "Students on the March: The Cases of Mexico and Colombia," *Sociology of Education*, XXXVII (Spring 1964), 218–19.

Williamson, *op. cit.*, pp. 400, 411. Walker, *op. cit.*, pp. 103–4. **Mexico:** Bakke, *loc. cit.* **Puerto Rico:** Liebman, *op. cit.*, pp. 163, 173.

89. This average was calculated from the results of the previously cited Comparative National Development Project Surveys in Colombia, Mexico, Panama, Paraguay, Puerto Rico, and Uruguay. High "no answer" proportions, ranging from one-third to slightly over one-half in Colombia, Puerto Rico, and Mexico, make the one-fifth figure more suggestive than descriptive. Nor should party membership levels be taken as indicators of strikes, demonstrations, and other radical forms of activism. The highest membership percentages—35 in Paraguay and 30 in Uruguay—occurred in two countries where such activity has been quite infrequent.

90. In 1963 in Nigeria, only 9 per cent and 13 per cent of samples at the Universities of Ife and Ibadan, respectively, belonged to a political party. (Ife: Day, *op. cit.*, p. 339. Ibadan: Hanna and Hanna, *op. cit.*, p. 26.) However, a multi-university survey in Nigeria two years later showed 23 per cent affiliated. (Rooks, *op. cit.*, p. 45.) In Ghana and Uganda in 1963, Finlay and the Hannas, respectively, found that 22 per cent of their respondents were members of a political party. (Ghana: Finlay *et al.*, Chapter 3, n. 54, above; Uganda: Hanna and Hanna, *loc. cit.*)

91. Comparative National Development Project surveys. Two separate questions were asked. The greatest disparity occurred in Colombia, where 77 per cent of the respondents justified university-centered strikes whereas only 24 per cent approved of strikes on national or international matters. The gap was narrowest in Panama, where the corresponding figures were 75 and 58 respectively, perhaps reflecting the salience of the Panama Canal issue. A large majority approved of university-focused strikes in each country, while in Mexico a plurality and in Colombia and Puerto Rico a majority disapproved of nationally or internationally oriented student strikes.

92. V. I. Lenin, "The Student Movement and the Present Political Situation" (1908), in Lenin, *The Young Generation* (New York: International Publishers, 1940), pp. 17–18. Italics in original.

93. Pamela Day, *op. cit.*, p. 336. Also see *ibid.*, p. 341; Rooks, *op. cit.*, pp. 49–50; Hanna, "Students," pp. 435–38; Hanna and Hanna, *op. cit.*, pp. 36–41.

94. Lyman, *op. cit.*, p. 291. Byung Hun Oh notes, however, that in Seoul the student of provincial origin may be courted by politicians from his home region who see in him, given the high status he enjoys in the province, an important potential supporter. Willame finds a similar phenomenon in the Congo: see Chapter 2 above.

95. Comparative National Development Project surveys. The majorities ranged from 65 per cent in Uruguay to 75 per cent in Mexico and Colombia. In another survey in the latter country, 62 per cent said that no political party fully represented their political views. "En minoría absoluta . . . ," *loc. cit.* (Note also the Chilean student criticism of *politiqueria* [dirty politics] reported in Chapter 9 above. Among the Panamanian law students questioned by Goldrich, however, 48 per cent reported a favorable attitude toward politicians, the remainder expressing dislike or indifference. (Goldrich, *op. cit.*, p. 35.)

96. Richard W. Patch, *op. cit.*, p. 3.

97. Kalman H. Silvert, *The Conflict Society: Reaction and Revolution in Latin America* (rev. ed.; New York: American Universities Field Staff, 1966), pp. 123–24. Reprinted by permission of the American Universities Field Staff.

INDEX

THE CONTRIBUTORS

HARSJA W. BACHTIAR received his B.A. and M.A. degrees from Cornell (1958, 1959) and is a candidate for a Ph.D. from Harvard. He is currently Lecturer in Sociology at the University of Indonesia and the Military Academy of Law, and a senior official of the Indonesian Council for the Sciences. He is the author of *A Study of Political Decision-Makers in Indonesia* and co-editor of *The Population of West Irian* (both in Indonesian).

CHARLES A. BALLARD, JR., holds a B.S. degree from St. Joseph's College (1964) and an M.A. from the University of Ghana (1967). He has also studied at Lincoln and Villanova universities. He is presently writing a book on the Ghana Young Pioneer youth movement.

DONALD K. EMMERSON received his B.A. from Princeton (1961) and his M.A. from Yale (1966). He is presently preparing his doctoral dissertation in political science for Yale as a Ford Foreign Area Fellow in Indonesia. His published work includes essays on national and continental student organizations in Africa.

DAVID J. FINLAY has a B.A. from Willamette University (1956) and M.A. and Ph.D. degrees from Stanford (1958, 1962). An Associate Professor of Political Science at the University of Oregon, he is currently on leave as a Postdoctoral Fellow at the Western Behavioral Sciences Institute in La Jolla, California. He is a co-author of *Enemies in Politics* and the author of articles on Ghanaian politics.

MYRON GLAZER received his B.A. from the City College of New York (1956), holds M.A. degrees from Rutgers and Princeton (1961, 1963), and obtained his Ph.D. from Princeton (1965). Currently Associate Professor of Sociology and Anthropology at Smith College, he is also affiliated with the Comparative Student Politics Project of the Harvard Center for International Affairs. He is the author of various articles on students and social-science research in Chile and co-author (with Frank Bonilla) of a forthcoming study of Chilean students.

WILLIAM L. HAMILTON received his B.A. from Harvard (1963) and holds M.A. and M.A.L.D. degrees from the Fletcher School of Law and Diplomacy (1964, 1965), where he is also a candidate for a Ph.D. His published works include an article on student politics in Argentina, in David Spencer (ed.), *Student Politics in Latin America*.

ROBERTA E. KOPLIN received her B.A. and M.A. degrees from the University of Oregon (1953, 1965). Presently Instructor in Political Science

443

at the University of Oregon, she is the author of an article on Kenyan student politics in a forthcoming study of students and politics in Africa.

BRUCE D. LARKIN received his B.A. from the University of Chicago (1954) and his M.A. and Ph.D. degrees from Harvard (1962, 1966). He is currently Assistant Professor of Government and Fellow of Cowell College at the University of California, Santa Cruz.

MARTIN LEGASSICK holds a B.A. (Hon.) from Balliol College, Oxford (1963), and is a candidate for a Ph.D. at the University of California, Los Angeles. Currently Assistant Professor of African History at the University of California, Santa Barbara, he is the author of various articles on Africa.

DAVID G. MARR received his B.A. from Dartmouth (1959) and his M.A. from the University of California, Berkeley (1966). He is presently completing a doctoral dissertation on Viet-Nam's early anticolonial movements as a Fulbright Research Fellow and a grantee of the Center for Southeast Asian Studies at the University of California, Berkeley. He was recently appointed Lecturer in the University's Department of History.

ROBERT O. MYHR holds a B.A. from Amherst (1960) and an M.I.A. degree from Columbia (1962), where he is also a candidate for a Ph.D. Presently Assistant Professor of Political Science at the University of Washington, he has published several articles on Brazilian student history and politics.

DAVID B. OTTAWAY holds a B.A. from Harvard (1962) and is presently completing work toward an M.A. degree at Columbia. His publications include *Algeria: The Politics of a Socialist Revolution* (forthcoming).

JOHN SHINGLER received his B.A. from Rhodes University in South Africa (1956) and his M.A. from Yale (1964). Currently Assistant Professor of Political Science at McGill University, he is a co-author of *Africa in Perspective*.

JAIME SUCHLICKI holds a B.A. and an M.A. from the University of Miami (1964, 1965) and a Ph.D. from Texas Christian University (1967). He is presently Assistant Professor of History and a Research Associate in the Center for Advanced International Studies at the University of Miami. He is the author of various articles on student politics in Cuba and Latin America.

JEAN-CLAUDE WILLAME received his *candidature* in law and a *licence* in social and political science at the University of Louvain (1959, 1962). An Associate Member of the Center for Research and Sociopolitical Information (Brussels and Kinshasha), he is currently associated with the African Studies Program, Institute of International Studies, University of California, Berkeley. His publications include a five-volume study, *The Provinces of the Congo,* and *Congolese Political Parties* (both in French).